Grow It

and

Cook It

Grow It

and

Cook It

Denis Wood and Kate Crosby

Faber

and

Faber

3 Queen Square London

First published in 1975
by Faber & Faber Limited
3 Queen Square London WC1
Printed in Great Britain
by Butler & Tanner Limited
Frome and London

ISBN 0 571 10571 8

for M J W
with love from us both

Contents

Line Drawings

Acknowledgements

WE acknowledge with much gratitude the ready help and advice which we have received from Mr T. Laflin of the National Vegetable Research Station at Wellesbourne, Warwickshire; Mr J. L. W. Deen of the Glasshouse Crops Research Institute at Rustington, Sussex; Mr Criddle of the Lee Valley Experimental Horticulture Station at Hoddesdon, Hertfordshire; Mr B. F. Self of the East Malling Research Station near Maidstone, Kent; Mr H. A. Baker, the Fruit Officer at the Royal Horticultural Society's Garden at Wisley, near Ripley, Surrey. We acknowledge also assistance from time to time from the Long Ashton Research Station of the University's Department of Agriculture and Horticulture, near Bristol. Also information gained from leaflets obtained through fellowship of the National Institute of Agricultural Botany at Cambridge. We record very grateful thanks to Mr H. Fraser, for permission to draw at length from his book *The Gardener's Guide to Pruning*; to Ward Lock Limited for permission to draw on *Fruit-Growing* by N. B. Bagenal; to Wm Collins Sons & Company for permission to quote a passage from *Pesticides and Pollution* by Kenneth Mellanby; to the Connecticut Agricultural Experiment Station, New Haven, U.S.A., for permission to quote from their leaflets, in particular *The Biochemistry and Methodology of Composting* by Raymond Poincelot; to Mr L. D. Hills of the Henry Doubleday Research Association for permission to quote from the H.D.R.A. pamphlets; and to The Hon. Margaret Mackay, Mr J. L. Toland, Mr Hugh Coates and Mr Edward Marshall for much help and advice.

We thank Mr Denys Baker for his excellent line drawings.

Other acknowledgements will, we hope, be understood through the bibliography on pp. 366–368. If we have inadvertently left

14 ACKNOWLEDGEMENTS

out some to whom we are indebted, we offer them sincere regrets and apologies.

We owe the greatest thanks to those who have typed and made, we hope, some sense of the manuscripts: in particular to Shirley Wills for inexhaustible patience and good humour, and also to Pamela Dancaster, Alison Edwards, Josephine Morris and Sheila Roberts.

Introduction

Growing good food and cooking it well is what this book is about. More and more ordinary people are tired of the tastelessness of the vegetables they can buy, and are turning to their own back gardens for fresh, crisp, homegrown produce to feed themselves and their families. They are worried by the loss of nutritional value in vegetables wilted and bruised by travelling and storage. They are concerned that everything they buy has been sprayed with lingering pesticides and fungicides. Crops grown like this on ground heavily treated with chemicals are different in kind, too—in the structure of their amino acids—from those grown organically. We are what we eat: shall we become chemically different in time?

Making things grow, whether in a real kitchen garden or in a city window-box, brings a very basic satisfaction and sense of achievement. By doing this organically, that is, by encouraging the microbiological action of natural composts to produce real fertility, we are making a positive contribution to the survival of the planet.

Gardening can be hard work, but it provides fresh air and exercise, and above all a change of pace, an awareness of the seasons, in this age of technology. We show from the beginning how to prepare, plan and crop your vegetable garden from scratch, saving money and striking a blow against pollution by composting your own household waste. We catalogue the seed varieties to plant to grow vegetables you can really taste; commercial growers choose their varieties for their thick skins and ability to travel. Growing the right variety means the difference between a leathery old lettuce and a crisp, green delicious one.

There is no conflict between good cooking and healthy cooking; every gourmet is interested in the taste of food, and that taste is

composed of the total components—vitamins, minerals, carbohydrates, protein and all—the more of these that are undamaged,
the better the flavour will be. Every mother wants to provide the
best start in life for her children, and sound nutrition is the first
requirement for them to grow up in good health—mental as well
as physical. Yet often she is ignorant of the basic rules of vegetable
cookery that make this possible. Old people, too, are at nutritional
risk through lack of knowledge as much as lack of money. There
is evidence that a poor diet encourages senile decay; there are
certainly old people today who are suffering from scurvy without
knowing it, for lack of vitamin C.

We explain in simple language the jargon of gardening and
cookery writers. We show from the beginning how to prepare
and serve vegetables and how to combine them in delicious and
unusual recipes. Cooking vegetables you have grown yourself
and serving them with their maximum nutritional value intact
makes feeding a family a positive pleasure instead of a daily grind.

This book is intended as a permanent part of your household.
First to read through for pleasure and inspiration, afterwards to
refer to for growing instructions and recipes.

PART ONE

Grow It

My vegetable love should grow . . .
ANDREW MARVELL

CHAPTER ONE

The Soil, Garden Compost and Growing Media

WITHOUT green growing things there would literally be nothing for us to eat, either directly or indirectly, through cattle or through vegetables. So, in fact, our health and well-being depend on the health and well-being of green things, and on the earth that supports them, on a far larger and more vital scale than a kitchen garden. Soil is the essential reservoir of nutrients, air and water, and it is the living space for the micro-biological population of bacteria and fungi, without which life cannot exist.

Besides providing anchorage for the roots of trees and plants, the soil is also the medium for the supply of everything which plants require, except sunlight. This works the everyday miracle of photosynthesis through chlorophyll in the green leaves of plants, enabling the plants to combine water and nutrients derived from the soil, with carbon dioxide from the air, producing the first stage of complex food materials.

Soil consists of a mixture of inorganic and organic materials; the first are mainly mineral, the detritus of old rocks, silt and clay; the second is organic material, some of it already converted to humus and the rest on the way to being converted. Humus is a dark brown, friable substance, made up of partly or entirely de-composed plant or animal materials. It is sweet smelling, the archetypal mould. The resulting mixture is something pulsatingly alive with micro-organisms which exert a two-way action, taking for themselves certain materials for their own nourishment and making it possible for the root-hairs of the plants to take up food materials from the soil. For these extraordinarily complex and miraculous functions to be performed, the micro-organisms and the root-hairs of plants need both air and water which can be, to a degree, mutually exclusive in that an excess of water can block up the minute capillaries from which air would otherwise reach down from the atmosphere to the plant's area of root activity. The preservation of the correct balance of air and water is dependent upon what is known as the structure of the soil, the provision of pores of the right size to accommodate films of moisture on their walls. Humus plays an important part in soil structure because it has the property of cementing together mineral particles, such as sand or clay, making them into larger crumbs, resulting in pore spaces which permit the entry of air and also the exit of excess water into lower levels. Beside this mechanical function, humus contains all the nutrients required by plants growing in normal conditions. It also has the function of drawing to the surface from lower levels worms for whom it is an important food. In their upward passage these earthworms enlarge the pore spaces for the access of air and water, and also for the extension of plant roots.

A 400-year-old oak tree has never had fertilizers given to it apart from what is left by cattle grazing in its shade, nor has an upland pasture that is cropped by sheep, yet both the tree and the pasture are whole according to their kind. They have no deficiencies of growth and no need of chemical fertilizers; they are part of the slow cycle of natural fertility. The tree with its deep roots brings up essential elements from the subsoil and deposits them on the land's surface in its fallen leaves; animal dung and urine replace the food materials taken out by cattle and crops. Under these natural conditions humus is produced slowly, perhaps over many years. Organic farmers with many acres at their disposal still find it possible to do without added fertilizers or manures, organic or inorganic, but in the restricted space of the ordinary kitchen garden and the consequent intensive cultivation that it needs, a natural renewal of humus does not occur to a sufficient degree. For this reason it is necessary to provide humus artificially, and this can be done by making compost, as will be seen later in this chapter.

Adequate drainage is essential to ensure that the soil pores are not obstructed by standing water. If this happens, the root hairs of the plant and the diminutive organisms which support these hairs, will be denied air and literally drowned. A gentle slope across the garden is the best of all drainage measures, but even on the flat most established and productive kitchen gardens drain well naturally and little or nothing needs to be done; in cases

where the drainage is slightly restricted it may be better practice
not to undertake large soil-moving operations which, by destroying existing pore spaces, make conditions worse. In such cases
massive applications of garden compost will make a great improvement through the crumb-producing action of humus and its
attraction to worms. In the absence of humus, other organic
materials, notably farmyard manure or 'fertile peat', or partly
decomposed chopped straw, will be effective but will probably
take rather longer to produce a noticeable improvement. Massive
dressings of lime are also useful in lightening heavy soils. Beside
all this, a first crop of potatoes or deep-thrusting vegetables like
salsify or parsnips will help to improve the drainage.

If you are faced with impossibly heavy clay and determined to
make a success of a kitchen garden, or any sort of garden, it will
probably be necessary to carry out major drainage. When this is
contemplated you should recognize that when the work is finished
it will take a year or more to re-establish a soil structure, a process
which can be hastened by adding garden compost or other organic
materials, and by planting deep-rooted crops. If the topsoil is
satisfactory or capable of being made so, stiff clay subsoils on
heavy ground can be mole-drained, provided that there is a
slope on the ground. Mole draining is done by agricultural con-
tractors and consists in drawing through the ground at a depth of
between 15–30 cm (6 in–1 ft) a metal 'mole' which is something
like the nose of a 10-cm (4-in) shell. This is attached to a piece of
steel like a knife; the combination of the slit made by the steel
and the tunnel made by the mole is effective in carrying away
surplus water for a number of years, depending on the plasticity
of the subsoil. It can, of course, only be used on sloping ground,
because it is impossible to vary the depth of the mole as it is
drawn across the ground.

Compost

The purpose of making garden compost is to produce humus for
the nourishment of plants and the conditioning of the soil. If
you can make enough garden compost it will be unnecessary to
use additional fertilizers of any kind. The word 'compost' has
become linked with the John Innes Institute through the mixtures
of sterilized soil, sand, peat, chalk and fertilizers which that

Institute propounded for sowing and potting. The garden compost we are now to consider is quite different, in that it results from the deliberately induced decomposition of organic materials and, when the process is finished, it is used without being mixed with any other ingredient, not even extra fertilizers of any kind.

There are different ways of making garden compost. One of the best is that devised by Sir Albert Howard at the Institute of Plant Industry, Indore, Central India, between 1924 and 1931, and named the Indore Process.[1]

The way to produce it in gardens in this country is to have one or, preferably, more wooden bins about 1·2 × 1·2 × 1·15 m high (4 × 4 × 3½ ft) (Fig. 1). The bins must be close-boarded

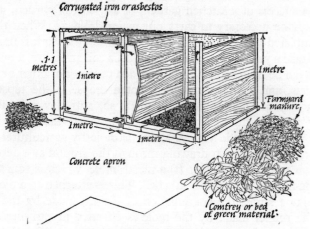

FIG. 1. Double compost bins

with no gaps, in order to keep in as much heat as possible. For the same reason, bins with wire-mesh sides are no use. It is convenient to make the front detachable simply by securing it to the two sides with strong hinged hooks at the tops and bottoms. This makes it easy to empty the bins and turn the compost from outside to inside, and from top to bottom. It is essential that these bins should rest on soil to give access for worms. A single line of bricks is laid underneath the four sides to give stability, and in front of the bin a hard concrete 'apron' 1·8 m (6 ft) square makes it much

[1] Sir Albert Howard, *An Agricultural Testament*, Oxford University Press, 1940.

easier to shovel back the contents after emptying bins in the course of turning the compost. As an alternative to wooden bins, bales of straw can be set down on the earth to form a square. In this country it is unlikely that added water will be necessary, and therefore an easily removable cover of wood, corrugated asbestos or iron sheeting should be put over the top to keep out the rain.

To make the compost, 30 cm (1 ft) of coarse vegetable material, twigs, prunings, Brussels sprouts stalks or similar waste, is put on first. The purpose of this is to provide access for air at the bottom. If, when the rest of the material has been converted to compost, these coarse foundation members have not been broken down, they can be picked over and put back into the next heap. Above this lower ventilating layer, vegetable material and household waste is put in to a depth of 15 cm (6 in); this can be almost anything that is, or has been, animal or vegetable. Cabbage stalks, nettles, potato, pea and bean haulms, tea leaves, orange peel, banana skins, lawn mowings, weeds, seaweed, fish bones, egg shells, waste scraps of meat, lobster shells (from well-heeled households), sawdust, wood shavings; paper, if finely shredded, and chopped straw are also useful, although if there is a high proportion of these two materials, the process will take longer. It is wise to bear in mind that the trees from which sawdust or wood shavings are derived may have been infected with honey fungus. Garden weeds are an important constituent, and other useful vegetable additions are nettles and green bracken cut in the spring and summer, and comfrey (much work has been done on comfrey at the Henry Doubleday Research Association at Bocking, Braintree, Essex). When this layer is 15 cm (6 in) thick, it is lightly pressed down and traditionally covered with a 13-cm (5-in) layer of animal material of some sort—farmyard manure, pig or poultry manure. Recently, organic activators have begun to be used, in particular materials derived from seaweed, such as Marinure, which needs to be sprinkled on at the rate of about 56 g (2 oz), or a handful to each layer. The late Miss Maye Bruce developed a herbal activator known as Q.R.[1] In the absence of any of these a light coating of concentrated organic material, such as hoof-and-horn meal or dried blood, can be used.

The very best and cheapest 'animal manure', if only we could

---

[1] M. E. Bruce, *Common Sense Compost Making*, Faber & Faber, 1973.

get past the coyness of the subject, is, in fact, urine. Sir Albert Howard writes lyrically of it in his *Agricultural Testament*: 'The key substance in the manufacture of humus from vegetable wastes is urine—the drainage of the active cells and glands of the animal. It contains in a soluble and balanced form all the nitrogen and minerals, and in all probability the accessory growth-substances as well, needed for the work of the fungi and bacteria which break down the various forms of cellulose—the first step in the synthesis of humus. It carries in all probability every raw material, known and unknown, discovered and undiscovered, needed in the building up of a fertile soil. Much of this vital substance for restoring soil fertility is either wasted or only imperfectly utilized. This fact alone would explain the disintegration of the agriculture of the West.'

Above the activating layer, 5 cm (2 in) of garden soil is then spread, covered, in turn, with a sprinkling of ground limestone or chalk. The process then begins all over again with a second layer of vegetable material, etc. When the top is reached, a final coating of animal manure is given. If properly made in this way, no chemical activator will be necessary and soon after filling the temperature will rise sharply to about 65°C (150°F). At this temperature, weed seeds, pest residues and many pathogens are destroyed. To achieve this, aerobic conditions must be maintained all through the material in the bin, which is simply done by pushing a stake right through the compost from top to bottom in five places—one in the middle and four towards the corners. It is convenient to have five stakes, leaving them in position but lifting and replacing them once every day. After this first aerobic process, an anaerobic stage follows which completes the transformation into humus.

Soon after filling, the contents will shrink in volume and can be topped up. Provided the high temperature of 65°C (150°F) has been reached, in three weeks the compost should be turned for the first time. To do this, one side is removed, the contents turned out on to the concrete apron, and then shovelled back so that what was the outside becomes the inside to heat up, and what was the bottom becomes the top. Light watering is advisable in the course of this process, but you must take care not to create sodden conditions. In another three weeks the second turn is done by emptying the bin and shovelling back the contents, outside to inside and top to bottom. Again, a little water will be necessary unless there is a high proportion of grass cuttings in the charge. Soon after the second turn has been carried out the compost will begin to ripen, and will be complete and ready for use in about three months. An indicator as to whether it is 'done' will be the presence of small, bright red worms. It should now be dark in colour and should be watered to give it the texture of a pressed out sponge.

In practice you will seldom find it possible to fill a bin with one charge; instead, it will be gradually filled up, perhaps over several weeks or even months, with the result that instead of a massive 'conflagration' there will be a series of small ones, and the contents of the bin will take longer to make compost. But, if it is turned two or three times over the month or six weeks that it may take to fill, it will still make good compost, although taking longer to do so.

There is a much quicker method of producing compost which is known as the Berkeley or 'Two-week' Process. Its rapidity depends on shredding the organic materials with a mechanical shredder, or by making several passes over it with a rotary mower. Dried blood is mixed into the heap, which has to be turned on the fourth, seventh and tenth day. After this the temperature drops, and in fourteen days the compost is generally ready for use. Fuller information is given in the American publication, *The Biochemistry and Methodology of Composting*,[1] which gives an analysis of the chief fertilizer nutrients in garden compost in dry weight percentage of finished material, as follows: nitrogen, 1·4–3·5; phosphorus, 0·3–1·0; potassium, 0·4–2·0.

The wonder-working properties of compost must depend upon it having been properly made, and made also with materials which will produce the nutrients in the finished product. The table on page 26 is again taken from *The Biochemistry and Methodology of Composting*. From this it is seen that grass clippings by themselves contain 2·41% nitrogen only, no phosphoric oxide and no potash; so a compost made entirely of grass clippings would be seriously deficient. On the other hand, the addition of weeds enables it to give a reasonable analysis.

The preparation of garden compost is a neat and economical process, putting garden and household waste to a positive and

[1] Raymond P. Poincelot *The Biochemistry and Methodology of Composting*, Connecticut Agricultural Experiment Station

satisfying use. It strikes a blow against pollution, since by composting your household rubbish you are reducing by at least one-third the amount of waste with which you would otherwise cumber

Nutrient Content of Common materials used in Home Garden Compost

Material	Per cent (dry weight)		
	Nitrogen (N)	Phosphorus as Phosphoric oxide (P_2O_5)[1]	Potassium as Potassium oxide (K_2O)
Blood Meal	10–14	1–5	—
Bone Meal (steamed)	2·0	23	—
Coffee Grounds	2·08	0·32	0·28
Cottonseed Meal	6·6	2·0–3·0	1·0–2·0
Eggshells	1·19	0·38	0·14
Fish Scraps	2·0–7·5	1·5–6·0	—
Garbage	2·0–2·9	1·1–1·3	0·8–2·2
Grass Clippings	2·41	—	—
Grass Clippings/Weeds	2·03	1·09	2·03
Leaves (freshly fallen)	0·5–1·0	0·10–0·15	0·4–0·7
Manure (dry) Horse	1·2	1·0	1·6
Cattle	2·0	1·0	2·0
Poultry	5·0	1·9	1·2
Meat Scraps	5–7	—	—
Salt Marsh Hay	1·10	0·25	0·75
Seaweed (dry)	1·68	0·75	4·93
Sewage Sludge (digested)	2·00	1·5	0·18
Wood Ashes (unleached)	—	1·0–2·0	4·0–10·0

[1] Phosphoric oxide, P_2O_5, is more often referred to in Britain as phosphoric acid, or simply phosphorus, similarly potassium oxide, K_2O, is called potash or potassium.

the land. The end product is far cheaper than bought fertilizers and infinitely better; the making and use of compost is a part of a kind of philosophy of living, self-sufficient within a private enclosure uncontaminated by the world outside.

Other Organic Materials

Provided it is properly made (see p. 23) and used in sufficient quantity, compost is the perfect material for fertilizing, mulching and soil conditioning, but as it is unlikely that you will be able to make enough of it to meet the requirements of all the crops in your kitchen garden, other bulk organic materials will have to be used as well.

Leaf soil can be produced simply by making a compound to prevent the stored leaves from being blown away. This compound can be made of straw bales, wooden sleepers, wire netting or Netlon (which is attractive to look at) or wattle hurdles. Even a heap in a sheltered corner of the garden will do. The reduction of dead leaves to fine mould is a much longer process, taking about a full year, because leaves do not heat up to the extent that green vegetable material does, but it still makes humus in its own good time. Layers of poultry, pigeon, rabbit or farmyard manure will hasten it a little. It is sometimes very acid—I have known samples with a pH of below 4·0, a figure which is low even for rhododendrons. If such a reading is seen, hydrated lime must be added before it is used on cropping grounds for vegetables.

Other bulk materials may have to be bought-in. One, fairly commonly available, is fresh cow manure mixed with straw. This is better stored for a few months to allow bacteria to begin decomposing the straw, and give time for the dung itself to dry a little and rot into a crumbly state from its original sloshy half-formed stools. When rotted and crumbly it is good for poor soils, and for crops that need a great deal of dung. A good dressing, 10 cm (4 in) thick, is equivalent to about 2 kg of cow manure per sq m (about 4 lb per sq yd). The proportions of nitrogen, phosphorus as phosphoric oxide and potassium as potassium oxide in an average sample of cattle manure are shown in the Connecticut Agricultural Experiment Station table on p. 26. The potassium content is very useful, potassium being the nutrient which is hardest to come by from organic sources.

Horse manure, before the world was cursed with the internal combustion engine, was the classic bulk material. Now, alas, it is difficult to come by unless one lives near riding or racing stables. Before forking in it should be stored for a few months to mature with its straw, and then used at the same rate as cow manure. The proportions of nitrogen, phosphorus and potassium in an average sample of horse manure are shown in the Connecticut Agricultural Experiment Station table on p. 26.

Fresh horse droppings were, in the past, and can still be used to make hot beds for cucumbers, mushrooms, etc. This is a useful method of getting early crops by making use of the heat generated in the course of fermentation, instead of paying for electric or coal heat. The way to make a hot-bed is first to obtain fresh stable manure with its straw, and mix it on the ground with a spade with an equal volume of leaves, because the heat generated from unadulterated droppings would be too intense. The mixture must then be turned every other day and, if it is dry, water added sparingly. It will give off a considerable amount of vapour, smelling at first of ammonia. When it has cooled down sufficiently and lost its ammoniacal smell, it is ready for use and can then be stacked where it is needed to a depth of 76 cm (2½ ft) over an area that can be covered by a light frame, or it can be stacked on greenhouse benches. In either case, it is covered with 30 cm (1 ft) of light soil into which pots are plunged before the seeds are sown. This can be done when the temperature falls to 30°C (86°F). For direct planting, seedlings can be knocked out of the pots or put directly into peat pots. When all heat is spent the hot-bed material can be used for forking in to the soil or applied as a mulch. It makes good material for the following year's vegetable marrow cropping ground. Fresh horse manure is composted with straw for growing mushrooms, see p. 109.

Poultry manure, when obtainable uncontaminated by antibiotics, is useful material but, having a high nitrogen content, must be used with discretion. So much so that in apple orchards it is not recommended that poultry should run free in an orchard of eating apples, because these will produce extensive growth at the expense of fruit. On the other hand, poultry are useful in an orchard of cooking apples because these require a greater supply of nitrogen. This material is an excellent addition to a compost bin, and useful also for composting straw and peat because it produces the nitrogen which the bacteria need, and take, to give them energy for dismantling the raw straw and peat. The proportions of nitrogen, phosphorus (as phosphoric oxide) and potassium (as potassium oxide) in an average sample of poultry manure are shown in the Connecticut Agricultural Experiment Station table on page 26.

Peat is much used as a bulky organic dressing, its special virtue being its water-holding capacity. There are two different kinds of peat: sphagnum peat, or high-moor peat, is very acid with pH values of between 3·0 and 4·5, whereas low-moor peat derived from sedges has pH values ranging from 3·5 to 7·0.[1] Either sort may contain from 1·5–3·5% nitrogen, and less than 0·1% phosphorus and potassium.

Temporary loss of existing nitrogen in the soil can be caused by the application of more or less sterile materials such as straw and some peats, because bacteria take nitrogen from the soil to give them energy for breaking down these materials. Therefore bulky dressings should have an adequate nitrogen content before being applied. This can be done by composting, stacking them with an activator such as animal manure or a seaweed product such as Marinure.

If peat is to be used as a substitute for garden compost, it can be fortified by mixing 35 g (1¼ oz) of hoof-and-horn meal, 35 g (1¼ oz of bonemeal and 70 g (2½ oz) of dried seaweed (or 21 g (¾ oz) of potassium sulphate) with each bushel (about 36 litres).

Alternatively, bales of peat can be opened, spread out and composted over many months with nitrogenous material—cow manure, horse manure, pigeon manure, rabbit manure, poultry manure, etc., or with dried seaweed. Having thus made up a store of what will be referred to in this book as 'fertile' peat, the material can be used in place of garden compost for digging in, having been spread to a depth of 10 cm (4 in) or as a mulch to remain on the surface at a depth of 5 cm (2 in).

Straw, when bought in a bale, is a fairly inert bundle of celluloses and hemicelluloses, but a potential reservoir of humus. In order to transform it, open the bale, spread out the straw and soak it thoroughly with water. Then either dress it with an activator known as Adco, formulated many years ago for this purpose by the Rothamstead Experimental Station, or with ammonium sulphate of which 8 kg, about 17 lb, will be needed per tonne together with an equal quantity of hydrated lime. These materials are spread over the wetted straw in alternate 15-cm (6-in) layers. It is turned only once and then left for another three months, by which time the straw should be decomposed and black, well on the way to becoming humus. Now that we have seaweed materials, straw composting can be carried out with them instead of making use of chemicals such as ammonium sulphate.

Sawdust and shavings are comparatively inert, but consist of

---

[1] F. W. Pauli, *Soil Fertility*, Adam Hilger Ltd.

lignins and celluloses which can be composted in the same way as straw, or by simply mixing them with poultry manure or pigeon manure, giving the heap an occasional stir and waiting until the worms begin to invade from below. If there are not enough leaves, sawdust or other slow-converting products to merit separate bins for each of them, they can all be put together in one compound and given what organic nitrogenous activators that you can come by, and left to mature, perhaps for a year before being brought into use.

Municipal compost may consist of dustbin refuse mixed with sewage sludge, or either of the two separately. It should be re-remembered that there may be a sufficiently high content of metals to be toxic to plant growth, and it does have to be used with care. Information on this and on the rates of application can be obtained from the supplier. The material varies considerably from district to district, but will usually make a good basis for the production of humus, activated by dried seaweed and diluted also with some stirrings of peat or sawdust.

Green manuring means sowing a quickly-growing crop with the sole intention of digging it in before it flowers. When this is done it simply returns minerals which it has taken out, but it also returns more valuable nitrogen in a form which continues to be available for some time, and carbon compounds which will form the basis of new humus. Seeds sown for green manuring include mustard, rape, rye, vetches, winter tares, lupins, buckwheat and comfrey, of which selected strains can be had from Henry Doubleday Research Association at Bocking, Braintree, Essex.

Litter was much referred to in old gardening books, and used in large gardens as a protection against cold winds and excessive transpiration, and worked rather like cellular string vests in maintaining micro-atmospheres. It is still useful material to have on hand and can consist of dried autumn bracken, straw and large leaves, piled together into a compound of wire-netting or Netlon about 60 cm (2 ft) high to stop the material being blown away. Toss the mixture with a pitchfork to stop it bedding down and beginning to make compost, which for once is not wanted. It is put over and round crops in autumn and can also be laid against crops in frames. When it is finished with in spring it can go into the compost bin.

What an old gardener understood by 'loam' was a slightly greasy, marly topsoil, which used to be bought in thick turves about 10 cm (4 in) thick, and stacked upside down, sometimes with layers of farmyard manure between. The stack was left to mature from four to six months and when needed for potting or propagating purposes, was chopped down with a spade and the loam sieved to the particle size required. It is probably almost impossible now to buy loam turves, but if some of the garden turf has to be stripped and discarded, try to cut it as thick as possible and carry out the process just described. Stacked loam, when mature, usually had a fairly low pH of 5·5–6·0. Therefore, if you intend to produce it for yourself, keep an eye on this, adding lime as required.

So-called 'mushroom compost' is generally horse manure which has been used to create a mushroom-growing hot-bed. The material varies considerably, the average pH being between 6·3 and 6·8, but some of it contains lump lime raising the pH higher than is needed for some garden crops, but not all. Some of it has residual formaldehyde and organochlorine insecticides, notably BHC. Others will have no residual insecticide, having been treated with a fugitive type of organophosphorus insecticide such as dichlorvos, which has entirely disappeared by the time the mushroom compost is delivered into a garden. There will soon be available a new form of this material, mushroom soil recomposted with a seaweed preparation, having no lump chalk and little if any residual insecticide or fungicide.

Growing Media

'Soil fertility . . . is a manifestation and measure of the success of the population in reaching a high standard of living. The sum is reflected in the structure of a soil', in the words of Dr Pauli.[1] In other words, fertility does not reside simply in weighing out doses of fertilizers, whether chemical or organic, but in other ingredients also, the population of micro-flora, the access to atmospheric oxygen and water, and fertile medium of humus which sustains them, and all make up a whole soil. It is evident that continued fertility must depend on continuing restoration of humus as it becomes drawn upon by the plants and removed as crops.

But it is useful to know the nutrient values of different materials that can be used either to make compost, or to fortify relatively

---

[1] F. W. Pauli, *Soil Fertility*, Adam Hilger Ltd.

inert materials like peat. The chief nutrients which plants require are nitrogen, phosphorus and potassium, and beside these, minute quantities of trace elements, of which at least twenty-eight occur in dried seaweed alone. There is a proprietary product, Frit 253A, which contains boron, manganese, iron, copper and molybdenum.

You will see from the table on p. 26 that, with the exception of seaweed and wood ashes, whose potassium is so quickly leached out as to make it of little use, the amount of potassium available from the organic sources referred to is small and, in fact, the maintenance of the proper amounts of potassium has been difficult until, in fairly recent years, processed seaweed has become available. Marinure, for instance, may be expected to contain approximately 1% nitrogen, 0·3% phosphorus and 2·7% potassium. Now that this is available, it may be used instead of potassium sulphate to boost potassium supplies to soft fruit. A common rate of application of potassium sulphate was 28–56 g per sq m (1–2 oz per sq yd). In order to put on the same amount of potassium it would be necessary to use Marinure at over 700 g per sq m, about 25 oz per sq yd, a rate much higher than recommended and certainly not in one dressing. It is better to use the seaweed product in three or four dressings at intervals of three or four weeks.

In the course of creating a fertile soil, the acidity or alkalinity has to be taken into account. This is measured by hydrogen-ion concentration, recorded in a pH scale. In this, the figures from 1–7 indicate acidity, and above 7·0 alkalinity. For most crops a pH of 6·5–7·0 (very slightly acid) is what is required. The pH of the sap of most plants is in the region of 6·0. Cabbages and other members of the *Cruciferae* family are high lime demanders and will do best and avoid one of their greatest afflictions, clubroot, at a pH nearest to 7·0, but some other plants, notably potatoes, raspberries and strawberries, will succeed best at a pH between 5·0 and 6·0. It is easy to increase the pH by adding lime in some form, either ground calcium carbonate or hydrated lime. As an approximate guide the table opposite indicates how much hydrated lime in grams per square metre is needed to bring up the pH to an average requirement.

To lower the pH is less easy. It may be done by dressings of ammonium sulphate which has a bad effect on the soil structure, and even by flowers of sulphur. The best way is to allow the pH

to descend by stages through the rotation of crops. For example, cabbages, which require a high pH, can be followed by peas, beans, etc., needing less lime, which in any case tends to be leached out of the top layers of the soil, and finally they in turn can be followed by potatoes which, as we have seen, require a more acid soil. If the descent of the pH does not occur naturally through the rotation, leaf soil and peat, particularly sphagnum peat, can be forked in. In order to get the best out of the soil by the regulation of its pH, buy yourself a simple soil-test kit (see list of suppliers on p. 363).

Lime Dressing (using hydrated lime) in grams per square metre
(28 g = 1 oz; 1 sq m = 1·2 sq yd)

	Light soils	Loams	Clay soils
Slightly acid (pH about 6·0)	112	168	224
Moderately acid (pH about 5·5)	168	224	280
Acid (pH about 5·0)	196	280	392
Strongly acid (pH about 4·5)	252	336	448
Very acid (pH about 4·0)	280	448	560

Note: If quicklime is used, dressings should be two-thirds of the above quantities.[1]

Sowing and potting can be done in quite ordinary, good, fertile garden topsoil if it is friable, just tacky but not wet or sticky, nor powder dry. Sieve it first from a 0·6 cm ($\frac{1}{4}$ in) mesh sieve, and then mix it with about half its volume of peat and clean sand, in equal parts. The John Innes potting compost (No. 1) is made up of 7 parts by volume of composted, partially sterilized medium loam; 3 parts by volume of peat; 2 parts by volume of coarse grit sand, and 21 g ($\frac{3}{4}$ oz) chalk and 113 g (4 oz) compound fertilizer to each bushel of the mixture. In practice, it has been found, since this was formulated, that the substantial clay fraction in soil when used for seed and potting compost, notwithstanding the addition of the grit sand, tends to make the whole material pack down and form a crust under repeated waterings. It was partly because of

[1] Remington & Francis, *Manure and Fertilizer Notebook*, Leonard Hill, 1955.

GICI—B

this that the newer soilless composts were introduced, based on peat and sand, and reinforced in varying degrees. To make up your own on these lines, use a mixture of 25% fine sand and 75% peat (not in this instance fertile peat) for sowing, and 50% sieved garden compost, 25% fertile peat and 25% fine sand for potting on.

Growing mixtures for plants in tubs, for example bush fruit trees, can consist of 50% sieved garden compost, 25% coarse grit sand (to keep the mixture open) and 25% of chopped loam or good topsoil, in this case for the sake of its clay fraction, to provide a firmer anchorage for roots than might be provided by compost alone.

CHAPTER TWO

The Kitchen Garden

Position and Aspect

Any piece of ground from a window-box upwards can grow something. Any vegetable or herb which you grow for yourself will improve your cooking and the nutrition of your family. Herbs such as parsley (which is not only one of the fundamentals of cooking but is also rich in vitamin C, iron and vitamin A), basil, chives and thyme can all be grown in window-boxes, in tubs or in large pots in sunny positions. Out in the garden extreme shade or bad drainage will be limiting, but you can overcome even these disadvantages with a little learning and some determination. Many kitchen gardens are made and successfully cropped in apparently unpromising situations—little cramped plots in town gardens, often badly shaded to start with, and indeterminate areas fitted as afterthoughts into a garden primarily designed to give priority to flowers and grass; sometimes, too, on exhausted soils, given new life by compost and perhaps lime.

An original and imaginative way with a small plot is to make the whole thing into a decorative kitchen garden after the manner of a French *potager*. Such a one might be enclosed by a hedge or a fence, and framed inside this by bush or pyramid-trained fruit trees standing in grass. It might have a wide *tapis vert* running through the middle with vegetable beds on either side, and also narrow borders of flowers for cutting, running along the length of the grass. The vegetable beds would have to be designed to be entirely productive and useful, but imagination and a sense of design could bring into play, the placing of plots of, say, red cabbage, beetroot and globe artichokes. None the less, the principles of the rotation of crops must be followed, and not subordinated to visual considerations.

The perfect position for a kitchen garden, whether decorative

or severely practical, is on a gentle slope facing towards the south
or south-west and protected from the north and east and also
from west and south-westerly gales by screens of trees, planted far
enough away to avoid shade or competition from their roots. A
hedge or a screen of trees, by filtering the wind, will materially reduce its speed and strength for a distance up to six times its
height, that is 18 m (59 ft) for a 3-m (10-ft) hedge, and double this
distance for a fairly modest 6·1 m (20 ft) high screen of Norway
maples. By comparison, solid barriers like walls or fences will
give good shelter for a horizontal distance equal to three times

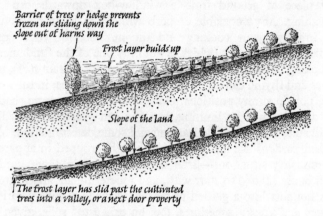

FIG. 2. Upper drawing shows way in which cold air builds up to produce typical frost pocket; lower shows how to avoid it

their height, thus a 3 m (10 ft) wall will give protection and calm
conditions for 9 m (30 ft), but create turbulence at a distance
greater than this. Even slatted fences, as seen in gardens near the
sea exposed to the wind, can be very useful. Within the garden
itself the use of quite low yew or box hedges defining the beds and
making compartments will create warm, tranquil micro-climates
for vegetables to grow in.

A south-facing slope will gather all the sunlight and warmth
that is going and, other things being equal, lead to earlier crops,
but make sure that there is no barrier, hedge or fence where a
frost pocket could be built up at the lower end of the slope to
arrest the downward progress of dense, cold air produced by

radiation frosts in the spring. Without any barrier this dangerous cold air will run away downwards, and either into a part of the garden where plants whose blossoms are susceptible to spring frosts are not being cultivated or, uncharitably, into the next man's garden (Fig. 2).

Undue importance can be attached to points of the compass. Plants in positions or beds facing the north or east are only severely prejudiced when there is a high wall or hedge, or a tree cutting off nearly all the southern sun. In cases where there is only a low wall or hedge behind, plants in beds which may be officially classified as facing towards the north will receive a reasonable amount of sunlight from directly above, and exposure to the north and east is no great detriment to ordinary hardy plants, including many vegetables, although their rate of growth may be slowed down.

Crop Rotation

During the Second World War Great Britain was able to maintain an exceedingly high standard of diet, due in part to the vigorous Dig-for-Victory campaign imaginatively and directly encouraged by a number of exemplary leaflets. In the first of these a cropping plan was worked out to produce a sequence of vegetables for an average household. The plot measured 27 × 9 m (90 × 30 ft), 250 sq m (300 sq yd exactly). This is the same size as the larger of the two model vegetable gardens laid out at the Royal Horticultural Society's Garden at Wisley in Surrey, and it is also the accepted size of an allotment garden. The cropping plan for both of these is similar and, if followed conscientiously, will produce a sound, relatively pest and disease free, if rather limited supply of vegetables throughout most of the year. Since our national health was so good in war time, it is worth taking these as a basis for present-day vegetable growing. Anyone who wants to investigate the higher reaches of the craft will add such epicurean delights as asparagus, globe artichokes and seakale, which occupy the same ground for several years, and other comparatively unusual vegetables: cardoons, chicory, Jerusalem artichokes, salsify, scorzonera, courgettes, and, in a greenhouse, cucumbers, green peppers and aubergines.

The aim of the rotation of crops is to ensure that the same plants, or those of the same family, are not grown in the same ground time and again, but are regularly moved around the garden in a simple three-year cycle. This is one of the first requirements for true natural fertility. One kind of vegetable will draw from the soil food materials that are either not needed, or needed in lesser quantities by the crop that follows it. Another may actually put in nutrients actively required by its successor. Many pests and diseases are specific to certain vegetables, thus the blackfly of broad beans will not, as yet, attack potatoes or beetroots, and therefore these are usually grown to succeed peas and beans. The influence of the rotation of crops on the pH has already been mentioned (see p. 32).

The simple system indicated in the Dig-for-Victory cropping plan provides for the following sequence, with the plot divided into three.

First year Dwarf peas inter-cropped with spinach and leeks, dwarf beans, onions followed by spring cabbage, shallots and broad beans, followed with winter lettuce and inter-cropped with summer lettuce and runner beans.

Second Year Main crop carrots, parsnips, early potatoes, followed by runner beans, main crop potatoes, spinach and spinach beet.

Third Year Main crop cabbage, savoys, Brussels sprouts, inter-cropped with early carrots and early potatoes, spring broccoli, kale, swedes, globe beetroot and a row of early peas.

This is still a good practical method to follow today.

Pest Control

By far the worst garden pests are birds, closely followed by slugs. Young seedlings can be stripped by chaffinches and sparrows; the best protection against these is black thread or cotton stretched between short canes. Wood pigeons will devastate a row of Brussels sprouts in a matter of minutes; the protection against these is sold as pigeon netting. The most practical way of using it is to support it on posts 1·8 m (6 ft) above ground, surrounding the whole cabbage patch all the year. Inverted jam jars on the tops of the posts will make it easier to pull the net over them before pegging it to the ground all the way round.

Bullfinches will destroy the buds of fruit trees; the protection against them is to grow the fruit trees inside a fruit cage, which means choosing varieties of apple or pear which crop well as dwarf pyramids, espaliers and cordons. The most effective kind of fruit cage is one 1·8 m (6 ft) high, surrounded by wire-netting of not larger than 1·9 cm (¾ in) mesh, with a gate. This is left uncovered until just before the birds show an interest in the buds, and it is then covered with string or nylon netting, supported on intermediate posts within the enclosed area.

The reason for not leaving the netting on all the year is that some insects and, in particular, their chrysalids, are good winter provender for Robin Redbreast and Jenny Wren (God Almighty's cock and hen), which do practically nothing but good in the garden throughout the whole of the year. Blackbirds, also, probably do more good than harm, although they will, if allowed to, take all the cherries before we can. Rooks, although they know precisely when to take our walnuts, are otherwise good allies, something which Richard Payne Knight (the great Picturesquer) recognized in his poem, *The Landscape*, of 1795, referring to them as dragging 'the embryo beetles from their holds'. A footnote to the poem adds: 'The farmers, when they see the rooks feeding on the fields that are newly sown, are apt to imagine that they are eating the seed-corn, and thence endeavour to destroy them; whereas they are in reality digging up the worms and slugs, and by that means doing the most essential service. The large white grub with a brown head, which, after lying three years in the ground, becomes the common brown beetle, and which is so destructive to the roots of grass and corn, while in this embryo state, is a favourite food with them;—whence those insects seldom appear near to rookeries.'

Little can be said for jays, who attack not only fruit, but even crops of beans. Moles, I suppose, if they really begin an invasion and cannot be driven away by putting holly into their runs or planting caper spurge, may have to be reduced by trapping; gassing is not a worthy way of trying to deal with them. Mice also may have to be trapped if their attentions to newly sown pea and bean seed become too insistent. As for the cold-blooded cohorts of insects which strike such terror into the breasts of well-meaning gardeners and contribute to the tinkle of shekels into the laps of beady-eyed scientists, some kind of *modus vivendi* has to be reached. The first step might be to read *Pesticides and Pollution* by Kenneth Mellanby (Collins), which is a reasoned, humane assessment of this subject. Towards the end of the book, Dr Mellanby writes:

Private gardens pose particularly important problems to-day. They are increasingly valuable refuges for wild life. Many birds are found there in greater numbers than in any other habitats. A great deal of damage is done by the over-enthusiastic amateur gardener if he is too liberal in his application of pesticides. The Ministry of Agriculture produces a shilling booklet called *Chemicals for the Gardener*; I find it a rather frightening compilation. Though excellent advice on the avoidance of dangerous practices is given, the reader finds himself advised to apply an enormous range of substances. He should use 2,4-D or MCPA on his lawns, simazine and similar long-lasting weedkillers on the path, dalapon to kill couch grass, paraquat instead of weeding the beds. Fruit trees may be sprayed with DNOC, tar oil, BHC, DDT, malathion and a host of other chemicals. Practically every other crop should receive one or more of these same insecticides. The question is, is this all necessary? The farmer has to control pests if he is to make a living. Most of our shops insist that fruit is unblemished and uniform, even if few questions are asked about its flavour. But does a little damage matter to the amateur, unless he wants to exhibit at his local flower show? No doubt if he sprays and sprays he will have 'clean' crops, and a higher level of pesticide in his, and his neighbours', tissues. He may find his wild birds are dying, and that eggs are left cold in the nests. Sometimes he will find that if he forgets to spray again he will have even more serious damage, for his garden will be devoid of predators. An unsprayed garden usually gives reasonable crops. A few apples may contain grubs but these can be cut out—some people think the rest of the flesh is all the sweeter! A garden, with diversity of trees, shrubs, grass and crops is unlike a huge area of agricultural monoculture. There are many beneficial insects. Biological control goes on all the time, not a hundred per cent successful, but sufficient to satisfy most householders who suffer more often from a glut than a shortage. They will find their friends appreciate their produce all the more, even if it bears a few marks of insects' jaws, if they know that it is free from pesticide residues. And there are now even some commercial shops which have discerning customers willing to pay more for slightly scabby apples with a good flavour and no organo-chlorine content. If our gardens could be kept free from at least the more dangerous pesticides, the effect on the wild life of Britain might be enormous.

The Ministry of Agriculture, Fisheries and Food publishes from time to time a list of approved products for the amateur gardener. These products include weedkillers, insecticides and fungicides.

Behind this is the Ministry's much larger booklet, produced for the Agricultural Chemicals Approval Scheme, the *Approved Products for Farmers and Growers*, which includes a very wide list of insecticides, etc., which are approved, although often with cautionary reservations, for use by professional and commercial growers. To read this, and to recognize how far we have come in our blundering, insensate tramline-path to overkill, is horrifying. Years ago Rachel Carson's *Silent Spring* set off the alarm, but still persistent organochlorine insecticides such as aldrin, BHC (lindane), DDT and dieldrin, are all given guarded recommendations. Organophosphorus insecticides, some of them systemic, also come into this chamber of horrors, albeit annotated with the best of all possible warnings; for instance, parathion, for the use of which protective clothing is obligatory—rubber gloves, face shield or dust mask, overall, rubber apron or macintosh . . . the Poisons Act applies to it. It should not be used by anyone under medical advice not to work with organophosphorus compounds; crops cannot be eaten within four weeks of application; animals and poultry must be kept away from treated crops for ten days; it is dangerous to bees, fish, livestock, game, wild birds and animals. Parathion is not approved for use by the private gardener and it is unlikely that he would ever get hold of it and try to use it, but malathion is another organophosphorus compound, contained in some of the products approved for use by gardeners. Malathion is probably the least dangerous of all the organophosphorus insecticides, a conclusion which Dr Mellanby came to when he wrote that 'it was chiefly dangerous when used by people who had been progressively exposed to low, and apparently harmless, doses of parathion (or to one of the other highly toxic organophosphorus compounds)'. If this is excluded, Dr Mellanby considers that: 'under most conditions—and, fortunately, most parts of the world have never yet been sprayed with any chemicals— malathion is a safe and useful insecticide'.

In the face of all this it would seem more becoming to restrict one's use of all chemicals to the absolute minimum. Each will decide how far he is to go; I will only suggest the following, which might be a reasonably acceptable list for those who are like hypochondriacs and alcoholics who cannot keep their fingers off a bottle of pills or a bottle of whisky.

Pyrethrum sprays, to be used against aphides, and **derris** for control of aphides and caterpillars. These are both fugitive, pyrethrum more so than derris. Both can safely be used on fruit blossom in the evenings when the bees are no longer present and will have dissipated by the time they return the next morning.

Bordeaux Mixture, which contains sulphur and copper, can be used against certain fungi, in particular peach-leaf curl and potato blight. The former may become chronic so that a gardener will have to decide whether to give up growing peaches and related fruits, or to spray them before the buds burst, and again a fortnight later, with Bordeaux Mixture, recognizing that Bordeaux sprayed over a number of years will drive away earthworms. Against mildews, **Sulphur** can be used either as dust or sprays.

Apart from these, organic methods of cultivation, proper rotation of crops, commonsense hygiene and growing immune varieties will generally make it unnecessary to undertake the expense and go through the unattractive motions of pumping evil-smelling chemicals on to one's growing crops. Apple scab, a fungus, can be kept in check by pruning away affected parts in the course of summer and winter pruning, and also by sweeping up infected fallen leaves and fruit and putting them on to the bonfire. Winter moth damage can be almost eliminated by putting grease bands round the stems of fruit trees in September, and apple-blossom weevil trapped in bands of sacking tied round the stems of the trees in early June. Lawrence Hills[1] has ingenious ways of dealing with many pests.

The poison most used against slugs and snails is Meta-fuel, sold under many different names. This is dangerous to children and pets, including the resident labrador, and the local hedgehog population which feeds on the poisoned slugs. Therefore, acceptable controls are: saucers of beer sunk in the ground (pick out and kill the inebriated slugs in the morning); orange and grapefruit hulls as a counter attraction, and an ingenious method consisting of crushed roasted egg shells scattered round the plants; also the old-fashioned remedies of soot and lime used in the same way— all dry and gritty materials discourage slugs' slimy progress.

An example of the Gadarene slope upon which we have embarked is the widespread adoption some years ago of tar distillate washes, sprayed in winter on to apple trees to kill the overwintering eggs of aphides. This was successfully accomplished, but along

[1] L. D. Hills, *Grow Your Own Fruit and Vegetables*, Faber & Faber Ltd, 1971.

with the aphides' eggs, predators, which fed on and kept down red spider mite, were wiped out, with the result that another, later, spray had to be devised against red spider. There is considerable evidence that pests and fungi develop strains resistant to the washes and dusts used against them.

Conclusion

In the beginning or soon after it, primitive man was a hunter, but he also ate berries, leaves and roots as he could find them. The plants which produced these were growing in some sort of equilibrium which changed from time to time, depending on climatic variations of ice, rainfall, temperature and wind direction. The bushes and plants which bore these berries, leaves and roots were, by our standards, poor specimens—aphides and fungi saw to that, but no one species of tree or moss dominated the whole landscape. In time, man himself began to exert influence on the environment by cutting down trees to make space to grow crops, by draining the land and planting hedges, resulting in a gradual but accelerating progression away from nature's *laissez-faire*; moving on to artificial cultivations by horse and tractor, the use first of the blood and bones of killed animals and the dung of birds and animals and, later, artificial fertilizers, the tidal wave of entirely chemical fertilizers and, in our own time, the use of organophosphorus and organochlorine compounds for killing insects.

Given the present state of civilization and economics, man cannot be expected to return to the state of imagined bliss in which he would be eating apples the size of golf balls, picking Good King Henry and cooking it instead of spinach, and painstakingly plucking fingernail-sized wild strawberries. In an attempt to establish some sort of philosophy, however tentative and even temporary, I suggest that, wherever possible, you cultivate vegetables and fruit in humus derived from compost, thus making them nutritionally satisfactory though not necessarily of exhibition quality. With this material it is possible to grow good, nourishing, if not prize winning, peas, beans, spinach, lettuce, carrots, beetroots, potatoes, onions, salsify and so on if they are spaced a little farther apart than they would be if they were grown more intensively, allowing their roots to draw on a larger volume of ground not much trespassed upon by plants in the same row. Vegetables resulting from such cultivation may be a little smaller than those forced up by fertilizers, ammonium sulphate, potassium sulphate and others, but they will be much better endowed with vitamins and other food values and they will be more resistant to insect and fungus attack, although they may not have so much shop-window appeal as those grown with full benefit of chemicals. An over-riding principle must be not to use cultural methods or chemicals which can cause damage to the environment outside your own garden.

CHAPTER THREE

Cloches, Frames and Greenhouses

W HEN you have explored the possibilities of growing out of doors in your kitchen garden you will want to widen your horizon with the use of some form of plant protection, especially if you intend to produce vegetables for the table all through the year. Cloches and a frame will help you to obtain the most from your soil and aspect, as far as plants that ordinarily produce vegetables or fruit in the northern hemisphere are concerned. When you add a greenhouse to your armoury, much of the vegetable world is spread at your feet.

The *Dictionary* of the Royal Horticultural Society succinctly describes cloches as: 'appliances for enclosing small areas to protect the plants therein from wind and rain and excessive transpiration, and at the same time to expose them to light and prevent loss of heat'. They are particularly useful for obtaining earlier crops of peas, beans, asparagus and lettuces, and also in prolonging them into the autumn. Young plants grown in greenhouses or heated frames and hardened off can be put out of doors some weeks earlier if they can be protected by cloches. Certain plants whose final harvesting in this climate may be doubtful can be given a longer period of growth by starting them early under cloches. This applies particularly to haricot beans and sweet corn.

Cloches

The word cloche is the word for the glass bell jars which were used in France in spring to protect and to hasten crops planted outside. These really looked like glass bells, and being made of fairly thick glass, were heavy enough never to be blown over by the wind, and they produced wonderful crops. In an old book published some years ago by the Daily Mail, called *The French Garden*, they are advertised in diameters of 14, 16, 18 and 20 in in cases of up to 300 cloches. There is a photograph in this book illustrating over 10,000, each holding one cos and four cabbage lettuces, and looking rather like a snowfall of little UFOs.

They were, however, expensive and in time were superseded in Britain by Chase continuous cloches, pieces of glass held in position by wire fittings. Single cloches in the shape of tents or barns were placed end to end to make a continuous row, the ends being closed with a pane of glass placed against the cloche at right angles to it (Fig. 3). Glass cloches of this type are still made in

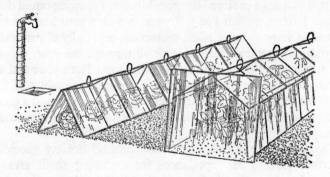

FIG. 3. Glass cloches can be tent like or barn shaped—those shown here are Chase cloches which can be dismantled and packed flat

large numbers and from a performance point of view are probably among the best. Glass not only transmits the radiant heat of the sun but retains a high proportion of it inside the cloche when the sun goes down. The disadvantages of such cloches are that they are heavy and awkward to move about, panes of glass can be broken fairly easily, and handling glass is generally not a pleasant occupation; it is very easy, for instance, to cut one's knuckles on the cloche corners.

Polythene is now very much used for inexpensive cloches any size, for example, 60 cm (2 ft) long, 60 cm (2 ft) wide and 45 cm (1½ ft) high; much lower strawberry cloches 75 cm (2½ ft) long, 45 cm (1½ ft) wide by 28 cm (11 in) high, and tall tomato cloches which I have used with some success with the variety Outdoor Girl, being 35 cm sq (14 in sq) by 1 m (3¼ ft) high. Polythene has disadvantages: although it has a higher light transmission than glass it does not retain the heat generated inside in the way that glass does (glass in fact acts as a partial one-way valve, letting in sun warmth, but not letting it out through the glass). Polythene is flimsy, tears easily and usually needs renewal at least every two years as it darkens under exposure to sunlight, reducing its light-transmitting potential.

Continuous polythene tunnels have been developed for commercial users, in particular for asparagus, lettuce and strawberries, and are now available to the private gardener. The arrangement is a length of clear flexible polythene film, supported over the crop

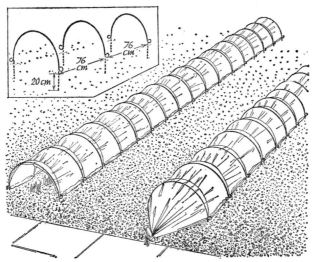

FIG. 4. Polythene tunnels are being much used instead of the conventional cloche

by stout wire hoops pushed into the ground and secured by wires to each hoop. The ends are drawn into the funnel shape and pegged down (Fig. 4). In spite of the disadvantages inherent in polythene, these tunnels will produce crops from ten to fourteen days earlier than plants which are unprotected. Plastic film is also used on the Continent as a mulch, amongst other crops, for asparagus and melons; for example at Aigue Mortes, polythene mulch increased the yield of asparagus by 39% and produced it eight days earlier.[1]

---

[1] Bulletin 11—Sept 71: Plasticulture Bulletin de Comité International des Plastiques en Agriculture.

PVC has better heat-retaining qualities than polythene, being thicker, but is more expensive. There is one particularly useful standard cloche made of corrugated PVC, bent in a half circle and retained by frames and end pieces, with a width of 1 m ($3\frac{1}{4}$ ft).

Frames

Frames are in practice larger and more effective cloches. Many vegetable plants can be sown in frames three or four weeks earlier than out of doors, some of them to be finished off entirely in frames, others to be transplanted. The traditional frame lights

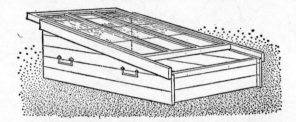

FIG. 5. A single portable frame, 1·8 × 1·2 m (6 × 4 ft), showing handles for lifting on to hot-beds

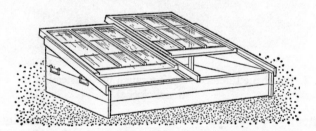

FIG. 6. Double portable frame, 1·8 × 2·4 m (6 × 8 ft)

measured 1·8 × 1·2 m (6 × 4 ft) or 1·2 × 1·2 m (4 × 4 ft) and were placed on walls of wood or brick so that they sloped down from back to front. They usually had three or four panes of glass. The lights had handles on either end so that in fine warm weather they could be pulled right back, to leave only one edge resting on the back of the frame, or the frame could be kept entirely closed except for a gap at the front edge where a brick or block of wood held the light up from the frame bed (Figs 5 and 6). Frames with wooden bodies were used, and still can be used, for covering hot-beds (see p. 48).

A Dutch light consists of a single standard size pane of glass 142 × 72·9 cm (56 × 28¾ in) (Fig. 7). This is a single light, easy to handle, but the large size of the pane makes it expensive to replace if it gets broken. Dutch lights are used as modules for some greenhouses today (Fig. 10).

Today frames are made in many different sizes and shapes. Some, for instance, have rigid PVC framing and acrylic panels; most of these are lighter and easier to handle than the old types. The heating of frames by a hot-bed is effective and apparently inexpensive, but involves rather dirty work. Much use is now made of soil-heating cable placed inside the frames, and run off a well-

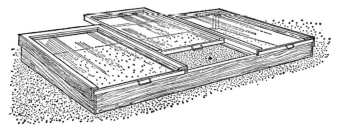

FIG. 7. Triple Dutch light frame; each frame has a standard measure-ment of 140 × 72 cm (56 × 28¾ in)

insulated mains voltage. They are laid on the ground and covered with 15–20 cm (6–8 in) of sand or soil. The installation is controlled by thermostat and is usually adjusted to give a soil temperature of 13–16°C (55–60°F). Makers do not advise making the soil bed above the wires of peat, vermiculite, fibre, ash, clinker, moss or other similar insulating materials as they might cause the cable to overheat and break down. Besides the soil-heating kind, there are also cables which can be used for air-heating inside the frame.

Greenhouses

A greenhouse is a glass box with all the elements under control; heat, humidity and available light. By beginning early enough, crops from sub-tropical or even tropical countries can be produced with the help of artificial heat. A cold greenhouse is useful in the way that a cold frame is useful for advancing by as much as eight

weeks the harvesting of crops such as strawberries and fruit trees
in pots (Fig. 8). By reason of its greater volume it is likely to be
less susceptible to rapid changes in temperature than a cold frame.
Greenhouses are also the only sure way of getting a sufficient
volume of crops which can just, but only just, in good weather be
produced out of doors, aubergines, peppers and melons for
example. Out of doors, tomatoes in a good summer can produce

FIG. 8. Fruit tree grown in a pot; drainage holes are needed in the base
as well as at the lower side

four trusses of the variety Marmande, but too often these will be
overtaken by the damp and the poor light after the autumn
equinox. On the other hand, perfect fruits of the varieties like
Alicante and Ailsa Craig will be produced from eight or more
trusses from June until October in a heated greenhouse.

But of course at a price: to start very early tomatoes it is necessary to keep up a temperature of 16°C (60°F) at night. This
may require what is known as a 'lift' of 27°C (48°F) above an outside temperature of − 11°C (12°F), i.e. 20°F of frost. Heating

systems are supplied with many small greenhouses; they are said to be capable of maintaining a temperature inside the greenhouse of about 7°C (45°F) against the outside temperature of −6·67°C (20°F)—a difference of 13·67°C (25°F). This difference is known as the 'temperature lift'.

Apart from exceptional winters such greenhouses will satisfactorily protect plants against frost.

A heated greenhouse will give the best results and be the most economical to run if exposed to the maximum of light. It is surprising how, after a night of continuous frost with heat being supplied nearly all the time, even the first rays of sun will quickly

FIG. 9. Lean-to greenhouse, making use of otherwise vacant wall; note the frame conveniently placed for hardening off plants, and the container for rain water, and the stand-pipe

raise the temperature so that the heating can be turned off. There must be a reservation about exposure. Some shelter from north and east which does not cause shade on the house is certainly useful. A span-roof greenhouse can be sited with its long axis running either north and south or east and west. The former used to be the most popular because from the middle of March to the middle of October the sun is high enough in the sky to shine down through the sides and the roof as it passes over the greenhouse at right angles to its long axis. On the other hand, a greenhouse running east and west with one side facing due south will collect more sunlight during the winter half of the year. A lean-to greenhouse against a wall ought always to face due south for the same reason: the wall at the back will be a good heat store (Fig. 9).

Nowadays, small greenhouses, particularly those made with metal frames, are generally constructed with glass to the ground. This is useful for growing crops at ground level, particularly tomatoes which need all the light they can get, including some on a level where the staging (slatted shelving) would otherwise have been. Cucumbers and peppers are also usually grown from ground level, but melons are more often placed on staging. Moderate-sized wooden-framed greenhouses are, for cheapness, often made on the standard Dutch light pattern, using as many as possible of these units (Fig. 10). The greenhouse with the base of brick or

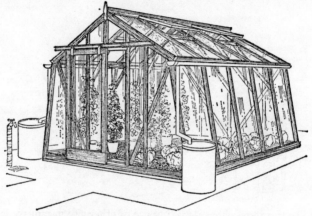

FIG. 10. A typical Dutch light greenhouse, measuring approximately
3·9 × 3·1 m (12⅔ × 10½ ft)

wood up to staging level is traditional, and warmer, because wood and brick are poorer conductors of heat than glass, permitting about half as much heat to escape. This requires staging, usually on either side of a central path about 75 cm (2½ ft) above ground level and from 60–90 cm (2–3 ft) wide, depending upon the width of the house. The width of 1 m (3 ft) is about as much as you can conveniently reach across when cultivating and tending the plants. Space under the staging is useful for packing in chicory, seakale and cardoons, for 'blindfolding' and blanching.

Ready-made greenhouses vary in size from about 2·4 × 1·8 m (8 × 6 ft) upwards (Fig. 11). Recently I realized that I had a space in my garden which would exactly take a small house of this size. It is not by any means perfectly sited because it is shaded by plants on the north and east, but it has been useful as a piece of experimental equipment. The frame is of aluminium with glazing to the ground and with very ingenious staging consisting of aluminium tray sections which can be lifted out and stored if crops are to be grown from ground level; this removal of staging can be done to almost any extent, all the staging on one side, half the staging on one side, two or three feet on one side and so on. The staging measures 60 cm (2 ft) on each side, leaving a central

FIG. 11. Small aluminium span roof greenhouse, with staging at one side. Size approximately 2·4 × 1·8 m (8 × 6 ft)

gangway 60 cm (2 ft) wide, a little cramped for the average-sized adult to keep turning round in, as for instance when watering. A good size for a general purpose greenhouse is 3·7 × 2·4 m (12 × 8 ft), but they can be obtained in different materials and in very many different sizes. A list of suppliers is given on p. 364.

If a lean-to greenhouse is built against a wall of a house, or if it is a conservatory it may just be possible, if there is some spare capacity on the central heating boiler, to connect the greenhouse heating to it, using the modern small bore pipes controlled by an independent thermostat. But generally the greenhouse will need some sort of heating plant of its own. Solid fuel boilers are still available. These employ low pressure, hot water pipes, usually 10 cm (4 in) in diameter. The boiler itself with its chimney generally stands outside the small greenhouse, but few people now are willing or able to take on the stoking commitment, and other forms of heating are much more widely used. Paraffin heaters in their simplest forms will keep out the frost if the right size and in sufficient numbers. The smaller of these need to be filled at periods between thirty and fifty hours of burning, but there are other more advanced types which are connected to an oil drum and will burn continuously for six to eight days, and there is at least one model which heats hot water in tubes, some control being exercised by a non-electrical thermostat. In this one, the fumes are removed by a flue running up through the roof.

There is a heater designed to burn natural gas which has the added advantage of enriching the air inside the house with carbon dioxide—something which tomato growers carry out with special equipment.

Electricity is on many grounds the most convenient method because it provides flexibility and simplicity of control. One or

FIG. 12. A typical electric fan heater for the greenhouse

more ordinary convector heaters can be stood on the floor like oil heaters, but the new turbo-heaters are more useful because the forced draught from the fan sends warm air probing all round the inside, and when the heating element is shut off by its own thermostat the fan continues to run, keeping up the circulation of air and making for a buoyant atmosphere (Fig. 12). These are rated at from 1 to 3 kw, and more than one will be needed in a greenhouse of any size. In large greenhouses they can be fixed to the sides at eaves' level so that they do not get in the way and litter the floor which they otherwise tend to do in a small greenhouse. This is one of the reasons why I prefer electric tubular heaters in banks fitted to the sides of the greenhouse. In the case of my own small greenhouse I have three 1·8-m (6-ft) lengths of tubing each side and under the staging (there is, as there should be, an air gap of about 7·5–10 cm (3–4 in) between the outer edge of the staging and the glass greenhouse wall) (Fig. 13). This gives 10·8 m (36 ft) total length of tubing at 60 watt per foot providing 2160 watts— 2·160 kw. These tubes are controlled by a separate rod thermostat

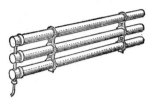

FIG. 13. Electrical heating tubes, usually placed under the staging against the wall of the greenhouse

fixed half way up the inside of the roof (Fig. 14). This kind of thermostat is much more accurate than the smaller wall mounted type.

When installing a new greenhouse it is essential to take the advice of the supplier on the heating equipment. If you explain the position of the greenhouse relative to wind and altitude the

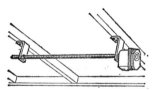

FIG. 14. A rod thermostat

suppliers, knowing the district, will work out the heat losses through the various materials of which the house is made: glass, metal, wood, brick, concrete, and then calculate the amount of heat needed to give a certain 'lift' in temperature. The lift provided for represents the capacity of the heating equipment to keep the temperature inside the house above the temperature outside the house by a certain number of degrees. The heating in most general purpose greenhouses is calculated to give a 13·67°C (25°F) lift which means that an inside temperature of 7°C (45°F) will be maintained against an outside temperature of −6·67°C (20°F) which is 12°F of frost, a fairly low temperature but by no means uncommon, particularly in the north of Britain. With this in mind a stand-by supplementary heater, such as a paraffin type, is useful to have on hand, and may save a whole greenhouseful of plants in a power cut.

This lift of 13·67°C (25°F) will not provide a high enough temperature inside to cultivate, for instance, early tomatoes. It is perfectly possible to increase the heating, but to heat the whole house to 18°C (about 65°F) from January to March or April would be very expensive. This can be avoided by providing much higher local temperatures for germination and early growing periods. Hot warming wires under some of the staging can keep the temperature of the soil at 16°C (60°F) while the air temperature inside the greenhouse is only 7°C (45°F). This, on the approved principle of 'warm feet, cool head', is excellent for germinating many seeds. Tomatoes, however, need not only high temperatures for germination, but an air temperature higher than 7°C (45°F). These conditions can be provided by some of the ingenious and often expensive propagators. One of the largest measures 125 cm (50 in) long by 66 cm (26 in) wide (this width should not be wider than the width of your staging) and gives a head room inside, under the plastic cover, of about 39–45 cm (16–18 in). Some of these propagators are heated by soil warming wires only, but these are perfectly capable of giving a 16–21°C (60–70°F) air temperature. A more sophisticated type has both soil warming and air warming cables. Tomato seeds sown in one of these devices in late January or early February would be put into pots three weeks later, kept in the propagator for a total of seven weeks and planted out in the greenhouse about the third week in March. The temperature would still have to be about 16°C (60°F), but at that time of the year the sun would provide much of the heat for you, and you would have saved the best part of seven weeks of high temperature for the whole of the greenhouse.

Ventilation is at all times important to create and preserve what is known as a buoyant atmosphere. This means the right degree of humidity related to the temperature, and as many changes of air as can be managed without causing the temperature to drop below what is required for cultivation. Plants get bored and sulky with dank unchanging air. Ventilation is effected by opening windows, known as ventilators in the roof, and in the sides of the greenhouse. The smallest houses, such as mine, have one vent only, and that in the roof. Far more satisfactory is to have at least two on each side of the roof, two on each of the sides and, as an extra luxury, what is known as bottom vents, sliding shutters or other means of inducing air to circulate from ground level. I find an automatic air controller very useful with my single roof vent. A greenhouse with four roof vents could make do with two controlled automatically, the others being hand operated, chiefly in the summer to increase ventilation on hot days. The equipment consists of a special bracket which replaces the standard opening stay, made from a tube filled with heat sensitive materials which, when they expand or contract, shorten or lengthen an arm fixed to the ventilator, thereby shutting or opening it, as the temperature rises or falls (Fig. 15). It is entirely self contained, and requires

FIG. 15. Automatic ventilator-opening gear

no electricity or other means of operation. It operates within a range of 18–40°C (65–105°F). This means in practice that it cannot be set to open below 18°C (65°F). I also have an extractor fan controlled by a thermostat and fitted into the end of the greenhouse opposite the door. To take an example, if the heating is set at 16°C (60°F), the automatic roof ventilator would open at 18°C (65°F) and the extractor fan start up at 21°C (70°F). If the temperature outside is such that the fan succeeds in bringing the temperature inside below 21°C (70°F) it will shut off, and if the temperature inside continues to drop the roof vent will shut at 18°C (65°F), and finally, the heat will come on at 16°C (60°F). In spite of this mild degree of automation there are times when recourse has to be had to hand operation. For instance, in winter when temperatures outside are about 10°C (50°F) and the temperature inside somewhere between 10 and 16°C (50 and 60°F) depending upon bursts of sunshine, the atmosphere inside the house can be stagnant because the automatic vent cannot come on below 18°C (65°F). In this case I override the fan to set it going and leave the door half open—my door has an adjustable stay so that this can be done.

We think so much about keeping up the temperature in winter and putting the greenhouse in the open to get the greatest amount of sunshine that we forget that at times there can be too much heat and too much sunlight. Lath blinds carried on runners above the roof can be specially made at great expense, but they are most effective because they filter the light, and being carried 15 cm (6 in) above the glass roof provide an insulating air space. Smaller houses now make use of green plastic blinds on spring rollers inside, or louvred Venetian blinds. A rough and ready and ugly looking way of shading is to spray a proprietary preparation like Summer Cloud on to the outside of the glass (or to make up your own with whiting and flour) and wash it off when the plants that need it are finished.

Much more use can be made of old greenhouses. Too many people, and wealthy ones in particular, throw up their hands at the imagined heavy expense, largely, I suspect, from inertia. But many greenhouses whose rafters and glazing bars are beginning to rot and the glass to fall out and whose old sectional anthracite boilers and 4-in pipes have long gone to their eternal rest, can still be made into something of practical use. A good deal of patching up, if only temporary, can be done by rough and ready repairs, by using polythene to replace broken glass, by making a partition to reduce the whole length and concentrating one's do it yourself resources at one end to produce a structure which is fairly air tight and as transparent as possible. To grow plants like peaches, nectarines and many fruit trees in pots, applies, pears, cherries and plums, all that is needed is heat enough to keep the temperature inside the jury-rigged house above freezing in February, March and April. Paraffin heaters, gas heaters and turbofan blowers will provide this small amount of extra heat.

CHAPTER FOUR

Growing Vegetables

THE methods described for growing the vegetables that follow are the very best ones, but if you are a novice gardener with small financial resources, do not be put off by the elaborate procedures and expensive equipment that is sometimes specified. Look around you: you cannot prevent green things growing. This same indomitable vigour will be your most valuable ally when you begin your vegetable garden; the plants will want to grow. Start small— a little care, water, sunshine and weeding will be enough to bring the simpler vegetables to your first and satisfying harvest.

You will not want to grow every vegetable we list here. Choose the ones that will be most useful to you, some from each section of the rotation of crops, and plan your ground accordingly. If you are a town or even a pot gardener, look for vegetables that will flourish under difficult conditions and in a measure of shade. If you have literally no growing ground at all, experiment with the different kinds of bean sprouts and mustard and cress that you can grow in the kitchen.

Build up your collection of equipment slowly, perhaps through birthdays and Christmases, as you begin to expand your horizon and feel the need for them.

I feel I would be less than honest if I ignored the pests and diseases that could attack each fruit and vegetable, so they are listed in some detail. Do not be daunted by them, they cannot all occur at the same time; they frequently do not occur at all.

Above all, make gardening not a chore but a delight.

Alfalfa seed see Sprouting Seeds

Artichoke, Globe and Chards   *Cyanara scolymus*
(*Compositae*)
Herbaceous perennial

Globe artichokes are some of the great delicacies of high summer,
with their unmistakable taste and texture when cooked. Perhaps the
greatest mystery is how anyone discovered the delectable fraction at the base of each leaf, and the superb heart inside the horrible
hairy centre of this giant bud. If the globes are not cut for the
table they will grow into handsome, violet-blue thistle-like
flowers which, with large, arching grey-green leaves, make it a
worthy contributor to a flower border.

The plant is probably a native of the Mediterranean region,
which accounts for its doubtful hardiness in cold districts of
Britain. Artichokes are much more common in France in summer,
and can redeem a long wait in the most unpromising-looking little
restaurant at a minor railway junction.

In Britain they are in season between July and September from
the open ground and, having a productive life of at least five years,
are a semi-permanent crop.

CULTIVATION   In March prepare the planting positions on a sunny
warm aspect away from shade and the drip of water from trees.
The plant is not reliably hardy outside the south of England. A
rich, deep soil is required, well-fortified with compost spread to
a depth of 10 cm (4 in) and lightly forked in, or decayed animal
manure, decayed leaf soil, seaweed or fertile peat (see p. 29).
The *p*H (see p. 32) should be about 6·5 and certainly not
below 6·0. Ensure that a supply of water is available close at
hand.

In April obtain offsets or suckers[1] 23 cm (9 in) high. These
should be short-jointed, sturdy and cut with a few roots attached
to their bases.

Plant these firmly 1 m (3¼ ft) apart in both directions in moistened soil. If young, keep a careful watch for the young suckers
flagging in hot, dry weather and be ready to give water as soon as
there are any signs of this.

This crop demands copious water in dry periods because its

---

[1] For names of suppliers see Appendix 2.

full productive growth is rapid. Hoe or pull out weeds in the early stages, but it will be found that as foliage develops and spreads, weeds will be suppressed by lack of light. A few globes may be expected in the August after planting, but in the interest of building up the strength of the crown, it is best to remove these as soon as they appear; in subsequent years the heads, five or more on each plant, are cut as required in July and August. Cut these before the bud scales open widely enough to show purple inside—if they are left on the plant at this stage and beyond, they are well past their best for eating. When picking the main crop of terminal globes, leave a 15-cm (6-in) length of stem above the top leaf. If the picked globes are not immediately required, store them with the stems in jars of water; renew this water every day, and slice off about 1 cm ($\frac{1}{2}$ in) of stem before replacing it in the fresh water. If stored in this way, the globes will remain in better condition than if they had been left on the plant.

The small lateral heads are a special delicacy. Remove them when they are as large as golf balls and cook as recommended on p. 293 or, like the Italians, eat them raw, or preserve them in olive oil. Take your own offsets by slicing off part of the stem base with roots attached, every other year, to maintain a ready supply of plants in prime condition. This can be done in November, overwintering them in cold frames in cold districts.

Chards can be a separate crop from this excellent vegetable. They are produced by cutting down in July plants which have borne a first crop of globes to a foot above the soil, putting on a generous mulch of compost or other organic material, and maintaining a generous water supply to encourage new shoots to grow from the base (it is, in miniature, a kind of coppicing).

When these new shoots are 60 cm (2 ft) tall—usually at about the end of September—tie the tops together and earth up the stems like cardoons and celery, by drawing soil up the stems in two or three stages of 7·5 cm (3 in) each. In six weeks—about the middle week in November—the blanched stalks are ready for cutting and cooking. The plants will resume ordinary globe production the following summer. As the plants are doubtfully hardy in some parts of the country, it is wise to give them protection in winter. A 10-cm (4-in) mulch of compost and leaf soil in October will be valuable, topped over with 15 cm (6 in) of litter (see p. 30), retained by 45 cm (1$\frac{1}{2}$ ft) of chicken wire or Netlon. When the need for the litter is no longer there, it should be removed, usually in early spring.

VARIETY   Vert de Laon.

PESTS AND DISEASES   None of any account.

Artichoke, Jerusalem

Helianthus tuberosus (Compositae)
Herbaceous perennial

Jerusalem artichokes are tubers (it is the globe artichoke whose flower heads are eaten) like knobbly irregular potatoes. They are tedious to peel for cooking but their flavour, especially in soup, makes them well worth the trouble. Although you can buy them more easily now than used to be possible, they are not yet as commonly seen as cabbages or peas, so there is good reason for growing your own. They are hard not to grow, once you have planted a few tubers.

Their name comes not from any biblical connotation but from a corruption of the Italian 'girasole', being a branch of the sunflower family that was introduced from the North American continent early in the seventeenth century.

In hot summers the Jerusalem artichoke will produce yellow flowers and is a handsome, decorative plant, useful to make tall temporary hedges up to 2·4 m (8 ft) high as windscreens and divisions between garden beds. If you like them for decoration you can leave a row of plants to renew themselves year by year, but if you need the ground for another crop you must dig out all the tubers, otherwise you will find occasional plants where they are not wanted.

The tubers are in season from October to December from the open ground. They have no particular place in the rotation of crops, and are often grown in spare corners of the kitchen garden.

CULTIVATION   In early February prepare a bed on fairly light sandy soil (this is not a plant for heavy soil) in an open situation. Fork in some compost or other organic material (see pp. 21–31).

At the end of February or early in March plant the tubers 15 cm (6 in) deep, 37 cm (15 in) apart, in rows 75 cm (2½ ft) apart.

Hoe out weeds. Make sure they have plenty of water. Draw

up soil round the stems to make room for developing tubers, as for potatoes.

In late October cut down the stems.

Dig up the tubers as you need them for cooking, until the end of December when the remaining tubers can all be dug and stored in sand in dry frostproof quarters.

Keep some of the tubers for planting back in February.

VARIETIES supplied as tubers:
Silver-skinned
Fuseau, said to be without the smoky flavour—if that is objected to.
Unnamed, but perfectly good varieties can be obtained from nurserymen.

Asparagus   *Asparagus officinalis* (*Liliaceae*)
                                                    Perennial

Asparagus is the most luxurious of all vegetables: the delicate green spears have an indescribably delicious flavour, and a sadly short season. They are extremely expensive to buy, so it is worth growing your own in terms of money as well as satisfaction. It takes time and care to establish your own asparagus bed.

Wild asparagus is a native of Europe, naturalized in Britain on sand dunes and in waste places. The cultivated varieties are usually sold not as seeds but as roots or 'crowns', of one, two or three years' growth. In the words of that great authority, Mr A. W. Kidner of Lakenheath in Suffolk: 'Transplanting is a major operation for a three-year crown, necessitating two years' convalescence'. You will gain nothing by yielding to the blandishments of nurserymen offering three-year crowns, so possess your gustatory soul in patience and plant one- or two-year crowns. Cut no buds in the first year, and in the second year cut for five weeks only. In later years cut for eight blissful weeks in May and June while the harsh world goes by. Your bed will provide a long-term crop, occupying the same ground for up to twenty years.

CULTIVATION Choose an open position, preferably on a southern slope, unshaded by trees, with good natural drainage, the

bed not less than 100 cm (3⅓ ft) above the highest water table
water level. If the drainage is poor, make up raised beds by digging
out alleys on either side and throwing the soil up to raise the bed.
The alleys will help the drainage and make useful service track-
ways for weeding, watering and harvesting.

In March, enrich the soil in the beds by forking in 15 cm (6 in)
depth of garden compost, or some kind of crumbly decayed
organic material, leaf soil if this is not strongly acid or, best of
all if available, chopped seaweed. The optimum pH of the bed at
the time of planting is 7·0—more alkaline than that needed for
most vegetable crops.

Early in April (the latter part of April is safer in northern
districts), buy one- or two-year-old 'crowns' and plant them in
two ways, half in each, as follows:

1. By the ridged system, in which you put the crowns 10 cm
(4 in) deep, 30 cm (1 ft) apart, in rows 1·3 m (4⅓ ft) apart. Ridge
up the stems as the plants grow, to blanch the lower parts of the
spears. This method will produce a higher proportion of thicker
spears.

2. 'On the flat'. Put in the crowns 10 cm (4 in) deep at a spacing
of 53 cm (21 in) in both directions. Do not ridge up. Asparagus
grown in this way will produce thinner, more flexible spears,
purplish green all the way down without the whitened inedible
'handles' of ridged plants. Their flavour is excellent, to my taste
better than that of the more usually seen spears with white
ends.

Plants grown in this way 'on the flat' produce spears for cutting
about a fortnight earlier than those grown on the ridged system,
because the crowns are nearer to the surface of the soil and respond sooner to the often rapid increase in soil temperature in
May and June. Therefore try half your crop on the flat and half
ridged up, to prolong the season. Earlier crops can be obtained
from cultivation under polythene tunnels (see p. 47).

Notwithstanding my insistence on free drainage, it is essential
that asparagus is supplied with plenty of water at all times, continuously percolating through the soil without any obstructions
to cause waterlogging or airlessness.

You must consistently remove weeds by hoeing or hand pulling,
in order to avoid competition for water and nutrients. This is
important in the early stages before the fern develops to give a

degree of shade to suppress weeds but this shade, such as it is, is relatively thin and you must keep a vigilant look-out at all times for weed development, especially perennial weeds. Apply repeated mulches of peat, leaf litter, seaweed, etc. after the soil has been thoroughly moistened.

The cutting period is from six to eight weeks, beginning about the end of May. Commercial growers stop cutting on the 20th June in order that shoots appearing after that date can develop into mature plants to build up the crowns for the following year's supply of spears.

You can raise asparagus from seed, but the process takes a year longer. Soak the seed first in lukewarm water overnight and then sow it in April on a nursery bed in drills 5 cm (2 in) deep and 30 cm (1 ft) apart. Thin the developing plants to 7·5 cm (3 in) when large enough to handle, and the following April put out the young crowns at one of the spacings referred to above.

Buy your crowns from local growers. They are cultivated on such a wide divergence of soils that success is most likely to come from plants propagated and cultivated in conditions similar to those existing in your own garden. In the Evesham district Yates' Giant Mammoth, available from Asmer Seeds, has shown promise at the Luddington Experimental Horticulture Station, near Stratford-on-Avon. The Kidner strains in East Anglia were outstanding; Mr A. W. Kidner has now retired from active growing, but some of his strains are still available from growers in Norfolk. Elsoms of Spalding have Limburgia, and Suttons of Reading have Martha Washington. Connover's Colossal has been a catchword for many years, but strains of it offered by a seedsman may have been raised in districts far away, so that before buying asparagus crowns you should first find out on what type of soil and in what district they have been raised, in order to determine whether they are likely to succeed in your garden.

PESTS AND DISEASES

Asparagus beetle The brightly-coloured black and orange adult beetle lays eggs on young shoots in spring. The eggs can be seen standing out like pegs, and may be laid before the end of the cutting season. Both larvae (greenish grey) and adult beetle feed on the foliage. The larvae pupate in the soil for ten days and several broods may occur in one season. Rub off the eggs by hand. The officially recommended sprays are persistent organochlorine insecticides, and unacceptable, but derris can be tried.

Slugs Take the measures against them suggested on p. 42.

Violet root rot A fungus which attacks the roots, covering them with violet or purplish threads, while the top growth turns yellow, and finally killing the plant. There is no cure, and diseased plants and those growing near them should be burnt.

SPECIAL REFERENCES
The Modern Approach to Asparagus Growing, Luddington Experimental Horticulture Station
Asparagus, Asmer Seeds Ltd
Asparagus, A. W. Kidner, Faber and Faber Ltd

Aubergine
Solanum melongena Egg plant, Jew's Apple, Mad Apple
(*Solanaceae*)
Annual

Aubergine or egg plant—the deep purple fruits are either long or much shorter and oval in shape—is a native of Africa and south Asia, known in England since the sixteenth century; modern plant breeders have produced varieties that will ripen their fruits in our climate. It is a vegetable that provokes mixed reactions: some people consider aubergines delicious sliced and fried, and an essential ingredient in ratatouille, others dismiss it as a useless, prestige-only vegetable, tasteless but with a repulsive, soapy texture.

Aubergines are essentially a greenhouse crop, although you may have some success in finishing them out of doors in a good summer. They are in season from July to October.

CULTIVATION Aubergines can be quite satisfactorily produced from a cool greenhouse, together with tomatoes, peppers, melons and cucumbers, provided that you do not expect very early crops. You will get the earliest and best results from growing them on their own at high temperature. The Lea Valley Experimental Horticultural Station emphasizes that aubergines are high temperature plants.

For those wishing to cultivate them in this way, the procedure is as set out in the following paragraphs. Those who have not either the greenhouse space or the money to pay for the extra heat can moderate the timings to produce fruit from July onwards, by sowing later (in late February or early March) and maintaining a lower temperature.

To produce the earliest crops, therefore, sow the seeds about 1st December in a seed compost in seed trays at a temperature of 18°C (65°F). When they are strong enough to be handled, transfer the seedlings to small pots, preferably peat strip-pots containing a soilless compost or a mixture of 50% garden compost, 25% sieved garden soil, and 25% sharp sand (all parts by bulk), and as soon as their roots are well round the pot, transfer them into the larger 30-cm (12-in) pots of growing compost, from which they will be fruited. The optimum temperature is 21°C (70°F) up to picking, which can be as early as the middle of May.

Do not stop the plants, but give them liquid compost made up as a spadeful of farm manure or garden compost in a bucket of water, or high nitrogen tomato feed at every watering. They grow fast and produce large leaves, their height at maturity may be about 60–90 cm (2–3 ft). Support them with short stakes if they become unsteady in their pots. Aubergines need a high temperature to set their fruit properly. If you are growing yours in a cool house together with tomatoes, cucumbers and so forth, you may find the pretty purple flowers wither and fall off without forming a tiny aubergine at all. If so, take a small paint-brush and hand-pollinate the fruits by transferring pollen from one flower to another, to encourage a good set, but do not allow more than four to six fruits to a plant.

VARIETIES New F₁ hybrids are Burpee Hybrid, Large Fruited Slice-Rite No. 23, and Short Tom. A promising variety at the Lee Valley Experimental Station which should be looked out for when it comes on to the retail market is Mammouth.

DISEASES AND PESTS
Grey mould Infects the embryo fruit and may be encouraged by falling petals. In any case, remove them, and raise the temperature inside the house.

Aubergines may suffer from some of the tomato diseases.
Red spider mite This can cause a good deal of trouble on aubergines, especially in summer, but maintaining some humidity and

68   GROWING VEGETABLES

spraying the top growth frequently with clear water will help to keep them at bay, and encourage fruit setting.

Bean, broad   *Vicia faba* (*Leguminosae*)
                                                        Annual

Broad bean plants are handsome in the garden, and the pretty black-spotted white flowers are especially favoured by bees.

The small, pale green beans, picked before they have acquired a leathery outer skin, are one of the pleasures of early summer; moreover they have a good vitamin C content. If you grow your own you can also pick them when the pods are only a couple of inches long, and cook them like mangetout peas. The delicate, bunched leaf tops that gardeners pick out to discourage the ubiquitous blackfly also make a good spring greens kind of vegetable, hinting at the taste of beans to come.

Broad beans are picked from the open ground in May and June. In the rotation of crops they are planted in freshly-manured ground, along with peas, onions, leeks, spinach and celery, after the brassicas and before the root crops.

CULTIVATION Prepare the ground by forking in 10 cm (4 in) depth of garden compost or other friable organic bulk material, some weeks before sowing.

In November, and again in February and March, sow the seeds 5 cm (2 in) deep in an alternated 'staggered' double row, 23 cm (9 in) between the plants. If cloches are available for November and February sowings, cover the rows with these. Broad beans are very hardy, but in cold northern districts their progress can be advanced a little if the plants are also protected by pea sticks, branches or litter, see p. 30.

Remove weeds and make sure that the plants receive plenty of water in dry weather in the spring. When the bean plants have reached their full height and are in full bloom, with the first flowers setting, pick out the tops to cook, and to discourage blackfly, and to direct the energy of the plant into making beanpods. After cropping pull up the stalks and roots for the compost bins—they are rich in nitrogen.

VARIETIES

Aquadulce (will produce the earlier crops and can be sown in
November or January but not later):
  Claudia
  Giant Seville
Longpods (the toughest, and better to plant in November):
  Imperial Green Longpod
  Imperial White Longpod
Windsors (best planted in February and March):
  Unrivalled Green Windsor
  Imperial White Windsor

PESTS AND DISEASES

Blackfly. Attacks and swarms over the tender upper leaves and
blossoms. Pinch out the tops, because these aphids are not as
partial to the tougher lower leaves. Autumn- and winter-sown
plants are much less susceptible because their upper leaves are not
as succulent as those sown in February and March.
Chocolate spot Causes brown spotted leaves. This is encouraged
by poor cultivation and lack of nutrients, particularly potassium.
If there is not enough good garden compost or animal manure,
use potassium sulphate at 28 g (1 oz) per sq m (sq yd) in October
for November-sown plants, and in December for February-sown
plants. Bordeaux Mixture will help to arrest its spread, but will
kill or drive away worms.
Slugs Protect against these pests, which may move in under
cloches or litter in cold weather, as suggested on p. 42.

Bean, French   *Phaseolus vulgaris* (*Leguminosae*)
                                                        Annual

French or dwarf beans are the aristocratic cousins of the more
pedestrian English runner. Their pods are more rounded, and
less hairy, and their flavour and texture exquisite when they are
picked small—something you can ensure if they are growing
in your own garden.

French beans are in season from the open ground in July and
August, continuing until the first frost. Cultivation under cloches,
and successional sowing will expand the season from June until the

end of September. If you are a real fanatic you can force an early crop in the greenhouse. In the rotation of crops, beans are planted in freshly-manured ground after the brassicas and before root crops.

CULTIVATION Choose an open, unshaded position, as warm as possible. Prepare the cropping ground in March by forking in 10 cm (4 in) of compost or other decayed, light-textured organic material. Make sure that there is lime enough to give a *p*H of 6·5–7·0.

Between the middle of April in the south and early May in the north soak the seeds in water overnight and then sow them directly into the cropping ground 5 cm (2 in) deep and 7.5 cm (3 in) apart in drills. This spacing is half that intended for the mature crop in order to provide for casualties from weather or slugs. Thin them to 15 cm (6 in) apart when they have a good hold on life.

If you have cloches, sow the beans as described, but from early April onwards. Make sure that the ends of the cloches are well closed up and be ready to cover with litter or mats, if late severe frosts threaten your seedlings.

Make a second sowing early in July to prolong the season of these most delicious vegetables. Keep a vigilant eye on watering, for preference using rainwater from a butt or storage tank at atmospheric temperature.

Pick the beans as soon as they are fully grown, but while still young.

For very early crops under glass, sow in March, in boxes 13 cm (5 in) deep, the seeds 15 cm (6 in) apart. If possible, have the boxes on the staging close to the glass. Maintain a temperature of 16°C (60°F) rising to 27°C (80°F) as the plants develop and the daylight lengthens.

VARIETIES
Sprite, pencil podded
Masterpiece
If you go to France and can pick up some of Vilmorin's seed, try for:
Mangetout Tendergreen
Beurre du Paradis
Beurre Crayon
Vilnel and Strinel are both immune to anthracnose.

PESTS AND DISEASES

Anthracnose. A fungus resulting in sunken, dark brown spots on the pods mainly, but also on leaves and stems. It is seed carried, and most likely in very cold conditions. Make sure of getting clean seed. If plants are infected, remove them and destroy them.

Bean, haricot or kidney   *Phaseolus lunatus (Leguminosae)*
                                                                  Annual

Haricot beans are the white or yellowish white dried beans used imaginatively in French cooking—particularly in the rich stews called *cassoulets* from south-western France. The bean pods are left on the plants until the ripe beans inside are harvested in September or October. These freshly-dried beans from your own garden are a great improvement on the hard little white stones of indeterminate age you usually get when you buy haricots in the shops. However, the beans mature so late in Britain that they risk being finished off by the frost, so it is advisable to cultivate them only in the warmer parts of the country. The variety called Comtesse de Chambord grows pods that can be eaten as a French bean first, so it is certainly worth planting a row of these, picking some and leaving some, and hoping for a mild autumn. In the rotation of crops they come after the cabbages and other brassicas and are followed by potatoes and other root crops.

CULTIVATION Sow the seeds in the middle of April directly into the open ground 5 cm (2 in) deep and 7·5 cm (3 in) apart in drills, the distance between the drills being 45 cm (18 in). When the plants have taken a hold on life, thin them to 15 cm (6 in) apart.

Continue cultivation as for French beans except for the climbing varieties which will need support like runner beans, q.v.

Harvest by pulling up complete plants when the pods are yellowing and the beans inside have reached full development, then hang them up to dry and later shell out the dried beans and store them in jars with open tops.

VARIETIES

Comtesse de Chambord, small, white round beans. Can also be cooked whole as a French bean.

Granda, stringless. Can also be cooked as a mangetout.

PESTS AND DISEASES   See French beans, p. 69.

Bean, runner   *Phaseolus coccineus* (*Leguminosae*)
                                                           Annual

Runner beans are the most reliable crop in the kitchen garden. Every country cottage sports its row of criss-crossed poles, almost buried in greenery and gay red flowers from midsummer until the first frost. Country housewives used to salt down their extra runners, in big earthenware pots, to supply them through the winter. Nowadays we can deep freeze a good quantity to preserve the vitamins and minerals in this delicious vegetable.

If you are growing vegetables in cramped or unlikely conditions, you can plant these good-natured climbers along a fence, or train them up a wall, or even decoratively over a town balcony.

You can start harvesting your runners from mid-July; pick them while they are young and tender. There is no pleasure in a bean that has become tough, stringy and full of parchment, and I have always found that continuous and almost brutal picking stimulates the crop. In the rotation of crops they are planted in freshly-manured ground after the brassicas, and before potatoes and other root crops.

CULTIVATION   Choose an open sunny position on well-drained soil (clay soils are usually too cold for this crop). Enrich the soil with 10 cm (4 in) depth of compost or bulky organic material, in April, then fix the supports in place. Use poles or canes 2·4 m (8 ft) long, pushed 30 cm (1 ft) into the ground 45 cm (18 in) apart in a double row opposite each other with, again, 45 cm (18 in) between them. These can be slanted towards each other and tied together 15 cm (6 in) below the tops, and horizontal canes or poles tied into and secured in the crotches (Fig. 16).

Another way which we saw at the Lee Valley Experimental Station is to slant the canes to meet about 105 cm (3½ ft) above ground, tying them there and fixing the horizontal canes or poles

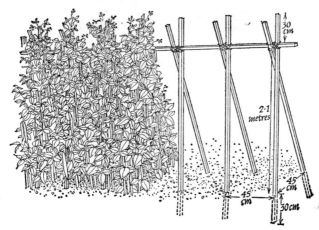

FIG. 16. Supporting runner beans by the conventional method of poles
or canes tied to a horizontal stake

as before—forming an X. This is slightly less stable in wind, but
it makes for much easier picking because the beans hang down from
the tops of the poles (Fig. 17).

A third method is to drive stout chestnut poles 2·7 m (9 ft)
long, 1 m (3¼ ft) into the ground, in a line at intervals of 3 m
(10 ft). A stout wire is then fixed between them and from this a
wide mesh net, known as a bean net, is hung (Fig. 18).

Between mid-May in the south and mid-June in the north,

FIG. 17. Runner beans supported on cross-rigged poles tied to canes

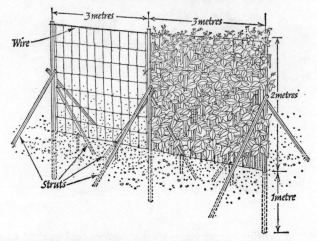

FIG. 18. Runner beans supported on netting

sow two seeds to each pole or cane. Put the seeds in 5 cm (2 in) deep. For earlier crops sow in peat-pot strips in a frostproof frame or greenhouse in April. Harden them off by increasing ventilation and plant them out from the end of May.

Keep the ground hoed and anticipate dry conditions by watering in good time; flower dropping without setting can be aggravated by dry soil, and also low night temperatures. The flowers are pollinated by wild bees. If they are not in evidence consider installing two or three hives of your own—more particularly if you also have fruit trees. Syringing with water, preferably at atmospheric temperature, will help to assist in setting the flowers.

VARIETIES
Enorma (Twenty one), long, dark green.
Scarlet Emperor, early, long.
Violet-podded (Climbing French), stringless. Tender pods, deep blue when harvested, turn green on cooking.

PESTS AND DISEASES
Slugs Protect the seedlings against these, as suggested on p. 42.
Aphides The array of organophosphorus insecticides against aphides is unacceptable, the more so since pollination depends so largely on bees, but fortunately trouble is seldom caused by either blackfly or greenfly.

Attacks by fungus will seldom be severe enough to make it necessary for plants to be pulled out and burnt, but plants which have been affected should be destroyed in the fire after harvesting.

Beetroot   *Beta vulgaris (Chenopodiaceae)*
                                   Biennial, grown as a hardy annual

Beetroot is a native, maritime plant which has been developed and selected for culinary use. Its distinctive dark red colouring as well as its sweet, delicious taste make it an interesting vegetable to eat. It is extremely easy to grow, and symmetrical plantings of beetroot are effective in a decorative potager. The leafy tops can also be cooked, like spinach, and supply much vitamin C.

Beetroot are in season from July to October from the open ground, and may be stored for use through the winter. In the rotation of crops they come after peas, beans etc., and before the brassicas.

CULTIVATION Beetroots prefer a light sandy soil, open to full sun, with no shade. Work the soil into good heart by forking in compost or other organic material. Sow the seed late in April, directly into the cropping position, 3·7 cm (1½ in) deep in drills 30–37 cm (1–1¼ ft) apart, having first soaked the seed in water, allowing it to dry and teasing out the separate seeds. Thin out to 23 cm (9 in) apart after about three weeks, or use pelleted seed which can be put in separately, 23 cm (9 in) apart. An adequate supply of water throughout the growing season will prevent the roots becoming hard and woody.

Pull early sowings as required as soon as they are large enough. Lift the remaining roots in October or before there is a frost, clean these of soil and twist the tops off, then store in sand. It is important to avoid bruising or damaging the skin, though breaking off the thin tap root does not matter.

VARIETIES
Globe varieties; the earliest are:
    Boltardy, less likely to bolt than many others, bright red colour.
    Avonearly, bred by the National Vegetable Research Station; a good early bunching beet for summer salads.
Long variety:
    Cheltenham Green Top, recommended for storing.

PESTS AND DISEASES

Beet carrion beetle Eggs are laid in the soil near the plants and young black grubs feed on the young leaves. Regular cultivation gives some protection.

Beet or mangel fly Maggots bore into the leaves which become blistered and withered. Hand picking and crushing mined leaves is the best remedy.

Beet rust Makes dark brown spots on the leaves. Burn infected tops and strictly maintain the rotation of crops.

Brassicas

In many gardens more space is given to members of this family than to any other, except potatoes. They have been developed from the wild maritime cabbage, *B. oleracea* (oleraceus means of the vegetable garden), and include broccoli, Brussels sprouts, cabbages, cauliflowers, kale, kohlrabi and savoys. Although they are a plebeian section of the garden population they are valuable providers of food, vitamins and minerals, particularly in winter when peas, beans, tomatoes and other delights of summer are over. Although the level of taste of the brassicas is commonplace, some of its members, the spears of sprouting broccoli for example, if cooked with élan and understanding, can approach the delicacy of sea-kale, or even asparagus. Some of them, unfortunately, in particular Brussels sprouts, may have a whiff of a distant sewage farm unless they are always gathered young and firm, and old soggy buttons and stalks promptly removed to the fire.

Since they have many characteristic requirements, ailments and afflictions in common, the following paragraphs will apply to all the vegetables in the family.

They all need well-limed soil, a pH of not much less than 7·0, for healthy growth and to keep at bay some of their particular pests and diseases. They need soil which has been enriched with compost or other decayed crumbly organic material three or four months before planting. They all need to be planted in well-firmed soil because they are top-heavy plants, and to ensure that they heart up well and solidly.

More than most other vegetables, they should not be cultivated in the same ground in succeeding years; their place in the rotation of crops is after potatoes, carrots, beetroots, parsnips and swedes, and they are followed in the next year by peas, beans, onions, leeks, tomatoes and celery.

With few exceptions, the seeds of all of them are sown first in nursery beds, cold frames or cool greenhouses, and later transplanted to their final cropping positions.

PESTS AND DISEASES

Birds Protect young seedlings by stretching black thread to small sticks or canes. Protect maturing and mature plants, especially Brussels sprouts, with pigeon netting.

Slugs Trap or deter these. See p. 42.

Cabbage white butterfly caterpillars Green and black caterpillars with a yellow line on the back. If possible pick these off by hand. Derris is the least dangerous of the many poisons recommended, but it will kill bees, and fish if the land slopes down to a stream. If the attack is severe, use derris late in the evening only, when the bees have returned to their hives.

Cabbage moth caterpillars Resembling those of the Cabbage White Butterfly but are smooth-skinned and not velvety. They bore into the hearts of the plants. Again, hand pick any caterpillars that are seen before they burrow into the hearts. Syringe the foliage briskly with water, or with 56 g (2 oz) of soft soap in 4½ litres (1 gallon) of water. As a last resort use pyrethrum or derris—but only in the evening after bees have gone.

Cabbage aphis Blisters and curls the leaves and produces honeydew and consequently sooty moulds. Young aphides hatch in early spring and feed on shoots and leaves until late summer. Burn stalks and stumps to destroy their overwintering premises. If the attack is severe, use derris dust in the evening when the bees have gone. Official approvals of organophosphorus and organochlorine contact and systemic insecticides are not acceptable.

Cabbage root fly Chiefly on cabbages and cauliflowers, the flies rather like houseflies, lay eggs from May to September on the stems of plants, particularly young plants just below soil level. The maggots hatch and bore into the roots, so that the leaves wilt, and the plant turns yellow. Tarred felt discs round the collar will help to prevent flies reaching the base of the stems.

Club-root A fungus which causes deformation and swelling of roots, and stunting of the top growth. Its occurrence only in acid soils is the best reason for maintaining a high pH. The long-term remedy is to apply massive dressings of hydrated lime of the order of 454 g (1 lb) to 0·8 sq m (1 sq yd). This will take a year or more to be effective, but rather than putting mercury into the soil by using calomel, dust or liquid, it is better to wait to plant brassicas or other crucifers until the soil pH is stabilized at 6·5–7·0, and in the meantime to use the ground for some other crops (not potatoes which need a low pH)—broad beans, other beans, or peas, or some of the stolid salsifies or scorzoneras. Take care not to be over exuberant in dressings of lime. Keep a check with your soil testing kit to ensure that the pH does not rise above pH 7·0, because wildly high pH readings can lead to iron and other deficiencies.

Broccoli, sprouting and Calabrese

Brassica oleracea botrytis cymosa,
B. o. italica (Cruciferae)
Annual

The Americans know how to appreciate broccoli, they consider it a delicacy almost equal to asparagus. In Britain we either ignore it or treat it like an obscure relation of the cabbage tribe. But the Americans are right. Besides being one of the most nutritious of all green vegetables (rich in vitamin A and vitamin C) broccoli is quite delectable, and deserves proper appreciation.

The name derives from the Italian *broccolo*, and in one or other of its forms can be harvested from September and sometimes earlier, until April, providing a much-needed green delicacy when others like peas and beans have vanished with the summer. Sprouting broccoli, unlike cauliflowers which have been bred to produce single, large, compact flower heads or curds, makes loose clusters both at the tops, and lower down between the leaves and the stem, which are harvested when about 15 cm (6 in) long. The Calabrese strains (green sprouting broccoli) can be picked as early as July and on into November, after which the early purple sprouting broccoli come in January and February, followed by the late purple sprouting right through until April.

In the rotation of crops, broccoli, with the other brassicas, comes after the root crops, and is followed by peas, beans, etc.

Early-maturing types—CULTIVATION In January, two or three months before planting, begin to prepare the cropping position in ground from which root crops have been lifted. Rake in compost or other bulky organic material spread at 10 cm (4 in). Make sure of adequate lime, a pH of between 6·5 and 7·0. Firm the ground by treading several times before planting.

In January and February sow the seeds of the earliest crops in a cold frame or cool greenhouse. Begin to harden these off in April, and plant them out from May onwards into the cropping positions 45 cm (1½ ft) apart, with the rows 75 cm (2½ ft) apart. Protect against pigeons and slugs, see pp. 38, 42).

Early varieties, harvested before hard frost, can be given a dressing of compost to a depth of 10 cm (4 in)—or if this is not available, hoof-and-horn meal and bonemeal, each at 56 g (2 oz) per 0·8 sq m (1 sq yd), in June–July.

EARLY VARIETIES
Express Corona (Calabrese) F₁ hybrid, September. One of the earliest of the Italian Calabrese.

Italian Sprouting (Calabrese), ready from September onwards.

Sutton's Autumn Spear (Calabrese), from September to November.

Later maturing types—CULTIVATION In late April or May, sow the seeds of later maturing kinds out of doors in nursery beds. Protect against birds with thread stretched between canes. Protect against slugs.

Transplant to cropping positions as above, in June and July, with the rows rather closer than the early ones, 60 cm (2 ft) apart, to afford mutual protection in the winter. Ensure that the ground is really firm to avoid wind-rock. Protect against pigeons and slugs.

These stand through the winter, and should not have nitrogenous dressings to encourage soft sappy growth to be subsequently damaged by frost.

LATE VARIETIES
Sutton's Early Purple Sprouting, ready in January and February.

Sutton's Purple Sprouting, ready in March and April.

Sutton's Late Purple Sprouting, ready in April.

PESTS AND DISEASES See brassicas, p. 77.

Brussels Sprouts

Brassica oleracea bullata gemmifera (Cruciferae)
Biennial

Brussels sprouts are in season from August to January and even later. Being rich in vitamin C, they are a valuable green crop in the winter months, yet we almost take them for granted, they are so plentiful in the shops. Brussels sprouts are delicious with all kinds of meat and fish dishes, and traditional with Christmas game and turkey.

If you grow your own you can choose a medium variety, and need not then be dependent on the huge torpedoes that agricultural botanists have developed for commercial growers.

In the rotation of crops, Brussels sprouts, being brassicas, come after potatoes and other root crops, and before peas, beans, onions, leeks, lettuces, tomatoes, spinach and celery.

CULTIVATION In January, two or three months before planting, begin to prepare the final cropping positions in ground from which root crops have been lifted. Rake in compost or other bulky organic material, spread at 10 cm (4 in). Make sure of adequate lime, a *p*H of between 6·5 and 7·0. Firm the ground by treading several times before planting. Firm ground prevents loose, 'blown' sprouts.

If you are starting with seed, sow it in a nursery bed out of doors, between the middle of March and the beginning of April in drills 1·9 cm ($\frac{3}{4}$ in) deep. Protect against birds with black thread stretched between canes. Protect also against slugs, see p. 42.

In late May or early June put in bought plants or transplant your own to their cropping positions in by now, well-firmed ground, 1 m ($3\frac{1}{4}$ ft) apart, in rows the same distance apart. If the weather is dry, water the plants in. For earlier crops sow at the beginning of March in frames or under cloches, and transplant in April. Protect these transplanted sprouts with large-mesh netting because sprouts are a preferred diet for wood pigeons. Protect also against slugs.

During the growing season, hoe out weeds. Pay attention to adequate watering.

Pick from the bottom upwards. Early varieties to be picked before hard frost will benefit from another dressing of compost, or hoof-and-horn meal and bonemeal, each at 56 g (2 oz) per 0·8 sq m (1 sq yd), put in in early July.

VARIETIES

Early Dwarf, 45 cm (1½ ft), ready October.

Peer Gynt F₁ Hybrid, ready in October. Short growing. Can be planted closer together, 60 cm (2 ft), and is useful when space is limited.

Prince Askold F₁ Hybrid, from November to January. Dark green, firm, medium-sized buttons.

Sutton's Market Rearguard, from December to March. Medium-sized sprouts, a heavy cropper.

PESTS AND DISEASES   See brassicas, p. 77.

Cabbage   *Brassica oleracea (Cruciferae)*
                                                    Biennial

Cabbage is a most maligned vegetable, yet it is a highly nutritious one, and when it is properly treated, delicious as well. There are times in the year when it is almost the only vegetable in the kitchen garden, so it is infinitely worth taking the trouble to grow it and then to cook it properly. If you enjoy cabbage, you can arrange for it to be available almost all the year round from your own kitchen garden. Winter cabbage is particularly useful, as it has a high vitamin C content.

The seasons for the various kinds of cabbage are as follows: winter cabbage from October to March, spring cabbage from April to June, summer cabbage from July to August. In the rotation of crops, cabbages, as part of the brassica family, follow potatoes and other root crops, and are themselves followed by peas, beans, onions, leeks, lettuces, tomatoes, spinach, spinach beet and celery.

Winter Cabbage—CULTIVATION   Either buy plants from local nurserymen in the summer or sow the seed in nursery beds out of doors in drills, 1·9 cm (¾ in) deep, in March and April. Protect the seed against birds with black thread or cotton stretched between canes. Protect the seedlings also against slugs, see p. 42. In June and July, transfer the young plants as soon as they are large enough to handle, into their winter quarters, in well-firmed soil at a *p*H of not less than 7·0, 60 cm (2 ft) apart. At no time apply quick-acting nitrogenous fertilizers because winter cabbages must stand through the winter and young sappy growth might be damaged by frost. Protect with wide mesh pigeon netting.

VARIETIES

Autumn Monarch F₁ Hybrid, solid heads, long standing.

Winter Monarch F₁ Hybrid, firm heads, late.

January King, one of the latest, a hardy drumhead, standing on until April.

Spring Cabbage—CULTIVATION Sow the seeds in July and August in nursery beds out of doors 1·9 cm (¾ in) deep in drills 23 cm (9 in) apart. Protect against small birds and slugs, see pp. 38, 42. Transfer the plants in September to ground which has been well fortified with compost or old rotted manure two or three months ago, and dressed with lime. Put the plants in at a distance of 45 cm (18 in) apart all round.

Do not use quick-acting nitrogenous fertilizers on spring cabbage, because they, too, must grow hard in order to survive cold winter weather. Protect against pigeons with wide mesh netting.

VARIETIES

Springtide, compact, with pointed hearts of moderate size.

Wheeler's Imperial, a well-tried, old variety, dwarf with small pointed heads.

Harbinger, one of the earliest spring cabbages, small hearted of good flavour.

April, dark green with pointed hearts, compact for close planting in restricted areas.

Flower of Spring, a little later than Harbinger with a larger heart.

Summer cabbage—CULTIVATION Sow the seeds under glass in boxes in a cool house or well-protected frame in January or February. Transfer the plants in May to the kitchen garden, and cover some with cloches for an early crop. Make sure that the ground is in good heart and recently manured, because a good proportion of nitrogen will be beneficial for these crops, which are gathered at the height of the growing season. Protect them from pigeons with wide mesh netting.

VARIETIES

Summer Monarch F₁ Hybrid, neat, solid heads.

May Star F₁ Hybrid, early ball-headed.

June Star F₁ Hybrid, ball-headed, rather later than May Star.

PESTS AND DISEASES   See brassicas, p. 77.

SPECIAL REFERENCES
Varieties of Spring Cabbage, Vegetable Growers Leaflet No. 7, 1970, National Institute of Agricultural Botany
Spring Cabbage, Advisory Leaflet No. 349, 1970, Ministry of Agriculture, Fisheries and Food
Summer and Autumn Cabbage, A.L. No. 351, 1971, M.A.F.F.

Cabbage, Chinese   *Brassica pekinensis* Pe-Tsai (*Cruciferae*)
Annual

Chinese cabbage is a brassica, a species of ordinary cabbage, which you can eat as a salad vegetable, or use like cooked cabbage. The thick white ribs of the leaves can also be served with melted butter as a first course. Chinese cabbage is available in August and September. In the rotation of crops it comes in with the other brassicas, after potatoes and root crops, and before peas, beans and so forth.

CULTIVATION   Sow the seeds in their cropping position 1·9 cm (¾ in) deep in drills 30 cm (1 ft) apart in May, or, for a later crop, in July. Thin the plants out progressively to 30 cm (1 ft) apart. The crop is less likely to bolt from later sowing.

VARIETIES
Chinese F₁ Hybrid, the leaves of this can be eaten uncooked in salad or boiled like ordinary cabbage.
Mi-Chihili
Pe-Tsai, sow in late July in cropping positions. The midribs can be cooked like asparagus.

Cabbage, red   *Brassica oleracea capitata* (*Cruciferae*)
Biennial

The deep red of this kind of cabbage is due to anthocyanin, the pigment which also gives autumn leaves their colours. It is easy to grow, decorative if you are planning a potager, and good to eat too. You can harvest red cabbage from September to March, and being a brassica it comes after potatoes and root crops, to be followed by peas and beans.

CULTIVATION Either sow the seeds in frames or in nursery beds out of doors, in both cases in September. Protect those sown out of doors with cloches if possible. Allow the plants to stand through the winter. In cold districts pack litter (see p. 30) around them, if you have it available. Prepare the cropping positions early in the following spring, forking in compost or well-decayed manure at 10 cm (4 in). Transplant the overwintered seedlings from frames or nursery beds in April to their cropping positions 60 cm (2 ft) apart.

Red cabbages can also be raised by sowing the seed out of doors in nursery beds between March and June, planting them out in June and July, and harvesting them the same year.

VARIETIES Sutton's Large Blood Red, a ball-headed variety.

PESTS AND DISEASES See brassicas, p. 77.

Cabbage, savoy   *Brassica oleracea bullata subauda* (*Cruciferae*)
Biennial

Savoy cabbages are the crinkle-leaved, solid-hearted cabbages, crisp to slice and the best for cole-slaw. They are extremely hardy, the leaves being made more tender by frost. None the less, do not put on quick-acting nitrogenous fertilizer to promote soft growth in the winter. The benefit of frost is on mature, hard leaves. Savoys are in season from November to April. Being brassicas, they come after potatoes and other root crops, and before peas, beans, spinach, onions, leeks, lettuces, tomatoes and celery.

CULTIVATION Sow the seed in a nursery bed in April and May 1·9 cm (¾ in) deep in drills 30 cm (1 ft) apart. Protect the seed against birds with black thread or cotton stretched between canes. Prepare the cropping ground as for brassicas, p. 77, three months before planting out. Do the latter in July and early August with a dibber or trowel. Put in the plants 60 cm (2 ft) apart in each direction. Keep weeds hoed out. Make sure that there is adequate water, never letting the plants begin to wilt or droop. Protect against pigeons with wide mesh netting.

VARIETIES
Sutton's Autumn Green, an early savoy, ready in October and November.
Sutton's Rearguard, good dark green colour, very hardy, picked between December and April.
Winter King, dark green leaf and head, ready November–December.
Ice Queen F₁ Hybrid, medium to large heads, mid-season, uniform in size and hardy.
Savoy King F₁ Hybrid, taller growing, even sized, prolific.

PESTS AND DISEASES See brassicas, p. 77.

Cauliflower *Brassica oleracea botrytis cauliflora (Cruciferae)*
Biennial, treat as an annual

The cauliflower is a vegetable that has been used for centuries, and continuously selected and developed to produce the large white head, or 'curd' we know today. It is an interesting member of the brassicas, particularly when partnered with cheese. Its creamy white flowering head needs to be carefully and quickly harvested, not permitted to become grimed and bruised in a vegetable market. It is surprisingly high in vitamin C, especially when eaten raw.

Summer cauliflowers are in season from July to September, autumn cauliflower from October to December, winter cauliflower from January to March, so you can organize an almost continuous supply. In the rotation of crops, cauliflowers with the other brassicas, come after potatoes and other root crops, and are followed by peas, beans, onions, lettuces, leeks, tomatoes, spinach and celery.

Summer cauliflower—CULTIVATION Sow the seed in a cold frame in October or in a heated greenhouse in January. Transplant to cropping positions in April after hardening off greenhouse seedlings. When possible, keep under cloches until the end of May or whenever damage from frost is still likely. Transplant at 50 cm (20 in) spacing. Protect against slugs and pigeons.

VARIETIES
Sutton's Classic, short growing, early June.

Sutton's Arcturus, dwarf growing, a little later than Classic, recommended for the epicure. June.

Snowball, compact, early, good quality. June–July.

Autumn cauliflower—CULTIVATION   Sow the seed in drills in nursery beds 2 cm (¾ in) deep out of doors in April and May. Sow the variety Flora Blanca rather later, in mid-May. Protect against slugs and birds. Transfer to cropping positions in June and July, 75 cm (2½ ft) apart. Protect against pigeons and slugs.

VARIETIES

Kangaroo, excellent Australian variety, maturing late September.

Boomerang, dwarf, maturing September.

Canberra, an Australian variety, maturing October–November.

Barrier Reef, dwarf, matures in late October.

Flora Blanca, matures in September, should be sown out of doors rather later than the others, in mid-May.

Winter cauliflower or headed broccoli—CULTIVATION   Sow the seed in drills in nursery beds 2 cm (¾ in) deep out of doors in late April to May. Transplant into cropping quarters as soon as they can be handled in June or July. Protect against pigeons and slugs, see pp. 38–42.

VARIETIES

Sutton's Autumn Protecting, heads in November or December.

St Agnes, Seale Hayne variety of Roscoff Broccoli No. 1 A6, heads in December and January. For Southern districts.

St Keverne, Seale Hayne variety of Roscoff Broccoli No. 4 DK7, heads March–April. For Southern districts.

Thane, heads in April.

Manston, heads mid May.

PESTS AND DISEASES   See brassicas, p. 77.

SPECIAL REFERENCE   *Varieties of Cauliflowers*, Vegetable Growers Leaflet No. 1, 1972, National Institute of Agricultural Botany

Kale or Borecole   *Brassica oleracea acephala (Cruciferae)*
Annual

Along with Savoy cabbages, kale is the hardiest of all winter greens, and is well suited to cold, northern districts. As with all the brassicas, correct cooking and serving makes all the difference between a dreary school-lunch vegetable and a delicious, fresh-tasting one, containing plenty of vitamin C.

Kale is in season from September to March. With the rest of the brassicas, it comes after roots and potatoes and before peas and beans, etc.

CULTIVATION   Sow the seeds of all varieties except Hungry Gap in a nursery bed, in drills 1·9 cm (¾ in) deep in early May, and protect the seedlings against slugs and birds. Transplant them into their cropping positions as described under brassicas, p. 77, in July. Ensure firm planting (Hungry Gap is sown straight into its final cropping position in early July, in rows 45 cm (18 in) apart). Keep the ground hoed and remove dead leaves. In harvesting, cut from the top, leaving sideshoots to produce more leaves. Pull the plants up when they begin to flower in April.

VARIETIES

Dwarf Green Curled, short growing, closely curled leaves, stout and compact.

Frosty Novelty (Frosty New), extremely hardy, 30 cm (1 ft) high, leaves carried above stems away from mud.

Thousand-headed, strong growing, prolific, used also for stock feeding.

Sutton's Extra Curled Scotch, dark green, densely curled, very hardy.

Hungry Gap, a late variety sown directly into its cropping position.

PESTS AND DISEASES   See brassicas, p. 77.

Kohlrabi   *Brassica oleracea caulorapa (Cruciferae)*
Biennial

Kohlrabi is known as the turnip-rooted cabbage: you can eat both the green tops and the roots. Kohlrabi matures from July to

October, and you can then store it for winter use. In the rotation of crops it comes with the brassicas, in well limed soil, after potatoes and other root crops, and before peas, beans, etc.

CULTIVATION In March prepare the ground as for turnips; in April sow the seeds in the cropping ground, in rows 39 cm (15 in) apart. Thin the seedlings progressively to 30 cm (12 in) apart. The thinnings can be spaced in adjacent rows, to make a second crop.

Water the plants thoroughly, and keep the surface open by hoeing. Dig up your kohlrabi when the roots are about 7·5 cm (3 in) in diameter. Store them for the winter like beetroot.

VARIETIES
Early Green
Sutton's Earliest Purple

PESTS AND DISEASES   See brassicas, p. 77.

Cardoon   *Cynara cardunculus (Compositae)*
                                Perennial, grown as an annual

The cardoon comes from the Mediterranean. It is a handsome plant, with purple thistle-like flowers similar to its relation, the globe artichoke, but with spinier leaves. Although it is a perennial, it is treated like an annual in the vegetable garden, and the whole plant dug up when it is used. Unlike the globe artichoke, it is the blanched leaf-stalks, not the flower heads, of cardoons that are eaten. They are yet another interesting vegetable that you can no longer find in the shops. When you grow your own they will be available from the open ground from the middle of October.

CULTIVATION   In early April prepare the cropping ground, on the flat if the soil is reasonably water-retentive. If conditions are likely to be dry, dig trenches 25 cm (10 in) deep as for celery, and put in 10 cm (4 in) of rotted manure.

Towards the end of April sow the seeds in groups of three, 45 cm (18 in) apart, in rows 1 m (3¼ ft) apart. Thin the plants to leave the strongest one in each position, and tie each one to a stake. Make sure they always have plenty of water. In August, when they are fully grown, begin to blanch them by gathering the leaves together and wrapping them round with bands of hay or corrugated cardboard and earthing them up. Some litter laid round the base of the plants will also help. The blanching will take about eight weeks. To harvest, dig up the plants and cut the blanched stalks.

VARIETY Improved White

PESTS AND DISEASES There are no particular pests and diseases.

Carrot
Daucus carota (Umbelliferae)
Biennial, grown as an annual

Carrots are native to this country; the wild ones usually have yellow or white roots. They are a marvellously easy, versatile vegetable to grow—it is not surprising that they have long been domesticated. Early varieties are in season from May to June and maincrop ones from September to March, bringing some colour as well as needed vitamin A and carotene to our winter diet. In the rotation of crops, carrots are grown after peas, beans and so on, and before the brassicas.

Early carrots—CULTIVATION The cropping ground for carrots should be manured from the previous crop, well drained, in an open, sunny position preferably facing south, because carrots appreciate a warm soil for germination and early growth. Do not apply additional fertilizer or manure, to avoid producing forked roots.

For earliest crops sow in boxes in a cool greenhouse in February or in a frame out of doors in March. Thin progressively to about 12 cm (5 in) and harvest this crop in May. Sow early varieties in their cropping positions out of doors at the end of March or early April in drills 1·2 cm ($\frac{1}{2}$ in) deep and 30 cm (1 ft) apart. Thin out progressively. These are harvested in June and July. Hoe to keep weeds under control.

VARIETIES
Sutton's Champion Scarlet Horn, length 10–13 cm (4–5 in,) cylindrical shape with little core.
Amstel, small cylindrical.

Early Nantes, small cylindrical, finger size.

Amsterdam Forcing, medium length, blunt-ended.

Paris Forcing, rapid growing, produces round-shaped roots, best used about the size of a golf ball.

Main crop—CULTIVATION   Sow in drills 1·2 cm (½ in) deep and 30 cm (1 ft) apart, from April onwards in cropping positions. Carrots are useful as catch crops to be sown after early potatoes and early peas have been taken out. For a late crop of small, tender carrots, sow early varieties again in July.

VARIETIES

Scarla, stump-rooted, cyclindrical shape, little core, stores well.

Sutton's New Red Intermediate, a long, pointed carrot, stores well.

Chantenay Red-cored, stump rooted, early main crop.

PESTS AND DISEASES

Carrot fly   This insect lays its eggs in the soil, and the maggots which hatch out from them eat into the developing carrots. Control can be, and is, commercially exercised by dressing the seed before sowing, and dusting on to the soil chlorinated hydrocarbons which, as explained earlier in this book, are not recommended, and there is no other sure method of getting rid of these pests. The spreading of lawn mowings on the soil surface round the carrots and the planting of onions close to them have been suggested. Late sown crops are unlikely to be attacked.

Violet root rot   This produces violet coloured fungal threads on the carrots. Remove and burn plants which are affected.

SPECIAL REFERENCE   *Varieties of Maincrop Carrots*, Vegetable Growers Leaflet No. 4, National Institute of Agricultural Botany

Celeriac   *Apium graveolens rapaceum* (*Umbelliferae*)
                        Biennial grown as an annual

Celeriac is a celery-flavoured root vegetable, useful in winter salads and also as a cooked vegetable. It is in fact a type of celery, the swollen root of which is edible, rather than the stems. It is available from the open ground from October, and being a root vegetable takes its place in the rotation of crops after peas and beans and before the brassicas.

CULTIVATION   In March, sow the seeds as for celery, in a warm greenhouse; the germination is slow. When the seedlings are about 5 cm (2 in) high, prick them into a bed in a cold frame 7·5 cm (3 in) apart. In March also, prepare their cropping positions *on the flat*, not in trenches like ordinary celery, with 10 cm (4 in) of garden compost or well-rotted manure raked into the soil. Celeriac does best in a slightly heavy soil. In June, put the plants in 30 cm (1 ft) apart in rows 45 cm (1½ ft) apart. Keep them well watered—this is very important—pick out sideshoots, old leaves and potential flowering shoots; protect them against slugs. Dig the roots as you need them in October and November, then dig the whole crop and store it like beetroot, removing the outside leaves only.

VARIETY   Globus

PESTS AND DISEASES   See celery, p. 93.

Celery   *Apium graveolens dulce (Umbelliferae)*
                                   Biennial, but treated as an annual

Celery is one of autumn's major delights, indispensable to a civilized existence. It adds its individual flavour to many meat dishes, and its crisp texture to the pleasures of all kinds of cheese, to stuffings and to winter salads. Celery is a native of Britain, although the derivation of its name is obscure. The Royal Horticultural Society's *Dictionary* gives the derivation of *apium* from *apon*, water, from its habitat. Dr Stearn, in his revision of A. W. Smith's *A Gardener's Dictionary of Plant Names*, refers to it as the classical Latin name for parsley and celery, possibly derived from apis, a bee. In the rotation of crops, celery comes after the brassicas and is followed by potatoes and root crops. It is in season from September to January.

CULTIVATION   Either buy plants from a nurseryman in late May or early June, or sow your own seeds in a loamless 'compost' in mid-March, in a heated greenhouse at a minimum night temperature of 10°C (50°F). The seed takes at least three weeks to germinate. Prick out the seedlings into boxes as soon as they can be handled, and when they have settled down transfer them to a cold frame to accustom them to outside temperatures.

For self-blanching types, prepare the ground by forking in

very liberal dressings of compost or organic material. Celery needs a rich soil, so rich that like cauliflowers, it will thrive in rotten manure alone. Put the plants out into this prepared soil in June, 30 cm (1 ft) apart, in rows 30 cm (1 ft) apart. Water them in generously.

For the blanching kinds, you must dig trenches 30 cm (1 ft) deep and 37 cm (1¼ ft) wide, loosening the bottom of the trench by gentle forking, and spread 10 cm (4 in) of compost or rotted manure on the bottom. Then fill the trenches to within 7·5 cm (3 in) of the top with the previously excavated soil, set the plants into these trenches at 30-cm (1-ft) spacings, and again water in thoroughly.

Keep the plants (both kinds) very well watered all the time they are growing. Celery needs water more than most other vegetables. Lack of water may be one cause of a check to the growth and lead to bolting. Keep weeds hoed out. When the plants have reached 30 cm (1 ft) in height, begin earthing up (not the self-blanching kinds). Protect the stems with brown paper or specially made celery collars. For the first earthing use only the soil previously excavated. Make sure that crumbs of soil do not fall into the heart of the plants. Later, as the plants lengthen, take out shallow trenches on either side and pile up the soil against the lengthening stems. Continue this process at intervals as the plants grow taller, until only the leaves and 2·5 cm (1 in) of stem remain uncovered. The blanching process takes from five to seven weeks. Celery is said to taste better after the first frost; this may be so in moderation, but severe frost will damage the plants, and if you are relying on some for cutting in the winter, they will do better with a cover of litter, see p. 30. Five to seven weeks after you have completed the earthing up, pull up early varieties for use.

Self-blanching kinds will be ready from early August until October; the colour of the outside types will be improved by putting boards round the bed, as they grow.

VARIETIES
Blanching:
Sutton's Solid White, large sticks.
Prizetaker White, crisp solid stems.
White Ice, crisp with little fibre.

Self-blanching
Avonpearl, raised by the National Vegetable Research Station, white.
Vert de Villeneuve, rather short, full-hearted, plump, tender, very productive.
Golden Self-blanching, dwarf and compact, solid crisp heads of good flavour.

Pink and Red
Sutton's Superb Pink, early, sweet flavour.
Sutton's Giant Red, later, lasting into the New Year.

PESTS AND DISEASES
Celery beetle Steely blue or pale yellow beetles, 0·3 cm ($\frac{1}{8}$ in) long. They migrate in July from their alternative host plants, other umbellifers, such as hogweed and cow parsley. Spray the plants with derris if the attack is severe, but only in the evening when the bees have gone. Remember that derris is harmful to fish.
Celery fly. The flies have iridescent wings and green eyes. The young maggots cause damage by mining into the leaves, making blisters. Remove mined and blistered leaves and burn them.
Celery leaf spot A disease fungus producing brown spots on leaves and stems. The disease is seed-carried, so make sure you plant treated seed; do not use such seed for flavouring in cooking. Some seedsmen offer untreated seed for this purpose. If, in spite of treated seeds, the disease appears, spray the plants with Bordeaux Mixture when you see the first signs. But remember that Bordeaux will kill or drive away worms.
Heart rot A fungus disease which destroys the plant by turning its centre into slime. It enters through wounds made inadvertently in hoeing, or deliberately by slugs, and it can occur through using too much lime. Celery is an umbellifer, not a crucifer like the brassicas, and will do with a pH of 6·0 or a little lower.
Slugs See p. 42.

Chicory   *Cichorium intybus (Compositae)*
                               Perennial, treated as an annual

Pale, forced chicory shoots, with their interesting tang of bitterness and their crisp texture, are a welcome salad vegetable in the middle of winter. As a wild plant chicory is a hardy perennial, native to

Britain, with a rather pretty blue daisy flower. The roots can be dried and powdered and added to coffee. There is a permanent confusion between the English and the French over chicory, because the French call it Endive. Our endive is the curly-headed salad plant which the French call *chicorées frisées*.

Forced chicory is in season from November to March; it has no recognized position in the rotation of crops, but would fit in with peas, beans, etc. in freshly-manured ground, after the brassicas and followed by root vegetables.

CULTIVATION   In May or June sow the seeds in the open ground in soil well fortified with garden compost or other organic material. Sow in drills 1·2 cm ($\frac{1}{2}$ in) deep, and 45 cm ($1\frac{1}{2}$ ft) apart. Thin the young plants progressively to 30 cm (1 ft) apart. Throughout their growing season hoe out weeds and keep the ground well watered; cut down potential flowering stems.

In October when the leaves die down, cut them off some 1·9 cm ($\frac{3}{4}$ in) above the root, taking care not to damage the central growing point, lift the parsnip-like roots and pack them 10 cm (4 in) apart in boxes of light soil. This is the stage at which the plants are blanched, and you must keep them completely in the dark by some means such as covering the boxes with inverted boxes of similar size or with damp sacks. The boxes, suitably deprived of light, can be put under the staging of a cool greenhouse or kept in a warm shed or garage or even a dark cupboard, but in all places maintain a temperature of about 13°C (between 50 and 60°F) in order to force up the blanched leaves from the crowns. This takes about four weeks, by which time the leaves will be 21 cm (8–9 in) long. Break them off and use them. The roots can also be stored after lifting, in a cool but frostproof shed, until required for forcing, doing this in succession through the winter.

VARIETIES
Witloef
Sugar Loaf
Red Verona, with reddish colouring in the forced leaves.

PESTS AND DISEASES   Chicory is not subject to any particular troubles.

Cucumber   *Cucumis sativus (Cucurbitaceae)*
                                        Annual

Cucumbers are incredibly fast-growing in the right summer conditions; the starry yellow flowers turn into green fruits hanging among the foliage almost overnight. When the fruits are fresh they have a dusty bloom on the skin, like grapes, and they are one of the most satisfying vegetables to grow for oneself; it is privately very pleasing to be in the position of having to give some away because there are so many.

They were originally a tropical climbing or trailing plant. Our garden varieties fall into two kinds: frame and greenhouse cucumbers which develop without fertilization of the flowers, (fruits from fertilized flowers are bitter and unpalatable), and ridge or garden cucumbers which require fertilization for the flowers to develop into fruits. Cucumbers can be picked from the open ground from August to the first frost, and from a heated greenhouse from June to October.

Outdoor or ridge varieties—CULTIVATION   Prepare the beds in May by forking in liberal quantities of compost and animal manure, then buy plants from a nursery and plant these 60 cm (2 ft) apart in early June (or in May if you have cloches).

You can speed up your outdoor cucumber production if you make a mild hot bed by removing from 30–60 cm (1–2 ft) of topsoil and replacing this with a mixture in equal parts of compost and fresh animal manure, covering this with 15 cm (6 in) of the previously removed topsoil.

Alternatively, instead of buying plants, seeds can be sown, two together, 60 cm (2 ft) apart between May and June in the prepared beds. The foliage will soon cover the ground and suppress weeds, and little hoeing will be necessary. Like all the cucurbits, cucumbers need a constant and ample supply of water all through their growing period. Pick them while they are still small, not more than 15 cm (6 in) long, except for Kyoto which will equal a greenhouse cucumber in length. The skins of outdoor cucumbers are often bitter and prickly, so must be peeled before you eat them. The insides are as cool and delicious as any hothouse variety.

VARIETIES
Petite Pepino
Kyoto Three Feet, long and thin, recommended for growing
up a tripod of poles.
Burpless Green King F_1 Hybrid, resistant to powdery mildew,
mosaic and bacterial wilt.
Burpless Early F_1 Hybrid
Nadir F_1 Hybrid
Suttons Baton Vert F_1 Hybrid

Frame varieties—CULTIVATION This depends on the availability of stable manure to make thoroughgoing hot beds. For each
frame measuring 1·8 × 1·2 m (6 × 4 ft) you will need about
1·5 cu m (2 cu yd) of fresh stable manure. Spread this to overlap
the frame area by about a foot all round early in March and at
the end of the month complete the planting bed with a layer a
foot deep of fibrous loam, then put the frames in position above
the prepared bed and sow the seeds 1 m (3¼ ft) apart early in April.
Keep the frame lights close to maintain a temperature of not less
than 16°C (60°F) at night. The day temperature under sunlight
can rise to 32°C (about 90°F) without harm, provided that the
plants are never allowed to get dry at the roots and that ventilation
is supplied by propping up the frame lights.
When fresh stable manure is not available, make use of the soil
under the frame, reinforcing this with whatever animal manure
may be available, or with compost. Sow the seeds as before in
April 1 m (3¼ ft) apart at one end of the frame and train them
towards the other. Keep the lights close at night and allow only a
chink of ventilation when the temperature inside reaches 27°C
(80°F) or more. At all times keep the plants well watered and the
atmosphere moist. Stop them as for greenhouse cucumbers. Pick
the cucumbers in June or July, when about 15–23 cm (6–9 in)
long.

VARIETIES (can also be grown in the greenhouse)
Sutton's Improved Telegraph, smooth fruit.
Butcher's Disease Resisting, medium sized, slightly ribbed. As
its name implies, resistant to some diseases.
Dobie's Topnotch F_1 Hybrid, smooth skinned, dark green.

Greenhouse varieties—CULTIVATION Early in February raise the temperature of the greenhouse to maintain a minimum of 16°C (60°F) at night. Fix wires to the sides and rafters of the house 22 cm (9 in) from one another and the glass. Fill your seed boxes with garden compost and leave the filled boxes for two or three days to warm up to the same temperature of the house, then sow the seeds 2·5 cm (1 in) deep. As soon as the seedlings can be handled, pot them on into 7·5-cm (3-in) pots, preferably peat fibre pots with a growing 'compost' (see p. 149), then prepare the final planting positions which can be either in boxes 30 cm (1 ft) deep or, better, 30-cm (1-ft) whalehide pots. Allow the soil in these to reach the temperature of the house before transplanting the young plants in their 7·5-cm (3-in) pots. From the moment the seeds germinate, water them carefully but ensure that no water runs round their stems, for they are very vulnerable to foot rot at this stage. If peat pots are used they can be planted pot and all, thus avoiding disturbance of the roots. Plants in clay or plastic pots will have to be knocked out before being transferred.

Tie the extending stems to the wires as they develop. Ensure that the plants are generously supplied with water and that the atmosphere is moist and buoyant. This is done by spraying with a syringe and pouring water on to the paths and the staging. For this purpose keep cans or buckets of water inside the greenhouse so that when given to the plants the water shall be at the ambient temperature. There is no need to begin opening ventilators until the temperature inside reaches 24°C (about 75°F).

Allow your cucumber plants to continue growing as long as possible within the limits of your greenhouse. You can pinch out the top when the plant threatens to overwhelm the space available, but from experience, it seems to do better with the growing point still growing. Your cucumber plants will soon start to produce flowers on the main stem. If you nip these off you will get a heavier, though later, crop from the sideshoots. It is difficult, especially within the confines of a pot, to achieve both. For an amateur grower I would recommend allowing the first two plants to crop off the main stem for some early fruit, and pinching off the rest for a heavier, later supply. When you have done this you will find your plants developing sideshoots with flowers on them. Nip these off beyond the leaf after the third fruit, and support them while the cucumbers develop. If you are not growing an all-female variety you must always nip off any male flowers—the ones without a small embryo cucumber at the back, or else the fruits will start to swell at the end and taste bitter. Like all pot-grown greenhouse crops, cucumbers are cropping in a highly cramped, artificial situation, and they will need heavy feeding, preferably with your own liquid compost, to give good results. The more diligently you do this, the more rewarding your crop will be.

VARIETIES   (can also be grown in a frame)
We highly recommend the all-female kinds, because although they are a little more expensive, they produce no male flowers to make the fruits bitter.

Femina F_1 Hybrid, all female, disease resistant.

Concorde F_1 Hybrid, resistant to fusarium.

Topsy F_1 Hybrid, all female, good flavour.

Sutton's Everyday, large smooth fruits.

Rocket F_1 Hybrid, all female, dark green, slightly ribbed fruits. Resistant to cladosporium and blotch.

PESTS, DISEASES AND DISORDERS *Canker or foot rot.* All parts of the plant soften and turn brown, starting from the base of the stem. This is best prevented by not watering the base of the stem. In fact, it is an advantage to plant the cucumbers on small mounds so that water drains away from the collar. A copper lime dust can be used to check the disease, which is bacterial in origin.
Anthracnose The stems and the leaves turn pale and then brown. This is encouraged by excess humidity, hence the recommendation for a buoyant atmosphere. Some control is exercised, but if the attack is severe, remove and burn affected plants.
Powdery mildew The main symptom is the typical powdery white deposit on the leaves. Use a sulphur spray for control.
Leaf blotch Appears first as pale coloured spots soon turning brown, causing the leaves to wither. The best remedy is to choose disease-resistant varieties, particularly Butcher's Disease Resisting.
Gummosis Light brown spots on the leaves and sometimes on the fruits, which when affected become gummy. Spray with a sulphur spray and reduce the humidity by ventilation.
Mosaic diseases These are virus diseases causing yellow and pale green mottling and marbling of leaves and fruit. When the fruits are affected, it is best to remove and destroy the whole plant.
Botrytis (grey mould) Remove any mouldy foliage back to healthy

growth, and increase the heat in your greenhouse to discourage any more.

Whitefly A minute white, fly-like insect. Use derris or pyrethrum.
Red spider mite Yellowing and withering of the leaves. Maintain damp conditions, and use derris if desperate.

Commercial growers are now beginning to control these last two pests with specially developed parasitic insects, which feed on red spider mites and whiteflies, and so control the populations. This is an encouraging development because it does not use any chemical insecticides. Gardeners who are members of the Royal Horticultural Society can also obtain *Encarsia formosa*, the white-fly parasite, from the Director at the Society's Garden, Wisley, Ripley, Surrey, otherwise they can write to Springfield Nursery Ltd, Pick Hill, Waltham Abbey, Essex. The parasite cannot, of course, exist without the pest—in fact a small degree of infestation must be accepted, otherwise the parasite will die.

Thrips Tiny 1 mm-long insects, dark brown to black, infest the growing points and debilitate the plant. They can be a means of spreading virus diseases. Spray them with derris or pyrethrum.

SPECIAL REFERENCES
Manual of Cucumber Production, Bulletin 205, Ministry of Agriculture, Fisheries and Food, 1969, H.M.S.O.
The Biological Control of Cucumber Pests, Grower's Bulletin No. 1, Glasshouse Crops Research Institute, Littlehampton, Sussex

Endive   *Cichorium endivia (Compositae)*
                                           Annual

Endives come from the same family as lettuce and chicory, and their unruly, curly heads provide a deliciously astringent winter salad. It appeals to those with a taste for the dry in wine, and is particularly good accompanying a fillet steak.

Endive is in season from September through into the early part of the winter and may be blanched to reduce its bitterness. It takes its place in the rotation with root crops, potatoes, etc., after peas and beans, and before the brassicas. Endive will grow well in partial shade and in cold positions facing north and east, so it is well worth sowing a row if you are gardening in cramped, unlikely places, or using it to fill up an awkward dark corner of your conventional vegetable garden.

CULTIVATION   In May and June prepare the cropping positions in light, dry, sandy soil well manured from the previous crop. Sow the seeds in drills 1·9 cm (¾ in) deep and 37 cm (1¼ ft) apart. Thin the plants progressively until they stand at 30 cm (1 ft) apart.

Successional sowings may be made until August. To reduce their bitterness, blanch the plants by excluding daylight for fourteen days, either by tying the leaves together with raffia or, better, covering them with inverted flower pots with the holes plugged to keep out all the light. The leaves are ready in three to four weeks after beginning the blanching.

VARIETIES
  Sutton's Exquisite Curled
  Sutton's Winter Lettuce-leaved
  Batavian Broad Leaved
  French Moss Curled

PESTS AND DISEASES   None of any real importance.

Fennel, Florence or sweet

Foeniculum vulgare v. *dulce* (*Umbelliferae*)
Annual

Sweet fennel or Florence fennel is the vegetable version of the herb. Its bulbous stem has the same aniseed taste, and it is useful as a cooked and as a salad vegetable.

CULTIVATION   In March prepare a bed in the vegetable garden; a rich soil is preferred. In April make drills 1·9 cm (¾ in) deep and 45 cm (1½ ft) apart and sow the seed, thinning it progressively to 45 cm (1½ ft). In the course of the growing season draw soil up to the stems and blanch them, and ensure that the plants always have plenty of water. Harvest the swollen stem bases at the end of the summer.

Garlic

Allium sativum (*Amaryllidaceae*)
Perennial, grown as an annual

Garlic was appreciated by Apicius and the ancient world, and has ever since been continuously recognized as indispensable to civilized cooking. It has also long been known as an internal anti-septic. It now appears, together with onions, to have the property of reducing the likelihood of blood-clotting, a cause of heart attacks and strokes. This was first discovered by French trainers who use garlic poultices to reduce the swellings in their horses' legs. Now some tests in a Newcastle hospital show similar results with onions in the blood of human beings.

It is very satisfying to grow your own garlic. You can supply your kitchen all the year round, lifting the bulbs in late summer and hanging them to dry in a frostproof shed or room until you need them. In the rotation of crops garlic, with onions and other root crops, comes after peas and beans and is followed by cabbages and the other brassicas.

CULTIVATION For cropping positions choose a sunny place and a light soil which has been fertilized by previous crops and fork in and spread garden compost or other organic material at a depth of 7·5 cm (3 in). Plant the offsets, or cloves as they are known, either in October or in March, in drills, pushing them in base downwards till all but the tip is covered, 23 cm (9 in) apart. Keep them free from weeds. Lift the new crop in August or early September when the leaves begin to wither. Lay them to dry on top of the soil if the weather is good, or in a dry shed.

VARIETIES (all as bulbs)
Best Italian
You can separate and plant the cloves from a supermarket or greengrocer's bulb, if you find them difficult to obtain otherwise. Others, such as Thermidrome and Rose, can be found when travelling in France.

PESTS AND DISEASES See onions, p. 115, but garlic is very rarely troubled.

Kale, see brassicas, p. 87.

Kohlrabi, see brassicas, p. 87

Leek   *Allium ampeloprasum porrum (Amaryllidaceae)*
                        Biennial grown as an annual

The Welsh traditionally wear the leek on St David's Day, 1st
March, to celebrate the victory of King Cadwallader over the
Saxons in A.D. 640, but the leek as the national emblem now seems
interchangeable with the daffodil, or Lent Lily. Parkinson reminds us that in the time of the children of Israel being in Egypt,
and no doubt long before, they did: 'feed upon Leekes, Onions
and Garlicke boyled with flesh', and goes on: 'they are much used
with us also sometimes in Lent to make pottage and as a great
and generall feeding in Wales with the vulgar Gentlemen'. Notwithstanding Parkinson, leeks are among the most civilized
vegetables, both for themselves, and as a catalyst vegetable, in-
forming many dishes with their own delicate version of the onion
flavour. The green tops contain much more vitamin A than the
blanched lower stem, so should be eaten whenever possible.

Leeks are exceedingly hardy and undamaged by the severest
of winters. They are available from the open ground between late
October and April. In the rotation of crops they come with peas,
beans, onions and spinach in freshly manured ground, after the
brassicas and before the root crops.

If you nip out the flower stems in the spring: 'the result of this
practice will be the formation on the roots of small roundish
white bulbs which make an excellent dish when stewed in gravy,
and may be used for any purpose in cookery for which onions or
shallots are employed. They are called leek bulbs and are obtainable only in early summer.'[1]

CULTIVATION In the middle of March sow seeds in shallow
drills in nursery beds. In July transfer them to final positions
when they should be 15 cm (6 in) high, the ground having been
fortified in autumn or winter with garden compost or bulky
organic material spread to a depth of 10 cm (4 in) and very lightly
pricked into the soil. In the absence of bulky organic material,
prick in hoof-and-horn meal and bonemeal, each at 56 g per sq m
(2 oz per sq yd).

Space the plants 23 cm (9 in) apart in rows 37 cm (1¼ ft) apart.
Make holes 3 cm (1¼ in) in diameter with a dibber, to a depth of

[1] Sutton's *Culture of Vegetables and Flowers*, 1902.

23 cm (9 in). Put the young plants into these holes as deep as the base of the leaves. *Do not fill the soil back round the young plants. They will be well set in by watering which must be done immediately after planting.*

Maintain regular hoeing to destroy weeds and maintain aeration. For the most delicate flavour, pull the plants when little more than finger-thick, but they can remain in the ground and be picked as required for the table until well into April or even early May for late Vichysoisse soup, or encouraged to make tiny leek bulbs.

VARIETIES

Musselburgh, good length, hardy.

Lyon, very hardy, tender white solid stems with good flavour.

Sutton's Early Market, the earliest. Not recommended for late crops.

Malabar, quick growing, new variety from France. For autumn use.

Sutton's Winter Crop, very dark green, hardy. Will stand until April.

Sutton's Royal Favourite, pure white, large stems, very hardy. Raised in the Royal Gardens at Windsor.

PESTS AND DISEASES

Leek moth A generation of overwintered moths appear in April and May, and lays eggs on the leek plants close to the ground. Caterpillars hatch from these and feed on the foliage. Organochlorine sprays and dusts are unacceptable. It is better to follow Lawrence Hills'[1] comforting advice: 'give the robins a chance at the chrysalids'.

See onion, p. 115, for other pests and diseases, but leeks rarely suffer troubles except for leek moth.

Lettuce   *Lactuca sativa (Compositae)*
                              Perennial, treated as an annual

Lettuce in all its variety of forms is the crop you will want to grow most of all. Nothing is more useful or more delicious than a continuous supply of crisp lettuce; it means that you have the

---

[1] *Grow Your Own Fruit and Vegetables.*

basis of almost every kind of salad on your doorstep all the time. If you have a frame or a greenhouse you can grow lettuce all the year round. If you have neither, you can still sow a row of corn salad, or lamb's lettuce in August, to provide you with some outdoor greenery in the winter months.

Lettuce falls into two categories, cabbage lettuce and cos lettuce. Cabbage lettuce, the Butterheads, have soft floppy leaves, such as Cobham Green and Borough Wonder; the Crisphearts have crisper-textured foliage, as in Avoncrisp and Great Lakes. Cos lettuce, which takes a little longer to mature, has long folding leaves with a central spine, a little like chicory.

In the rotation of crops, lettuces grown in the open ground go with peas, beans, etc., after cabbages and other brassicas, and before potatoes and root crops. You will also want to plant lettuces as catch crops between rows of later-developing vegetables like peas, and later, to keep the kitchen supplied, after early potatoes, peas and carrots. It is much more useful to plant your lettuces in small successional rows, than have one large crop run to seed before you can eat it all. Lettuce likes partial shade.

The open ground—CULTIVATION (*a*) In March sow the seed in the cropping position in soil well-manured from a previous crop, well supplied with lime, at a pH of 6·5–7·0. Sow it 1·2 cm ($\frac{1}{2}$ in) deep in short drills, 30 cm (1 ft) apart, and repeat at fortnightly intervals until early August to give a succession. Thin the seedlings first to 7·5 cm (3 in) apart when they are an inch high and progressively to 25 cm (10 in). The thinnings can be planted out 25 cm (10 in) apart to make a succession crop conveniently delayed by the check in transplanting—you should aim to achieve a few lettuces maturing at one time. Protect them against birds with black cotton or thread or wire pea-guards, and against slugs, see p. 42. Cut the lettuces from May onwards.

(*b*) At the end of August or September sow the seed in the open ground in cropping positions as above. Thin the plants to 7·5 cm (3 in) apart in early October and leave them at this distance through the winter. In early spring carry out a final thinning to 25 cm (10 in) apart. The plants should be ready for cutting in March and April. Their progress can be speeded up by covering them with cloches after thinning.

VARIETIES
Butterhead (Cabbage):
  Cobham Green
  Avondefiance, bred by the National Vegetable Research Station, resistant to mildew and root aphis.
  Salad Bowl
Crispheart (Cabbage):
  Avoncrisp, bred by the National Vegetable Research Station.
  Great Lakes, stands up well to drought.
  Webb's Wonderful, large, unlikely to bolt even when hot and dry.
Cos:
  Lobjoits Green Cos, large, self-folding heads.
Corn Salad:
  Large Leaved Italian—pull the leaves like spinach, through the winter.

Cloches—CULTIVATION Put the cloches into position on the cropping ground towards the end of September, about a fortnight before the seeds are sown. In early October lift the cloches and sow the seed in drills 1·2 cm (½ in) deep. In the middle of January transplant the seedlings to ground previously warmed up for a fortnight under other cloches. Plant them 15 cm (6 in) apart for small varieties, 25 cm (10 in) apart for larger ones and 30 cm (1 ft) apart for cos lettuces. These can be cut from the end of February or the middle of March depending on the district. Cabbage lettuces will need little watering, but cos varieties will require watering several times before being harvested.

VARIETIES
  Attractie
  Hilde

Frames—CULTIVATION Sow the seed in drills 15 cm (6 in) apart in early October under frames. Transplant the seedlings in mid-December inside the traditional frame or in Dutch lights, 23 cm (9 in) apart. These are ready for cutting in March. For later crops, for cutting in April and May, sow in mid-January under frames and transplant 25 cm (10 in) apart into cropping positions previously warmed up under frames when they are about 2·5 cm

(1 in) high. For autumn crops from frames for cutting in October and November, sow the seed in the open ground in nursery beds in the first week in August. Transplant the seedlings to frames over previously warmed up ground 25 cm (10 in) apart in the middle of September.

VARIETIES
  Winter Crop
  Arctic King

Cold, frost-protected greenhouses—CULTIVATION Sow the seed in small nursery beds inside a cold greenhouse from August to early February. Transplant them between October and January to cropping beds in the same greenhouse, 30 cm (1 ft) apart. These can be cut from December to April.

VARIETIES
  Seaqueen, butterhead cabbage, bred by the Glasshouse Crops Research Institute.
  Emerald, a smaller variety for restricted space.

Heated greenhouses—CULTIVATION Sow the seeds from the middle to the end of September. Thin them to 25 cm (10 in) apart in cropping beds previously warmed up to the ambient temperature in a greenhouse at 10°C (50°F). Cut these lettuces from mid-December to early February.

VARIETIES
  Kordatt
  Valentine and Neptune are promising varieties at the Glasshouse Crops Research Institute, but not yet available in the retail trade; they should be noted when on general sale.

PESTS AND DISEASES
Lettuce root aphis Yellowish, with white wool covering it. The roots and the junction of roots and stems are attacked, resulting in wilting and rapid decline. A primary host of this aphis is the poplar tree, from which winged aphides migrate to lettuces and other plants. The most effective control is to choose a variety resistant to aphis attack, such as Avondefinance, otherwise practise prompt hygiene by pulling up and burning affected plants.
Slugs See p. 42.
Downy mildew Mainly occurs under glass, and can be avoided by

proper control of watering and ventilation. Crowded seedlings, as well as mature plants, may be infected.

Bacterial spot Causes browning of the margins of the leaves, and if the attack is serious, degeneration of the leaves into a sodden mass. It can be avoided by maintenance of a dry atmosphere under glass.

Grey mould Can cause collapse and rotting of the entire plant, and is mainly troublesome under glass. Outside leaves are infected first. To prevent it avoid overwatering, and too damp atmosphere, and too low temperatures.

Mosaic A virus disease, seed borne. Affected plants should be removed and destroyed, there being at present no cure, but seedsmen should be asked to provide mosaic-tested seed.

Marrow and Courgette *Cucurbita pepo ovifera (Cucurbitaceae)*
Half-hardy annual

Visitors to Britain are puzzled by our predilection for marrows— curious, watery vegetables that grow very fast and are most prized when they have reached inedible proportions. Natives appreciate their delicate green taste. Courgettes, which are really only small marrows, also called zucchini, concentrate their flavour and are a much more universally acceptable vegetable. If the marrows in your garden threaten to overwhelm you, you can keep them in check by picking them as courgettes.

Marrows and courgettes are in season from July to October from the open ground, and from early June, from frames over hotbeds. Marrows have no recognized position in the rotation of crops. Success in cultivating them will depend on your preparation of the growing soil and conscientious supply of water all through the growing period. There are various ways of cultivating them.

CULTIVATION For picking from the end of July to October, make up a bed in mid-May of rich compost and animal manure dug into the upper foot of good fertile vegetable-garden soil in a warm corner, fully exposed to as much sunlight as possible. Then at the end of May, sow the seeds in groups of three, the groups being 60–90 cm (2–3 ft) apart. If there is danger of frost, or cold wet weather, keep the seedlings covered with inverted pots at night and sometimes even in the daytime until early June

Choose the strongest seedlings from each group and remove the other two weaker ones. Keep the plants well watered as they develop. Take out the tips of the main shoots, if trailing, when 90 cm (3 ft) long, to encourage sideshoots, which produce more female flowers. Pollinate by removing the male flowers, pulling off or folding back the petals and pressing the stamens in the centre into the female flowers, which can be recognized by the very small marrow-shaped swelling at the base of the flowers.

To obtain earlier crops, you can do one of two things. You can buy plants in June which have been raised in heat and hardened off, and set them out 1 m (3¼ ft) apart for bush varieties, and 1·5 m (5 ft) apart for trailing varieties, thereafter keeping them pollinated and watered. Alternatively you can raise your own plants in a warm greenhouse by sowing the seed in March directly into 7·5-cm (3-in) pots, preferably peat pots such as the Jiffy kind which, when the time comes, can be planted, pot and all, in the cropping positions. While the seedlings are developing, the pots are best plunged into a 7·5-cm (3-in) bed of fertile peat (see p. 29) or compost to make sure that they do not get dry. Stand the peat pots on a hard bottom of slates or asbestos to prevent them rooting into the peat or compost underneath.

Plant these out in the prepared beds in June in the same way as plants bought from a nursery.

Considerable refinement can be made in the preparation of the bed for cropping. One method is to make an old-fashioned, mounded hot-bed (see p. 27), in this case composed half of stable manure and half of leaves topped off with a 23-cm (9-in) casing of good loam. Plants will grow very well on this mounded hot-bed, but it is not convenient to try to arrange cloches on a mound and, therefore, when cloches are available it is better to make a raised rectangular-shaped bed where there is good natural drainage below it. Make this 60 cm (2 ft) high and retain the sides with boards or wire netting. Cover the young plants with cloches —the simple tent type will do for a few weeks—but barns or one of the many plastic types will be needed as the bush plants grow taller.

Always pick marrows in the bloom of their youth, 25 cm (10 in) should be the largest size, and 10 cm (4 in) for courgettes (zucchini) which are cooked whole.

VARIETIES
Bush types:
  Prokor F₁ Hybrid, dark green, medium sized.
  Sutton's White Bush.
  Baby Crookneck F₁ Hybrid, small, yellow with curved or crooked necks, early.
  Custard Pie, round, flattened, white, scalloped edges.
  Gold Nugget, orange-yellow, the size of a coconut.
Trailing types
  Long Green Striped
  Long White Trailing
  Little Gem, round, the size of a large orange. Cut while still green. From South Africa.
Courgettes
  Courgette F₁ Hybrid, bush habit, early. Pick when 13 cm (5 in) long.
  True French, pick at 7·5 cm (3 in).
  Zucchini F₁ Hybrid, early, deep green, cylindrical. Pick at 15 cm (6 in), but will grow into a recognized marrow if left to 30 cm (12 in).
  Cocozelle, Italian Zucchini, dark green.

PESTS AND DISEASES
Powdery mildew White coating on leaves and stems. Keep plants well watered, and dust with sulphur every two weeks, if the disease begins to get a hold.
Grey mould Infects flowers, and fruit at blossom end, caused by dropping flowers. Remove infected parts, and cut off some leaves to improve circulation of air.
Mosaic Yellow mottling of leaves and fruits, puckering of leaves and stunting of shoots. Destroy infected plants, and always use seed from virus-free plants.

Mung bean, see Sprouting Seeds

Mushroom   *Agaricus Campestris, A. bisporus*

Mushrooms, the most mysterious of vegetables, once much associated with magic (perhaps from their way of appearing fully-grown overnight), have now become as tame and domesticated as any other vegetable. Commercial growers produce huge, continuous crops, and we can use mushrooms as we please to lend their unique flavour to all kinds of dishes. You can grow your own mushrooms all the year round if you are prepared to construct a special growing house. In the open they can be cropped from March until June and again from September to November. If you like to dabble in mushrooms rather than make them a way of life, you can grow them very easily, by the bucketful, as described below. They are not concerned in the rotation of crops.

CULTIVATION The simplest way of obtaining home-grown mushrooms is to buy one or more of the plastic buckets available in garden centres ready filled with growing 'compost', spawn and casing. All that is necessary is to spread about half the casing material over the ready-spawned compost, give it about half a cupful of water and keep it in cool, rather dim light—darkness is not necessary. After the first crops have been picked in a few weeks, more of the casing material is put on and it is possible to get up to half a dozen successive crops at intervals.

The craft of producing mushrooms on any scale lies in the preparation of the growing medium, whether in beds in the open, or in boxes in outbuildings, cellars or even large cupboards indoors. First obtain fresh stable manure from horses kept up, hunters or race horses, add additional straw in the proportion of 1 part of straw to 10 parts of fresh manure, mix together with water and stack in a round based pyramid with the top cut off, or in a rectangle with the sides tapering inwards up to a flattened top, on a hard base, there is no need to cover it. Considerable heat will be developed. In about ten days take the temperature with a soil thermometer. It should reach 65°C (150°F), at which temperature unwanted fungus spores will be reduced. When this temperature has been reached, turn the heap from inside to outside and from top to bottom, and in the course of doing so add 14 kg (30 lb) of calcium sulphate (gypsum) to each 1000 kg (0·98 ton) of compost, to prevent the compost becoming greasy. Water the heap from a can and after a few days turn the heap again from top to bottom using a fork so that the final heap is built up in flaky layers. By this time the compost should have lost its ammoniacal smell. If not, it will be necessary to turn it once again.

Obtain boxes—fish boxes are suitable—and fill these with

prepared compost to a depth of 20 cm (8 in). When the temperature
has dropped to 24°C (75°F) proceed to spawn the bed by taking
the spawn from its cartons, breaking it up into pieces 6 cm (2½ in)
wide and pushing these into the compost 25 cm (10 in) apart,
afterwards closing up the holes into which the pieces of spawn
have been pushed. Do not use a dibber, because it leaves smooth
cavities which hold up the progress of the mycelium. The spawned
compost should be kept in subdued light.

Out of doors cover with straw to keep in the heat. When the
white threads of the mycelium start growing, proliferating all
through the prepared compost, put on a 5-cm (2-in) casing of soil,
preferably shredded and sieved medium loam or a light sandy soil.
Leave this for two days and then firm it with the back of the spade.
In warm dry weather give a very little water, but not enough to
percolate through the casing to the manure below. When this is
done put on a covering of straw (for outside beds) to a depth of as
much as 45 cm (1½ ft), less than this in summer, to keep in the
heat. Aim to maintain a temperature inside the bed of 16°C
(60°F) till picking time. The first mushrooms can be expected to
appear about six weeks after planting. In the absence of horse
manure, mushroom hot-beds can be made from straw first thoroughly wetted and then doctored with a chemical activator or
boost. Follow the same procedures as with the horse manure
compost until the temperature drops to 24°C (75°F). When this
happens put in the spawn and case it over.

The easiest way for those who have fields and pastures is to
plant directly into the fields, preferably those which have long
been down to pasture and have a high organic content. A turf
sod about 30 sq cm (1 sq ft) and 3·7 cm (1½ in) thick is cut out
with a spade and a further 10 cm (4 in) of soil dug up and laid
aside. A piece of spawn and generous half spadeful of manure
are put into the hole, and the turf then replaced and trodden down.
Repeat this at 90-cm (3-ft) spacings.

SPECIAL REFERENCES
How mushrooms should be grown, W. Darlington & Sons Ltd,
Rustington, Sussex.[1]
Growing your own Mushrooms, Samuel Dobie & Son, Llangollen,
Denbs., N. Wales.[1]

---

[1] Also suppliers of spawn.

Mustard and Cress

Mustard: *Sinapis alba (Cruciferae)*
                                                          Annual

White Mustard is the variety with cress. It is also sometimes used
to make the condiment mustard, but for this black mustard,
Brassica nigra is more common.

Cress: *Lepidium sativum (Cruciferae)*
                                                          Annual

Mustard and cress are every child's introduction to growing things.
Both of them will sprout almost anywhere—on a flannel or a sheet
of blotting paper if you are totally garden starved—but they
should not be sown together. Cress takes three to four days longer
than mustard to be ready for cutting, so time your plantings accordingly. Mustard and cress take no part in the rotation of crops
and you can grow them all the year round.

CULTIVATION   In boxes, fill seed trays with home-made compost, or commercial seed compost, water well and sow cress seeds
thickly, press the soil down with a piece of wood but do not cover
with any more soil. Cover with glass, shade from bright sun in
summer and stand on the staging of a cool greenhouse, a windowsill or anywhere else that is convenient. Four days later sow the
mustard seeds. Cut the seedlings with scissors at the cotyledon
stage for salads and sandwiches. You can also sow mustard and
cress in the open ground, but don't forget them or they will grow
to huge and inedible plants!

Onion   *Allium cepa (Amaryllidaceae)*
                                                          Biennial

A bed of onions with the foliage turned down, and large bulbs
partly showing above the surface of the earth, is a satisfying sight
in the vegetable garden, and it is a pleasant autumn task to twist
them into heavy plaits and hang them up for use throughout the
winter. Onions are an essential ingredient of many, many recipes
and it is necessary to have a good supply at hand.

You start to pull the small salad spring onions from March, and you can arrange a steady supply with successional sowings. You must plant these separately if you are growing the larger bulb kind from bought sets (small bulbs) as in Method Four, the easiest one. If you are growing onions from seed, or growing pickling onions, you can use the thinnings as spring onions. Pickling onions and the larger bulb kind are dug from August to October and stored to provide a supply until the next year's crop. In the rotation, onions are grown on freshly-manured ground, with peas, beans, leeks, lettuces, tomatoes, spinach and celery, after the brassicas and before root vegetables.

CULTIVATION   There are four methods:
Method One   Onions need an open position exposed to full sun for the ripening of the bulbs. Avoid soil that is likely to be waterlogged, or if such conditions are likely to arise, slightly raise the beds by throwing up soil in the course of digging, making alleys on either side of the beds.

Between October and January prepare the cropping positions by digging in substantial quantities of compost or other bulky organic material spread on the top to a depth of 10 cm (4 in). Leave the ground rough dug to be weathered by frost.

In early February knock down the clods when the ground is dry and rake to a rough tilth. Tread the ground firmly and rake once more to a friable tilth.

Between the middle of February and the end of March draw out drills 1·9 cm (¾ in) at right-angles to the alleys. Sow the seed in these and cover it lightly with the soil pushed aside in the course of making the drill. If the soil is in a state of friable grace, firm it lightly with the back of a spade. If not, leave it alone because compaction at the top will make it difficult for the first weak onion 'grass' to push through. Thin progressively to 18 cm (7 in), the second thinnings can be used for spring onions.
Method Two   In January sow seeds in boxes in seed compost in a cool greenhouse, frame or cloches. Harden these off before planting them out in April, 20 cm (8 in) apart, in the cropping ground prepared as described above. Ailsa Craig is well adapted to this method; it can produce very large bulbs.
Method Three   At the beginning of August in the south and towards the end of the month in the north, sow the seed out of doors

in shallow drills in a nursery bed and allow the seedlings to stand through the winter. Thin them at first to 5 cm (2 in) apart. Do not allow them to become over-crowded but leave them close enough to afford mutual protection. In early March prepare their cropping positions by liberally enriching the soil with compost or animal manure (pigeon manure is famous for this purpose), then draw out drills to make rows 37 cm ($1\frac{1}{4}$ ft) apart and plant out the seedlings 23 cm (9 in) apart. These will make very large bulbs.

Method Four In April choose a cropping ground less richly manured and plant out onion sets 30 cm (1 ft) apart. Onion sets are small bulbs lifted at the end of the summer and carefully stored at a temperature as high as 24–27°C (75–80°F). Plant these 15 cm (6 in) apart and pull the soil up to the tops of the bulbs, leaving the necks uncovered. Then follow the maintenance routines described above for spring-sown onions. The chief advantage of using sets is that they seldom, if ever, 'bolt'. Plants from sets are sometimes thought to be less tender (to the tooth, not the frost) than those produced from seed but they are often easier to cultivate, particularly in the north.

Hoe out the weeds; water is not often needed. Onions require less artificial irrigation than many other vegetables but do not overlook the matter entirely in periods of prolonged drought. Only a very little excess watering can prevent the ripening of the bulbs and certainly by the time the bulbs have nearly reached maturity, watering will do more harm than good.

In Sutton's old book, *The Culture of Vegetables* (my copy is dated 1902), is written: 'When Onions are doing well they lift themselves up and sit on the earth, needing light and air upon their bulbs to the very axis whence the roots diverge. If weeds spread amongst them the bulbs are robbed of air and light, and their keeping properties are impaired. But in the use of the hoe care must be taken not to loosen the ground or to draw any earth towards the bulbs. When all the thinning has been done, and the weeds are kept down, it will perhaps be observed that in places there are clusters of bulbs fighting for a place and rising out of the ground together as though enjoying the conflict. With almost any other kind of plant this crowding would bode mischief, but with Onions it is not so. Bulbs that grow in crowds and rise out of the ground will never be so large as those that have plenty of room, but they will be of excellent quality, and will keep better than any that have had ample space for high development. It is a pity to touch these accidental clusters, for the removal of a portion will perhaps loosen the ground, and so spoil the character of those that are left, for fine Onions are rarely produced in loose ground, and hence the necessity for care in the use of the hoe.'

After the middle of August, bend down the tops of the foliage to encourage ripening. The tops will then turn yellow and the necks shrink. Now lift the bulbs and, if the weather is fine and dry and the forecast good for the next three or four days, lay them out on the soil to dry. If, on the other hand, the weather is wet or doubtful, lay them out in a shed, well ventilated and open as much as possible to the sun.

When they are dry store them in a cool, dry, airy shed or twist them into skeins so that they look like the bundles of onions which Breton onion sellers carry around the country and sell to well-to-do housewives for an exorbitant price.

VARIETIES

Ailsa Craig Selected, the largest onion.

Superba F_1 Hybrid, early, will keep until May.

Autumn Spice, strong flavour.

Giant Zittau, flattish shape, stores until summer, susceptible to white rot.

James Long Keeping, globe shaped, red-brown skin, keeps well.

Sutton's Solidity, for autumn sowing, long keeping, not likely to bolt.

Bedfordshire Champion, old, well-tried variety, heavy cropping, keeps well. Susceptible to downy mildew.

Sutton's A1, large flat bulbs, suitable for sowing under glass in January, keeps well.

Red Globe, deep red flesh, long keeping.

Blood Red, red colour, mild flavour.

White Lisbon, mild spring onion for successional sowing from March to September. Susceptible to white rot. Immune to downy mildew.

Paris Silverskin. For pickling, small bulbs, sow from March to June. Use the thinnings as spring onions.

PESTS AND DISEASES

Onion fly The flies lay eggs in spring close to the bases of the bulbs or seedlings, and the white maggots bore into the young bulbs which, in the worst cases, can be reduced to liquefaction. The flies are attracted to fresh manure. This is the reason for manuring the beds in the winter well before the seeds are sown. Take out and burn badly-infested plants. Soot or bonfire ash spread around the seedlings will give some protection. Transplanted onions are much less affected. The pest would appear to need a spring-sown crop for its well-being.

Onion thrips These feed on the foliage and cause mottling and bleaching.

Onion downy mildew The leaves develop pale spots and die downwards from the tips into the bulb. Follow the rotation of crops because resting spores from the fungus may persist in the soil. If the attack is severe spray with Bordeaux Mixture, but remember that it drives away worms. If you are intending to keep bulbs for sets examine them rigorously and discard any that show signs of this infection. The variety White Lisbon is immune, Ailsa Craig rather less so. James's Keeping and Bedfordshire Champion are very susceptible.

White rot At the end of the summer plants are seen to have decaying roots and the base of the bulbs is infected with the typical white mould of the fungus. Destroy affected plants.

Eelworm (Onion Sickness or Onion Bloat) The bulbs show a brownish colour and when cut horizontally exhibit concentric dark coloured rings. This is similar to the eelworm which attacks daffodils. Lift and burn infected bulbs. Adhere closely to the rotation of crops. Suttons A1 and Bedfordshire Champion are moderately resistant. Ailsa Craig, Giant Zittau and White Lisbon are susceptible.

Grey mould (Botrytis) A fungus disease which may affect autumn-sown onions. It exhibits white spotting on the foliage. Spray with Bordeaux Mixture if the attack is very severe.

Neck rot Can also cause serious damage to onions in store. This often follows damage caused by incorrect lifting and storage. Prevent by making sure that bulbs are well ripened and do not get wet after being lifted. Do not apply fertilizers late in the growing season. These can make the plant sappy and delay ripening.

Soft rot A bacterial disease which may attack onions in store, causing them to degenerate to slime. The remedy is to ensure proper ripening and storing.

Onion smut Causes dark streaks on the leaves. These streaks swell and burst, releasing black spores. It is a notifiable fungus disease. If it is suspected get in touch with the Horticultural Advisory Officer of your local branch of the Agricultural and Development Advisory Service.

Parsnips   *Pastinaca sativa (Umbelliferae)*
                                                     Biennial

The parsnip is native to Britain, and arouses violent likes and dislikes. Some dismiss it as 'a repulsive vegetable', others enjoy its distinctive sweetish flavour and faintly fibrous texture, and find it the most delicious of the winter root vegetables. Parsnips will be ready in the garden from September, and can be kept in store until March. In the rotation of crops, parsnips, with other root vegetables, are cultivated in ground previously manured for peas, beans, onions, tomatoes and so forth, and are followed by cabbages and the other brassicas.

CULTIVATION Between November and February prepare the cropping ground in an open position. Dig the soil deeply to 1 m (3¼ ft) to provide a growing medium easily permeable for the long roots. Do not enrich the soil.

In March sow the seed in the cropping positions in drills 2·5 cm (1 in) deep, 45 cm (1½ ft) apart. Thin the young plants progressively to 23 cm (9 in).

Hoe out weeds. Maintain an adequate supply of water.

Pull up the roots as required for cooking. The crop in general will keep better in the ground than out of it, but when the land is required, lift the remainder of the crop and store it in sand in a frostproof shed.

VARIETIES
    Hollow Crown. Improved, long rooted.
    Avonresister, short, thick roots, bred by the National Vegetable Research Station, resistant to canker, suitable for shallow soils.
    Offenham, early, for shallow soils.
    Tender and True, resistant to canker.

DISEASE
Canker The upper part of the root turns brown and cracks. Prevent by sufficient lime in the soil, pH 6·5–7·0, by not preparing

too rich a soil, and maintaining adequate moisture throughout the growing season. Later-sown crops are less susceptible. Grow resistant varieties.

SPECIAL REFERENCE
Advisory Leaflet 151, 1970, Ministry of Agriculture, Fisheries and Food.

Pea   *Pisum sativum (Leguminosae)*
                                             Hardy annual

There is something about frozen peas, their year-round availability, their ubiquitousness, their unlikely colour, that makes me glad to see the fresh ones in the garden. It is a peaceful, almost Edwardian afternoon task to sit down with a basket of peas to shell. Surprisingly, our ancestors may have originally grown peas for their ripe dried seeds—not the tender fresh green ones we all enjoy today—for pease-pudding and pottage. Andrew Knight (brother of Richard Payne Knight, initiator of the Picturesque in landscape gardening, whereby gardens were to be made to look like the paintings of Claude and Poussin) of Downton Castle in Herefordshire conducted experiments with peas which led to the development of wrinkled-seeded peas, the kind we now prefer to the round-seeded type.

You can grow peas in the open ground from June to September. In the rotation of crops, together with beans, onions, leeks, lettuce, tomatoes, spinach and celery, peas are planted in freshly-manured ground and come after the brassicas and before root crops.

CULTIVATION Between November and January prepare the cropping ground. When weather conditions permit it to be worked easily, dig in compost or other bulky organic material previously spread to a depth of 10 cm (4 in). Ensure that the soil has an adequate lime content—pH 6·5–7·0, but no more.

In early February in open weather when the soil is reasonably dry, roughly level off the ground.

In early March prepare a seed bed, if possible with a grainy but not dusty tilth. Draw out flat drills 18 cm (7 in) wide and 7·5 cm (3 in) deep. Regulate the distance between the drills (which will become the rows) according to the height of the mature pea plants, making the distance between the drills/rows a little more than the height of the plant, for example rows of Hurst's Green Shaft which grows to a height of 65 cm (26 in) should be 1 m (3¼ ft) apart. Where space is very restricted choose shorter growing varieties. Sow the seeds 7·5 cm (3 in) apart alternated (staggered) in three rows. Pull back the soil from the drills to cover the seeds. Catch crops of lettuce can be raised by sowing in between the rows. Make successional sowings at intervals of three weeks of first earlies, second earlies and main crop varieties, up to the end of May, after which make one or two sowings of early varieties for final autumn crops. Peas take all of fourteen weeks from sowing to production. Protect against birds either with wire pea-guards or cotton or thread tied to sticks. Hoe out weeds. Keep the growing plants well watered, increasing the water supply as the stems (haulms) lengthen.

Dwarf varieties will not need support, although they will benefit from the protection against wind given by pea sticks. All varieties growing to 75 cm (2½ ft) or more require pea sticks. The best are hazel branches put in a foot apart on either side of the rows. When hazel branches are not available use nylon netting stretched between 1·75 m (5–6 ft) posts.

Protect your peas against pigeons by driving poles, 2–4 m (8 ft) long, into the ground to a depth of 60 cm (2 ft), leaving 2 m (about 6 ft) standing above ground, and over these drape pigeon netting. Reasonable protection can be obtained by simply draping the netting over the pea sticks.

Pea crops can be considerably advanced by putting cloches over the young plants until they reach the underside of the glass or polythene.

To obtain even earlier pea crops, in November sow the seeds two to each pot, in peat pots in a frame or cold greenhouse and in March plant them out, pot and all, 8 cm (3–4 in) apart in the cropping ground as described above.

VARIETIES
Round-seeded   These are hardier and can be sown earlier, particularly in northern districts. Generally the flavour is not so good as that of Wrinkled or Marrowfat Peas.
First Earlies
Feltham First, can be sown in late autumn in open ground like broad beans. 45 cm (1½ ft) high. Does not need sticks.

Pilot, can be sown from January to March. Large pods. 1 m
(3¼ ft).

Meteor, very hardy, suitable for cold, exposed positions and for
sowing between November and January like broad beans. 45 cm
(1½ ft) high. Does not need sticks.

Wrinkled or Marrowfat

First Earlies

Pioneer, prolific, suitable for continous sowing between March
and June. Resistant to mildew. 60 cm (2 ft).

Little Marvel, sow from March to June, small peas like French
Petit Pois, succeeds under cloches. 50 cm (1⅔ ft).

Second Earlies

Hurst Green Shaft, heavy cropping, matures in fourteen to
fifteen weeks from sowing, resistant to downy mildew and fusarium. 70 cm (about 2⅓ ft).

Onward, a reliable heavy cropper, probably the most generally
cultivated pea. 60 cm (2 ft).

Main crops

Recette, prolific, three pods on a stem, matures in 10 to 11
weeks. 1 m (3¼ ft).

Senator, heavy cropping, pods in pairs. 1 m (3¼ ft).

Alderman, a heavy cropper. 1·5–2 m (5–6¼ ft).

Continental types

Gullivert (Petit Pois), the true French Petit Pois. Sow from
March to June. 1 m (3¼ ft).

Cobri, small, round peas, Pick young. Cook first and shell
afterwards. Sow March to May. 60 cm (2 ft).

Carouby de Mausanne Mangetout; this has no parchment in its
pods. Pick before the peas are mature, before their shape can be
seen outside. 1·5 m (5 ft).

Dwarf Sweetgreen Mangetout. Fleshy, sweetly flavoured pods
1 m (3¼ ft).

PESTS AND DISEASES

Pea and bean weevil   The grubs feed on the roots and root nodules,
and the small grey adults eat the leaves, producing rounded notches
in the margins. Dust the foliage when dry with soot in May and
June when the winged insects are in flight laying their eggs.

Pea moth   These cause maggoty peas. The adult moths lay eggs
on the plant from mid June to mid August. There is no effective

acceptable control. The best precaution is early sowing to obtain
a crop before the moths are active.

Pea thrips Thrips feed on and disfigure the flowers, haulms and
pods spoiling the latter and producing silvery patches and streaks.
They are tiny, narrow black or yellow insects. The recommended
organophosphorus contact and systemic insecticides are not acceptable. It is better to put up with the pest which is worse in dry
seasons, and hot weather.

Damping off The base of the plants is affected and the plants may
collapse. This is not often serious. A preventive is to maintain
a light texture in the soil and ensure adequate under-soil drainage.

Foot rot and black root rot Brownish discoloration at the roots,
due to soil-borne fungus diseases. Prevent this by maintaining
the rotation of crops, and do not overdo the liming in the preparation of the ground.

Powdery mildew A fungus disease which takes the form of a white
powdery deposit on leaves and pods. Spray with Bordeaux Mixture, if the attack is severe, but recognize that the chemical will
reduce or eliminate the worm population.

Mosaic A virus disease evidenced by mottling and marbling of
leaves and flowers. Pull out and burn affected plants.

Peppers   *Capsicum annuum (Solanaceae)*
                                                    Annual

Peppers came originally from tropical America and settled happily
all around the Mediterranean area. Our increased national interest
in exotic vegetables has led to the development of varieties that are
rewarding to grow in Britain, and with their extraordinarily high
vitamin C content—especially when they are red and ripe—we
need them. These are the sweet peppers, large-fruited, 10–15 cm
(4–6 in) long, used in salad, cooked in ratatouille or giving a bite
to stews. Green peppers are unripe red peppers; they often go
through an intermediate yellow stage. Chillies are *Capsicum
frutescens*, much smaller (about 5 cm, 2 in) with pronounced tails.
These are very hot indeed, and used to make cayenne pepper,
chilli con carne, chilli sauce and other spicy Spanish-American
dishes.

    Peppers are in season from July to September in a heated greenhouse. They are not concerned in the rotation of crops except that, belonging to the *Solanaceae* family like tomatoes, they may be susceptible to the same diseases, and therefore should be grown in fresh soil each year, when they are cultivated in pots. If you grow them in frames or cloches out of doors, keep them well away from potatoes and tomatoes.

You can grow your green peppers, along with cucumbers, aubergines and tomatoes all together in a greenhouse as small as 3·6 × 2·4 m (12 × 8 ft) if you do not expect them all in great quantity or very early in the season. It is really exciting to watch all these unusual and often expensive vegetables growing in your own back garden, and finally set your first all-home-grown salad on the table.

CULTIVATION Peppers need conditions similar to tomatoes. In February or early March, raise the temperature of your greenhouse to a minimum of 16°C (60°F) at night—as for starting tomatoes in a cool house. Fill individual peat pots or seed boxes with compost, and leave them in the greenhouse to reach 'room temperature'. Plant the seeds, one to a pot, or space them well in the boxes. Maintain the temperature at 16°C (60°F), or if possible raise it to 21°C (70°F). Make sure they have plenty of water, and syringe the developing foliage to discourage red spider mite.

At the end of April, tranfer the young plants (peat pots and all if necessary) to larger, 30-cm (1-ft) clay (with some broken pottery pieces in the bottom) or plastic pots, and filled with sieved garden soil mixed with plenty of compost, or John Innes Potting Compost No. 3, or if you want to be really professional, the growing compost recommended by the Glasshouse Crops Research Institute.[1]

Set the plants in their pots some 60 cm (2 ft) apart, because they will grow tall and bushy, to a height of 45–60 cm (1½–2 ft). Pay

---

[1] This is made up of 75% Irish Moss Peat, 25% fine sand, with the following fertilizers added and mixed carefully with every 36 litres (1 bushel): 28 g (1 oz) potassium nitrate, 56 g (2 oz) superphosphate, 84 g (3 oz) ground chalk, 84 g (3 oz) magnesium limestone, 14 g (½ oz) ammonium nitrate, 14 g (½ oz) Frit 253A. This last is manufactured by Ferro Enamels Limited and can be bought from garden centres and horticultural shops, also Medlock Chemicals. It contains trace elements such as boron, zinc, manganese, iron, copper and molybdenum.

attention to watering and syringing. They will be slow to grow in the first few weeks, and watering should not be overdone. Feed them either with your own liquid compost (a spadeful of animal manure or garden compost in a bucket of water) or a proprietary high potash tomato liquid fertilizer, or the liquid feed recommended by the Glasshouse Crops Research Institute for tomatoes (p. 11). Growing green pepper in pots is a highly artificial method, bearing little relation to the way they would grow in nature. The cramped roots will need intensive feeding—the Glasshouse Crops Research Institute feed their peppers at every watering—and it is true to say that the more you put into them, the more fat, glossy fruits you will receive. If you skimp on this your results will be disappointing. At the end of the season you can throw away the exhausted compost in the pots, to reconstitute itself in an unneeded corner of the garden.

You can also grow peppers out of doors, by transferring the young plants in their peat pots into a bed in a warm sunny position, when all danger of frost is past. Fork in 10 cm (4 in) of compost or decayed animal manure, or other bulky organic material, first. Feeding with a liquid fertilizer once a week will speed up the production of fruit, which you can pick either green or leave until they turn red. You need a frame or cloches in a poor summer.

VARIETIES

Canape F1 Hybrid. Suitable for finishing in frames, cloches or out of doors in warm positions in the south.

New Ace F1 Hybrid. Early, high yielding under glass.

PESTS AND DISEASES

Red spider mite Syringe regularly with water, preferably at greenhouse temperature.

Fruit spot Spots in red depressions. Spray with Bordeaux Mixture. Remove infected fruits.

Grey mould (Botrytis) Increase the heat and ventilation, and pick out and remove infected leaves in order to avoid having to resort to a systemic fungicide like benomyl.

Blossom end rot Large sunken brown-black patches in the skins, due to irregular drying out and watering.

Potato   *Solanum tuberosum (Solanaceae)*
                                              Half-hardy perennial

Potatoes probably originated in the subtropical regions of the
Andes. They were introduced to England through Spain in the
sixteenth century and have caused the greatest impact on our
eating habits of any single vegetable. Whether or not Sir Walter
Raleigh really had a hand in bringing the potato to the British Isles
is not certain. If he did, he makes an interesting spoke in the whir-
ligig of time, for he lived in 1588-9 at his house in Youghal,
County Cork. Cork was later to be the scene for some of the worst
episodes in the great 1845 potato famine in Ireland, which in turn
started massive emigration to America.

'With the addition of milk or buttermilk, potatoes form a satisfactory diet, as the physique of the pre-famine Irish proved,' says
Cecil Woodham Smith,[1] 'the potato was . . . the most universally
useful of foods. Pigs, cattle and fowls could be reared on it, using
the tubers which were too small for everyday use; it was simple
to cook; it produced fine children; as a diet it did not pall.' No-
one has to exist entirely on potatoes any more but, properly cooked,
they can bring many more nutrients beside starch, in particular
vitamin C from early potatoes. The Irish today like their potatoes
big, white and floury, the kind for baking and mashing. The
French grow firm, waxy textured varieties, good for salads.

Potatoes are harvested from the open ground from June to
November and can be stored until June in the following year. In
the rotation of crops, potatoes, with other root vegetables, are
grown in soil which has previously been heavily manured for
crops of peas, beans, etc. They are followed by the cabbages and
other brassicas.

CULTIVATION The crop is grown from 'seed' potatoes (rather
small potatoes specially grown in 'clean' soil conditions and free
from disease).

In October and November dig the cropping ground. It is
unlikely that lime will be required; a low *p*H of 5·0 is satisfactory.
Leave the surface rough for the winter.

At about the time of Christmas, order the seed potatoes.

---

[1] *The Great Hunger.*

In February take delivery of seed potatoes of certified stock. These should be about the size of a duck's egg; if larger than this, cut the seed potatoes in half, but make sure to leave eyes in both halves.

Correctly, you should 'chit' or sprout the potatoes by placing them in single layers on slatted trays or special chitting boxes and keeping these containers in a shed or other building at a temperature of between 4·4°C (40°F) and 10°C (50°F). Note that this temperature is critical because sprouting will not start at a temperature of below 4·4°C (40°F). Subdued light is necessary; keeping the door and windows of the shed open is satisfactory when the outside temperature is above 4·4°C (40°F). Complete darkness will encourage long white weak shoots. When sprouting is in progress, keep an eye on the potatoes and discard at once and burn any that show signs of disease. The sprouting process takes from four weeks for early rapid sprouting types such as Arran Pilot and from eight to ten weeks for others. The sprouted potato is ready for planting when the shoot measures about an inch and has begun to develop small green leaves at the top and is also showing the first side growths.

If you have no trays or frostproof place, seed potatoes can be planted directly in the soil without previous chitting, but this cannot be done before the end of February or March (Good Friday is traditional in the gardener's calendar) for earlies and in April for main crops.

At the end of February, get the roughly-prepared cropping ground ready by forking it to a fairly fine (but not dust-fine) seed bed 37 cm (1¼ ft) deep.

Plant the early varieties between the end of February and the middle of March—in northern districts early April is more prudent. Dig trenches for each row, 23 cm (9 in) deep and 60 cm (2 ft) apart, leaving alleys between the rows. At the bottom of the trenches spread 15 cm (6 in) of compost or very well rotted manure, topped off with 5 cm (2 in) of fertile peat (see p. 29). Push the tubers into this with the sprouts upwards or, if it has not been possible previously to sprout them, with the eyes facing upwards, then cover them with fertile peat and fill in the rest of the trench with excavated soil. Plant early varieties 30 cm (1 ft) apart.

Plant the main crop potatoes in the same way during April, 37 cm (1¼ ft) apart. Make the rows for these a little further apart

75 cm (30 in). After filling back the trenches, draw in a little more soil to leave the planted rows slightly mounded.

Hoe systematically to keep away weeds. Pay careful attention to watering. When the green shoots are 15 cm (6 in) long, begin earthing up by drawing up more soil from the sides of the rows with a hoe. Use this hoe also to keep the soil loose, because potatoes need a good supply of atmospheric oxygen. Pay special attention to watering earlies, particularly in May and June, and main crops particularly in June and July.

Another method of growing potatoes does away with the need to ridge; the best soils for this are light or sandy. The surface is raked down to remove large lumps and stones, and tubers are put in, one each to a 15-cm (6-in) deep hole, 30–37 cm (12–15 in) apart, in rows 75 cm (2½ ft) apart. After filling the holes with fine soil, lengths of black polythene sheeting are put over the rows lengthways and held down with soil or stones. When the shoots begin to push up the polythene, cut holes in the appropriate places to let the growth through. Use this method for early varieties only.

The first earlies, new potatoes, can be dug as required in June or a little earlier, while they are immature, before the haulm (the stems, leaves and all the above ground parts) dies down. Main crop potatoes are at first also drawn upon as required, and the crop finally cleared, usually in September, when the skin of the tubers is set, i.e. when the skin cannot easily be rubbed off, and when the tops have died down. Private gardeners will find it best to store them in boxes in dry frostproof sheds in darkness. If they are exposed to light they will begin to turn green and become poisonous.

VARIETIES

First earlies:

Arran Pilot, recommended by the N.I.A.B.[1] Immune to wart disease. White skin and flesh, kidney shaped. It can be cultivated as a second early if allowed to grow to full maturity. A heavy cropper, it begins to sprout rapidly and should be put into its trays or boxes immediately it is received from the suppliers.

Sutton's Foremost, white-skinned and oval in shape. Awarded a Certificate Commendation by the Department of Agriculture for Scotland.

Ulster Chieftain, recommended by the N.I.A.B. Immune to

---

[1] National Institute of Agricultural Botany.

wart disease. White skin and flesh, oval in shape. Recommended for early lifting because of cracking at maturity.

Home Guard, recommended by the N.I.A.B. Immune to wart disease. White skin and flesh, oval in shape. Early, rapid sprouting.

Second early:

Maris Peer, recommended by the N.I.A.B. Immune to wart disease. White skin and flesh. Oval-shaped, medium size.

Main crop:

Desirée, recommended by the N.I.A.B. Immune to wart disease. Red skin, lemon-yellow flesh. Kidney-shaped. Early main crop. Good cooking quality.

King Edward, recommended by the N.I.A.B. but not immune to wart disease and may be withdrawn. Skin partly coloured pink, kidney-shaped. 'Edwards' always command the highest price for main crops. The variety needs good growing conditions.

Majestic, recommended by the N.I.A.B. Immune to wart disease. White skin. Kidney-shaped. Generally the most popular potato for baking.

PESTS AND DISEASES

Potato root eelworm Causes what is known as potato sickness, resulting in small leaves, a poor root system and few and small tubers. Symptoms caused by the larvae boring into the young roots. The remedy is to adhere closely to the rotation of crops so that the eelworms are starved out during intervening years—even extending the rotation to keep potatoes off an infected piece of ground for eight years.

Colorado beetle This is now very rarely seen but if it should occur must be reported immediately to the Ministry of Agriculture, Fisheries and Food, at Hatching Green, Harpenden, Herts. The beetles, which are generally yellowish in colour and about a quarter of an inch in size, have ten black lines on their wing cases and black spots on the thorax. They would be seen in late July and August, feeding on the leaves. The dark red, black-dotted grubs hatch from eggs laid at this time, and when present in sufficient quantities feed on the foliage so as to destroy an entire crop. Both beetles and larvae can overwinter in the soil.

Potato blight This first appears as dark brown patches on the leaves. In wet weather a white mould becomes visible and soon after this the haulms turn black and give off an unpleasant smell.

Spores falling to the soil infect the tubers to produce brownish patches in the flesh and slightly sunken grey-brown areas of skin above these patches. If the disease occurs in one year it may be carried over through tubers being left in the ground, and the remedy for this is careful and thorough digging at the time of lifting and strict adherence to the rotation of crops. If there is reason to suppose that the disease is likely to occur from an attack in a previous year or from nearby crops, the preventive measures recommended by the Ministry of Agriculture, Fisheries and Food are to spray the crop with Bordeaux Mixture first, just before the disease would begin to spread if it were left unsprayed; this will be in mid-June in the south-west of England, early July in the south and the latter half of July in the midlands and the north. Two or, at the most, three applications of Bordeaux Mixture, at intervals of seven to ten days, may be necessary, and more on susceptible varieties in really wet seasons.[1]

Wart disease Warty growth develop on the tubers, generally around the eyes, and may extend also to the stem. This is another notifiable disease to be reported immediately to the Ministry of Agriculture, Fisheries and Food. Infected tubers should be immediately burnt. There is at present no treatment, but certain varieties are immune (see the list of varieties).

Potato powdery or corky scab Scabs will be present on the skin, and in bad cases the tubers will be covered with canker-like growths. No effective treatment is so far known. The remedy is to rest the soil for at least six years. A too high pH may encourage the spread of this disease, therefore it is wise to maintain a low pH down to 5·0 as previously recommended.

Potato blackleg The plants are stunted in growth and the foliage becomes yellow; black rot sets in at the base of the stems and infected tubers will begin to rot, with subsequent wilting of the foliage. This disease is transmitted through 'seed'. It is important, therefore, always to buy certified seed and never to keep any tubers about which you are suspicious.

Potato common scab This fungus produces scabby processes on the skins of the tubers, but no rotting. There is at present no known preventive spray. The best precaution is to ensure a good

---

[1] *Potatoes*, Bulletin 94, 1965, Ministry of Agriculture, Fisheries and Food.

supply of humus and to maintain a low pH as already mentioned. Maris Peer has a good resistance to it.

Potato dry rot This disease may make itself evident in seed potatoes being chitted. It causes shrinkage and premature decay. It can to an extent be avoided by immediately unpacking deliveries of seed potatoes, putting them into their trays for sprouting and not leaving them lying about in the box in which they were delivered. If the disease is noticed, remove and burn infected tubers immediately.

Potato skin spot This fungus produces tiny, non-rotting spots on stored tubers. It may cause non-sprouting in seed potatoes and, if this occurs, discard and destroy the non-sprouters.

There are other fungus diseases from which potatoes can suffer. For some of them no immediate spray remedy is known and the best precaution is to discard and burn seed potatoes in particular and all tubers exhibiting suspicious symptoms.

There are two functional disorders of particular interest to the gardener:

Potato hollow head The tubers, particularly the larger ones, exhibit hollow centres. This condition may be due to a prolonged lack of rainfall, then followed by heavy rainfall, as a form of second growth, or to a deficiency of potassium. The remdy is to water regularly and to make sure that the potassium supplies are adequate.

Potato jelly-end rot The heel end of the tuber becomes translucent, and later softening, and finally destruction of the whole tuber may occur. It is due to insufficient humus and lack of water at a critical time, followed by heavy rain. The remedy is to maintain proper irrigation and to ensure that adequate humus is provided.

SPECIAL REFERENCES

Bulletin 94, *Potatoes*, 1965, Ministry of Agriculture, Fisheries and Food, H.M.S.O.

Farmers' leaflet No. 3, *Recommended Varieties of Potatoes*, 1972, National Institute of Agricultural Botany

Radish   *Raphanus sativus (Cruciferae)*
                                                                    Annual

After mustard and cress, radishes are the easiest crop in the vegetable garden. The seed germinates fast enough to interest small children, and the little red radishes bring colour and texture to summer salads from May to October, or earlier if you have cloches. Winter radishes are bigger, and available in December and January. Their long roots are good piercers of the soil, bringing up minerals not only to the roots themselves but to the tops of the plants which end up in the compost bins.

Radishes have no fixed position in the rotation of crops, but belonging to the *Cruciferae* family, could be included with the brassicas. In reality, you can sow them as catch-crops where and when you can, to ensure a small but continuous supply. The roots ought to be pulled while still young—except for the winter radish.

CULTIVATION Between March and May sow the seed in cropping positions thinly in shallow drills 15 cm (6 in) apart in open ground. The seeds germinate rapidly and the crop can be harvested in twenty to thirty days after having been sown (radishes germinate so quickly that their seeds are sometimes sown as indicators of where other slower developing seeds have been put in, notably parsley). Thin out progressively, harvesting the later thinnings. Plants arising from seeds sown in summer will bolt instantly and are useless.

Attend conscientiously to the supply of water. Protect from birds with cotton or thread. Hoe out weeds if there are any which grow more quickly.

Sow winter radish varieties in July and thin to 45 cm (18 in) apart. Pull up the roots in winter as required.

VARIETIES
Summer radishes
    Cherry Belle, globe shaped, scarlet flesh.
    French Breakfast, olive shaped, white flesh.
    Sutton's Red Forcing, round early, suitable for cloches.
Winter radishes
    China Rose, oval, rose-coloured skin, white flesh.
    Round Black Spanish, round, black skin, white flesh.
    Long Black Spanish, tapering, black skin, white flesh.

PESTS AND DISEASES
Club root As for brassicas and other members of the *Cruciferae*, make sure that the lime content of the soil is adequate, giving a pH of 6·5–7·0.

Damping-off and downy mildew These may also occur. For treatment see brassicas, p. 77.

Flea beetle Use derris dust when the beetles are seen, in the evening when wandering bees are safely home. Remember that derris is harmful to fish.

Salsify (see also Scorzonera) *Tragopogon porrifolius (Compositae)*
Biennial, usually grown as an annual

Salsify is sometimes known as the vegetable oyster, because of its faintly fishy flavour: it has roots that are hairy, white and spindly, making them tiresome to scrape, but the trouble taken is well worthwhile. It is another vegetable that has simply fallen into disuse—it was common in Mrs Beaton's day. The roots are available from the garden between November and March, so they provide something in the lean months. Salsify has no recognized place in the rotation of crops, but being deep-rooted and a member of the *Compositae*, can take its place with carrots, potatoes and other root crops, in soil manured from a previous crop.

CULTIVATION In March prepare the cropping positions by raking the soil where last year's peas and beans have been cultivated. Draw out drills 1·9 cm (¾ in) deep and 37 cm (15 in) apart. Sow the seeds directly into the cropping positions. Thin the young plants progressively to 25 cm (10 in) apart. Maintain water supplies and keep weeds hoed out. Leave the plants' roots undisturbed to allow them to penetrate as deeply as they will, probably 30 cm (1 ft) and, in doing so, gather minerals from lower soil levels.

In early November if the ground is required for other crops, lift the roots and store them in sand, otherwise leave them in their cropping positions until they are required for the table.

VARIETIES
Sutton's Giant
Mammoth Sandwich Island

Scorzonera *Scorzonera hispanica (Compositae)*
Biennial, usually grown as an annual

Scorzonera is better described by its alternative name, black salsify. It has a black skin, but is otherwise very similar in shape and taste.

to ordinary salsify. It was once used in Spain for the treatment of snake bites, hence perhaps its name, from 'scurzon', a serpent; it is also called common viper's grass. It has yellow, dandelion-like flowers, whereas salsify has purple, thistle-like ones.

Scorzonera is in season from September onwards. It has no particular place in the rotation of crops, but it can, like salsify, be included with the other root crops.

CULTIVATION   In March prepare the cropping ground as for salsify. Make drills 37 cm ($1\frac{1}{4}$ ft) apart. Sow the seeds and thin the young plants progressively to 25 cm (10 in) apart. Hoe out weeds. Pay careful attention to watering.

Begin to lift the roots in September as required for the table. If the ground is needed for other crops, lift all the roots in November and December and store them in sand in a frostproof place— a shed, outhouse or cellar.

Seakale   *Crambe maritima* (*Cruciferae*)
Hardy herbaceous perennial

Seakale is a native plant; cultivated strains have been selected from the wild plant seen—increasingly rarely—growing on coastal cliffs and beaches. Seakale is one of those vegetable delicacies which head gardeners took great pains to produce to perfection for our hedonistic grandparents, whose taste, whatever it may have been in fine art, was, in the matter of food and other applied arts, always impeccable. It is still a vegetable which might well be cultivated again in our quiet search for the excellent. It has a near non-taste so delicate as to need the appreciation of an experienced connoisseur, to be taken quietly, alone, with pheasant and one of the last few bottles of claret which were boys when he was a boy.

Seakale is in season from November to March, in the open ground. Established beds, like beds of rhubarb, will last for many years and take no place in the rotation of crops.

CULTIVATION   In October prepare the bed in an open situation on soil well fortified by spreading 10-cm (4 in) depth of compost, well-rotted farmyard manure or seaweed (this is particularly good for seakale). The lime content must be the same as for cabbages— seakale, like them, belonging to the *Cruciferae* family. A pH of 6·5–7·0 is required. Allow for one row of seakale plants 60 cm

(2 ft) apart in the middle of a 1·2-m (4-ft) bed, with alleys for servicing and harvesting on either side, or using a bed 3·0 m (10 ft) wide, plant in three rows, 60 cm (2 ft) apart, the bed being raised a few inches by throwing up soil from the alleys.

Between November and early March, buy plants. These will be grown from suckers or 'thongs' and should have pieces of root attached to the base. Plant them in trenches 30 cm (1 ft) deep with their crowns 5 cm (2 in) below the surface. In the first year the spaces between the seakale plants can be used for catch crops of lettuce (the considerable watering needed by seakale will not be suitable for onions).

Through the summer maintain a generous water supply and hoe out developing weeds. Remove any flowering stems.

In the late autumn when the leaves have died down, begin to blanch the stems. This can be done *in situ* on the growing ground by covering the plants to exclude light. This was once done with specially-made seakale pots 40 cm (about 16 in) tall, and the same in diameter, with removable covers. Rhubarb pots were of the same diameter, but about 60 cm (2 ft) high; if either of these can still be found they are perfect for the job, otherwise use very large pots turned upside down with their drainage holes covered up to keep out the light, or inverted boxes, or even sections of drainpipe if these are wide enough. Failing all of these, blanching can be done by piling on soil 23 cm (9 in) deep, covering with litter another 7·5–10 cm (3–4 in) deep and surrounding it with wire netting or Netlon to prevent it from being blown away. It will then be ready for harvesting in March–April.

Another method is to lift the plants bodily in October. Trim the roots to about 15 cm (6 in) long and pack them in leafmould or very well rotted manure in boxes, and keep them at a temperature of between 12 and 16°C (50 and 60°F). Higher temperatures than this can result in thin unpleasantly wiry stems. Keep them in complete darkness for five or six weeks until Advent. Plants which have been lifted and forced in this way are of no further use. Consign them with blessings and thanks to the compost bins.

The trimmings from the roots can be used to supply root cuttings for the next crop; they should be 12–15 cm (5–6 in) long, and can be stored in moist sand until the following March, when they are planted with the top end about 2½ cm (1 in) below the surface.

If you want to start from seeds, they can be sown either directly in the cropping ground prepared as above and thinned progressively to the distance required, or in nursery beds, and transplanted to cropping grounds a year later. In both cases the sowing is done in March. Plants grown from seed will take two years to produce a crop.

VARIETY Lily White, obtainable as seed. Specialist growers may have their own strains to offer as thongs.

PESTS AND DISEASES
Club-root This should not occur if the land is correctly limed. If the disease should develop, take up and destroy affected plants.
Violet root rot The symptoms are a violet-coloured network on the roots. If this becomes serious, lift and destroy affected plants, but it is rarely seen.
Black rot Causes weakened crowns which, when lifted and the stems cut across, show black rings in the diameter of the stem. Lift and destroy affected plants.

Shallot   *Allium cepa ascalonicum (Amaryllidaceae)*
                                                         Biennial

Shallots are like small onions, but instead of growing one large bulb, each plant produces a ring of several little bulbs around the central set. They are propagated by these sets, or small bulbs. Shallots have a milder flavour than onions so they go well with fish—in *sole bonne femme*, for example. You can also pickle them, or use them instead of button onions to add to stews. However, they are tiresome to peel and chop in any quantity, so we recommend that you grow only a few shallots for these specialized purposes.

The plant may have originated in Syria or Palestine and has been known here since the middle of the sixteenth century. The old countryman's practice of planting shallots on the shortest day and digging them on the longest is still valid, but the February planting and July harvesting we recommend below is safer in cold districts. In the rotation of crops they are included with onions, that is with peas, beans and leeks, after cabbages and the other brassicas, and followed by potatoes, carrots and so forth.

CULTIVATION   Between November and January dig the ground
in an open, well-drained position. Fork in compost or other bulky
organic material, previously spread 10 cm (4 in) thick on the soil.

Early in February when the ground is dry, prepare a planting
tilth by knocking down any large clods and raking the surface.

In February, when this has been done, draw out shallow drills
30 cm (1 ft) apart, push the bulbs into the fine soil 15 cm (6 in)
apart and firm the soil around them. The tops of the sets should
be just above the surface of the soil. If birds tend to tweak them
out by their tops, protect with netting or black cotton.

Keep the weeds hoed out, water in dry conditions, but take care
not to overwater this crop.

When the leaves turn yellow and a ring of new bulbs has developed, usually in July, lift the bulbs, and if the weather is fine
lay them on the top of the soil to dry in the sun. In wet weather
lay them out in a shed or other dry place. When they are dry, put
some aside for next year's planting in February; the remainder
should be tied together and hung up for use in the kitchen as required. They can be kept dried until May or June.

VARIETIES   The following are all sold as sets by the pound:
Dobies' Longkeeping Yellow
Dutch Yellow
Jutland Yellow AA Grade, golden yellow and produced in a
virus-free area.

PESTS AND DISEASES   Shallots may be attacked by the same
pests and diseases as onions, see p. 115.

Sorrel   *Rumex acetosa*, wild English sorrel (contains potassium
                oxalate) *R. scutarus*, French sorrel (rather less acid)
                                                    (*Polygonaceae*)
                                                        Perennial

Sorrel is so sadly neglected by the British that you have to grow it
yourself if you want to use its interesting flavour in your cooking.
In France it is properly appreciated and you can buy it in the
shops. It is only one of many good vegetables that have fallen into
disuse in this century, and our supermarket palates are the poorer
for it.

Parkinson writes:

Sorrell is much used in sawces both for the whole and the sicke, cooling
the hot livers and stomackes of the sicke, and procuring unto them a
appetite unto meate, when their spirits are almost spent with the vio-
lence of their furious or fierie fits; and is also of a pleasant relish for
the whole, in quickning up a dull stomacke that is overloaden with
every daies plenty of dishes. It is divers waies dressed by Cooks, to
please their Masters stomacks.

CULTIVATION Sow the seeds[1] out of doors in shallow drills
37 cm (1¼ ft) apart during April and May, where they are to
grow. Thin the plants when 7·5 cm (3 in) tall to 30 cm (1 ft)
apart, and pick the leaves as you need them from midsummer
onwards. Pick out the flowering stalks to encourage leafy growth,
and your sorrel bed will serve you well for several years.

Soy beans, see Sprouting Seeds

Spinach   *Spinacia oleracea (Chenopodiaceae)*
                                                          Annual

Spinach is a member of the *Chenopodiaceae*, the goosefoot family,
which includes cultivated beetroots and also Good King Henry, a
wild plant once much used as a vegetable. Spinach has been
known here since the middle of the sixteenth century, and probably
came from the eastern Mediterranean. It is not quite the universal
nourishment that nanny used to pretend, because it is a lock-out
vegetable. Spinach is a valuable source of iron and vitamin A, but
its calcium is made unavailable to us because it combines with the
oxalic acid in spinach (oxalic acid is present in chocolate and
rhubarb too) to form undigestible calcium oxalate. However, the
oxalic acid does not combine with any calcium outside the vegetable,
so you can make good this loss by cooking it in milk.

You can grow both summer and winter spinach, if you like a
good supply. Summer spinach can be picked between June and
September, winter spinach between October and March. In the
rotation of crops, spinach is planted on freshly-manured ground

[1] For names of suppliers see Appendix 2.

and included with peas, beans and so on, that is, after the cabbages and brassicas and followed by potatoes, beetroots, etc. It may also be sown as a catch crop between peas and beans.

Summer spinach—CULTIVATION   If there is in the kitchen garden a position which, although open, tends to be moist, this will suit spinach very well. To prepare it, in January or February fork in compost or decayed organic material previously spread 10 cm (4 in) thick on the ground.

Between February and May rake out a fine tilth and in this draw shallow drills 2·5 cm (1 in) deep and 30 cm (1 ft) apart. Repeat the process about once a fortnight to give successional crops. Sow the seed and thin progressively until the plants are about 20 cm (8 in) apart. Spinach bolts (goes to seed) at the slightest opportunity, but can be slightly deterred from this by giving ample room for development of leafage. Hoe out weeds and water the plants diligently.

Winter spinach—CULTIVATION   In August choose an open position; some shelter from north and east is an advantage but, unlike summer spinach, winter spinach likes a drier situation. Prepare the ground, but without generous quantities of nitrogenous manure, because the plant has to stand through the winter, and over-lush growth promoted by heavy nitrogenous fertilizing might be damaged by frost. Sow the seeds immediately, 2·5 cm (1 in) deep and 23 cm (9 in) apart, as for summer spinach, and make repeated sowings until mid-September. Thin progressively, but only to about 15 cm (6 in) so that the plants shall stand a little closer together and afford each other some protection.

Hoe out weeds regularly. Maintain a good water supply, but do not cause waterlogging of the soil. Pick as the leaves develop between October and March.

VARIETIES
Summer Spinach
    Longstanding Round
    Victoria, slow to seed
Winter Spinach
    Sutton's Greenmarket
    Virkade
    Longstanding Prickly

PESTS AND DISEASES

Downy mildew Dull yellow patches appear on the upper surface of the leaves—the underside of these produces a violet-grey mould.

Blight or mosaic The leaves turn yellow and become distorted. This is a virus disease and may be spread from neighbouring plants such as vegetable marrows.

Leaf spot Evidenced by brown patches and spots.

With all of these, lift badly-affected plants and burn them; the virus-infected plants should be lifted as soon as seen to prevent further spread. Plants slightly affected by mildew and leaf spot need only have infected leaves removed as soon as seen.

Spinach beet   *Beta vulgaris cicla*, Swiss chard, perpetual
spinach
(*Chenopodiaceae*)
Perennial

Spinach beet or Swiss chard is related to ordinary spinach, and to beetroot, also a member of the *Chenopodiaceae* family. Like spinach, this plant is cultivated for its leaves, not its roots. The leaves provide yet another useful supply of greenery for pulling as you need them in the kitchen and are available all year round. In the rotation of crops it is usually included with ordinary spinach, but would be better alongside beetroot, its close relation. This would be after peas, beans, leeks, celery and ordinary spinach and be followed by the brassicas.

CULTIVATION   In March prepare the cropping ground by forking in compost or other bulky organic material previously spread to a depth of 10 cm (4 in) or failing these, equivalent organic fertilizers, see p. 26.

From April to July sow seeds in drills 2·5 cm (1 in) deep and 45 cm (1½ ft) apart. Thin progressively to 20 cm (8 in) apart, hoe out weeds, maintain a good water supply and cultivate generally as for ordinary spinach. The early sowings will provide leaves in summer and autumn; those in July for winter and spring.

Pull leaves as they are required for the kitchen; do not allow a surplus of leaves to remain on the plant, because these will become coarse and be of more use in the compost bins.

VARIETIES
   Swiss Chard Vintage Green F₁ Hybrid
   Ruby Chard
   Perpetual or Spinach Beet

Spinach, New Zealand   *Tetragonia expansa* (*Aizoaceae*)
                                                          Annual

New Zealand Spinach is another member of the spinach family, a
frost-tender, creeping, spreading plant, with delicious spinach-
tasting leaves. It is also known as 'cut and come again spinach'
because it lasts all summer long and does not bolt to seed in hot
weather like ordinary spinach.

CULTIVATION   In March, sow the seeds in 7·5 cm (3 in) pots
in a cold frame and transfer the hardened off plants to the open
garden in May, as for ordinary spinach, but planting them 60 cm
(2 ft) apart in both directions. Pick the young shoots and leaves
for the kitchen as soon as they are large enough.

PESTS AND DISEASES   None of any account.

SPECIAL REFERENCE   Advisory Leaflet 419 *Spinach*, 1971.
Ministry of Agriculture, Fisheries and Food.

Sprouting seeds: Mung Beans or Green-gram
                             Phaseolus aureus (*Leguminosae*)
                                                          Annual

Sprouting seeds, Mung beans, alfalfa seeds, wheat seeds and soy
beans can all be grown in a dark cupboard or a jar, and need
no garden, pot or windowbox to provide a small and continuous
supply of vegetables. 'These sprouts have a useful vitamin content,
and in time of famine can be used as a source of Vitamin C for the
avoidance of scurvy', says *The Oxford Book of Food Plants*. They
take no part in the rotation of crops and you can sprout them at
any time of the year.

CULTIVATION   Use a Kilner jar that can be covered with a circle
of muslin in place of the metal disc, or an earthenware crock with
a piece of muslin secured over the mouth with a rubber band.

Put two tablespoons of the seeds into the jar and cover them with warm water and cover the jar with muslin. Let them soak for eight hours, then drain off the liquid. Continue to rinse and drain the seeds two or three times a day—they should not dry out—placing the jar on its side in a dark cupboard between rinsings (there is not sufficient water in the jar to run out). Two days later bring the sprouts out into the light to turn green and a day or two later they will be ready to eat.

VARIETIES
    Chinese Bean Sprouts
    Other varieties available at health food stores

PESTS AND DISEASES   There are no particular troubles.

Swede   *Brassica napus napobrassica* (*Cruciferae*)
                                                              Biennial

Swedes are peppery-tasting, orange coloured root vegetables; they have their detractors as well as their supporters, but they are useful in the winter vegetable garden. The *Oxford Book of Food Plants* thinks they may be a hybrid between a turnip and a cabbage which appeared as late as the seventeenth century. Swedes are also cultivated for feeding livestock, but they should not be confused with the other root crop for cattle, the mangel-wurzel which is a variety of beetroot of the *Chenopodiaceae* family.

In the spring your overwintering swedes will sprout orange coloured shoots which were once considered a delicacy almost on a par with asparagus. Nowadays few people have heard of them, and you must grow your own if you want to try them.

Swedes are root crops harvested from October, which can be stored for three or four months in sand. In the rotation of crops they are included with turnips, potatoes, carrots, beetroots and parsnips. They follow crops of peas, beans, etc., for which the ground has been well manured with organic material. They, in turn, are followed by the brassicas, cabbages, etc.

CULTIVATION   In February prepare your beds in an open situation and well-limed soil (swedes are members of the *Brassica* family). Fork in compost or well-rotted animal manure or, in the absence of these, bonemeal at 56 g to the sq m (2 oz to the sq yd).

In March sow the seeds in the open ground where they are to crop, in drills 1·9 cm (¾ in) deep and 45 cm (1½ ft) apart. Thin the plants progressively to 30 cm (1 ft). Hoe out weeds. Pay particular attention to adequate watering. This crop is susceptible to lack of water, and if allowed to get dry may bolt to seed and fail to make proper sized roots.

If you require a second crop sow again in July for harvesting in late winter.

Swedes are best left in the ground and dug up as required, but if you need the ground, dig them in November–December and store them in sand in boxes in a dry, airy shed.

VARIETY Chignecto, purple-topped, round-rooted and resistant to club-root.

PESTS AND DISEASES
Club-root The best prevention is maintenance of a *p*H of 6·5–7·0 and strict observance of the rotation of crops.
Soft rot The insides of the roots soften and liquefy, though the outside appears healthy. Again, practise proper rotation. Do not leave pieces of root in the ground after harvesting the crop.
Black rot Turns the insides of the roots dark brown or black. Prevent by taking the same measures as for soft rot.
Powdery mildew A grey-white, dusty appearance on the foliage, particularly in dry seasons. Bordeaux Mixture has been recommended for this, but it is likely to destroy or drive away worms, and it is probably better in the long run to maintain moist conditions and to remove very badly affected plants.
Turnip or flea beetle Very small beetles which feed on the leaves of seedlings and young plants in May–June, producing a large number of small round holes. Eggs are laid in the soil or on swede leaves between June and August, and the subsequent adults feed on summer- and autumn-sown crops, thereafter hibernating until the spring. Some control is exercised by dusting with derris—which will kill bees, and is likely also to kill fish if water from the treated cropping area can drain or percolate into ponds, ditches or streams.

Sweet corn   *Zea mays* (*Gramineae*)
                                                    Annual

Said to have been introduced into Spain by Columbus in about
1500.

We have imported our taste for sweet corn from America.
The table varieties are little known or grown on the Continent
where it is widely despised as 'food for cattle'. However, there is a
difference between cattle maize and the selected and inbred form
of it that we call sweet corn. Ordinary maize has a sort of unpleasant
bready taste; you sometimes buy it unwittingly in supermarkets.
Even domestic sweet corn will become less sweet and juicy if it is
not cooked almost immediately it is picked—a chemical reaction
sets about turning sugar into starch.

In the warmer parts of Britain you can harvest your sweet corn
at the end of summer, from August to October. Although even with
the varieties that plant breeders have developed for our climate the
success of your crop will depend greatly upon the summer it is
grown in. An early frost will also finish off a promising crop.
However, it is always worth planting a row or two, because it is so
delicious when it succeeds. It has no recognized position in the
rotation of crops, but could be alternated with tomatoes.

CULTIVATION In April choose the sunniest position in the
garden and dig in compost or well-rotted organic material previously spread at 10 cm (4 in) thick.

Early in the same month, sow the seeds in the smallest peat
pots, Jiffy strips for instance, in a warm greenhouse. These peat
pots, though rather expensive, are essential for sweet corn which
greatly dislikes any root disturbance, such as being knocked out of
solid pots when they are planted out.

Plant these in the prepared ground 37 cm (15 in) apart, either
in the second week of May under cloches or in the first week of
June without cloches. It is advisable to start these plants as early
as possible because they need a long, growing period in maximum
sunshine.

If no glass of any sort is available, sow the seed directly in the
cropping positions in the open ground at the end of May; two seeds
together 37 cm (15 in) apart in shallow drills 1·9 cm (¾ in) deep.

The plants do best if they are planted in blocks 37 cm (15 in) apart—they pollinate one another better than in long rows. Keep weeds hoed out. Be vigilant with the water supply. In windy places fix canes to prevent the young growths from being blown over.

The cobs develop from the female flowers low down in the axils of the leaves. The stigmas which protrude as silky fronds are known as the 'silk'. When this silk turns from silvery white to black, about a month after it first appears, the cobs are ripe for picking.

VARIETIES
Early Extra Sweet F_1 Hybrid
John Innes Hybrid No. 2 (F_1 Hybrid)
North Star F_1 Hybrid
Earliking F_1 Hybrid

PESTS AND DISEASES
Rooks Can cause damage by pulling up the seed and can be deterred by black cotton strung across the rows.
Frit-fly Lays its eggs on soil round young seedlings; feeding of the larvae on young plants can cause distorted growth in heavy attacks. The recommended controls are both organophosphorus derivatives, which are dangerous to everything, but fortunately, if trouble occurs, it is seldom bad enough to warrant using a chemical control.

Tomato   *Lycopersicon esculentum* (*Solanaceae*)
                              Perennial grown as an annual

The tomato is a native of the lower western slopes of the Andes in America. In nature it is a perennial, rambling over the ground and producing random trusses of fruit along its length. It was introduced into Europe through Italy at the end of the sixteenth century, at first as an ornamental plant; as love apples, tomatoes were once held to be aphrodisiac. Mediterranean cooking must have been very different without them.

Red-ripe and warm from the plant is the only way to taste the full flavour of tomatoes. Fresh, they have a delicate sharp savour that is actually the smell of their foliage; it fades with the withering of the calyx. Fruit from the shops, unless locally grown and

gathered the same day, will have been picked 'pink' or even green
if it has had to come far, and its ripening, such as it is, has taken
place in the course of transit and shelf life. Taste is a very secondary consideration in most commercial varieties—they are grown
for their uniformity of size and their ability to stand up to packing
and travelling. Full of flavour, often oddly shaped and cracking
with ripeness, a home-grown tomato is almost a different vegetable,
and certainly one of the most rewarding to grow for yourself.
Crops from the open ground can be expected between August and
October, and from heated greenhouses between May and October.
In the rotation of crops out of doors, tomatoes are included with
peas and beans, in freshly-manured ground. They follow crops
of brassicas, and are followed in turn by root crops such as potatoes.
They need full exposure to sunlight.

Out doors—CULTIVATION The plants may be bought from
nurserymen or local garden centres, in which case the choice of
varieties will often be restricted and conservative, but if you have
a slightly heated greenhouse, or even just a heated propagating
unit, plants can be raised at home from seed and a much wider
choice of variety is available. The procedure is that at the end of
March or early in April, seed boxes should be prepared, filling
them either with a home-made mixture of half garden compost
and half good garden soil uncontaminated by herbicides (because
tomatoes are very susceptible to weed-killers, particularly the
hormone types) or with one of the proprietary loamless seed composts. The mixture recommended by the Glass house Crops Research Institute is described on p. 149. Two or three days before
sowing, raise the temperature to at least 16°C (60°F) and, if
possible, up to 21°C (70°F), in order to raise the temperature of
the sowing compost to that of the air inside the house. Sow the
seeds about 2·5 (1 in) apart in boxes or, better, directly into 3·7 cm
(1½ in) peat pots or strips.

As soon as the young plants exhibit two true tomato leaves,
not their cotyledon leaves, transplant them into 7·5-cm (3-in) pots
preferably, again, peat pots. Plants from seed trays have to be
handled very carefully and will suffer a little check, but those in
the strips are put into the larger pots, strip and all. These 7·5-cm
(3-in) pots will hold the plants until they are ready to be planted
out of doors, pot and all in the case of peat pots, thus saving another

check. Time the planting out of doors for about seven weeks after sowing the seed, subject to frost danger.

In the propagation period keep the greenhouse as warm as possible by leaving the ventilators shut on all but the hottest days. The temperature can rise to 22°C (72°F) before it is necessary to give even a crack of air.

Before planting out of doors begin to harden the plants off by progressively increasing the ventilation in the daytime, and for the last three days leaving the ventilators open all night, provided there does not appear to be a danger of frost.

In May prepare the cropping positions in as warm a situation as can be made available, subject to the rotation of crops. Spread 15 cm (6 in) depth of garden compost or other organic material on the soil and fork this into the surface. Tomatoes will not withstand the slightest frost, therefore wait until all risk of this is over, usually by the 1st June in the south of England, and a week later in the north, and then put out plants, either bought-in or raised at home, 60 cm (2 ft) apart in rows 90 cm (3 ft) apart.

At the time of planting push a 2-m (6½-ft) cane alongside, leaving 1·2 m (4 ft) of it above ground, and immediately make the first loose tie with soft string, making a 5-cm (2-in) loop to allow the stem to grow. Repeat these ties at intervals of 10-15 cm (4–6 in) as the stems lengthen. Tall polythene cloches are available and are useful in speeding up early growth.

Pay very careful attention to watering. Tomato plants in full career need a good supply of water.

Take out sideshoots as they occur. These are the green shoots growing out of the joints between the main stem and the branches. Hoe or pull out weeds. Protect against snails which may climb into the plants and eat the developing shoots (see p. 42). When two trusses (sprays of flowers) are formed, apply another 10-cm (4-in) depth of garden compost.

When the flowers have formed in the fourth truss, 'stop' the plant by taking out the main leading shoot at the first leaf above the fourth truss. Four trusses are the most that can be expected from outdoor plants (and sometimes only two) before the first cold weather and shortening daylight sets in. This stopping is done to concentrate the plant's energy into fruits which can be ripened, and to divert this energy from the extension of leaves and shoots.

When all trusses intended to produce fruit have 'set', that is, formed fruits, immature though these may be, remove all the leaves below the first truss because a full spread of tomato leaves for some reason operates, photosynthetically, less efficiently than a reduced spread, and if some leaves are taken away the remaining ones perform at their maximum potential. Another reason for this is that the reduction of leaves reduces the unwanted shading effects in fruits which ripen best when fully exposed to the sun. In October when frost threatens, pick the last green fruits and store them in a dark place while they turn red, or make green tomato chutney.

VARIETIES for outdoor cultivation

Those needing cane support

Harbinger, early, good crops of fairly small fruit. Can also be grown under glass.

Marmande, large irregularly-shaped fruit, typical Continental type like those seen on holiday in markets in Spain, France and Italy. Good flavour, solid flesh with few seeds. Not recommended for cultivation under glass.

Outdoor Girl, very early, medium-sized fruits of good flavour, fairly thin-skinned. One of the easiest to grow and possibly the best all-rounder.

Bush types

These are raised in the same way as ordinary kinds but are planted out 90–105 cm (3–3½ ft) apart in both directions. Lay straw around plants to keep the fruits above the soil. Protect against slugs (see p. 42). Do not take out sideshoots. These types do not need support from canes because they spread sideways. They can be cultivated entirely under large cloches.

Sutton's French Cross F₁ Hybrid, fairly early, heavy crops of good-sized fruit.

Sugarplum (Gardener's Delight), small fruits, sweet flavour, can also be grown in pots on a terrace and look very decorative. Suitable for cultivation in a cold greenhouse.

Tiny Tim, very small fruits 1 cm (½ in) in diameter. Can also be grown in a window-box.

A cool greenhouse—CULTIVATION The reason for growing your own tomatoes under glass is to pick them early in the year and to harvest larger crops from each plant, which can give eight trusses or more compared with, at the most, four out of doors.

From a cool greenhouse, with what is known as a 'lift' of 14°C (25°F) (see p. 56 for basic information on greenhouse heating) above outside temperature, ripe fruits can be expected in late June–July. The propagation of plants from seed is the same as for those to be cultivated out of doors, except that seed sowing can be in early February and the date of planting inside the greenhouse can be early in April. Put the young plants into containers at ground level after removing the staging, if this exists. The cropping medium can again be a home-made mixture, this time consisting of three-quarters garden compost and a quarter loam, or one of the proprietary soilless composts, or the special mixture recommended by the Glasshouse Crops Research Institute. Put this into 25-cm (10-in) pots, or boxes about 40 × 35 × 12 cm (16 × 14 × 5 in). Or, instead, put the plants into one of the commercially available compost-filled plastic bags, such as Tombags, Bio-bolsters or Gro-bags.

Before the growing seedlings get in your way, put the supports in position. These can be 2·4-m (8-ft) canes pushed into the boxes or pots, or into the ground alongside the bags or bolsters, and tied at their tops to one or more horizontal wires previously fixed on the inside at eaves' level, and one or two more wires fixed to the underside of the slanting roof below the glass, at right angles to the eaves' wires, so that the extending tomato 'vines' will turn inwards, thus making use of the maximum length of growth. Alternatively 4-ply fillis can be used, tied in a loose loop round the base of the stem with the other end attached to wire or hooks in the roof of the greenhouse; the plants and the fillis are then twisted round one another as the plants grow.

When the compost in the containers has reached the same temperature as that of the air inside the house, usually in three or four days, put in the young plants and immediately make the first loose tie to the cane. Continue ties as for outdoor plants, and also take out sideshoots but, in this case, do not stop the plants until six or eight trusses are formed. Be careful not to remove a truss in mistake for a sideshoot. Keep weeds under control.

More intensive feeding will be needed. Use one of the proprietary tomato liquid fertilizers with a high potassium content in accordance with the directions, usually once a week. Flavour is dependent on a good supply of potassium. If you prefer, when the plants are growing strongly and have made one truss, the feeding can be further intensified by using at every watering the mixture recommended by the Glasshouse Crops Research Institute, described in the notes on cultivation for a heated greenhouse.

VARIETIES for the cool greenhouse

Alicante, early, moderate-sized fruit of bright colour, thin-skinned, resistant to some forms of leaf mould (Cladosporium, a fungus disease).

Ailsa Craig, the classic tomato for flavour, moderate-sized fruit.

Davington Epicure, thin-skinned, moderate-sized, good flavour.

Small Fry (F1 Hybrid), delicious tiny fruit, sometimes seen for sale in punnets like strawberries. Can also be grown out of doors in a window-box.

A warm greenhouse—CULTIVATION Professional growers sow the seed in November in a temperature of 21°C (70°F), never dropping below 16°C (60°F), to start picking in March, until cropping is over in August. This requires a great deal of heat through the coldest time of the year, and implies a temperature lift of something between 22 and 33°C (40 and 60°F) above outside temperatures of 6°C (20°F) and −18°C (0°F), respectively.

The heating installation of the usual small greenhouse is often calculated to give a 14°C (25°F) lift to provide a temperature of 7°C (45°F) inside the house (safely above freezing and providing a little margin against penetrating winds) when the outside temperature is −7°C (20°F), 12°F of frost, which is not unusual in the south of Britain. This sort of greenhouse will be good for cool house cultivation referred to earlier, but to obtain substantially earlier crops at the end of May or June it is necessary to increase the heating capacity considerably and it would not seem to be worth doing this unless you can afford a lift of 22°C (40°F). This will provide 16°C (60°F) against −7°C (20°F) outside and should enable seeds to be sown in January, possibly squeaking by with an extra paraffin heater or a fan blower plugged in if hard frost should seem likely in early March.

Having decided on how much heating you wish to install and the time of sowing the seed, the procedure can be the same as for growing in a cool house referred to earlier. But if the best advantage is to be taken of the extra heating, more sophisticated growing media and feeding techniques can be used as at the Greenhouse Crops Research Institute, who have kindly allowed us to make use of their recommendations as follows. Sow the seed in a mixture of equal parts by volume of granular sphagnum peat and fine sand, lime free, grading 0·05–0·5 mm (this is much finer than the grit used in the John Innes compost). To every 36 litres (1 bushel) is added: 28 g (1 oz) 18% superphosphate, 14 g ($\frac{1}{2}$ oz) potassium nitrate and 112 g (4 oz) ground chalk or limestone. Cover the seeds with 0·6 cm ($\frac{1}{4}$ in) of the sowing mixture.

For potting use a mixture of 75% sphagnum peat and 25% sand as above, to which is added per 36 litres (1 bushel): 28 g (1 oz) potassium nitrate, 56 g (2 oz) superphosphate, 84 g (3 oz) chalk, 84 g (3 oz) magnesium limestone, 14 g ($\frac{1}{2}$ oz) frit 253A and 14 g ($\frac{1}{2}$ oz) ammonium nitrate. Frit 253A contains such trace elements as boron, zinc, manganese, iron, copper and molybdenum.

After the first watering-in with plain water, use a dilute nutrient solution at every watering made up by diluting the stock solution given (following) at the rate of 1 part to 133 parts water. To 180 litres (40 gallons) of water add: 21·3 kg (47$\frac{1}{2}$ lb) potassium nitrate, 3·9 kg (8$\frac{3}{4}$ lb) urea[1] and 3·6 kg (8 lb) magnesium sulphate.

Straw substrates in a warm greenhouse—CULTIVATION Bales or wads of straw can take the place of pots, boxes or polythene bags filled with compost. Wheat straw is better than barley or oat straw, but whichever kind is used it must be uncontaminated by herbicides.

While the seeds are germinating, lay out straw bales or wads in a line on the greenhouse floor on a layer of polythene, and allow them to take the temperature of the air inside the greenhouse. This should be 10°C (50°F) or above, then wet the straw thoroughly with several waterings every two or three days, applying a total quantity of about 40 litres (9 gallons) of water per bale. When the straw is thoroughly wetted, shut the ventilators and activate fermentation by applying the following mixture. To 50·8 kg (1 cwt) of dry straw add: 0·9 kg (2 lb) nitrate lime (Nitro-chalk or Nitra-shell), 340 g (12 oz) triple superphosphate, 670 g (1$\frac{1}{2}$ lb) potassium nitrate, 340 g (12 oz) magnesium sulphate and 170 g (6 oz) commercial ferrous sulphate.

Water in the mixture over the whole of the bale, make depressions in the top of the bales and fill these with good garden soil for the planting positions. The fermentation should produce a

[1] Before planting substitute 5 kg (11$\frac{1}{2}$ lb) ammonium nitrate for urea.

temperature of 43–45°C (110–113°F) within three to five days. When this drops to 38°C (100°F) and no more ammonia fumes are given off, begin planting. Make the first ties to the supports loose enough to allow for two or three inches of sinkage in the bale as it rots so that the roots are not left hanging in the air. Pay careful attention to watering, as straw can dry out unexpectedly quickly. Regular feeding with a proprietary liquid fertilizer high in potassium must be carried out at the supplier's recommended intervals, waiting until the plants have been planted a week before giving the first feed.

VARIETIES for the heated greenhouse

Amberley Cross F_1 Hybrid, early, vigorous, resistant to leaf mould. Free from greenback. Suitable also for cold or cool greenhouse production. Descended from Ailsa Craig, one of the best for flavour. Recommended by the Glasshouse Crops Research Institute.

Ailsa Craig, smooth, medium-sized, best for flavour.

Alicante, thin-skinned, free from greenback, resistant to some forms of leaf mould.

PESTS AND DISEASES   Being highly developed and intensively cultivated, tomatoes are subject to many afflictions, all of which are more frequent and more serious under glass.

Blight   This is the same disease as the one which produces potato blight, and is the reason for keeping these crops apart. The symptoms are brown spots and blotches on the leaves, and grey patches on young fruits. It occurs most often on outdoor plants. If considered necessary and if past attacks have been serious, spray with Bordeaux Mixture, but recognize that this will kill or drive away earthworms.

Damping off   Seedlings collapse under glass. Water with Cheshunt Compound; this will not eradicate one kind of damping off, *Corticium solani*, which is controlled by corrosive sublimate—far too dangerous to have on hand. Damping off is kept at bay by keeping up the temperature, not allowing the plants to get chilled with cold water, and not overwatering. Also, thinly sown seed is much less likely to be affected.

Sleepy disease   The plants wilt as a result of infection of the roots by a soil-borne fungus disease. The treatment is to increase the temperature to 25°C (77°F) for a fortnight, shade the glass, and spray the plants overhead frequently with clear water. A mulch of peat close against the stems will encourage the production of new, clean roots—the peat should be kept moist.

Leaf mould (Cladosporium) Typified by yellow spots on the upper surface of the leaves, with white mould rapidly becoming brown, on the undersides of these spots. This disease is discouraged by ensuring adequate ventilation and moisture at the roots, removing infected leaves and, above all, by cultivating resistant varieties such as Amberley Cross.

Grey mould (Botrytis) Characterized by grey mould on the leaves, sometimes spreading to the fruit, particularly the calyces and the blossom end. Reduce the moisture in the atmosphere inside the house by not damping down the paths or benches, and increase the ventilation as much as possible without reducing the temperature. Remove affected leaves and fruits.

Stem rot or stem canker A fungus disease which produces a dark brown shrinkage at the bottom of the stem which can eventually result in death of the plant. Other discoloured patches are also sometimes seen at the leaf joints higher up the stem. Remove and burn affected plants.

Spotted wilt A virus disease. The leaves at the tops of the plants develop brown spots and turn downwards. The growth of the plant may be arrested completely. Remove and burn affected plants. The disease may be spread by thrips feeding.

Mosaic A virus disease, in which the leaves have dark and light green areas, and blisters. Destroy affected plants and, in future, plant only resistant varieties, e.g. Amberley Cross.

Enation mosaic A virus disease characterized by the suppression of the leaf growth so that the leaf blades are reduced to long thin threads which may be curled or twisted. Plants are usually stunted. Plants cannot be cured, though growth can be improved a little, by giving extra food and mulching. Keep greenfly under control, and do not handle healthy plants immediately after touching infected ones.

Greenback A functional disorder in which that part of the fruit near the stalk remains green. It may be caused by insufficient potassium. The remedy is to make sure that the right proprietary liquid food is used, or the GCRI nutrients systematically applied with each watering. Grow resistant varieties such as Alicante and Amberley Cross.

Blossom end rot or black rot   The fruit may develop a dark sunken, roundish patch at the end furthest from the stalk. It is caused by irregular supplies of water. Sufficient water must be supplied at all times.

Red spider mite   Causes yellowing and blotching of the leaves, chiefly on the undersides, accompanied by webbing. It results in inefficient photosynthesis, and leaves may wither and die. The pest is less liable to establish itself in moist conditions, therefore syringe regularly with clear water, and damp down floor and staging, under glass. Use derris, remembering that it kills bees and fish, only when desperate. Red spider mite predators can be obtained from the Hortic. Training Centre, Dartington Hall, Totnes, Devon, and from the Royal Horticultural Society if you are a Fellow, by writing to the Director, the R.H.S. Garden, Wisley, Ripley, Surrey.

Thrips   The upper surfaces of the leaves are mottled and the undersides covered with a black liquid. The chief damage caused by thrips to tomato plants is in the spreading of the virus disease spotted wilt. Syringe with plain water. In stubborn cases and under glass, use derris, which is harmful to fish and bees.

Tomato moth   Green to light brown caterpillars cause damage to fruits and leaves; pick them off when they are seen, usually from July to September. Recommendations to use organochlorine and organophosphorus insecticides are not acceptable.

Whitefly   This attacks the foliage and appears as a white cloud when the leaves are shaken. The young live and feed under scales on the underside of the leaf and are difficult to destroy with chemicals, but it is now possible to obtain supplies of *Encarsia formosa*, a wasp parasitic on whitefly from either the Director, R.H.S. Garden, Wisley, Ripley, Surrey, if you are a Fellow of the Society, or from Springfield Nursery Ltd, Pick Hill, Waltham Abbey, Essex.

Turnip   *Brassica rapa* (*Cruciferae*)
                                                              Biennial

Turnips are an almost Dickensian winter root vegetable, but not to be despised when there is little else in the vegetable garden. If you love turnips, you can begin to grow them in March, and harvest them some six weeks later, when they are small and tender, something between the size of a hen's egg and a tennis ball. For winter use, leave them in the ground until you need them. You can also eat leafy turnip tops in early spring, as a nutritious alternative to spring greens. In the rotation they go with potatoes, carrots and other root crops, in soil which has been previously manured for a crop of beans or peas, and are followed by the leaf brassicas.

Summer turnips—CULTIVATION   In mid-February prepare the ground in an open situation.

In mid-March work the soil down to a fine tilth and make drills 30–37 cm (12–15 in) apart, 7·5 cm (3 in) deep and of an equal width. Spread in these rotted garden compost or manure almost to the top. Cover this with a little fine soil to keep the newly-sown seed off the compost or manure in the early stages. Sow the seed, and lightly cover this with sifted soil. Thin gradually to 15 cm (6 in) apart. Turnips should be grown rapidly for tenderness. Hoe out weeds; maintain the water supply to prevent bolting. Lift them when they are small.

For *winter turnips*, make a sowing in July, and thin to a final distance of 30 cm (1 ft) apart.

For *turnip greens*, make a sowing in late August or September and do not thin the seedlings. The tops are tender in early spring, and can also be blanched by earthing them up like seakale.

VARIETIES
 Tokyo Cross Hybrid, semi-globe shaped. Can be harvested in from five to six weeks from sowing.
 Sutton's White Milan, flat rooted, medium size.
 Sprinter (from Clause), very early good for frames.
 Sutton's Golden Ball, hardy, yellow-fleshed. Can be left in the ground for some time. Stores well,
 Sutton's Green-top White, good for turnip greens.

PESTS AND DISEASES   See swedes, p. 140.

Wheat seed, see Sprouting Seeds

CHAPTER FIVE

Growing Herbs

OF all the vegetable garden plants, herbs are among the most satisfying to grow, and even if you have no garden at all you can experience this quiet pleasure. Herbs are near-species, and have not been cultivated intensely in an attempt to produce bigger and better varieties; so they have not grown 'soft' and they are seldom afflicted by pests and diseases. Some of them thrive in shady corners, in window-boxes or pots, on kitchen window-sills or out in dim city backyards. Herbs are to be enjoyed for their interesting foliage and for the distinctive aromatic scents they release. Few herbs have startlingly bright flowers, but each one that you grow will add interest and pleasure to your cooking. Experiment with a collection of your favourites in whatever growing space is available to you.

Most herbs will flourish happily together, with the exception of mint which should be planted separately for its rampant root system will soon force out its companions. This will do well by itself in a box or pot outside and it does not mind some shade. If you are unable to start from seed, buy herb plants and pots from a local nursery,[1] or beg roots and seedlings from country friends. Remember that over-watering is as bad as no watering, and cut your herbs gently until they are well established. Plants need some overhead light so if those you have in pots indoors start growing leggy, switch them to the outside to recover.

If you have a garden you will want to set aside a separate space for growing these plants, preferably near to the kitchen so that they can be collected easily and are a constant reminder to the cook to make use of them.

Many herbs are perennial, so once you have established your

---

[1] Also see Appendix 2 for supplier of herb plants.

herb garden it will need little care and maintenance beyond re-sowing the annuals like parsley, dill and so forth.

'In the smallest gardens, Mint, Parsley, Sage, and both Common and Lemon Thyme, must find a place. In gardens which have any pretension to supply the needs of a luxurious table there should be added Basil, Chives, Pot and Sweet Marjoram, Summer and Winter Savory, Sorrel, Tarragon, and others that may be in especial favour.' So says Sutton's old *Book of Gardening*, dated 1902. Many of the herbs are propagated from seed sown directly in their permanent positions, and only a few have to be started in nursery beds. An examination of the natural orders is interesting, the *Umbelliferae* and the *Labiatae* being about equally represented.

Many herbs were once used as simples in medicine, and old herbals attribute many virtues to all manner of plants, as Gerard in his *Herball* of 1597 on Rosemary:

The distilled water of the floures of Rosemary being drunke at morning and evening first and last, taketh away the stench of the mouth and breath, and maketh it very sweet, if there be added thereto, to steep or infuse for certaine daies, a few Cloves, Mace, Cinnamon, and a little Annise seed.

The Arabians and other Physitions succeeding, do write, that Rose-mary comforteth the braine, the memorie, the inward senses, and restoreth speech unto them that are possessed with the dumbe palsie, espicially the conserve being made of the floures and sugar, or any other way confected with sugar, being taken every day fasting.

The floures make up into plates with Sugar after the manner of Sugar Roset and eaten, comfort the heart, and make it merry, quicken the spirits, and make them more lively.

Herbs were also used as strowing herbs to make a carpet to tread on, and in doing so crush the leaves and release their scents. The commonly held theory that they were also used heavily in cooking to disguise the taste and smell of putrescent meat has lately been questioned. Another opinion suggests that Roman cooking, and mediaeval cooking which was in the Roman tradition, were more akin to true Eastern cookery, with its use of subtle blends of herbs and spices by choice, not necessity. The roast beef of old England kind of cooking with plain boiled vegetables and plain boiled puddings took over in the eighteenth century.

Angelica   *Angelica archangelica* (*Umbelliferae*)
Perennial, treated as a biennial

Handsome anywhere in a herb garden. Sow towards the back of a herb or mixed border as it grows 1–1·5 m (3¼–5 ft) tall. Attractive to bees, it succeeds in partial shade.

CULTIVATION Sow the seeds out of doors as soon as ripe, i.e. in August or early September, as they lose their viability quickly. Transplant to cropping positions, putting them in 45 cm (18 in) apart, as soon as they can be handled. This is important because this herb transplants badly if allowed to grow large.

Harvest the young stems in April or May, for crystallizing, and the leaves in May to June.

Basil, sweet   *Ocimum basilicum* (*Labiatae*)
Annual

From tropical Asia. (*O. minimum*, the bush basil, is more compact in form—20 cm (8 in).)

CULTIVATION In March or April, sow the seed under glass in warmth, then prick out into boxes, harden off and in late May or early June plant out into warm cropping positions 20 cm (8 in) apart, in light but rich soil. Maintain a good water supply and remove competing weeds. Pinch out the tips to encourage leafiness. Prick out a few plants into pots to put into a greenhouse later to keep a supply of fresh leaves during a poor summer and on through the winter. Both kinds are used for this. When the flowers appear, cut off the stems, tie them in bunches and dry them in a dark cupboard.

Bay, sweet   *Laurus nobilis* (*Lauraceae*)
Shrubby tree

The laurel crown of poets and conquerors, the bay is an evergreen bush or tree cultivated for the flavour of its aromatic leaves. In sites which suit it, it will grow to 7·5 m (25 ft) and more. It is capable of living in Britain to 100 years or longer in a mild climate, but it can be killed in a hard winter, particularly when grown in tubs above ground level, when frost gets at the roots. For kitchen purposes it is advisable to have a small plant in a tub that can be trundled into a frostproof shed when a hard winter threatens.

CULTIVATION In April buy plants and plant one in the ground and one in a tub, small enough to move into shelter in winter. A sunny position, sheltered from cold winds, and most soils will suit it. Make sure tub-grown plants do not run short of water. You can increase your plants if you want to by taking half-ripened shoot cuttings and rooting them in warmth.

Bergamot *Monarda didyma* Oswego Tea, Bee-balm (*Labiatae*)
Perennial

This makes a well-mannered front row plant in a mixed border, growing to 60 cm (2 ft) and more, preferring moist soil and partial shade. It was named in honour of Nicolas Monardes of Seville, fl. 1571. It is a favourite with bees.

CULTIVATION In March buy plants and put them in 60 cm (2 ft) apart in a herb garden (I use one of the decorative cultivars such as *Monarda didyma* 'Cambridge Scarlet', in a mixed border). Pick the leaves as they are required throughout the summer. Increase by dividing in autumn or spring.

Borage *Borago officinalis* (*Boraginaceae*)
Annual

Borage and courage were impossible to separate in mediaeval prosody. In his *Herball*, Gerard has '*ego borago gaudia semper ago*'. It is another favourite with bees. Its bright blue flowers, from June onwards on stems up to 90 cm (3 ft) tall, make it an attractive plant for the mixed border.

CULTIVATION In March, sow seeds thinly and thin later, or buy plants and put them in 1 m (3¼ ft) apart in threes in a sunny place. Pull off the leaves as you need them. Borage will seed itself, and once you have planted some you will always have a random supply in the garden.

Caraway　　　　　　　　　*Carum carvi (Umbelliferae)*
　　　　　　　　　　　　　　　　　Biennial

This is the plant which provides the seeds for the familiar caraway
cake of the Edwardians, and grows 30–60 cm (1–2 ft) tall. Its leaves
are feathery, and in June of the year following sowing it has white
flowers.

CULTIVATION　In March sow the seeds directly into the cropping ground in a herb garden in rows about 30 cm (1 ft) apart;
when the seedlings have grown 5–7 cm (2–3 in) high, thin them to
25 cm (10 in). The young plants will not like winter waterlogging.
In the following year pick the umbels when they are fully developed. Lay them to dry on paper and shake out the seeds.

Chervil　　　　　　　　　*Anthriscus cerefolium (Umbelliferae)*
　　　　　　　　　　　　　　　　　Annual

A native of Britain and a garden escape. *Cerefolium* means waxen-
leaved, according to W. T. Stearn in his revision of the *Gardeners'
Dictionary of Plant Names*. It is a parsley-like, hardy annual,
whose leaves are used much as parsley is, with a delicately-
aromatic flavour.

CULTIVATION　Sow in cropping positions in March, thinning
the seedlings to 23 cm (9 in), and make repeated sowings if required. This plant will succeed in light shade, and must be
watered in dry weather. Remove flowering heads. For winter
supplies, sow in pots in late summer and take indoors.

Chives　　　　　　　　　*Allium schoenoprasum (Amaryllidaceae)*
　　　　　　　　　　　　　　　　　Bulbous perennial

Chives are pulled from the garden between April and October.
They will also flourish in a pot or a window-box. The delicate
onion flavour of the leaves is very attractive used in recipes where
only a suggestion of onion is wanted.

CULTIVATION　In April sow the seeds in a nursery bed and a
year later lift and divide the roots and plant in permanent positions,

which can be edgings to kitchen garden beds or, if necessary, separate beds in a herb garden. A supply of chives is usually started by begging a few roots from friends. Covering with cloches in winter will ensure leaves for most of the year.

Coriander   *Coriandrum sativum* (*Umbelliferae*)
Annual

A native of southern Europe, possibly introduced by the Romans, and naturalized in Britain. Has been much used in medicine, as well as in cookery. The seeds are powdered, and used in both savoury and sweet dishes.

CULTIVATION   In April prepare cropping positions by working up a light soil with small amounts—5 cm (2 in) deep—of compost or organic material. Later in April sow the seeds in drills 1·9 cm (¾ in) deep and progressively thin the plants to 25 cm (10 in) apart in both directions. Germination will be slow. If desired repeat or make sowings twice more in the spring and early summer. This plant at first has a disagreeable smell but this disappears as the small fruits ripen and gives way to a pleasant aromatic scent. When this occurs it is time to gather the plants and hang them up to dry. Shake out the seeds and keep them in a stoppered jar.

Dill   *Anethum graveolens* (*Umbelliferae*)
Annual

An infusion of the seeds was the basis of dill water to calm colicky babies. Dill is a plant native to the Mediterranean region, and is easily grown in Britain, though it does not transplant well.

CULTIVATION   In March, prepare cropping positions out of doors, sowing the seeds in shallow drills 1·9 cm (¾ in) deep and 23 cm (9 in) apart. Thin the seedlings to 23 cm (9 in) apart. Harvest the plant as the flower heads ripen; hang them up to dry and shake out the seeds. Keep them in an air-tight jar. Through the summer pull off the very thin young leaves and use these green for flavouring fish, soups and sauces.

Fennel   *Foeniculum vulgare* (*Umbelliferae*)
                                                    Perennial

Fennel, with its tall feathery foliage, is a handsome border plant, particularly the bronze or black variety, which is admired by flower arrangers. Southern Europe is its home, but it is naturalized in Britain, especially in coastal areas. It grows to at least 1·5 m (5 ft) tall.

CULTIVATION   In April lightly fork up a sunny bed in your herb garden. Later that month prepare shallow drills 1·9 cm ($\frac{3}{4}$ in) deep and 45 cm (18 in) apart and sow the seed, thinning to about 30 cm (1 ft) apart.

To renew beds, divide roots of old plants and space them out as above. To produce the tender new leaves or 'grass', cut the stems down two or three times in the course of the growing season so that the plant soon puts out new growth. The 'seed'—really fruit—can be harvested, dried and stored.

Geranium, see Pelargonium

Horseradish
        Armoracia rusticana (syn *Cochlearia armoricia*) (*Cruciferae*)
                                                    Perennial

According to Dr W. T. Stearn, *armoracia* (f) is the classical Latin name of a related plant. Horseradish is a crop worth growing, although it is a long-term project. The grated root is the part used in horseradish sauce.

CULTIVATION   In March prepare the cropping ground by deep digging, making trenches 75 cm (2–2$\frac{1}{2}$ ft) deep, to allow for development of the long root. Manure it well with bulky organic material and fine soil. Later in the same month plant pieces of root 30 cm (1 ft) apart and 35 cm (14 in) deep.

To avoid the labour of digging trenches, you can use your existing soil conditions and make holes 35 cm (14 in) deep with a crow bar, pushing pieces of root to the bottom with a stick and then filling up the hole with fine soil mixed with bonemeal and hoof and horn meal.

Hoe out weeds, remove sideshoots, leaving terminal growth. The roots will grow to be 25–30 cm (10–12 in) long when pulled for use and this will usually take two to three years. The roots can be pulled as required or the whole crop lifted during the winter and stored in sand in a dry, frostproof building. The plant is exceedingly invasive (native of eastern Europe and naturalized in Britain) and ought to be confined in some way, either by making a bed with brick sides as recommended by Dawn Macleod,[1] or in the raised beds referred to in the R.H.S. *Dictionary of Gardening.*

Lemon Balm   *Melissa officinalis* (*Labiatae*)
                                           Perennial

A long-term crop. The word *melissa* is the Greek for a honey bee, and the plant is popular with bees. The leaves are attractively scented with lemon.

CULTIVATION   In early April prepare cropping positions in light warm soil fortified with compost or other organic material. Later in the month sow the seeds directly into their final cropping positions in shallow drills 1·9 cm ($\frac{3}{4}$ in) deep. Alternatively, sow the seeds in boxes in May and plant out when 5 cm (2 in) high. One or two plants will be enough for the ordinary herb garden, as it grows into a substantial bushy plant, about 60–120 cm (2–4 ft) tall. Plants can be renewed from divisions made in autumn.

Lemon Verbena   *Lippia* (*Aloysia*) *citriodora* (*Verbenaceae*)
                                           Tender shrub

Introduced into Britain towards the end of the eighteenth century, lemon verbena is a tender exotic from Chile. A garden plant valued for its strongly lemon-scented leaves, which can also be used for flavouring.

CULTIVATION   In April prepare the cropping position by forking in 10-cm (4-in) depth of garden compost or other organic material. Between the middle and the end of May buy plants, or use plants raised from cuttings from your own stock, and put them in, preferably against a wall and facing due south. Take a few

[1] Dawn Macleod, *A Book of Herbs*, Duckworth, 1968.

stem cuttings each year as an insurance against the plant out of doors being killed by a hard frost.

Lovage

Levisticum officinale (*Umbelliferae*)
Perennial

A native of Europe, including Britain, it flourishes in partial shade and you can pick the celery-flavoured leaves all summer. Its name implies that it was once considered an aphrodisiac. It grows much too tall for a pot or window-box.

CULTIVATION 1. To start a supply, in September draw out drills 1·9 cm (¾ in) deep and sow the seeds in nursery beds in sheltered positions; progressively thin the plants to 20 cm (8 in). In March, prepare the cropping positions in a herb garden in a shady situation in moist soil. Towards the end of March transfer the young plants to these beds, 90 cm (3 ft) apart. One or two plants will be enough for a small herb garden, as they grow tall—sometimes to 180 cm (6 ft)—and take up much space.

2. To renew the existing crop, divide and replant old roots, at the same spacing as indicated above, in spring.

Marjoram, sweet, knotted or garden

Origanum majorana (*Labiatae*)
Half-hardy perennial treated as an annual

A native of Portugal and North Africa, long loved and used by British herbalists. *O. vulgare* is the wild species, native to Britain, commonly called oregano, and *O. onites* is pot marjoram, a small, shrubby plant. *O. vulgare* is the least trouble to grow but *O. majorana* is the most aromatic.

CULTIVATION 1. To begin a crop: in March prepare cropping positions in a herb garden on light friable soil moderately tempered with 2 cm (1 in) of garden compost, in an open position where the plant will gather all the warmth from the sun.

In April sow the seed in 1·9-cm (¾-in) drills and thin the plant to 30 cm (1 ft) apart. If required make repeated sowings in the late spring and early summer. Keep the young plants free of weeds.

2. To increase from old stock, lift and divide roots, pot them up

and keep under cover through the winter, then plant out at the spacings indicated previously in May.

Pull the fresh green leaves as required for the kitchen until just before the plant comes into full flower. Hang up the plant to dry and rub the leaves into small pieces to be stored in air-tight stoppered bottles.

Mint *Mentha* spp. (*Labiatae*)
Perennial

This indispensable herb appreciates moist conditions and partial shade and it is a useful plant to fill darkish, dampish corners, including window-boxes and unlikely backyards. It is a long-term crop. Mint is native of Europe, including Britain.

CULTIVATION In February prepare the cropping positions in deep, rather moist soil. In early March obtain roots and plant them 5 cm (2 in) deep and 30 cm (1 ft) apart. If kept well watered they seldom fail to establish and are likely to become invasive. The crop can be kept in check in boxes or raised beds like horseradish. There are many kinds of mints, and 'collectors' enjoy growing several of them in different parts of the garden. The pineapple mint is inclined to be tender in severe winters.

VARIETIES
Mentha spicata—the common green spearmint
M. piperita—peppermint
M. pulegium—pennyroyal
M. requienii—carpeting or Corsican mint, peppermint scented
M. × *gentilis*—ginger mint
M. citrata—bergamot mint, and variety Eau de Cologne
M. rotundifolia—apple mint or Monk's Herb
M. r. variegata—pineapple mint

Parsley *Petroselinum crispum* (*Umbelliferae*)
Biennial

Not a native of Britain and not officially introduced until the sixteenth century, probably from central and southern Europe. The nutrient content of this plant is interesting. You can harvest its foliage and stalks through the year and grow it in pots in the kitchen or greenhouse, or in window-boxes, to keep a continual supply. It is a hardy biennial and needs to be renewed each year.

CULTIVATION   In late February prepare the cropping ground in deep soil, well fortified with compost or organic bulky material at a pH of about 6·0. In March sow the first row of seed at a shallow depth of only 0·3 cm ($\frac{1}{8}$ in) and with it, in the line, a scattering of radish seeds as indicators, because parsley seedlings take from three to six weeks to show above ground. An old countryman will say it has to go down to the Devil and back. Make drills 30 cm (1 ft) apart. Thin the plants to 7·5 cm (3 in). Make further sowings in May and July. This is possibly the most important of all the flavouring herbs, and so you may need to cover a row or two of parsley with cloches, in October, to maintain fresh supplies during severe winters. There is a belief that the seeds take better if the drills are first watered with hot (*but just not quite boiling*) water. If, despite protection by cloches, the plants show signs of dying down, pick them and parch them in a cool oven until crisp and then rub the leaves into small particles and store them in air-tight jars. Sadly, these are a poor substitute for fresh parsley.

VARIETIES
   Sutton's Curly Top
   Claudia D.4, good in cold weather
   Sutton's Imperial Curled
   Hamburg Parsley, parsnip-shaped edible root, plain leaves.

Pelargonium   *Pelargonium* spp. (*Geraniaceae*)
                                              Half-hardy perennial

Some of the scented-leaved geraniums can be used in cooking. They are tender plants from the Cape of Good Hope and although they will flourish out of doors in the summer in the same way as the familiar flowered geraniums like 'Paul Crampel', they need protection in a cool greenhouse in winter.

CULTIVATION   In April prepare the ground by making a space of about 60 × 60 cm (2 × 2 ft) for each plant in light soil with a minimum of organic enrichment, in full sunlight facing, if possible, due south. At the end of May either buy plants or make use of ones propagated at home from cuttings, and plant these—two plants will provide quite enough scented leaves for an ordinary family's modest needs.

These scented geraniums are best put into what was once pompously known as the 'flower garden', mixed with petunias, tobacco plants and heliotrope in beds against the house. They are frost-tender plants and need to be lifted and potted up and put into a cool greenhouse before winter. Cuttings can be taken in September and grown in a cool greenhouse until the following May.

A good variety for cooking is: *Pelargonium denticulatum*, pheasant's foot geranium. It has lemon-scented foliage with background hints of camphor. When grown in a pot inside, it is said to repel flies. It was once known as the water closet geranium, from the small room where it carried out its doleful duty. It is an excellent plant to mix with emphatic summer bedding geraniums, 'King of Denmark', 'A. M. Mayne', 'Gustav Emich' and others.

Rosemary *Rosmarinus officinalis* (Labiatae)
Shrub

This is the obvious species for the herb garden, but there are varieties of rosemary which have individual interest when planted in a mixed border, for example, the fastigiate 'Miss Jessop's Variety', and a dwarf form 'Severn Sea', with arching branches and brilliant blue flowers. There are also 'Tuscan Blue; more tender than the others, with broader leaves and brighter flowers, and *R. lavandulaceus*, the most tender of all, prostrate and full of flowers.

Rosemary is a small shrub used for its aromatic foliage. Sometimes tender even in the south of England. It is a long-lived shrub, but one which it would be prudent to be able to replace with young plants in case of casualty from very severe winters.

CULTIVATION In March prepare the ground for three or four plants, by lightly forking the soil and bringing the pH to about 6·5. No organic manure or other fertilizer will be needed, but mingle a sprinkling of sedge peat which will comfort the roots in

the course of their establishment. In April put in the plants 60 cm
(2 ft) apart, and in the first summer ensure that the soil is just
moist enough for the roots to make biological contact with the
surrounding soil. Once the plants are established, withhold water
unless there are signs of distress.

Sage   *Salvia officinalis* or Common kitchen sage (*Labiatae*)
Shrub

An evergreen bush herb with strong fragrant leaves. It is a long-
lived shrub, provided winters are not severe; southern Europe is
its place of origin.

CULTIVATION   In March prepare the ground in an open sunny
position by lightly forking in 2·5 cm (1 in) of compost, and ensuring
that the *p*H is between 6·0 and 7·0. In April buy plants or scrounge
seedlings and put them in, or sow seeds, which germinate readily.
Keep an eye on watering until the roots have established themselves, but thereafter maintain only a minimum of water supply
because these plants had their origins on Mediterranean hillsides
exposed to full sunlight and little rain. Hoe as required to eliminate weed competition. Gather the leaves as required. They are
exceedingly pungent and one or two plants should be enough for
even a large household.

OTHER SPECIES AND VARIETIES   Among related garden plants
is *Salvia lavandulifolia*. A good plant for a mixed border, having
narrowish leaves, bright blue flowers and a prostrate habit of
growth.

Salvia Officinalis purpurascens (the purple sage) is a vigorous
plant with purple foliage; good for planting among roses where it
hides their bare legs and wreckage in the winter. It is exceedingly
vigorous and can be invasive, and therefore probably better
propagated and put in fresh each spring.

Savory, summer   *Satureia hortensis* (*Labiatae*)
Annual

A good bee plant. An annual herb requiring to be re-sown each
year. More trouble than the perennial winter savory, but worth it
if you have space for both.

CULTIVATION In March prepare the ground in lean soil in full sunlight, and a *p*H of not less than 6·0. Lightly rake the surface and make drills 1·9 cm ($\frac{3}{4}$ in) deep.

In April sow the seeds and progressively thin the young plants to 15 cm (6 in) apart. Be patient and expect slow germination. Cut some of the leaves in June for use as fresh flavouring. Leave the remainder until the flowers have developed and then pull up the whole plant and tie it in bunches for use through the winter.

Savory, winter *Satureia montana (Labiatae)*
Perennial

A very useful herb in that it is a perennial evergreen, and its fresh leaves are available from the open ground all the year. A bee plant. Both summer and winter savory were supposed to give relief from the stings of bees and wasps; both come from southern Europe. A long-term crop.

CULTIVATION In March prepare the cropping ground in full sun in lean, well-drained soils with *p*H of 6·0–7·0. A rich soil will produce lush growth which will not withstand the winter.

In April or May put in plants 30 cm (1 ft) apart, or alternatively sow the seed in shallow drills in April out of doors in the cropping positions, and thin them to 30 cm (1 ft) apart.

Tarragon *Artemisia dracunculus (Compositae)*
Perennial

A herbaceous perennial, inclined to be tender even in the south of England. There are two varieties, a Russian and a French, which has very smooth dark green leaves, and a more delicate flavour. According to Dawn Macleod, French tarragon was Charlemagne's favourite herb.

CULTIVATION In April prepare the ground in dry, light and friable soil in a warm south-facing aspect. In late April make drills 1·9 cm ($\frac{3}{4}$ in) deep and sow the seed, dividing the plants progressively to 30 cm (1 ft) as they develop. Put on a thin mulch 5 cm (2 in) of compost or fertile peat and above this a protecting layer of 15 cm (6 in) of litter (see p. 30) between mid-October and the end of March. Harvest the leaves as required.

Thyme   *Thymus vulgaris*, garden thyme (*Labiatae*)
                                              Perennial shrublet

A long-term evergreen herb, cultivated for its tiny aromatic
leaves. There is a hybrid called *T.* × *citriodorus*, which has lemon-
scented foliage.

CULTIVATION In March prepare the ground in light lean soil
with a *p*H of 6·5–7, only very lightly laced with compost on a
south-facing warm sunny aspect. Make sure that there is satisfactory under-soil drainage. At the end of March or in April put in
bought plants 23 cm (9 in) apart. Water them sparingly until
they are established, and after this only give water if there are
signs of distress. These plants come from the Mediterranean, and
probably get more water than they need from our skies.

Established plants can be increased by taking cuttings in April–
May, or by dividing. Seed can also be used, sowing out of doors
in late April.

CHAPTER SIX

Growing Fruits and Nuts

FRUIT is less commonly grown than vegetables in private gardens—with the possible exception of the conventional soft fruit. Yet fruit is expensive to buy because it is expensive to harvest; it takes a great deal of labour to pick it and pack it and get it to the shops. At the East Malling Research Station I was told that cherry growing is becoming so financially prohibitive to commercial growers that we may very well *have* to grow our own if we want to eat them at all in the future.

Every garden needs shade from trees of some sort, so they might as well be fruitful ones. I include rather exhaustive instructions on the pruning of these trees, because the quality of your crop is very dependent on the care you take with this. If possible, ask an expert to show you how to prune; it is a great deal easier to demonstrate than to describe.

It may take a little time for your trees to begin bearing, but I am reminded of the ageing French Marshal, veteran of the Napoleonic Wars, who summoned his gardener to discuss an elaborate tree-planting scheme. 'But', the gardener said tactfully, 'does M. le Maréchal realize that these trees take a very long time to grow?' 'In that case,' replied the Marshal, 'we must begin today.'

When space is limited in the open or against a wall, fruit trees can be grown in large pots (Fig. 8). The crop is, of course, small, but it can be of excellent quality because the small trees can so easily be kept watered, free of pests, pruned and fertilized. They can be taken into the greenhouse when the fruit buds form, to protect them from birds and to hasten the crop a little. They are decorative when stood on a terrace; apples and pears can develop their fruits out of doors, but cherries would be at risk from black-birds.

Apple   *Malus pumila (Rosaceae)*
                                                                  Tree

The apple has been a powerful symbol in mythology in many cultures and countries, starting with Adam and Eve. It must have once been a much rarer and more mysterious fruit than the abundance of every variety we take for granted today. But perhaps a little of this distinguished aura still clings about the everyday fruit, and the characteristic apple shape with upward stalk and a single leaf, is still widely used as a design motif.

Most established country gardens already have a couple of old incumbents—usually bearing cooking apples—already planted. If you are contemplating installing some of your own, choose the kind of trees (both size and variety) that will serve your needs best, and choose compatible kinds that will successfully pollinate each other.

Apple trees are a permanent part of the garden; thirty years for dwarf pyramids, espaliers and cordons, and a hundred years for standards and half standards. The earliest kinds of apple will be ripe to pick from the tree in July. The later ones are stored for use through the winter and early spring.

CULTIVATION Choose positions in deep, well-drained soil which will favour free root development. If such conditions do not exist, improve the drainage and bring in fresh soil. Early in November dig a hole 60 × 60 × 60 cm (2 × 2 × 2 ft)—if the soil below the hole is retentive, make the hole deeper and put hardcore or some broken mortar rubble or ballast in the bottom, if necessary laying a length of tile-drain connecting to an outlet on lower ground, the slope on the line of the drain being not less than 1 in 100. Put a shovelful of very well rotted manure or garden compost in the bottom. This will be enough because apple trees do not need rich planting ground. When a stake is necessary drive it into the ground at the bottom of the excavated hole to a depth of 60 cm (2 ft), leaving about 2 m (6 ft) standing above ground level, then plant the tree. The best material to complete the filling is stacked loam (see p. 30) or, failing that, good deep soil, consolidating by treading after each shovelful of soil is thrown in. On completion of planting, secure the tree to the stake with tree-ties.

Trained trees need the support either of a wall or a framework of wires. If you intend to grow the trained trees inside a fruit cage then the height of the posts to support the three training wires ought not to be more than 1·8 m (6½ ft) above ground. Either fix the end posts in concrete or provide struts as shown in Fig. 19. At East Malling I saw this system, the trees being planted in rows at least 1·8 m (6 ft) apart on three lines of wires supported by posts 2·4 m (8 ft) apart, the trees being 60 cm (2 ft) apart in rows.

A few trained trees in a garden will usually take pot luck with the vegetables in their general cultivation, but remember that apple trees need sunny, open but sheltered situations, and good soil, not over-rich, and therefore they should not be planted very close to beds which are regularly strongly manured for certain vegetable crops. Cooking apples need more nitrogen than eating apples, but both can do with a good level of potassium, 0·9 kg (2 lb) of dried seaweed per tree or 28 g potassium sulphate per sq m, about 1 oz per sq yd, in winter. An indication of potassium deficiency is when the older leaves show brownish red edges, which curl upwards, from early July onwards.

Apples, together with most fruits, do not tolerate a high lime soil content, which will lead to chlorosis, iron starvation and deprivation of other trace elements such as manganese. In their early stages apples need nitrogen to stimulate leaf growth, thus increasing the area of leaves exposed to the sun to carry out photosynthesis and promote the growth, extension and formation of the framework of the tree. This nitrogen can come from compost, animal manure and, in the early stages only, from poultry manure. Later when the tree is ready to come into bearing, nitrogenous manure should be reduced and potassium applied. A seaweed preparation such as Marinure is suitable.

TYPES OF TREE   The form or shape of the tree—standard, bush, spindle, dwarf pyramid, espalier or cordon—is important, particularly in small gardens. The shorter the tree the easier it is to look after, and forms which can be kept below 1·8 m (6 ft) can not only be included in a fruit cage and protected from bullfinch attack on their buds in spring and blackbird damage to the fruit in the autumn, but can be pruned and picked largely from ground level with only occasional recourse to a soapbox.

The nurseryman can be relied upon to sell you trees budded on the right rootstocks, but it may be helpful to have an outline knowledge of these mysteries. Apple trees, like roses, are produced by grafting the scion (the variety you want to cultivate) on to a stock, a sort of humble wet-nurse, but a wet-nurse whose function persists throughout the life of the tree and influences its growth characteristics. Some of these stocks make tall, spreading trees like standards and half-standards, taking seven or eight years to come into bearing, and being difficult to manage. These are the trees seen in the old and beautiful orchards of Kent and Hereford-shire. At the other extreme, what are known as dwarfing stocks produce small trees from the same variety of apple. These may come into bearing within two or three years, and are much easier to manage.

Stocks were developed at the East Malling Research Station in Kent and used by commercial growers for many years. These stocks have been given 'M' numbers (M for Malling). At present the most dwarfing rootstock available is M9 and a tree on this stock is short in stature and comes early into bearing. Its root anchorage is poor and therefore such a stock is most suitable for cordons and espaliers, which are tied to wires. If used for dwarf pryamids the trees must be staked. Other dwarfing or semi-dwarfing root-stocks are M 26, M7 and M106. M 26 also has poor root anchorage, and it may be that the best stock after M9 would be M106.

Cordons on M9 will start to produce fruit within two to four years, and when in full bearing produce up to 4·5 kg (10 lb) per tree. It is usual to grow them as oblique cordons, that is at an angle of 45° in order to reduce the apical dominance of the leading bud (Fig. 19). Plant them 60 cm (2 ft) apart and at each planting position fix canes to the wires at an angle of 45°. Plant the tree with the graft union 10 cm (4 in) above ground and the scion part of the union uppermost, so that the union is not pulled apart when the tree is fixed to its slanting cane. More use of space and a more attractive appearance is obtained if the young trees are put in 1·2 m (4 ft) apart alternately on either side of the wires, giving a latticed effect.

Varieties for cordons should be of moderate vigour, producing spurs readily. Some of these are: Cox's Orange Pippin, Egremont Russet, Epicure (Laxton's Epicure), James Grieve, Ribston Pippin, Edward VII, Lane's Prince Albert, Royal Jubilee and Grenadier. The last four are culinary varieties.

Dwarf pyramid trees are upright with main stems from which branches about 4·5 cm (1½ ft) long radiate all round. Dwarfing stocks will come into bearing within three or four years, and when mature should produce about 6·7 kg (15 lb) of fruit per tree. Plant them 1·2 m (4 ft) apart in rows 2·4 m (8 ft) apart. Their height is usually about 2·1 m (7 ft), but they can be kept down to 1·8 m (6 ft) if you want to grow them in a fruit cage. They look much better on their own and can be very decorative on either side of a formal kitchen garden on the lines of a French potager. *Espalier* trees can be bought with one, two and sometimes three tiers ready

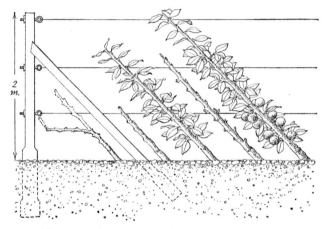

FIG. 19. Oblique cordon method of training apples and pears; useful where space is restricted

formed. The distance apart at which they are planted depends very much on the stock upon which they have been budded, and may vary between 4·5 and 6 m (15 and 20 ft). When in full bearing they can produce 9 to 13 kg (20 to 30 lb) of fruit a year. Espalier apple trees are best planted against wires, because when planted on walls they are prone to red spider mite.

The spindle bush starts with a young tree, something like a vertical cordon, from which laterals from 15 to 25 cm (6–10 in) long grow in all directions from about 30 cm (1 ft) above the union and 10–15 cm (4–6 in) apart. In the first summer after planting the lateral shoots are tied down horizontally to stakes fixed round the tree. It is not such an attractive form as the dwarf pyramid, but productive, producing about 22·5 kg (50 lb) per tree on dwarfing stock

and up to 54 kg (120 lb) per tree if on MM10b; it is easy to prune.
Spacing makes a difference to the yield.

Bush trees are bought as two-, three- or four-year-old trees.
They will grow to 3 m (10 ft) or more and are planted from
3·6 to 9 m (12–30 ft) apart, depending on the stock upon which the
trees have been budded, and can produce from 27 to 45 kg (60–
100 lb) of fruit, again depending on the stock.

Standard trees with clear stems of from 1·5 to 2·1 m (5–7 ft) and
half standards on a shorter leg are still offered by many nurserymen, and on different stocks. Plant them from 9 to 12 m (30–40 ft)
apart. They can be expected to yield up to 180 kg (400 lb) per
tree when in full bearing, which may take ten years or more.

PRUNING   For these notes I have had the advice of my friend
Mr Henry Fraser, who, after being a student gardener at the
Edinburgh Botanic Garden, was a lecturer at the then East
Anglian Institute of Agriculture at Chelmsford, later becoming
the head of the Department of Horticulture there, and then for
twenty-one years a Lecturer in Horticulture at Reading University. I have been very grateful to him for his skilled advice and
permission to quote, in some cases verbatim, from his book *The
Gardener's Guide to Pruning*, now, unfortunately, out of print,
but probably available in public libraries.

Cordons   No shaping is needed for oblique cordons as they are
not cut back in their first winter, nor are their leaders shortened
until they reach the topmost wire (it is possible to allow them to
lengthen beyond this by untying them, pulling them down and
retying them at a more acute angle). Leaders are then cut back
to the length required in May. Maintenance pruning of cordons
is done in summer. There are many different methods, but one
which is more generally used now is known as the modified
Lorette system. About mid-July any laterals that arise directly
from the main stem and have matured are cut to three leaves
beyond the basal cluster, or in other words to a length of 7 or
10 cm (3 or 4 in), or about the width of the pruner's hand—a most
convenient gauge. Other matured shoots arising from existing
laterals or spur systems are pruned to one leaf beyond the basal
cluster of leaves, which means to 3 or 5 cm (1 or 2 in). Any shoots
that mature later in the season are pruned in the same way, in
mid-September, and any secondary shoots resulting from the July

pruning are removed completely at this time. Harm may be done
if the pruning is carried out too soon. The leaves of the shoots
to be pruned must have assumed a deep green colour and the
base of each shoot should have become stiff and woody. It may
be noted that even tip-bearing varieties respond to the system
outlined.

Dwarf Pyramids These are upright and usually kept to no more
than 2·1 m (7 ft), with a central stem from which branches about
45 cm (1½ ft) long grow out in successive tiers, so that a more or
less pyramidal shape is produced eventually. A start is made in
winter by pruning the maiden tree back to a height of 50–60 cm
(20–24 in) depending on the position of any 'feathers' that may
be present. If any are present they are shortened to about 12 cm
(5 in) to a downward pointing bud. They will be removed
ultimately. Then four or five buds suitably spaced are selected
and a notch is made above each of the lower three to stimulate
them into growth. No pruning is done during the first summer.

In the winter of the second year the new growth from the central
leader of the tree is shortened so that 20 cm (8 in) or so of new
wood is left, the cut being made to a bud pointing in the opposite
direction to that of the bud at the previous cut, the object being
to keep the central leader as straight as possible. New growth on
branch leaders is cut back to 12 cm (5 in) to a downward pointing
bud to promote horizontal extension. In mid-July following the
second winter, laterals arising directly from the branches are cut to
three leaves from the basal cluster. Those that arise from laterals
and spurs that form in later years are cut to one leaf. In other words,
the modified Lorette system of summer pruning is practised.

In subsequent years the central leader is pruned as in the second
year in winter, but branch leaders are pruned in summer only
and the summer pruning practised is the same throughout the
life of the tree. Early cropping is encouraged because it helps to
restrict growth and so does the close planting that is characteristic
of this intensive way of growing apples. Blossom buds, however,
that may form on the central leader are removed until the tree
reaches the desired height. When that height has been attained the
central leader itself is removed completely in May, and so is the
leader of any branch that extends more than 45 cm (1½ ft) from
the main stem. Thinning of branches and spurs may become
necessary as the trees become older and this work should be done

during the winter. Figures 20 and 21 show a pyramid and a bush side by side.

Espaliers A tree of this form consists of a vertical main trunk from which side branches are trained along the wires to right and left, about 37 cm (1¼ ft) apart. When the desired height is reached the main stem is cut off at a point level with the top tier of branches. Espalier trees are useful in a garden to grow alongside pathways and as thin screens or divisions between one part of the garden and another. Only moderately vigorous varieties should be grown in this way and these should be on semi-dwarfing rootstocks.

If maiden trees are chosen for planting, and before the actual planting of a tree, it may be worthwhile selecting two buds on the stem nearly opposite each other and about 37 cm (1¼ ft) above ground level so that these point in the direction of the first tier of branches. The tree is cut back to the first bud above the two selected side buds. All shoots are suppressed except those from the three buds specified. The shoot from the terminal bud is trained vertically, while the other two shoots are trained diagonally during the growing season. If one grows more strongly than the other the stronger shoot is depressed and the weaker is raised to equalize the vigour. At the end of the growing season they are brought down to the horizontal. The following winter the vertical shoot is cut to an upward pointing bud about 5 cm (2 in) above the next support-ing wire and the whole process is repeated. Two buds are selected to give another tier and these may be notched to stimulate growth. All other buds on the main stem are removed. The side leaders each year are pruned to a downward pointing bud, the amount of wood removed depending on the strength of the shoots. The sum-mer pruning of laterals on the horizontal branches is exactly as for oblique cordons, the modified Lorette system being preferable. Four or five tiers of branches are usually considered sufficient nowadays.

Spindles Structurally the spindle bush stands halfway between a bush tree and a vertical cordon, and also has some features in common with the dwarf pyramid. The treatment of the lateral shoots appears to be the characteristic feature of the method, for this consists of tying down lateral shoots horizontally and not summer-pruning them. Not surprisingly, this has proved conduc-ive to spur and blossom-bud formation, and under good conditions the tree will begin cropping two or three years after planting. The rootstock M9 is used most frequently for spindle bushes.

The grower usually has to start with a tree supplied by the nursery which is like a vertical cordon, from which laterals 15–25 cm (6–10 in) long issue in all directions from about 30 cm (a foot) above the union and at a distance little more than a hand's breadth apart. After planting the tree, its lateral shoots of pencil thickness or more are cut back to four buds and thinner ones to three or two buds, each shoot being cut to a downward facing bud as this favours horizontal elongation. The leader is cut back to four, or at most six, well-developed buds on the current season's growth. A pyramidal shape is aimed at from the start so that lower branches are not unduly shaded.

In the first summer after planting the lateral shoots are tied down to the horizontal plane before lignification sets in, and are left unpruned until the winter. The ties are fixed to a short stake placed near the stem of the tree. Shoots must not be tied lower than the horizontal plane. When pruned in winter the weaker one-year-old lateral shoots are cut back to from three to five buds and the stronger ones from five to eight buds. If all the buds grow out moderately well after the pruning it is a sign that it has been well done, and this response is wanted from the winter pruning in later years. Evidently the most valuable fruits are obtained from spindle bushes of moderate vigour producing annual shoots 20–40 cm (8–16 in) long. Should a tree grow too strongly in its third or later years the repeated production of forks in the branches, by shortening them, is considered a good way of reducing vigour and promoting fruitfulness and is also helpful in preventing excessive development of shoots from fruiting wood after a poor cropping year. By the time the spindle bush is ten years old the need will arise for the gradual renewal of the fruiting branches.

Bush trees The open-centre tree is favoured by many growers and is one in which the primary branches arise over a relatively short length of stem giving an open cup-shaped branch system. Some degree of spacing out of primary branches is now customary. Assuming a start is made with a maiden, this is cut back to a prominent wood bud at the desired height, so determining the length of stem the tree will possess. This first cut is often referred to as heading back. If a stem 75 cm ($2\frac{1}{2}$ ft) long is wanted the maiden tree is cut at 105 cm ($3\frac{1}{2}$ ft) from the ground. This presupposes a well-grown maiden. The bud near the first cut may be called number one. Buds two and three will give rise to narrow-angled shoots, so they are removed (a narrow or acute angle between the branch and the main trunk is a source of weakness, and such a branch is much more likely to snap off when it has a crop of fruit on it). This is best done in late May when growths from these buds are 2 or 3 cm (1 or 2 in) in length. This deferment seems to result in wider angles being made by the growths from the buds below. An angle of 45° is wanted. Bud four is allowed to remain, but growths from buds five, seven and nine are removed otherwise they may prevent shoots arising from six, eight and ten.

If a 'notch' is made above a dormant bud at a right angle to it, it will encourage growth from that bud and is another way of getting the desired result, but is not always successful as varieties differ in their response to notching. Furthermore, shoots arising from notched buds may be too upright. Notching is done by removing a small wedge-shaped piece of bark (down to the wood) immediately above a bud. To discourage growth a nick is made with a knife at the base of a bud deep enough to cut the vascular strand leading to that bud.

Pruning in the second winter will consist of removing the top central shoot, then shortening the four primary branches by removing one-third to a half of their length, cutting to an outward pointing bud. This shortening will increase the number of primary branches and it will be practised until no further increase in branch numbers is required. It will be advisable later to retain a few branches near the centre of the tree to serve as replacements in the event of the lower branches being pulled too low by heavy crops. Unwanted laterals on the stem of a bush tree may be removed entirely when a start is made with forming the head of the tree, but on trees with longer stems they may be left for a year or so, though cut back to two or three buds. To make sure there are no narrow angles the final selection of shoots can be left until they are 10 or 12 cm (4 or 5 in) long.

After the second winter, the regulated system of pruning can be followed, thinning crowded branches, and shortening others to keep the centre open. No leader tipping is done.

In the *delayed open-centre* system of pruning a maiden tree is cut to 105 cm (about 3½ ft) from the ground. The topmost bud is retained to make the extension of the central system. The second bud is removed, the third and fourth buds are likely to grow normally at right-angles, and further down the stem two buds are selected and a notch made above each. Shoots that appear below are not required. In the second year there will be a central leading shoot and four laterals; any of these tending to become upright are removed, preference always being given to wide-angled shoots. Those growths chosen to make branches will usually need shortening by a half or a third of their length. The central leader is shortened to leave its top bud 30 cm (1 ft) above the highest side-shoot. Buds on this leading shoot are treated in the same way as those on the maiden tree.

The process is repeated with the central shoot in subsequent years until no further extension is required. When this occurs, the centre is finally opened by cutting back the central leader to a well placed branch.

Standards and half-standards In the half-standard and full standard the head of the tree is formed at heights above ground level, varying from 105 cm (3½ ft) up to 2·1 m (7 ft). The full standard form is mainly used for trees worked on vigorous root-stocks and planted in a permanent grass orchard, possibly grazed by stock. Half-standards are also strong growing varieties, planted as permanent trees.

To shape either of these forms, heading back is delayed until the stem is well above the height at which the head is to be formed, so a maiden tree must be grown on to the two-year stage to attain the necessary height. During the time the single stem is growing any laterals that appear are reduced to within 2·5–5 cm (1–2 in) of the base in winter, and pinched back to five leaves in the summer. The additional leaf area these laterals or feathers provide assists in the thickening and strengthening of the stem. They will be removed in the third year. Treatment after heading back is the same as that for the bush form, though pruning of leaders may be continued longer to make sure of providing a rigid framework of main branches.

The pruning involved will consist of removing or shortening any crowding or crossing branches, especially any tending to congest the centre of the tree. Extra long laterals are shortened to balance growth but no general leader tipping is done. Laterals on the outside of the tree may be left full length. During the early years a good deal of shoot thinning has to be done, but as the tree comes into full bearing less of this will be required, although it will be understood that those that are badly placed will have to come out.

Older branches may be removed periodically, provided replacements can be made where necessary. The number of fruiting laterals will need to be reduced as the tree gets older in order to maintain sufficient vigour, and to keep the size of the fruits up to the accepted standard. In general this system is most suitable for varieties such as Bramley's Seedling and Blenheim Orange.

VARIETIES   To obtain good crops of apples, varieties must be chosen which will cross-pollinate each other which, in turn, means varieties which produce their flowers at the same time in the spring. In the list which follows a letter is placed after each one indicating its earliness or lateness of flowering, A being early, at the beginning of May or even earlier, and F being late, in early June. Therefore, if only two apple trees are to be planted, both should flower at the same time. A further complication arises with what are known as triploids (most applies being diploids), whose pollen will not pollinate the flowers of any other apple tree at all, although its own flowers can be fertilized by pollen from a tree which flowers at the same time. But if only one pollinator is planted, this cannot itself be pollinated by a triploid. Consequently, in practice, one triploid needs two diploids to make a satisfactory working partnership of three. Many of these triploids are well worth having, including such well-known varieties as Bramley's Seedling, Blenheim Orange, and Ribston Pippin.

Cooking apples

Bramley's Seedling. C. Triploid. November–March. Large, green-yellow, sometimes with red flush and streaks. The best-known cooking apple. Suitable for standard or bush. It needs two pollinators which could be Grenadier or Emneth Early, or any two of the eating apples in the same flowering period, except triploids.

Crawley Beauty. H. December–March. Large, round, green with red stripes. White flesh, tart and juicy. Crops well and stores well. Suitable for standard, bush or espalier.

Edward VII. G. SCAB RESISTANT. January–April. Large, roundish, pale yellow, lightly flushed. Flesh firm, juicy and sharp. Tends to crop lightly. Stores well. Suitable for espalier, dwarf pyramid, cordon and standard forms. Note late flowering time. It would probably be pollinated by Crawley Beauty or the eating apple Court Pendu Plat.

Emneth Early (syn. Early Victoria). C. July–August. A medium-sized, yellowish green, codlin type of apple, cooking to a pale froth. It should be used soon after picking as it does not store well. Suitable for cultivation as dwarf pyramid or cordon.

Grenadier. C. SCAB RESISTANT. August–September. Medium size, light green to pale yellow, crisp and juicy. A good cropper, but should be used soon after picking as it does not store well. It is a tip bearer, and most suitable as a standard or bush.

Lane's Prince Albert. D. SCAB RESISTANT. November–April. Large, roundish, light green-yellow, flushed and striped red. Tender white flesh, juicy and sharp. Good cropper. Stores well. Suitable for espalier, dwarf pyramid, cordon and standard. Note flowering time. It is pollinated by the eating apples Orleans Reinette, Ellison's Orange or Duke of Devonshire.

Lord Derby. E. November–December. Very large, green turning to yellow, firm yellowish flesh, juicy and sub-acid. It crops well and regularly and stores well, and cooks red. Suitable for standard, bush, espalier, dwarf pyramid and cordon. Late flowering, pollinated by Royal Jubilee.

Royal Jubilee. C. October–December. Large, golden-skinned apple, firm, yellow, sub-acid flesh. Crops well and stores well. Suitable for bush or espalier. Pollinated by Lord Derby.

Eating apples

Ashmead's Kernel. C. SCAB RESISTANT. December–January. Medium size, greenish yellow skin, faintly flushed with brown and russeted. Flesh white, tinged green, juicy, aromatic. A moderate to poor cropper. Susceptible to canker. An old apple dating from about 1720, from Gloucestershire. Interest has been revived in it because of its resistance to scab and its excellent flavour. Stores well. Dwarf pyramid, espalier, cordon.

Belle de Boskoop. C. Triploid. SCAB RESISTANT. December–April. Medium to large. Greenish yellow skin with red flush. Flesh yellow, acid and aromatic. Espalier, bush and standard. Being a triploid it will need two pollinators chosen from Wyken Pippin, Charles Ross, James Grieve, Ashmead's Kernel, Discovery, Tydeman's Early Worcester, Cox's Orange Pippin, Rosemary Russet and Golden Delicious.

Blenheim Orange. C. Triploid. November–January. A fine dual-purpose eating and cooking apple. Stores well. Edward Bunyard wrote of it: '. . . the Blenheim flavour, a nutty warm aroma which is to my taste the real apple gust; in fact, I take a

Blenheim as a test case. The man who cannot appreciate a Blenheim has not come to years of gustatory discretion; he probably drinks sparkling Muscatelle.'[1] Standard, bush, espalier.

Charles Ross. C. SCAB RESISTANT. September–November. Large, round, greeny yellow with red stripes and some russeting. A very handsome apple, brisk, sweet and juicy. Can be 'woolly' if not eaten when ripe and immediately after picking. Does not store. Susceptible to canker and capsid bug. Bush or pyramid. Good in a pot.

Crispin (syn. Mutsu). B. Triploid. November–January. A new Japanese variety. Large, oblong, bright green, ripening to greenish yellow. Flesh firm, white and juicy. Regular cropper. Stores well. Bush, dwarf pyramid, espalier, cordon. Included in the Ministry of Agriculture, Fisheries and Food Bulletin 207, *Apples*. An early-flowering triploid, it would need both Egremont Russet and Margil for pollination.

Court Pendu Plat. F. SCAB RESISTANT. December–April. Smallish, yellow skin, dull red flush and slight russeting. Yellow flesh, rich flavour. Crops well, stores well. One of the latest to flower. More likely to escape spring frosts. Pollinated by Edward VII and Crawley Beauty. Tolerates clay soils. Standard, bush. Said to have been cultivated since Roman times.

Cox's Orange Pippin. C. October–January. Medium size, orange-red skin, russeted. Greenish yellow flesh, aromatic. Crops well, stores well. The favourite apple, but it needs good strong, deep soil (not clay), and sheltered warm position. Far from being a universal apple. Bush, dwarf pyramid, espalier, cordon. James Grieve is a good pollinator.

Discovery. C. August–September. Comparatively new apple. Medium size, greenish yellow, flushed bright red, creamy white flesh. It stores well for such an early apple. Probably suitable for bush, espalier, dwarf pyramid and cordon.

Duke of Devonshire. D. SCAB RESISTANT. February–March. Small to medium size, dull golden yellow, russeted. Flesh pale greenish yellow, aromatic. Crops well, stores well. Standard, bush, dwarf pyramid, espalier, cordon. Pollinated by Ellison's Orange, Orleans Reinette.

Egremont Russet. B. SCAB RESISTANT. October–December. Medium size, round greenish flesh, crisp, nutty. Does not store

---

[1] E. A. Bunyard, *The Anatomy of Dessert*, Chatto & Windus 1933.

well. Early flowering, pollinated with Margil which, with Egremont Russet, would be needed to pollinate Crispin and Ribston
Pippin. Standard, bush, dwarf pyramid, espalier, cordon.

Ellison's Orange. D. October. Large roundish, green-yellow,
red russeted. Tender yellow aromatic flesh; some people detect a
hint of aniseed in its flavour, which is quite distinctive. Standard,
bush, dwarf pyramid or cordon. This is fairly self-fertile, a heavy
and regular cropper, and if only one apple tree is to be planted,
this would be best to choose.

Golden Delicious. C. December–February. Medium size,
greenish yellow, sometimes with russeting. Creamy flesh, crisp and
juicy. Crops well, stores well. Bush, dwarf pyramid, espalier,
cordon. This originated in West Virginia, U.S.A., and is not always successful in Britain, probably because it requires higher
temperatures, a greater light intensity and a longer period of
maturation, nearer to 200 days as opposed to the 136 required for
Cox's Orange Pippin. Imported fruits are probably better than
home-grown ones.

James Grieve. C. September. Medium size, roundish, yellow
when ripe and lightly striped red. Soft flesh, sweet and juicy. It
should be eaten off the tree. Does not store. Inclined to canker.

Margil. B. October–January. Medium size, yellow with red flush,
some russeting. Very good flavour. Dwarf pyramid, espalier, cordon.

Mutsu, see Crispin.

Orleans Reinette. D. December–February. Medium to fairly
large. Golden yellow with slight red flush and russeted. Flesh
yellow, very crisp and juicy, aromatic. Crops well, stores well. This
was Edward Bunyard's favourite apple. He wrote of it: 'Its
brown-red flush and glowing gold . . . very easily suggest that if
Rembrandt had painted a fruit piece he would have chosen this
apple. In the rich golden flesh there is a hint of the Ribston flavour,
much of the Blenheim nuttiness, and an admirable balance of
acidity and sweetness which combine, in my opinion, to make the
best apple grown in Western Europe.'[1] Standard, bush, dwarf
pyramid, espalier, cordon. This apple deserves to be grown more,
not only because of its excellent flavour but also because it flowers
later than many others. It is pollinated by Duke of Devonshire,
Ellison's Orange and the cooker Lane's Prince Albert.

---

[1] E. A. Bunyard, *The Anatomy of Dessert.*

Ribston Pippin. B. Triploid. October–January. Medium size, greenish yellow skin, russeted brown. Yellowish white flesh. Crisp, aromatic. Moderate cropper, stores well. Susceptible to canker. Being an early-flowering triploid it needs two others for pollination such as Egremont Russet and Margil.

Rosemary Russet. C. December–March. Small to medium, roundish. Yellowish green skin with a slight red flush and lightly russeted. Fresh, crisp, yellow flesh, very well flavoured, aromatic, with other russets sometimes thought to have a hint of fennel in its taste. Crops well, stores well. Standard, bush, espalier, cordon.

Tydeman's Early Worcester. C. August–September. Bright crimson skin and juicy, white firm flesh. Suitable for standard, espalier or bush.

Wyken Pippin. C. SCAB RESISTANT. December–March. An old variety. Small, roundish, greenish yellow skin. Tender, yellow, aromatic flesh. Crops well, stores well. Standard and bush.

PICKING AND STORING The simple rule for picking apples is to wait until the fruit stalk parts easily from its twig on being lifted and given a tentative half turn. If it does not come free without a pull it is not ripe for picking. Early apples like Discovery, Tydeman's Early Worcester, Charles Ross, James Grieve, Ellison's Orange and the cooker, Emneth Early, are at their best when picked in this way and eaten or cooked almost directly from the tree. For these only limited and temporary storage is needed, a cool cellar, cupboard or attic.

Most of the others will be picked as the leaves fall from the tree, and before any quantity of them become windfalls. This is usually towards the end of October. To reach their best these need a period of quiet ripening, laid out in a single row, never piled, not touching each other, in a dark cool place. In more spacious days special fruit rooms were made with double walls filled with sawdust, thatched roofs and an earth floor. These buildings were practically frostproof and in them it was possible to maintain the perfect temperature of about 5°C, just over 40°F. These are beyond the reach of nearly all of us now, and we have to make the best of what storage facilities can be adapted and made available. Cellars are suitable, and so might a spare room be on the north side, or a shed in the shade. Attics tend to warm up quickly in autumn sun and drop their temperature alarmingly fast in the winter. Dry atmospheres should be avoided as the fruit will shrivel rapidly. The truth might have to be faced that, unless you have somewhere to store apples in the conditions indicated, it would be better not to attempt to cultivate varieties which need long storage beyond December.

Choose only sound fruit for storing. Lay them on a slatted rack or newspaper over a wire netting shelf. Discard any fruit that is even slightly damaged to avoid the spread of disease, particularly brown rot, which can affect a whole shelf or tray. Another convenient method of storing apples is to place four or five at a time in clear polythene bags; they create their own humid atmosphere, and keep very well in this way.

ORCHARD MANAGEMENT If you are making a new orchard, windscreens must be one of your first considerations. Lines of willow and alders have been found satisfactory, and probably Norway maples might be even better planted in a double alternated row, 6 metres (about 20 ft) apart, in the rows. The water drainage must be seen to, generally a slope on the land will accomplish this, but if the orchard is flat and particularly if it has ground running down to it, land drains will be necessary, discharging into a ditch or, as a last resort, into one or more sumps, if they can be constructed above a free-draining subsoil. Frost drainage must also be considered. When radiation frosts occur in the spring the temperature above the ground cools very quickly and actually becomes heavier, with the result that cold and even freezing air will, as it were, run down a slope. If its progress is arrested by a wall or a thick hedge it will build up and cause freezing air conditions as high as the blossoms of a fruit tree. The remedy is always to provide air drainage by removing any possible barriers, so that the heavy freezing air can go on downhill beyond the blossoming trees. If neither drainage, nor a good soil on a good aspect can be provided, it will be as well to reconsider the whole project of making an orchard.

In the early years the bases of the trees should be kept free of grass and weeds, to avoid competition for water and nutrients, in particular nitrogen, which young trees need while they are making shoot growth and developing their mature stature. At some stage, however, it becomes necessary to control the uptake of nitrogen so that the trees will reduce vegetative growth and concentrate their energies on flower and fruit (reproductive) growth. Grass is a good ultimate cover for orchards. This conserves the fertility of the soil in it, protecting it from the harmful effects of direct sunlight, and from frost, and it also harbours useful predator insects. In orchards of standard trees it can provide grazing for cattle and ponies and also for free-running hens. If this is intended, it would be best in the first place to plant all the cookers together and all the eaters together, so that a temporary wire barrier could be put down and the hens concentrated into the cooking apple section, for the reason that their dung is very rich in nitrogen, richer in fact than is good for eating apples. When it is not grazed the grass in an orchard should be mowed with a rotary type of mower once or twice a month, and the cuttings left to lie. If there is scab disease, sweep up fallen leaves and burn them and pick up all fallen fruit. Most of it may be useful for cooking, but put infected fruits into the incinerator.

PESTS AND DISEASES The full orchard spray programme undertaken by commercial growers is formidable, involving dormant sprays in the winter, sprays against red spider mite in February and early March, at least three sprays against scab at green-bud, pink-bud and petal-fall stages, and probably at least two more scab or mildew sprays and a caterpillar spray by the end of June. This is beyond anything that the private grower could contemplate and, in the end, also nugatory.

Aphides Different kinds hatch in the spring from overwintering eggs (black and oval) laid on shoots and spurs. It was to kill these overwintering eggs that tar distillate winter washes were first used, and although the control of aphis eggs was excellent, useful predators were also killed, resulting in a proliferation of red spider mite, which then had to have a special spray of petroleum oil to control it. Commercial growers continue to use tar-oil washes, amongst other sprays, but for a private grower it is, apart from disturbing a sort of cold war balance between pest and predator, tedious and expensive, and very difficult if not impossible to manage where trained apples are grown in close proximity to vegetables.

Summer pruning of trained trees removes much of the aphis population congregating in the young, soft growth. Many others can be simply washed off with a strong syringe of plain water. In desperation, spray derris as late in the evening as possible when the bees have retired. Any sprays used should contact both leaf surfaces in order to have greatest effect.

Capsid bug   In the spring the young wingless bugs looking at first rather like aphids, but much more active, hatch out from eggs laid in the bark of twigs and branches, and feed on the foliage and young fruit. The latter, as a result, becomes distorted and pock marked. Mr Hills, in his humane and responsible book, *Grow Your own Fruit and Vegetables* (Faber & Faber Ltd), recommends spraying vigorously with plain water to dislodge them. Grease bands will stop them crawling back up the tree. Capsid damage on the fruit results in corky scars a little like those caused by the scab fungus, but pale brown in colour. They are of little consequence in apples which are to be peeled before being cooked or eaten.

Codling moths   The moths lay their eggs on the young fruit at the beginning of June, after petal-fall. The dull pinkish caterpillars hatch and bore into the centre of the apple, where they feed on the pips and core, causing serious damage and maggoty apples. Caterpillars may be present until the end of August. There is a whole string of poisons, organophosphorus, lead arsenate and so on, which can be used. The best that can be done is to tie strips of sacking 10–15 cm (4–6 in) wide round the trunks in August to catch the larvae who have either fallen in windfall apples (infested apples ripen and fall prematurely), or have unintentionally fallen off and are crawling back up the tree to find pupation quarters. Remove and burn the sacking bands in October.

Red spider mite—fruit tree   This pest has increased since the use of the tar distillate washes, but it will not be found on totally unsprayed trees. Eggs are laid in autumn on twigs and hatch into young mites in early May which feed on the underside of the leaves, debilitating the leaf function and turning it a pale sandy colour. They are too small to be seen clearly without a hand lens; feeding can continue until autumn. This pest is normally held within acceptable balance by predators, *Anthocoris nemorum*, hover flies, ladybirds and, curiously, a black-kneed capsid bug.

Sawfly, apple   Eggs are laid at the base of flowers in May while the trees are in bloom. The larvae hatch to feed on the fruitlets, boring into the flesh from the side and often leaving a ribbon-like corky scar on the skin. Sawfly is one of the causes of maggoty apples and more serious and damaging than many other pests.

Derris can be sprayed on to the trees about four days after petal-fall, but even this may kill some of the beneficent predators. Hand picking of infested fruits does much good. The systemic organophosphorus insecticides are not acceptable.

Sucker, apple Overwintering eggs hatch out into insects resembling aphides. These suck the sap in the flower buds, which may fall off and so destroy the crop. This is one of the pests for which tar distillate washes were used. Again, Mr Hills finds that spraying the foliage with a hose after petal-fall will 'bring down thousands', together with the apple fruit weevil (not the apple-blossom weevil) and will at any rate safeguard next year's crop.

Weevil, apple-blossom The adult insects overwinter in the bark and emerge in spring to lay eggs in the blossom buds, on which they also feed. The eggs hatch into the larvae which cause the most damage, destroying the blossom and producing the brown 'cap' on unopened buds. Trap the beetles in bands of sacking or corrugated cardboard put on in late June to catch the adult weevils on their way down the trunk to pupate on the ground. The organochlorine and organophosphorus treatments are not acceptable. Unless an attack is very bad, however, control measures will generally not be necessary, and indeed the weevils may have a beneficial thinning effect.

Winter moths Wingless females crawl up the trunks of the trees from October onwards during the winter to lay their eggs singly on the twigs, and the caterpillars hatching from these feed on the leaves, buds and blossoms from early spring. They are often known as 'Looper' caterpillars and are green in colour—a similar species is brown. Fix grease bands round the trunks to catch the females as they crawl up, doing this before the end of September.

Woolly aphis This is responsible for the white woolly patches seen on the bark of the shoots, branches and trunk. Painting with methylated spirit, preferably using a wire brush, removes it and, being very localized, does not have bad side effects. The best time to do this is May or early June, or as soon as the white wool is seen.

Scab A widespread fungus disease arising chiefly in the spring, infecting the fruit and the leaves in the main. Infection is at its worst in wet warm weather. The disease produces the familiar, circular depressed black 'scabs' on the surface of the fruits. Some ways to avoid or control scab are first by choosing scab resistant

varieties such as the cooking apples Grenadier, Lane's Prince
Albert and Edward VII, and the eating apples James Grieve,
Charles Ross, Egremont Russet, Wyken Pippin, Belle de Boskoop,
Court Pendu Plat, Duke of Devonshire and Ashmead's Kernel.
Next, by keeping a sharp eye open for attacks when summer
pruning is being done. Scab will infest new shoots, producing
blistered and later cracking bark. Cutting out all such shoots will
help to prevent the disease overwintering. This is a good reason
for growing apples and pears as dwarf pyramids, espaliers and
cordons, which are summer pruned. Thirdly, by practising what is
known as orchard hygiene and preventing the spread of what may
start as only a minor infection. This means picking up at once
fallen scabby fruit and putting it into the incinerator. Also, if there
is scab in the trees, not allowing fallen leaves to lie but gather these
and again putting them into the incinerator and not the leaf
compound. For years the standard precautions have been at least
three sprays of lime sulphur, which annihilated some of the best
predator insects, killed the bees and could scarcely have been inviting to the worms. Nowadays there is an even more serious
battery of fungicides, including the systemic benomyl, which is
known to kill worms.

Mildew A powdery mildew which gives the leaves a whitened
appearance, and causes the flowers to become a sickly yellowish
white. Infection begins in the spring, overwinters in the dormant
buds and begins again the following spring. Infected winter buds
will be grey, thin and pointed instead of plump and brown. The
disease starts at the tips of shoots and works back down them;
some buds may be killed outright. This, like scab, can be held in
check by summer pruning which will cut out most of the infected
buds. Further tip cutting may be necessary in winter. Infected
leaves and flowers should be removed as soon as seen in spring.
Worcester Pearmain, Tydeman's Early Worcester and any with
Worcester blood in them, are resistant to mildew. Unfortunately
Lane's Prince Albert, although resistant to scab, is very susceptible
to mildew, which will also attack Cox and Bramley. The disease
causes most trouble in the drier part of the country, i.e. the eastern
half.

Canker A fungus causing sunken and discoloured patches, and
cracking and flaking bark. Infection occurs through pest damage or
wounds, often wounds left by pruning, which should be painted

over with Arbrex or white lead. Trees struggling to grow in unsuitable conditions, such as too heavy soil and bad drainage, are
most susceptible, and Cox and James Grieve are particularly
likely to be victims. The remedy is to pare or cut away the cankers,
burn them and paint over the cuts.

Brown spot   Concentric rings of brownish grey pustules on brown
rotting on the outside of the fruits. The disease is the cause of
mummified fruits hanging on the tree all winter. The action is to
collect all affected fruit and burn it, and make quite sure that no
apples showing incipient signs of the disease, nor apples with any
kind of injury whatsoever, are put into the fruit store.

Bitter pit   Bitter tasting, brown spots in the flesh of the apple,
occurring beneath sunken areas in the skin; worst in seasons when
the soil moisture varies considerably, and on young trees and
where there is much available nitrogen in the soil. Prune lightly,
improve the soil structure and try spraying with a 1% solution of
calcium nitrate at three-week intervals from mid-June to late
August (not Crispin). This is a new treatment and trouble on some
varieties in some seasons may occur as a result of it, so it needs to
be used with caution, but it can have some good effects.

SPECIAL REFERENCES
Bulletin 207, *Apples*, 1972, Ministry of Agriculture Fisheries and
Food, H.M.S.O.
Short term leaflet 77, *Promising Cultivars of Hardy Fruits*, 1972,
Ministry of Agriculture, Fisheries and Food, H.M.S.O.
Fruit Present and Future, Vol. II, 1973, Royal Horticultural Society.

Apricot   *Prunus armeniaca (Rosaceae)*
                                                    Tree

Apricots have long been cherished and cultivated in Britain. They
are the 'dangling apricocks' in *Richard II*; they are part of the
plot in *The Duchess of Malfi*. Warm from the garden wall, ripe,
faintly furry in the palm of the hand, they are much more delicious
than the hard, green-picked woolly-tasting ones which are frequently the only kind you can find in the shops.

You can pick apricots from plants growing out of doors against
warm walls in August. They are not greenhouse crops, but they

need the protection of a wall because their flowers rashly open in February.

CULTIVATION Apricots are propagated by budding desired varieties on to seedling plum stocks.

The fan shape is the universal method of training against a wall with wires fixed 15 cm (6 in) apart. Allow 6·0–7·5 m (20–25 ft) between the plants.

In autumn, no later, dig planting positions 1 × 1 × 1 m (3¼ × 3¼ × 3¼ ft). Ensure adequate drainage. If necessary lay a short length of agricultural tile-drain from the bottom of the planting position to a lower level or to a sump connecting down to free draining subsoil. Fill the bottom of the excavated position with 30 cm (1 ft) of coarse material, broken stones, lime mortar rubble, coarse chalk or coarse bones. Cover this with a layer of reversed turves (grass side down) and complete the filling with good strong topsoil; light sandy soil is unsatisfactory. In the coarse of planting keep to hand a supply of sifted topsoil to scatter over the roots. Set the tree in the same position relative to the surrounding soil level as it was when growing in the nursery. Make sure that the graft or bud union is 10 cm (4 in) above the final soil level. Shake the tree up and down as the fine soil is thrown round the roots. Tread the filling every 10 cm (4 in), and at each treading throw in a handful of coarse limestone. Water liberally, but remember later that apricots resist drought better than peaches or nectarines. After about three months tie the branches in to their fan shape, on to the wires as for peaches, and continue the training in the same way as for peaches (see p. 216).

A double thickness of netting will give some protection to the flowers against frost. Make sure that the nets are not of such close mesh as to exclude pollinating bees. In any case, it is advisable to supplement the bees' activity with a rabbit's tail or a paint brush pushed into the open flowers. Muslin can further be draped over the netting in the ripening period to keep out wasps.

The general cultivation of apricots, manuring and watering, is similar to that of peaches.

VARIETIES
Hemskerke, early August. Yellow with red blotches.

Moorpark, August. Large, round, deep orange. Skin flushed brownish red. Flesh orange, firm and juicy.

PESTS AND DISEASES

Die-back   This attacks Moorpark and other varieties; one of the branches first, and later, one whole side of a fan-trained tree, begins to die in a late frost. Protect with nets as indicated previously.

For other troubles, see peaches and nectarines, p. 216.

Blackcurrant   *Ribes nigrum (Saxifragaceae)*
                                    Perennial shrub

An old gardener told me that eating blackcurrants made him sweat under the eyes. They are certainly rich in vitamin C, a delightful fruit that is easy to grow and an essential part of every English country summer.

CULTIVATION   You can pick your blackcurrants from the end of June until early August. The bushes occupy the ground for ten years or more. They need protection from birds in a fruit cage or with netting. Choose a position sheltered from the north east and not in a frost pocket because blackcurrants are very susceptible to spring frost damage. Also choose a position sheltered from strong winds from any direction as the bees will not work the flowers in windy conditions. The best soil is a deep medium or well-broken down heavy loam at least 45 cm (1½ ft) deep. Before planting dig in farmyard manure or garden compost, if so much of the latter can be spared, previously spread to a depth of 15 cm (6 in). Put the plants in preferably in October, or between October and March. Buy one- or two-year-old bushes and plant them 1·5 m (5 ft) apart in rows 1·8 m (6 ft) apart. Plant them deeper than they were growing in the nursery so that the 'stools' are formed to produce new growths from the base of the stems.

Immediately planting is done, prune the stems down to leave one or two buds. This means no fruit in the first summer; the reason is to concentrate the plant's energies in the production of new growths for fruiting in the second summer.

After planting apply more manure as a mulch 5 cm (2 in) deep. If the soil is not warm defer putting on the mulch until April.

In the autumn after planting cut out the weakest of the new summer shoots to permit strong growth for the following summer. In subsequent years continue to cut out weaker shoots, and those that have fruited, doing some of the pruning immediately after picking and the remainder in November. In pruning do not aim at an open centre but keep the bush fairly thin and open to light and air. Most of the fruits are borne on wood of the previous year's growth.

At all times keep down weeds by hoeing, but avoid damage to the roots, which are near the surface. Alternatively, cover the soil with a thick layer of straw, in spring and again in autumn. This will prevent weeds from growing, and will rot down to provide humus. This is a hungry crop and must be consistently satisfied with farmyard manure or other fertile mulching material in large quantities, applied in spring.

VARIETIES

Boskoop Giant, the earliest to ripen. Large, sweet fruit. Susceptible to big bud. Makes a large bush.

Mendip Cross, early, hardy, crops heavily.

Wellington XXX, a heavy cropper and well flavoured. Mid season.

Baldwin, hardy and vigorous. Said to be one of the richest in vitamin C. Late but very heavy cropping.

Amos Black, a late variety, often fruiting into August.

PESTS AND DISEASES

Aphides Up to six different species of aphides (and a capsid) attack blackcurrants. One species produces disfiguring red blisters on the leaves by feeding, but does little real damage. However, the leaf-curling aphides at the shoot tips can stunt growth seriously, and if present in large numbers should be dealt with as soon as hatching starts, when the leaves begin to unfold. Derris in the evening is preferable.

Currant gall mite The feeding of these mites in spring and summer causes the notorious Big Bud. Hand pick swollen buds as soon as seen, and burn badly affected plants; choose, as far as possible, immune strains. These mites carry reversion, a virus disease.

Currant clearwing moth, the magpie moth and gooseberry sawfly. The caterpillars of the first named bore into the stem of new shoots, those of the last live and feed on the leaves. All can be sprayed with derris or pyrethrum in the evenings when the bees have gone home.

American gooseberry mildew   Besides gooseberries, this will now attack blackcurrants, producing white patches of fungus, which later turn brown, on all parts of the plant. Cut out affected parts as soon as seen. At East Malling Research Station resistant strains are being developed by crossing back with the garden flowering currant *Ribes sanguineum*, a cross which also gives resistance to the fungus disease leaf spot.

European gooseberry mildew   A white mildew on the leaves, usually not on the fruits. Cut out infected shoot tips in autumn, and with the routine cutting out later in the winter, keep the bushes well thinned out in the course of pruning, and collect up fallen leaves. Remove infected leaves in spring as soon as seen.

Rust   Small orange-brown raised spots on leaves and fruit. Burn infected prunings.

Reversion   A virus of which the vector is the gall mite. It causes elongation of the leaves, a reduced crop and finally death of the plant. The symptoms are most noticeable in June. Dig up and burn the whole plant when the infection is seen.

Cherry
Prunus avium, sweet cherry, *P. cerasus*, acid cherry (*Rosaceae*)
Tree

'Loveliest of trees, the cherry,' was so described by A. E. Housman for its blossom, not its fruit. But a cherry is a beautiful tree in the garden at any time of year, and now that commercial growers are becoming scarce because of the greatly increased labour cost of picking the fruit. Sweet cherries are picked from the end of June to August. Acid cherries, chiefly morellos, from July to September, both from trees growing out of doors. Earlier crops of either can be obtained from plants in pots under glass.

CULTIVATION   More than other fruits, cherries demand free drainage, and a fertile soil, but not a high lime content; soils containing free lime may lead to deficiencies of iron and manganese. They do need a generous water supply but not, perversely, just before the blossoms open, nor in July when fruit is filling out and ready to pick. But at all other times a good supply of water is necessary.

They need shelter from east winds, and positions where they will be above possible frost pockets at blossom time.

They are budded or grafted on to the wild cherry, the lovely mazzard or gean, which makes the vigorous, tall, widespreading trees seen in the beautiful cherry orchards, from which fruit is expensive to pick in these days. They maintain their vigour and rampageousness even when trained as fans for walls, and large, tall, wide walls are really necessary. In 30–35 cm (12–14 in) pots they are much more controllable. They are plunged under ashes for most of the year, but brought into a cold greenhouse in January for pollination and protected from frost at the critical time.

To plant a cherry out of doors either as a fan-trained tree or as a free-standing one, dig a planting position 1 × 1 × 1 m (3¼ × 3¼ × 3¼ ft) and fill the bottom with 30 cm (1 ft) of coarse drainage material as for peaches and nectarines, and make sure that there is free exit of water from the planting pit as previously indicated. Then lay reversed turves over the coarse material and begin to refill the hole with fibrous loam, turves that have been stacked for three months or, failing this, good topsoil. Have on hand a supply of sifted soil, granular and a little damp but not dusty, sprinkle this round the roots, lifting and shaking the tree as this is done, and as the first shovelfuls of soil are put in. A stake will have to be driven into the bottom of the hole before planting begins. If the planting is against a wall, arrange for the stem of the tree to be 23 cm (9 in) away from the base of the wall, and previously fix training wires as for peaches. To grow in pots, first obtain if possible plants which are already established in pots; at least one grower offers these. Then taking a 30-cm (1-ft) pot, put in a 5-cm (2-in) layer of broken crocks, cover this with a reversed turf, cut to fit and begin the filling with decayed fibrous loam. Transfer the pot-grown plant at such a level that the base of the 'leg' or stem is 5 cm (2 in) below the top of the rim of the pot. Then complete the filling to within 5 cm (2 in) leaving this space for watering and subsequent dressing.

Sweet cherries—PRUNING. The delayed open-centre system to pruning (as for apples, see p. 178) can be applied successfully to sweet cherries and, by selecting laterals over a relatively long length of stem, branches are developed of the required mechanical strength and so arranged that the production of a V-shaped crotch in later years is obviated, thus preventing the formation of a favourite point of entry of the bacterial canker organism. To minimize the danger from infection of the silver-leaf fungus, young trees are pruned in spring after bud burst and mature trees in summer immediately after picking.

The actual amount of pruning given to sweet cherries is small, after the head of the tree has been formed. The framework of branches is built up by cutting back the leaders to about half their length to buds pointing in the required direction. No shortening of laterals is done. Having obtained the requisite number of strong, well-shaped branches very little leader tipping will be done thereafter, though varieties with a pendulous habit will require this treatment for two or three years longer than others.

The fruiting habit of sweet cherries is different from that of other tree fruits. The fruit is borne laterally on very compact spurs, formed along the whole length of the two-year-old wood, hence when the branch framework has been built up pruning will consist of removing inward growing, crossing or crowded branches to prevent congestion. This is best done quite late in the pruning season after growth has started in order to minimize the danger of infection by silver-leaf disease. Where circumstances make the growth of the standard or bush forms of sweet cherries worth while, early cropping should be encouraged to help in the restriction of growth. The annual pruning of mature trees will amount to no more than the removal of dead, broken or crossing branches, preferably after picking the crop. The danger of silver-leaf infection is at its minimum between June and August, and as far as it is practicable pruning operations should be arranged with this in mind.

Established cherry trees tend to become bare near the centre and it is a good plan to dehorn such trees a little each year. This is done by cutting tall branches back, as in the apple, to a suitable horizontal branch, and if the cuts made are pared over and properly sealed, and few in number, it is not likely that the trees will suffer any harm. This system of dehorning may begin while the trees are still relatively young because cherries do not make fresh shoots readily and it is useless to cut back to very old wood; also, large cuts on cherry wood are slow to callus over.

Wall-grown trees Trees with this form have short stems, and the branches are spaced out a foot or so apart radiating outwards in the shape of a fan. The training and pruning are the same as for a fan-trained peach tree in the initial stage of development, and the placement of branches will always be similar, but much of the routine pruning will be different as the fruiting habit is very different. As the growth of a young cherry tree is normally vigorous, four good shoots may be formed the first year. The centre of the fan will remain unfilled until the side branches are well established.

The pruning of dessert cherries on walls should consist of shortening laterals to five or six leaves in July, and then shortening these again to three or four buds in September. Shoots which appear on the wall side of the branches should be rubbed off while they are small. Dessert cherries do not produce nearly so many laterals as apples and pears—one factor which makes them easier to manage—but they possess other features which make them difficult. Walls of considerable height are a prerequisite when sweet cherries are to be grown upon them, for if the walls are low the leading shoots of the trees soon overtop them and become unmanageable. Bending them over and tying them down for a year is usually helpful as it is then often possible to shorten the leaders back to a weak lateral. Cutting them hard back will only make the problem of control more difficult.

Surprising though it may seem, it is possible to grow sweet cherries as single cordons, spaced 60 cm (2 ft) apart, and inclined at an angle of 45°. One-year-old trees, budded low, are planted and left unpruned to encourage fruiting. Any lateral shoots that appear are kept pinched back to promote spur formation. A cherry cordon will reach a greater length than a cordon apple or pear and it follows, therefore, that a high building or wall is needed to accommodate them if several are grown to serve as a decorative feature, quite apart from the utilitarian aspect. Needless to say, bamboo canes are needed to keep the stems straight. One great merit of cherries on walls is that the fruit can be protected from birds.

Acid cherries—PRUNING Acid cherries may be grown as bush trees on a stem 60–90 cm (2–3 ft) long and having either a traditional open-centre head or, what is preferable, a delayed open-centre head. They fruit mainly on wood made the previous year, and the aim of the grower is to maintain plenty of young wood throughout the tree, and to avoid as far as possible having little but bare branches near the tree's centre. Fortunately, acid cherries can be induced to make fresh growth from dormant buds in old wood, so once the tree is established a certain number of branches are cut back annually into three- or four-year-old wood to maintain vigour and a constant supply of fruiting shoots. This pruning is best done in April after buds have burst, as it is then easier to see the position of dormant buds in the old wood, and the risk of silver-leaf infection is reduced if cuts are made at that time of the year.

Wall-grown trees Acid cherries lend themselves to growing on walls, and the pruning and training they receive when grown as fan-like trees is very similar to that given the peach when grown in the same form. The early treatment is exactly the same, the aim being to establish the side branches first and to fill up the central part of the fan later, making sure also that the base of the tree is sufficiently well furnished by gradually lowering some of the side branches when these are strong enough.

From what has been written it will be appreciated that a good supply of laterals (potential fruiting wood) is wanted on wall-grown acid cherries. Quite often there is a shortage. The best remedy for a shortage is to cut back a number of the older branches each year, and to tie in the young shoots resulting from this pruning, and other young shoots present, leaving only 7·5–10 cm (3–4 in) between each when the tree is unfastened from its supports in the winter, given what pruning is needed and replaced in position again. Any stubs that have failed to produce new growths are cut out carefully and wherever possible older branches are pruned away before they become too thick. In winter a wall-trained peach tree and a wall-trained acid cherry tree will look very much alike. The only difference noticeable will be the somewhat closer spacing of the young wood of the cherry.

VARIETIES

Sweet cherries The flowering periods and incompatibility groups of sweet cherries are perverse and idiosyncratic in the extreme. The matter is treated with much thoroughness in the Royal Horticultural Society's *The Fruit Garden Displayed* and succinctly also in the Ministry of Agriculture's Bulletin No. 119, *Plums and*

Cherries. In order to try to simplify this, I have set out after the description of the varieties groups which are compatible. The letters A to F refer to the time of flowering, A being early, and F being late.

Bigarreau de Schrecken. B. Late June. Large, black fruit. Pollinated by Merton Heart, Waterloo.

Early Rivers. A. Mid–late June. Large, black fruit. Pollinated by Merton Heart, Kent Bigarreau, although flowering a little before this.

Elton Heart. C. July. Heart-shaped, pale yellow, mottled red. Pollinated by Merton Glory, Roundel Heart, Merton Bigarreau.

Kent Bigarreau (Amber Heart). D. Early July. Medium size, pale yellow, with red cheeks. Pollinated by Napoleon Bigarreau.

Merton Bigarreau. C. Mid–late July. Large fruit, black with dark red flesh. Pollinated by Merton Glory, Roundel Heart, Elton Heart.

Merton Glory. C. Mid-July. White. Pollinated by Roundel Heart, Merton Bigarreau, Elton Heart. This is what is known as a universal donor and will pollinate any other C.

Merton Heart. B. Late June–early July. Very large, almost black fruit. Pollinated by Bigarreau de Schrecken, Waterloo.

Napoleon Bigarreau. D. Late July. Large black fruit. Pollinated by Kent Bigarreau.

Roundel Heart. C. Early July. Large, black fruit. Pollinated by Merton Glory, Merton Bigarreau, Elton Heart. This was raised by Sir Thomas Andrew Knight at Downton Castle, Herefordshire.

Waterloo. B. Late June–early July. Small black fruit. Pollinated by Merton Heart, Bigarreau de Schrecken.

In order to make the pollination as simple as possible, I have bracketed the varieties which should be grown together. To grow any one within each bracket you will need at least one other from the same group.

⎧ Bigarreau de	⎧ Merton Glory	⎧ Napoleon Bigarreau
⎪ Schrecken	⎪ Roundel Heart	⎨ Kent Bigarreau
⎨ Merton Heart	⎨ Merton Bigarreau	⎩ Early Rivers
⎩ Waterloo	⎩ Elton Heart	

Cooking (acid) cherries

Morello. Large, round, deep black fruit. August–September. A good tree for a north wall. Self-fertile.

Kentish Red Cherry (Scarlet Morello). Self-fertile, but crops better if cross-pollinated, by Morello. July.

May Duke. Large, deep red-purple. Rich flavour. End of June. Slightly self-fertile, but better if cross-pollinated by Morello.

PESTS AND DISEASES

Slugworm   See pears, p. 229.

Winter moths   Greaseband as for apples. Poultry free-ranging in a cherry orchard will eat most of these.

Blackfly and other aphides   Leaves and tips of shoots severely distorted and curled; particularly damaging to young trees. Spray thoroughly with derris in the evening when the bees have gone.

Bacterial canker   A serious disease which is difficult to eradicate. Leaves may have small, round 'shot-holes' in them from late spring onwards. The bark of shoots and branches shows sunken areas, which crack and gum. The leaves in the portion above the canker turn yellow, and the branch will gradually die. Cut out affected parts as soon as seen, and paint wounds at once with Arbrex or other wound sealing compound. Spray with Bordeaux Mixture, if the disease continues, just as leaf fall starts, and again the following spring at green cluster stage, remembering that continued use will decimate the worms eventually.

SPECIAL REFERENCE   Bulletin No. 119, *Plums and Cherries*, 1961, Ministry of Agriculture, Fisheries and Food, H.M.S.O.

Fig   *Ficus carica* (*Moraceae*)
                                                                      Tree

Grown in the open against sunny walls, fig trees will, with good weather and good management, bear one crop of fruits each year—in July and August. Under glass they can bear two crops—in June and August. Unlike apples and other fruits which mature after picking, figs are no good if picked early and hopefully sent on their travels to be eaten in faraway places. Therefore wait until the fruit is fully ripe and think of its ancient history in Greece and Palestine.

Figs are a permanent crop—trees continuing for forty years.

Generally they are supplied in pots and best planted in the spring as follows.

CULTIVATION In March choose a position in front of a south-facing wall not less than 2·4 m (8 ft) high and preferably up to 3 m (10 ft) in the warmest corner of the garden. Dig a hole 1·2 m (4 ft) square and 1·2 m (4 ft) deep. Line the four sides with brickwork, or slates or stones on edge and pack and ram into the bottom crushed brick or gravel to a finished depth of 30 cm (1 ft)— or excavate only 1 m (3 ft) deep and lay flat stones or slates on the bottom with only minimal chinks between them to let water out. Then put in thick turves in two layers each of 15 cm (6 in) grass side down. Plant the small tree and fill in firmly all round with chopped fibrous loam lightened a little with bean-size crocks or mortar rubble, or sharp shingle. Pack this in tightly below the tree. The reason for this is that if it is to bear fruit, the fig's very strong tendency to make leaf and shoot growth must be checked by putting it thus into purgatory. Add no manure or fertilizer. Water the plant only every ten days in its first summer, but never let it go short of water (water, without bread, is its penal diet), and remember that all plants growing against walls get less water from rain than those out in the open, because rain seldom falls conveniently vertically. It may bounce off and miss the roots; also the heat retained in the wall not only dries the soil but increases transpirational loss of water from the leaves.

Train a young tree by selecting and training out to wires five or six of the main branches in a fan shape. The number of 'ribs' in the fan can be increased later because there are plenty of side buds waiting their chance to grow outwards. The first crop of any year is borne on well ripened shoots of the previous year. The second crop may be borne on shoots of the current year, and the third crop on the laterals of those shoots which have produced the second crop. Three crops in a year is too much to expect even under glass in these latitudes. So when the first crop is gathered, all weak shoots are cut out leaving only the best of the current year's growth for a possible second crop. After the second crop has been harvested, the same routine is observed in thinning out weak growths for the following year.

Protect the base from frost with litter, see p. 30. If possible drape a double thickness of netting, or a sheet of hessian, from the top of the wall in frosty weather—but do not leave these drapes in position when the weather is mild. In a greenhouse, plant the young tree in the same way, but rely on the heating system to keep the frost away.

Figs are decorative in pots—kept in the greenhouse all the winter, and for some of the summer too, but brought out on to a terrace for occasions.

Plant them in 25-cm (10-in) pots with drainage material at the bottom, a part of a reversed turf cut to fit, and a filling of fibrous loam, again with a little mortar-rubble or sharp shingle run through it to keep it open. Watch the watering—particularly when the plant is brought out on to the terrace.

Wait until figs are fully ripe on the tree, 'with a tear in their eye', before picking and eating them, usually from mid-August onwards.

VARIETIES
Brown Turkey, for out of doors.
White Ischia, for a greenhouse.

PESTS AND DISEASES   None of any account.

Gooseberry   *Ribes grossularia* (*Saxifragaceae*)
Shrub

Gooseberries for dessert still make me shudder when I remember the, one hopes, apocryphal story of the Edwardian hostess entreating her guests in the garden not to throw away the gooseberry skins because: 'they make such splendid jam for the servants'.

Gooseberries are a popular cottage garden fruit, for they fruit abundantly, needing no elaborate cultivation. The large red or yellow dessert gooseberries are seldom seen in shops nowadays, the smaller green cooking varieties being the only ones available. Gooseberries are high in nicotinic acid.

They are picked from the open ground in late June and July, and later still if grown on north-facing walls. They are usually cultivated as bushes on short legs, but can also be grown as single and double cordons. They do best in cooler areas of the country, even mountain districts.

CULTIVATION   In September prepare the ground in an open position on friable, easy working soil, by forking in garden compost if it can be spared, or otherwise rotted farmyard manure previously spread to a depth of 15 cm (6 in). Make sure that perennial weeds are completely removed.

In October or, if this is impossible, between October and March, plant the bushes 2 m (6½ ft) apart in both directions. Put them in at the same depth as they were growing in the nursery, but make sure that the planting holes are wide enough to accommodate the roots without folding them.

After planting, prune the plants back hard, removing about two-thirds of each shoot and cutting back to outward pointing buds. Three to five of the strongest shoots only should be left, and the remainder cut out completely. In the second winter cut back all but six to eight shoots to 2·5 cm (1 in). Continue thus each year until ten or twelve main branches have formed to provide a permanent framework. Maintain an open centre. Thereafter routine pruning can consist of spurring back the sideshoots to leave them 2·5 cm (1 in) long and cutting the leading shoots back by half the new growth, until they have grown to the height wanted, when they are treated like the sideshoots. Alternatively, some sideshoots only need be spurred as described, others left unpruned if they are not more than 15 cm (6 in) long, and some of the stronger ones also left uncut. Gooseberries will provide fruit at both the base of young wood, and on the spurs of older wood. Wear gloves, and in the course of pruning try to leave space around the branches for the fruit to be picked without a great deal of scratching and catching. Cut away all drooping growths and maintain a leg. Routine pruning is best done as soon as the fruit is picked.

Hoe out weeds gently, the merest tickling with a hoe, because the roots are near the surface.

The plants need potassium, therefore give potassium sulphate at 28 g per sq m (1 oz per sq yd) or Marinure in January or February, and do not give massive dressings of nitrogenous material to the extent advised for blackcurrants.

Plant cordons 30 cm (1 ft) apart and double cordons 1 m (3¼ ft) apart against a wire framework 1·8 m (6 ft) high, consisting of two wires. These can be included inside a fruit cage.

VARIETIES
Careless, large white, early.
Early Sulphur, yellow, hairy, early.

Lancashire, large, red.
Leveller, yellow, mid- to late season.
Whinham's Industry, red, mid-season.

PESTS AND DISEASES

Gooseberry sawfly   The green, black-spotted caterpillars will first appear in May and can defoliate the bushes completely. Second and third generations may come in June and August. Pick off, or shake off, larvae on to sacks spread underneath the bushes. Spray with pyrethrum.

Magpie moth   Spray with derris against the black, white and yellow caterpillars in spring. Only one brood will be produced.

Aphides   Feed on young leaves and shoots, and severely stunt new growth. Spray with derris, but not when the bees are working.

Die-back   Due to infection by grey mould (*Botrytis cinerea*). Shoots may wilt and die one by one; if the main stem is affected low down, the whole bush may die. Single shoots should be cut out, well below the diseased part, or the entire plant destroyed.

American gooseberry mildew   White patches on leaves on the under-surface, also on shoot tips and berries. Later they become brown felted. Cut off infected parts as soon as seen, and do not give excessive amounts of nitrogenous fertilizers. Mildewed fruits can safely be eaten. Prune to let in light and air. Grow resistant varieties.

European gooseberry mildew   White patches on the upper surface of the leaves, seldom on the berries. Treat as for American mildew.

Grapes   *Vitis vinifera (Vitaceae)*
                                                   Perennial climbing plant

Grapes were widely cultivated in the ancient world, mostly to be pressed for wine but also, according to Apicius, to flavour and sweeten food when reduced to concentrated wine and grape juice.

Wine making is one of the oldest arts of the husbandman—vines were grown in Britain in Roman times. This crop is to some extent being revived today, and you can buy varieties of grapes especially for wine-making.[1] The wine grapes are small and un-

---

[1] For wine-making in England, read Edward Hyams' *Vineyards in England*, Faber & Faber, 1953.

impressive compared with the opulent Hamburghs and Muscats of our grandfathers' vineries. They took immense pains with their dessert grapes. 'I would request no better meat than a dish of ripe grapes,' said the Duchess to Dr Faustus, and she was right.

From a heated greenhouse, grapes can be picked between July and December; from a cold house, from August. Grown out of doors, grapes are ripe for picking from early September. This is a long-term crop, and plants last for many years.

OUTDOOR CULTIVATION To grow them out of doors in open ground choose a position on a south-facing slope, if possible, with a lime-rich soil over free-draining subsoil. In October put in two-year-old plants, 1·2 m (4 ft) apart, in rows about 75 cm (2½ ft) apart, and spread some litter over the plants for protection in the first winter. The following March cut back to brown wood. Keep weeds hoed out and ensure an adequate water supply.

The Guyot method of pruning, as outlined in the R.H.S. *Dictionary of Gardening,* is to allow two shoots to develop each year from the stump, and in winter to cut one of these shoots back to 1·2 m (4 ft) and bend it horizontally. The other shoot is cut back to two buds, to produce two more shoots for the following season. In the first summer, the longer one which has been bent horizontally is intended to bear fruit from all the shoots on its buds. Prune these to 15 cm (6 in) above the bunches of fruit. In winter after fruiting, cut out the longer shoot. You are then left with two shoots to prune as before.

If cloches with a headroom of 60 cm (2 ft) are available and deployed over the plants, the production of grapes can be advanced by three or four weeks. Vines can also be grown on a house wall and look classically beautiful. Unfortunately, they seem more prone to mildew.

GREENHOUSE CULTIVATION For cultivation under glass in a heated greenhouse, the vine border needs to be about 3 m (10 ft) wide to allow for the spread of roots over the years. This requires a fairly wide greenhouse, but it has also long been the custom to make vine borders up against the *outside* of the house with the vine's rods coming in through brick arches or specially made apertures. This results in the soil temperature above the roots being much cooler and slightly retarding development of the vines. It is most important that soil drainage is adequate, and ideally the border should therefore be dug to 120 cm (4 ft) deep, the soil broken up below this, and drainage material placed on the forked-up soil, with turves grass side downwards on top. Fill in the border with a mixture of stacked fibrous loam, well rotted manure, and a sprinkling of bonemeal and wood ash. Tread the soil firmly and plant the fruiting canes early in the New Year, 1–1·2 m (3–4 ft) apart, 45 cm (1½ ft) away from the wall. Then cut back to 45 cm (1½ ft) of ripe brown wood. In the first summer do not restrain the growth of the main shoot, but in the second winter cut back its new growth by about half, or slightly more. In the summer which follows remove unwanted sideshoots completely. Those that remain should be spaced about 23 cm (9 in) apart, alternately on the main stem, not directly opposite one another. These will be the the start of spur formation, which will gradually lengthen over the years. In the third winter cut the leader back hard to about half its length and prune the sideshoots back to one or two buds, removing the one which is obviously the weakest when growth starts in spring.

Thereafter give routine pruning as follows. In summer stop the shoots carrying a bunch of fruit at two leaves beyond the bunch or, if no fruit, at the 4th leaf; any sub-laterals are stopped so that one leaf only remains. During the winter cut all the sideshoots and the leader back hard to leave one or two buds only, aiming to finish the pruning (as with all winter pruning) by Christmas. When the vine begins to grow, remove the weaker shoot as soon as both are seen to be growing. In spring remove all the new shoots from sideshoots and leaders so as to leave one per spur. This method of training is for a single vertical rod.

In the first year after planting do not put heat into the greenhouse, but in subsequent years varieties such as Black Hamburgh and Muscat of Alexandria will need a night temperature of 10°C (50°F), rising another 10°F just before the bunches come into flower. After this, Muscat of Alexandria will need a higher temperature than Black Hamburgh.

Keep the house well ventilated and maintain a buoyant atmosphere by keeping the soil moist and frequently syringing the foliage. Top-dress with garden compost just after flowering. Thin the bunches out when they begin to develop berries, to one bunch to about every 30 cm (1 ft) of cane, and also thin the berries within the bunches, when just set, and again when just small pea size.

Once the fruit is picked, give as much air as possible, until growth is to be started again. Top-dress with rotted manure, garden compost or good loam in early spring every year. Water heavily when growth starts, and again just before the flowers open. Otherwise water with caution, to avoid fruit cracking and splitting. Outside borders need not be watered unless they begin to be obviously dry.

VARIETIES
Out of doors

Golden Chasselas, pale gold berries, best for warm walls. For eating.

Pirovano 14, red to black, early fruiting. For eating.

Précoce de Malingre, early white grape. For eating and wine-making.

Siebel 13053, black. For wine-making.

Greenhouse (all for eating)

Alicante, large black berries, late, perhaps a little coarse.

Black Hamburgh, black grapes for warm or cool houses. Will succeed in a mixed vinery.

Buckland Sweetwater, white, large, for a mixed vinery.

Gros Colmar, large black for a warm house.

Madresfield Court, black for a warm house.

PESTS AND DISEASES

Red spider mite Attacks by this pest on plants under glass often occur; leaves become discoloured and withered, but regular spraying and a humid atmosphere will discourage its appearance.

Mealy bugs and scale A traditional trouble on vines; scale shows as small brown lumps on the shoots, and mealy bugs live beneath a white fluffy wool. They can be scraped off together with loose bark, and the shoots painted with a mixture of soft soap and sulphur.

Mildew White powdery patches on young shoots in spring and on the berries. Thin out the shoots and leaves and give a little extra heat.

Grey mould (Botrytis) Berries infected with grey fur; remove and give extra heat to dry out the atmosphere and increase the warmth.

Shanking Stalks of berries turn brown and berries shrivel. Due to unsatisfactory growth conditions, often to do with the soil, such as dry roots, or waterlogging.

Sun scald Berries become scorched and sunken on one side, due to too much moisture on the skin during hot sunshine. Keep a higher night temperature, and ventilate well during the day.

Loganberry and blackberry

R. × *loganobaccus* (loganberry), R. *ulmifolius* (blackberry)
(*Rosaceae*)
Climbing or spreading shrubs

The loganberry is a hybrid, which orginated in America, thought to be a cross between a blackberry and a raspberry. The fruits are large and luscious, but to my mind the flavour is not so good as that of the ordinary blackberry. These are plentiful in the hedgerows, of course, but it is pleasant to grow a supply within easy reach of the kitchen.

The berries are ripe for picking in July and August, and on into October for blackberries. Country people say the Devil spits on these on the 1st October, when they start to taste woolly and dead.

CULTIVATION   Prepare planting positions as for raspberries (see p. 137). Fix supporting wires in the same way. Blackberries can also be planted against a fence or wall, securing the growths to the wood with twine and nails.

Remove weeds thoroughly, particularly persistent weeds, like couch grass which will be difficult to hoe out later without damaging the roots of the crop which are near the surface.

In November (or between November and March) put in the plants much further apart than raspberries, 2·4 m (8 ft) apart, in rows the same distance apart. Use bulky organic manure or garden compost as a mulch to a depth of 10 cm (4 in) in spring and again in autumn while the ground is warm.

Loganberries and some blackberries bear fruit on young canes of the current year. These die after bearing—cut them off at the base and burn them. In the autumn tie in the new canes, either in a fan shape, which is best, or by the rope method, with several canes tied together along the wires. This is rough, but quick to do.

The Himalayaberry has persistent canes which fruit in successive years; it is a kind of giant blackberry, ripening early. Take out the oldest canes after fruiting and burn them. Tie in new canes in winter.

VARIETIES
Loganberry LY 59, large dark fruit.
Himalayaberry, very vigorous, makes canes 3 m (10 ft) long.
John Innes, ripens before wild blackberries.
Boysenberry, large, dark red to black fruit. Sharp, distinctive flavour.

PESTS AND DISEASES See raspberries, p. 238. The common green capsid is kept at bay by derris sprayed in the evenings.

Medlar   *Mespilus germanica* (*Rosaceae*)
Tree
With mulberries and quinces, medlars make up a trio of fruits of Merrie England. Even Edward Bunyard did not appreciate the raw fruits, but he did say that Professor Saintsbury considered 'The Medlar the ideal fruit to marry to Port'. Perhaps its chief value is its decorative appearance on a lawn. The fruits are picked in the middle of November and stored until they soften.

CULTIVATION Medlars will succeed best in positions in the open, preferably with some shelter from cold winds. Ordinary good, fairly deep garden soil is satisfactory. They do not need such moist conditions as quinces. Plant as for quinces (see p. 235) in prepared positions 3 × 3 × 3 m (3¼ × 3¼ × 3¼ ft) deep. Standard trees are spaced from 4·5 to 6 m, about 15–20 ft, half-standards are planted 5 m (17 ft) apart and bushes 3 m (10 ft) apart.
Prune by removing crossing branches, keeping the centre open and thinning twiggy growth.
Pick the fruits from the end of October to the middle of November while they are still green. Store them in a cool fruit shed until they begin to turn reddish brown. This process was known as bletting, from the French word *blettir*—to become over-ripe. Bletting is really a progression towards what many would call rottenness.

VARIETIES Dutch, very large fruit, rich russet-brown. The tree has an attractive, slightly weeping head of growth.
Nottingham, small fruit, the flavour considered by connoisseurs to be better than the Dutch.

PESTS AND DISEASES None of any importance.

Melon   *Cucumis melo (Cucurbitaceae)*
                                    Annual climbing plant

Refreshing, juicy and delicious, melons are summer favourites with
almost everyone, and another fruit that our discerning grandparents cultivated with great determination and enthusiasm. This
may still be done today, although the melon remains a fruit that
prefers a much hotter climate than ours. According to Bunyard[1]
the word cantaloupe 'comes from Canteluppi, a Papal villegieatura
near Rome, where, it is said, this variety first arrived in Europe
from Armenia in the fifteenth century'.

Melons are in season from May to November from a greenhouse
or frame. They can also be grown entirely under cloches with a
kind of hot-bed, and they can often also be finished in the open in a
very warm corner. They are not subject to the rotation of crops,
although they belong to the same family, *Cucurbitaceae*, as marrows
and courgettes.

OUTDOOR CULTIVATION   If they are to be finished out of doors,
just produce young plants from seed in a greenhouse (see p. 211) or
buy or beg some.

Prepare a rich bed in a warm corner with the equivalent of 30 cm
(1 ft) of organic material, garden compost and farmyard manure—
old, cooled hot-bed material is excellent.

In June, put in plants on shallow mounds 60 cm (2 ft) apart and
keep them well watered. Cover with cloches if you have them.

Train and stop and pollinate as for frame cultivation (see below).
Rest the fruits on slates or small pieces of wood.

Edward Hyams[2] has a way of raising seedling plants in a propagator, like a miniature greenhouse, heated usually by electricity,
and stood on a greenhouse bench or inside a sunny window indoors. These are transferred to a kind of mild hot-bed consisting of
farmyard manure or straw packed into a trench, and barn cloches
put over them. Put a mound of soil on top before planting out the
young melons and keep the cloches on.

FRAMES OVER HOT-BEDS—CULTIVATION   In January make
up a hot-bed (see p. 27) 1 m (3¼ ft) deep. Cover it with 30 cm (1 ft)

---

[1] E. A. Bunyard, *The Anatomy of Dessert*.
[2] Edward Hyams, *The Cultivation of Melons under Cloches*, Faber &
Faber, 1953.

of soil and put a frame on top. Pack the hot-bed material round the outside of the frame to keep up the temperature inside to 18°C (65°F) for as long as possible.

For May crops sow the seeds in 7·5-cm (3-in) pots plunged into the soil over the hot-bed material.

For July–September crops, make up the hot-bed later, at the end of March, and sow the seeds in April. When they have developed their first true leaves, take up the seedlings and put them into cropping positions in the same frame. Plant them a third of the way from the back of the frame, on small mounds of soil, to raise up the centres of the young melons in order that when watering, water will not accumulate round the collars and provoke the development of canker.

Do not allow fruits to develop on the main stem. Stop the growing point of each plant at the third leaf. Encourage two laterals to grow forwards; when six leaves have been formed by these laterals, stop them at the fourth leaf and then stop the sub-laterals at the third leaf. By now there should be some female flowers recognizable by the swollen bases of the stalks. Pollinate these by picking off the male flowers, either folding back or pulling off the petals, and pushing the remains of the male flower on to the stigma in the middle of the female flower.

Under frames look out for two (only two) young fruits of about equal size on each plant—persevere with these; rest them on little squares of wood, or on tiles.

HEATED GREENHOUSE CULTIVATION To produce fruits in May: early in February raise the temperature of the greenhouse to 18–21°C (65–70°F). Fill peat pots with a seed compost (or make your own with ¼ finely sieved garden compost and ¾ screened loam —parts by volume) and plunge these into a bed on the greenhouse staging retained by boards 10 cm (4 in) deep. This plunging bed is to stabilize fluctuations of moisture and temperature in the soil inside the pots. Make the bed of fertile peat, see p. 29, or garden compost if there is enough.

Allow three to four days for the plunging medium and the soil in the pots to reach the temperature inside the greenhouse, then plant the seeds in the pots, one in each, covered with their own depth of soil.

While the seeds are germinating, fix wires horizontally to the sides and the undersides of the sloping roof about 23 cm (9 in) apart, and the same distance from the glass, in order that as they grow and lengthen, the 'vines' can be tied to canes fixed at right angles to the wires.

Then make up a cropping bed on the staging, 30 cm (1 ft) deep, retained by boards and, if possible, immediately above hot water pipes, electric tubes or soil-heating wires, in order to gain bottom heat.

First put a layer of crocks on the staging, which must have provision for drainage, either through holes drilled through corrugated asbestos or corrugated galvanized iron, or through slats in timber.

Cover these crocks with grass turves 10 cm (4 in) thick, which will be all the better if they have been stacked for three months out of doors. Allow at least a week for the soil to come up to the temperature inside the greenhouse. When the young plants have made two rough leaves stand them in their pots 50 cm (20 in) apart on the soil cropping bed, and surround them with garden compost, or well-rotted animal manure, not over-rich. Last year's hot-bed material would be suitable. Ensure an adequate lime content, a pH of 6·5–7·0 is best. In the course of planting, push the pots into small mounds, so that water cannot collect at the collar and provoke an infection of canker. Keep the night temperature as near 16°C (60°F) as possible (a good rod thermostat, controlling a properly planned heating installation, will see to this). The day temperature can rise, through sun heat, to 27°C (80°F). If it exceeds this, increase the ventilation. Syringe with water from cans which have been standing in the house. This syringing will usually provide enough water at the roots for a day or two. Melons do not need as much water as cucumbers—but none the less do not ever let them get dry at the roots.

Stop the plants at 15 cm (6 in) and then allow them to develop two stems to grow on side by side without further stopping. Give a little extra water as they begin to come into flower, but stop watering on to the soil when the flowers begin to open. After this continue with syringing only in the evenings before shutting the ventilators. The reason is the continuing importance of not getting water on to the collar.

Pollinate the female flowers as detailed under cultivation in frames. Try to find four fairly even-sized fruits, and encourage these by removing smaller or disproportionately large ones. Thin out the foliage to allow light to reach the fruits. As these develop, take their weight off the vine either by suspending them in specially-made melon nets tied to the wires in the roof, or by making small wooden platforms about 20 cm (8 in) square, and hanging these from the roof wires with flexible copper or flexible lead wire, and resting the fruits on these platforms.

Leave the fruits on the plants until they are ripe, when the undersides will yield a little to gentle pressure and when a typical melon scent will be noticed. Fine hair cracks will also appear round the stalk.

VARIETIES

Canteloupe These have a rough skin, not reticulated. Often with deep grooves and usually with orange-coloured but, less commonly, green flesh. These are the best types to grow in heated frames. They can also be attempted, often successfully, in cold frames or under cloches if plants are previously raised in a greenhouse, hardened off and put out in June.

Sweetheart F_1 Hybrid, pale green skin, bright orange flesh.

Ogen, small, round 15-cm (6-in) fruits, green flesh, from Israel.

Charantais, small, orange fleshed. This is the one grown in large numbers round Cavaillon in Provence.

Winter melons Smooth or with only shallow corrugations. Thick skins, not reticulated. These will keep for about a month after picking.

Honeydew, good for cold frame cultivation.

Musk melons The skins are reticulated, that is, covered with a raised network. The surface may be smooth or segmented. They are oval and even in outline. These are the usually grown hothouse melons.

Superlative, orange fleshed.

Hero of Lockinge, white fleshed.

Emerald Gem, green fleshed. Bunyard[1] wrote of its 'cool, transparent, jade interior'.

PESTS AND DISEASES

Grey mould (Botrytis cinerea) Remove and burn badly-affected plants, otherwise cut off infected parts, and thin out shoots and foliage.

---

[1] E. A. Bunyard, *The Anatomy of Dessert.*

Powdery mildew Powdery white patches on leaves and stems. Prevent this by giving enough ventilation and avoid too much moisture. Some control can be exercised with a sulphur spray.

Canker Causes slimy degeneration at the collar and is encouraged by overwatering, see cultivation. Make sure the plants are put on little mounds. When the trouble occurs, remove badly affected plants.

Leaf blotch A fungus disease causing pale spots which soon increase and may, in the end, kill the leaves.

Fusarium vasinfectum Infects roots and is a soil-borne fungus disease. Causes wilting of the plant. Remove infected plants, together with a good depth of soil.

Verticillium albo-atrum Similar to fusarium and also causes wilting of the plant. It occurs at low temperatures and improvements can be made by increasing the temperature.

Mulberry
Morus nigra (*Moraceae*)
Tree

The mulberry is a handsome, unusual garden tree which can be planted with quinces and medlars to make a Jacobean assembly. It came originally from western Asia, but has been cultivated in Europe for centuries. The tree will slowly reach some 6–9 m (20–30 ft) in height and is very long-lived. The deep red berries, which look a lot better than they taste, are gathered in July and August. The leaves of the white mulberry, *M. alba*, are the ones used for feeding silkworms. King James I attempted to establish plantations of these to set up a silk industry in Britain, but the attempt failed, probably because the white mulberry could not endure the cold and damps of this country.

CULTIVATION Mulberries enjoy an open sunny position, in good deep garden soil. Plant trees in November in holes not less than 60 × 60 × 60 cm (2 × 2 × 2 ft) deep, but enlarge this if necessary to accommodate the full root spread of the tree when delivered. Be careful to avoid damaging the roots, as they 'bleed' easily. Before planting fix a stake, and secure the tree to it afterwards. If planting more than one, allow a distance of 6 m (20 ft) between them.

Prune in winter by reducing the new shoots to four or five buds, and thereafter by removing dead wood, crossing branches and excessive twiggy growth. Prune as little as possible, as top growth, like the roots, will 'bleed' when cut.

When the fruits begin to fall on to the grass in July and August, pick them up by hand or spread sheets of paper round the tree and shake it.

VARIETY Black Mulberry

Nuts (cob, filbert and hazel) Corylus spp. (Betulaceae)
Tree

A brake of nuts, or a nut walk, can be a pleasant shady place in a garden, underplanted with hellebores and hostas, grape hyacinths, snowdrops, crocuses, aconites and lilies of the valley. The cobnut or hazel is Corylus avellana, the filbert C. maxima—its nuts are longer and proportionately narrower than those of the cob, and set in longer husks. The nuts of both are ripe in the autumn but you have to outwit the squirrels, to gather and store them for the winter.

CULTIVATION Hazels thrive best in open positions with, if possible, some shelter from the north and east, on well-drained soils which can be a little stony and gravelly without detriment. Bushes on a short leg, 45 cm (18 in), are satisfactory forms in which to plant them, 4·5 m (15 ft) apart in November.

After planting, cut the new growth back to an outward pointing bud leaving two or three other buds below it. This 'coppicing' is repeated in each autumn until the trees are 1·8 m (6 ft) high, in order to encourage development of laterals. Thereafter defer the pruning of these laterals until March by which time the male catkins will have produced pollen scattered in the wind to the female flowers. At this time, therefore, cut back the longest sideshoots to a catkin a few inches above the base. Cut out some of the older stems each year leaving the small twig-like wood of the previous year's growth to bear fruit.

VARIETIES
Pearson's Prolific (Nottingham Cob).
Lambert's Filbert (Kentish Cob), nut very large and long, good flavour.
Red Filbert, like the white filbert except for its red skin covering.
White Filbert, one of the latest of the filberts.

PESTS AND DISEASES

Nut weevil These feed on the leaves and nutlets in May and June, and lay eggs in the soft shells of the nuts up to mid-July. The resultant grubs feed on the kernels. One way to discover them and also to eliminate them is to shake the branches of the tree over a sheet on to which the weevils will fall. The Ministry of Agriculture leaflet referred to gives an organochlorine product as a control measure.

Nut drop and bud rot Both fungus diseases. The use of phenyl mercury chloride preparation can scarcely be undertaken by a private gardener. Therefore, if the attack is severe, cut out the affected parts and burn them.

SPECIAL REFERENCE Advisory leaflet 400, *Cobnuts and Filberts*, 1966, Ministry of Agriculture, Fisheries and Food.

Peach and Nectarine   *Prunus persica* (*Rosaceae*)
                                                              Tree

'A man who eats a peach, for example, is first of all agreeably impressed by the smell emanating from it; he puts it into his mouth and experiences a sensation of freshness and acidity which incites him to continue; but it is not until the moment when he swallows, and the mouthful passes beneath the nasal channel, that the perfume is revealed to him, completing the sensations which every peach should cause. And finally, it is only after he has swallowed that he passes judgement on the experience and says to himself, "That was delicious." ' Brillat Savarin was actually analysing the sense of taste, but he also describes the pleasure of peaches. They are yet another luxury fruit once elaborately cultivated, and now that they are so prohibitively expensive to buy, can certainly be again.

You will be able to pick your peaches and nectarines from the open ground out of doors from the middle of July until the end of September, or a little earlier from a wall, or from a cold greenhouse where they can be successfully grown in pots. Peach trees themselves are generally hardy in Britain, but the very early flowers are at risk from frost, and the fruits need warm weather to ripen them.

OUTDOOR CULTIVATION   Scions of peaches and nectarines are grafted on to plum stocks for small-sized trees, corresponding a little to dwarf apple stocks; on to Mussel stocks for moderate-sized trees, and on to Brompton stocks for the largest trees.

Out of doors peaches are generally trained in a fan shape against a wall, this being the best way to cultivate them. But they can also be grown as free-standing bush trees for which a warm climate in the south is best.

Nurserymen sell them as maidens, in which case the gardener has to do the preliminary training himself, but they also offer fan-trained trees with from five to twelve branches, bushes in the open ground, and pot-grown bushes.

For fan-trained trees, planting distances are from 4·5 to 7·5 m (15 to 25 ft) depending upon the stocks. They can be expected to produce from 9 to 15 kg (20 to 33 lb). Bush trees are planted at about the same distance, again depending upon the stocks.

If possible plant, while the ground is still warm, in mid-October, or as soon as the trees can be obtained. First fix training wires at 15 cm (6 in) vertical spacing as described for espalier apples. Put fan-trained trees 15 cm (6 in) away from the foot of the wall on a south-facing wall. Dig out a planting position $1 \times 1 \times 1$ m ($3\frac{1}{4} \times 3\frac{1}{4} \times 3\frac{1}{4}$ ft) deep. If the natural drainage is not entirely free, lay 7·5-cm (3-in) agricultural drain pipes to an outlet at a lower level, or if this is impossible, make a sump $2 \times 2 \times 2$ m ($7 \times 7 \times 7$ ft) deep, provided that there is access from the bottom of the sump to a relatively free-draining subsoil. If the drainage in the natural soil is severely restricted and it is not possible to improve it by methods suggested above, construct a large raised bed at least 1·8 m (6 ft) wide, retained by bricks or stones with deep holes at the bottom. Failing all these, it might be best not to attempt to cultivate the plant.

Fill the bottom of the excavated hole or brick box with 30 cm (1 ft) of coarse material; the best would be lump chalk, but the legendary mortar rubble used by our forefathers, if it can still be obtained, is very satisfactory. Otherwise stone ballast is suitable. Then begin to fill with good loam which has been stacked or, failing this, the best type of soil available mixed with a quarter of its bulk of farmyard manure.

Plant the tree at the level at which it had been growing in the nursery with the graft union 15 cm (6 in) above the soil. In the course of planting sprinkle fine soil round the roots, and as you fill in the soil tread it, in 15-cm (6-in) layers to make sure that the soil settles round the roots and no air pockets are left (roots need atmospheric oxygen, but they need it through the ordinary capillaries in the soil and not trapped in pockets round the roots where water could collect and fail to get away).

Do not begin to tie the branches to the framework for at least three months, to allow for sinkage. The tying of trees already trained is done by canes tied in a fan shape to the wires along the lines of the existing branches. Use long canes extending nearly to the top of the wall to avoid having to fix any new canes as the growth lengthens in the years ahead. Mr Fraser's (see p. 13) recommendations for training a maiden tree are as follows. On planting, first cut back the stem to within 30 cm (1 ft) of the union between scion and rootstock. In the spring, as the buds begin to grow, all of them are rubbed off except two near the top that are suitably spaced on opposite sides of the stem. These two should have a narrow space between them to avoid unequal development of the shoots which will be produced from them. Upright or nearly upright shoots always grow more vigorously than those down near the horizontal, so the lower side branches of the fan should be established first. The vigour of the shoots retained can be balanced by depressing one, should it threaten to outstrip the other. Both shoots are tied out, opposite each other, at an angle of 45° along bamboo canes, fastened to the lower wires of the supporting trellis. Once they are growing strongly the stump above them is cut out carefully and cleanly.

In winter the two primary shoots are brought down nearer the horizontal and are shortened by about half. In spring, shoots are encouraged to grow from the pruned primaries, one at each end to give extension growth there, one on the upper side of each branch equally spaced, and one on the lower side of each branch, so that by autumn the tree will consist of two main branches and six secondary branches. In the following February the six new branches are cut back by a third of their length, causing more buds to break into growth and, from these, three additional shoots per branch are encouraged, thus giving a total of eighteen new shoots. All other shoots that appear are unwanted and are rubbed off. Shoots retained are carefully spaced out at the approved distance and angle, and are tied to bamboo canes previously fastened to the wires. In February of the fourth year the eighteen branches are tipped again, more lightly this time, and during the summer selected laterals can be tied in and left to ripen their wood so that by the fifth year the first useful crop of fruit can be obtained.

By adopting the procedure outlined all the space is filled, the lower part equally with the upper and the central part equally with the sides. It should be noted that the central area is furnished last. The number of leaders will depend on the area to be covered. In general, they should be 30–45 cm (1–1½ ft) apart at the tips, to allow for the tying in of laterals. When no further leader pruning is required the extension shoots are pinched back in summer or they may be pruned by cutting to a replacement shoot in winter.

Pruning the mature tree When pruning the fan-shaped peach or nectarine, it has to be borne in mind that fruit is carried on shoots of the previous year's growth, and to all intents and purposes these shoots bear once only, and are cut out after fruiting; new shoots grown for the purpose are tied in to replace them for fruiting the following year. These young growths are left at the time of de-shooting and are trained in evenly and as straight as possible during the dormant season. They are tied about 13 cm (5 in) apart on to supporting wires which should be provided, whether the trees are in a greenhouse or on a wall outside.

The growths which are tied in position for fruiting carry buds, some of which are single, some in pairs and some in threes. The single buds are wood buds, and generally one of a pair and two out of a trio are fruit buds. If all the wood buds were allowed to grow unchecked, there would be too many shoots and serious congestion would result. Consequently a proportion of them have to be removed, when the growth from them is an inch or two in length.

When de-shooting is being carried out one good basal shoot is retained for succession, as it is upon this type of growth that the following year's crop is produced. All terminal shoots are left as 'sap-drawers', but unless they are required for further branch extension their growing points are pinched out just beyond the fifth leaf. On an extra long fruiting lateral another shoot might be retained about half-way between base and apex. Apart from these, all other shoots are removed completely, with the exception of those growing close by a fruit. These are pinched back to two leaves. Any sub-laterals appearing on the growths that are left are stopped at the first leaf. It should be mentioned here that all 'fore-right' shoots, i.e. those growing straight outwards from, or inwards towards, the wall are removed first and when the work of de-shooting is started, it is advisable to begin at the top of the tree. It is time for the young laterals to be tied temporarily when the peach or nectarine fruits are nearly full size.

When winter pruning is undertaken, almost the entire tree will be untied and the laterals that have borne fruit are pruned away, making the cut each time at the point where the replacement shoot arises. On mature trees each leader will also be pruned back to a replacement shoot. Younger trees that have not covered all the space assigned to them will have their leaders cut to provide laterals or more leaders as the case may be. On completing the pruning the tree is retied, putting the main branches back in position and evenly spaced out first, following with the lesser ones, and finally the laterals.

The untying, pruning and retying of a tree on a garden wall may be done by dealing with a few branches at a time; under glass, where it will be necessary to clean the glass and framework of the house, the individual tree had better be treated as indicated already. Several branches may be looped together loosely and slung aside and this is repeated until the whole tree has been made safe from damage done by careless handling. Retying is an excellent wet-day operation.

Thin out the fruits to 23 cm (9 in) apart when they are about 2 cm ($\frac{3}{4}$ in) in size, spacing the thinning over about three weeks. Conscientiously maintain an adequate and regular supply of water, to avoid dropping of fruit and stone cracking, and keep up the lime content.

COOL HOUSE CULTIVATION   Our forefathers cultivated peaches in cool houses under glass. This can still be done by those willing to keep old greenhouses in repair and to undertake the small amount of heating that is required. There must be many old peach houses abandoned because the rafters and glazing-bars are rotting and the glass falling out. Some of these may not have gone entirely beyond recall and can be patched up, even if only temporarily, by rough and ready repairs to woodwork, and by tacking on polythene to replace broken glass; by making a partition to reduce the whole length and concentrating one's amateur do-it-yourself resources at one end, a structure can be produced that is fairly air-tight and covered with glass or polythene. The old 10-cm (4-in) heating pipes and sectional anthracite boilers will have rusted beyond reasonable economic repair, but for these crops all that is needed is a source of heat strong enough to keep the temperature inside the house above freezing in February, March and April. Gas heaters, or electric tubular heaters, would be best, but turbofan blowers and paraffin heaters can also do what is needed.

The training of peaches and nectarines in a greenhouse is done against the back wall in the same way as out of doors. A thorough going peach border used to be made up above a 30-cm (1-ft) layer of coarse drainage material, mortar rubble, coarse bones or ballast, all above an outlet so that water could drain away. The border, or what we now call the growing medium, consists of half garden compost and half stacked, chopped loam at a pH of 6·5–7·0. For preference, the width of the border should be from 1·8 to 3 m (6 to 10 ft), but this will depend upon the space available. If there is no natural provision for good drainage, make a bed raised 1 m (3¼ ft) above ground level behind a brick retaining wall alongside the greenhouse path with weep-holes at its base every 1·2 m (4 ft).

Do not let the night temperature drop below 7°C (about 45°F) from February onwards, and allow it to rise to 16°C (60°F). As the season advances open the ventilators in the day-time to prevent as far as possible the temperature rising much above 23°C (about 75°F) due to sun heat.

PICKING Pick peaches with solicitude. Assess the ripeness of each fruit by gentle pressure at its base, not at the sides. If it yields a little to pressure at the base, put your fingers round the base of the fruit and pull gently. Do not grip the sides. The stalk of a peach ready for picking will part easily from the branch.

VARIETIES Peaches and nectarines are self-fertile. They do not require separate pollinators like apples, pears, cherries and plums.
Peaches
Amsden June. Mid-July. Greenish white skin with a red flush. Greenish white flesh, melting, good flavour. Large stone clinging a little.
Peregrine. August. Crimson-red skin. Yellowish white flesh. Juicy, richly flavoured.
Bellegarde. Early to mid-September. Skin yellow with crimson flush. Pale yellow flesh. Red at the stone. Rich Noyau flavour.

Dymond. Mid- to end of September. Skin pale yellow with deep flush and mottling. Flesh pale yellow. Red at stone. Stone free.

Royal George. End of August. Skin pale yellow with a deep red cheek. Flesh pale yellow. Red near stone. Stone free. Rich flavour.

Nectarines

Early Rivers. Mid-July. Skin greenish yellow. Flushed with brilliant red. Flesh pale yellow. Rich flavour. Stone free.

Elruge. End of August. Skin pale greenish white with dark purple flush. Flesh greenish white, red at the stone. Stone free.

Lord Napier. Early August. Skin pale yellow, deep crimson flush. Flesh very pale green. Brisk and rich flavour. Most delicious. Stone free. Provide shade under glass in bright sun because of the thinness of its skin.

PESTS AND DISEASES

Peach aphis Eggs are laid in leaf axils and hatch in April. The aphides feed on the leaves and cause them to curl. When aphides attack, the leaves curl without thickening (in peach leaf curl, a fungal attack, there is thickening of the leaves). The remedy for peach aphis is to spray with derris after the flowers have dropped their petals and in the evening, when the bees have gone back to their hives.

Peach scale This insect pest can be controlled with tar distillate washes in the dormant season, but these washes have undesirable side effects and are seldom convenient in a private garden. If things get really out of hand, scrape off as many scales as can be seen with the back of a knife and spray thoroughly with derris when the bees are no longer about.

Red spider mite Troublesome on trees under glass and in the open where conditions of soil and/or atmosphere are dry. Maintain the moisture content at all times, particularly in hot weather. Introduce the predator (see p. 99) where possible.

Peach leaf curl A fungus disease in which the leaves curl and blister, are thickened and turn red. Later a grey powdery bloom is evident on the thickened areas. This disease can be so chronic that it may be necessary to decide whether to spray with a fungicide containing copper or to give up trying to grow peaches. The disease may be controlled by picking off and burning affected leaves as soon as seen, and by spraying with Bordeaux Mixture in February as the buds begin to swell and again a fortnight later, and a third time in autumn just as the leaves begin to drop. Bordeaux Mixture will, if systematically applied, kill or drive away worms and build up a copper concentration in the soil which is not desirable.

Peach mildew   A white powdery-looking covering on the fruits and young shoots in June and July. The remedy is to cut off the affected shoots and fruits as soon as seen, and if driven to extreme measures, spray with Bordeaux Mixture in the dormant period.

Silver leaf   A fungus disease commoner on plums but sometimes affecting peaches. The best course is to prevent its occurrence by painting wounds from pruning or accidental damage immediately with Arbrex or white lead paint.

Pear   *Pyrus communis* (*Rosaceae*)
                                                       Tree

In the long history of the pear, the year of 1849 stands alone in importance . . . on the sunny banks of the Loire, a pear seed had germinated some years before and in the Spring opened its first blossoms to the April skies.

The fruit grew slowly to maturity and eager pomologues watched its green fade to yellow, waiting for the moment of degustation. Happy those who were present when Doyenné du Comice first gave up its luscious juice to man. . . . Here at last was the ideal realised, with perfect combination of flavour, aroma and texture of which man had long dreamed.[1]

E. A. Bunyard's description must make all other eager pomologues hurry to plant some pears of their own. Like other fruits, pears need some thoughtful selection and a little care if they are to bear satisfactorily.

Pears are picked from July, the early ones are eaten more or less from the tree; some kinds picked later can be stored until January and beyond. Even more than apples, mid-season and late pears need careful storage to bring them to perfection. Pears generally do best under warmer conditions than apples need, and also need more shelter, partly because their blossoms open about a fortnight earlier. They are a permanent crop, having a life of from fifty to

---

[1] *The Anatomy of Dessert.*

sixty years as standards and twenty to thirty years as dwarf pyramids, espaliers and cordons.

CULTIVATION Prepare planting positions exactly as for apples, p. 170.

TYPES OF TREE Pears are grafted on to one of three different stocks. Malling quince C, the most dwarfing of these, promotes rather earlier fruiting, and shy bearers may be more prolific, but this stock needs good rich deep soil, well textured and well supplied with water (quinces like to have their roots near water moving through the ground). It is shallow rooting, and pear trees budded on it do best with support, as is given to espaliers and cordons. Quince A is now the most frequently-used rootstock. It is recommended for dwarf pyramid, espalier and bush. Pear stock is used for standards and half standards. A process of double working has to be carried out by nurserymen on some varieties whose scions are incompatible with quince rootstocks. Among these is Williams' Bon Chrétien. The procedure is first to bud another, compatible scion, Pitmaston Duchess is one, on to the quince stock, and when these have united, and made a season's growth, to bud the quince-incompatible-Williams on to the bridging Pitmaston Duchess stock.

Pears are supplied by nurserymen in the following forms.

Cordons These will produce 1·8–5·4 kg (4–12 lb) fruit in a season. Planted like apples 60–90 cm (2–3 ft) apart. These can be trained as oblique or vertical cordons, double cordons, double U or treble cordons. Good varieties to be trained in this way are Easter Beurré, Beurré Superfin, Conference, Doyenné du Comice, Olivier de Serres.

Espalier These can produce from 6·3 to 12·6 kg (14 to 28 lb) per tree. Planted 4·5 m (15 ft) apart on quince C stock, 5·1 m (17 ft) on quince A stock, and 7 m (15 ft) apart on pear stock. Varieties suited to espalier training are Beurré Hardy, Doyenné du Comice, Glou Morceau, and Williams.

Dwarf pyramid Need good conditions, and will produce about 3–6 kg (7–14 lb) of fruit. Plant these 1·2 m (4 ft) apart in rows 1·8 m (6 ft) apart. Good varieties for dwarf pyramids are Doyenné d'Été, Beurré Superfin, Conference, Doyenné du Comice, Williams Bon Chrétien.

Bush These are planted 4·2 m (14 ft) apart and yield 45 kg (100 lb) per tree on quince A stock (Figs. 20 and 21).

Standards They are planted 6 m (20 ft) apart and yield about the same or rather more than bushes.

PRUNING In general there is little to differentiate between the pruning and training of apples and pears. The methods are essentially the same for both kinds of fruit. Summer pruning as well as winter pruning is carried out on trained trees. Summer

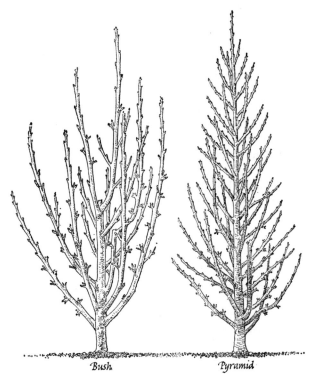

FIG. 20. Bush form of pear tree

FIG. 21. Pyramid form of pear tree

pruning is generally performed in July or when the young shoots have become woody at the base, but are still soft at the tip.

VARIETIES Like apples, most pears require pollinators, varieties whose flowers open at the same time. Some are diploid, some are triploid, but the matter is complicated in that there are incompatible groups in pears. To make this clear we have set out against

each recommended variety the names of other varieties which will
act as pollinators. The letters refer to the time of flowering, A being
early and D late.

Cooking pears

Black Worcester. C. November–February, keeping until April.
Large, brown russet. Grown since Roman times. Figures on the
arms of the City of Worcester. Perhaps the three pears on the
covers of Francis Brett-Young's novels. Pollinated by all other Cs
except the triploids.

Catillac. D. Triploid. December, keeping until April. Very large
green fruit. Scab resistant. Pollinated by Beurré Hardy, Gorham,
Doyenné du Comice, Glou Morceau, Winter Nelis, but not Pitmaston Duchess.

Pitmaston Duchess. D. Triploid. October–November. Large,
pale yellow with light brown russet, cooks amber red. Susceptible
to scab in wet atmospheres. Pollinated by any two of Beurré
Hardy, Gorham, Doyenné du Comice, Glou Morceau and Winter
Nelis.

Vicar of Winkfield. B. December–January. Large, green colour,
turning yellow in February. Vigorous. Pollinated by Doyenné
d'Été, Seckle.

Eating pears

Beurré Hardy. D. October. Large coppery russetted fruit, white
flesh, tender, with rose water flavour. Pollinated by Doyenné du
Comice, Glou Morceau, Gorham, Winter Nelis.

Beurré Superfin. C. October. Yellow with patches of russet,
flesh pale yellow, sweet and perfumed. According to Bunyard[1] one
of the best half-dozen pears. It begins to ripen at the core, and
should be gathered a little early and carefully watched in store.
Pollinated by any other C except Jargonelle.

Conference. C. October–November. Pick this one in late
September; calabash shaped, dark green fading to pale yellow with
considerable russetting. Flesh pale yellow, pinkish, juicy and
sweet. Pollinated by Beurré Superfin, Joséphine de Malines,
Merton Pride, Olivier de Serres, Thompson's. Prolific but below
first class.

Doyenné du Comice. D. November—pick in October. Large,
skin pale yellow with fine russet. Flesh also pale yellow, melting

---

[1] *A Handbook of Hardy Fruits, Apples and Pears.*

and delicate. Pollinated by Beurré Hardy, Glou Morceau, Gorham, Winter Nelis. This is the pear of all pears. One can be catty about Cox, but never about Doyenné du Comice.

Easter Beurré. B. February–April—pick before it is ripe and store. Skin pea green, fading to yellow-green, russetted. Flesh white, sweet and musky. Pollinated by Doyenné d'Été, Vicar of Winkfield.

Glou Morceau. D. December–January—pick in October. Skin pea green changing to greenish yellow. Flesh melting white, good flavour. Pollinated by Doyenné du Comice, Beurré Hardy, Gorham, Winter Nelis.

Gorham. D. Late September–October. Long, pale yellow, russetted, good flavour; a seedling from Williams' and less prone to scab. Pollinated by Beurré Hardy, Doyenné du Comice, Glou Morceau, Winter Nelis.

Jargonelle. C. Triploid. August; should be eaten straight from the tree. Calabash shaped, greenish yellow with a slight dark reddish flush. Flesh pale yellow, tender and juicy, sweet, a little musky. Pollinated by Black Worcester, Beurré Superfin, Joséphine de Malines, Merton Pride, Olivier de Serres, Thompson's.

Joséphine de Malines. C. December–January. Small, pale green skin fading to yellow, with a russet patch round the stem. Slightly pink flesh. Melting sweet; a little perfumed. Pollinated by Conference, Olivier de Serres, Thompson's. This is a tip-bearing tree, best cultivated as a bush, leaving the leading shoot unpruned. Not summer pruned, apart from the removal of canker and scab.

Merton Pride. C. Mid to late September. Pollinated by any C except Jargonelle.

Olivier de Serres. C. February–March. Round apple-like shape. Skin green covered with russet. Flesh white, musky. Pollinated by Beurré Superfin, Conference, Joséphine de Malines, Thompson's. This pear gives of its best on a wall.

Seckle. B. October–November. Small, dark brownish red with conspicuous white dots. Tender yellow flesh, sweet and rich. Apparently a favourite pear of Walt Whitman. Pollinated by Doyenné d'Été, Easter Beurré, Vicar of Winkfield, but not by Williams'.

Thompson's. C. October–November. Large, pale golden yellow with russet marking. White flesh. Melting and buttery. Pollinated by Beurré Superfin, Conference, Joséphine de Malines, Merton

Pride, Olivier de Serres. This is one of the pears which are best double worked.

Williams' Bon Chrétien. C. September. Golden yellow with russet dots and faint red stripes. Flesh white, juicy and sweet, musky. Partly self-fertile, but pollinated by any C (except the triploid Jargonelle and Seckle). Will not pollinate Seckle. Bunyard wrote that it should be gathered when still green and ripened in the fruit room. The musky flavour is less pronounced when grown on a north wall.

Winter Nelis. D. Late November–early March—pick in early October. Skin greenish yellow, russetted, flesh greenish white, juicy and sweet. Pollinated by Beurré Hardy, Doyenné du Comice, Glou Morceau, Gorham.

PICKING AND STORING Pears, like apples, are picked when, having lifted the fruit in the hand, taken the weight from the stalk and given it a tentative twist, it comes readily away from the twig. With the early varieties like Jargonelle this will be in August, and Gorham and Williams' in September; with the last two, the ground colour changing to yellow will also be a sign to pick. With some exceptions annotated in the foregoing descriptions, the others will not be ready until October, some to be eaten within a few days, and others to mature in slow dignity until well into the New Year. They are stored in the same way as apples, but it is even more important to have an even temperature, 10°C (50°F) or a little lower, but not below 4·4°C (40°F), and to maintain humid conditions. In this way 'sleepiness' and shrivelling will be prevented. Take care not to bruise the fruit; handle it with greater care than Dresden china, than which it is far more precious, and do not allow individual fruits to touch each other—never pile them on the shelves. It is better not to wrap pears. To quote from Bunyard once again on the subject of Comice: 'when the green colour begins to change to yellow the moment of watchfulness arises, and when the whole fruit is of an even yellow, the moment has arrived'.

PESTS AND DISEASES
Apple aphis Rather larger than the green aphis. It has a blue or purple mealy appearance and can cause considerable damage. It feeds on the young leaves and shoots, and also on fruitlets, migrating in July to plantains and other weeds, and returning in

autumn to apple trees. These aphides can largely be kept down by
summer pruning, which is a better alternative to winter washes of
tar oil distillates and the formidable battalions of organophosphorus
and organochlorine insecticides. Vigorous syringing or spraying
with a hose will also detach a fair number.

Common green capsid   As with apples, this causes corky scab dis-
figurement. For control, see under apples, p. 187.

Weevil, apple-blossom   See apples, p. 188.

Winter moth caterpillars   See apples, p. 188.

Codling moth caterpillars   See apples, p. 187.

Pear and cherry slugworm   These are the larvae of a sawfly, and
leave behind them a dark slime. Two broods may be produced,
which feed on the upper surfaces of the leaves in late June and in
August, making brown blotches and skeletonizing the leaf, and
sometimes causing severe defoliation. Derris is a good control and
as it would be used at times when the pear blossom is past and
over, will probably cause no harm to bees but, even so, would be
better put on in the evenings.

Pear midge   Midges lay eggs in the blossom in April, from which
the larvae hatch and bore into the fruitlets. There the white maggots feed and the fruitlets become deformed and enlarged; they
generally decay and fall off the tree prematurely. This pest is
difficult to control except with the worst of the organochlorine
insect dusts. The best that can be done is to collect and destroy
infected fruit as soon as it is seen. In large orchards stocking with
poultry in April, May and June will catch many of the maggots
escaping from the fallen fruits to burrow into the soil for pupation.

Pear scab   This is different from apple scab in that it can overwinter on the twigs for three years or longer, whereas apple scab
mostly survives only one winter. It can be kept under control by
summer and winter pruning, and maintaining proper orchard
hygiene as suggested for apple scab.

Blossom wilt   A fungus disease. The small leaves around the
blossom begin to wilt noticeably about two weeks after flowering
has started, and the disease spreads into the trusses, working down
from the flower stems. Cut off and burn spurs that are affected.

Brown rots   Rings of grey-white pustules appear on the surface of
brown rotting of the fruits which then dry (mummify) and remain
on the trees. Collect and destroy these affected fruits, so that the
infection cannot overwinter.

Sooty blotch   A fungus disease. This has some resemblance to scab in appearance, affecting the skin of the fruits, but is easily rubbed off and does not cause rotting. It occurs chiefly under conditions of overcrowding and bad drainage, and should be guarded against at the time of planting.

Fireblight   A bacterial disease which can affect both pears and apples. The disease was first recognized on pears in this country in 1957 on the variety Laxton's Superb, which appears to be very susceptible and has now been withdrawn from nursery lists.

Late produced blossoms are infected first, and killed, and the disease moves into the shoot from them, and down into the branches, so infecting the main trunk in due course. Infected leaves and shoots turn black, looking as though they have been burnt, hence the name. Bark becomes cankered and the disease can spread very rapidly so that a tree may be killed in two seasons. If the presence of the disease is suspected, you *must* tell your local Plant Health Inspector or Divisional Office of the Ministry of Agriculture immediately, under the Fireblight Disease Order, as it is a notifiable disease. If the disease is confirmed, grubbing out will be necessary.

Plum   *Prunus domestica (Rosaceae)*
                                                              Tree

Plums grow in such a delicious variety—greengages, quetsches, big pink Victorias, small blue-bloomed damsons—and each one has such a distinctive character and flavour that it is well worth selecting some compatible trees to produce fruits for your table—especially as the plums you can buy today all seem to be of the same dubious-Victoria family, picked either very sour or pulpy and overripe.

You can pick plums out of doors from the end of July to October.

CULTIVATION   Plums are propagated by grafting or budding on to plum stocks. They are cultivated as standards, half-standards, bushes, pyramids and fans. Cordons are not advised as the restrictive pruning involved would not be conducive to fruitfulness. Recommended spacing, if you intend an orchard, is: standards, 5·4–6·0 m (18–20 ft) apart; half-standards, 4·5–5·4 m (15–18 ft) apart; bush, 3·6–4·5 m (12–15 ft); pyramid 2·4–3·6 m (8–12 ft); fan trained, 4·5–5·4 m (15–18 ft).)

Plant them in October or early November by digging a hole as for peaches, but adding a 10-cm (4-in) layer of rotted farmyard manure in the bottom of the hole above the reversed turves. Standards and half-standards need stakes, and so also may bushes and pyramids in their early years. Fix these stakes firmly in the bottom of the hole before refilling with soil and planting the tree.

Plums have roots nearer to the surface than apples and pears, therefore take care not to disturb these roots in hoeing or weeding. They require good supplies of nitrogen, so maintain a heavy mulch of garden compost on the top. They do not grow well in grass.

Plums grow well in pots that are for the most part kept out of doors, but taken into a greenhouse at flowering and fruiting time. At least one grower supplies pot-grown bushes.

Thin the fruits to 6 cm (2½ in) apart when they have reached a size of 1 cm (½ in), spacing the thinning over several days. Leave dessert fruits on the tree until they are fully ripe. Pick cooking plums when they begin to turn colour.

PRUNING Plums carry their fruit on the wood of the previous year and on older wood, and pruning is relatively simple. To prune for what is known as the delayed open centre, the procedure is similar to that which is followed when pruning apples. Upright-growing varieties lend themselves to this kind of training. The maiden tree is headed back close to a good bud to leave a stem 23 cm (9 in) taller than the open-centre tree. Counting from the top bud on the maiden stem, buds four, six, eight and possibly ten are allowed to grow and all the rest are removed. This is done to give shoots well spaced on the stem, growing at a wide angle and away from one another. The top bud is allowed to grow and the resulting shoot is tipped back to about 45 cm (18 in) in the next winter. By following the same selective method a tier of branches is formed and the process can be continued for a third year if necessary before allowing the centre to open out. It is advisable not to have the branches directly above each other. A light tipping of the branches will probably be needed for a year or two and all of them should be kept growing in an outward direction. Any strong-growing, upright shoots are cut out at the base. For trees which naturally form wide angles between shoots and main stem, it may be enough simply to remove unwanted buds at pruning time, to encourage vigour in the growth of shoots required to form branches.

Regulated pruning When plum trees are established they are allowed to grow freely under a system of regulated pruning carried out annually, and little more than the removal of crossing and crowded branches is needed. Shortening back the drooping ends of branches of those that have this pendulous growth characteristic is also a pruning item that calls for attention periodically. Again, because of silver-leaf trouble, leader tipping and other pruning operations are performed in spring or even in June and July. All dead wood should be cut out and burnt before the middle of July to reduce the possibility of infection by silver-leaf disease. Broken branches should always be cut out as soon as the breakage occurs and the wounds covered promptly with a bituminous emulsion paint.

GROWING PLUMS AGAINST WALLS The training of plums on walls—and they should be high walls—closely resembles the training of peaches and nectarines when these fruits are grown as fan-shaped trees. The main object is to get the wall adequately furnished with branches of medium strength, properly spaced and well provided with fruiting wood from top to bottom. Balanced growth in the primary stages will be obtained by depressing a shoot that is too strong and raising a shoot that is barely strong enough. Shoots suggestive of extra vigour should be removed while still young and any that are upright are likewise removed.

When further extension shoots are needed it is usually better if they come from the lower side of the parent shoot in order to curb any upward tendency and to help to moderate their vigour. Plums are not submitted to de-shooting treatment like peaches, but shoots appearing on the wall side of the branches and others that are superfluous are rubbed off while they are small.

To assist in keeping the trees in a manageable state, summer pruning is a routine practice. New laterals not wanted as leaders are pruned in early July, or later if the season is wet, to five leaves from the base (the width of the pruner's hand). At the first opportunity after the fruit has been picked, shoots which were reduced to five leaves are given a further shortening and are left as stubs a few centimetres (inches) long. Natural short spurs which are produced need no pruning. Crowded or badly-placed spurs should be cut away then and weakened spurs cut back to an appropriate bud cluster which contains a growth or vegetative bud. Such a bud will be thin and pointed, rather than round and plump. This is to ensure that the spurs will remain alive and not die back through faulty shortening.

VARIETIES Plums have pollination vagaries. Many are self-fertile and will produce fruit unassisted and can be planted alone. Others are partly or entirely self-sterile, and others again form groups of incompatibles. All this is set out with excellent clarity in the Royal Horticultural Society's *The Fruit Garden Displayed*. As with apples and pears the flowering times are indicated here by the letters A to E, A being early and E being late.

For convenience, varieties suggested below are nearly all self-fertile.

Cooking plums

Czar. B. Early August. Small, purple-black, hardy and reliable. Susceptible to silver leaf.

Marjorie's Seedling. E. Late September. Large, black. Good for dessert if eaten fully ripe.

Pershore. C. End August. Medium size, good shape. Yellow skin and flesh.

Purple Pershore. C. Mid to late August. Purple skinned, yellow flesh.

River's Early Prolific. C. Self-sterile. Late July. Medium size, black skin, yellow flesh. Good for bottling and jam. Cross pollinated with Jefferson (B). Also pollinates the eating variety Kirke's.

Victoria. C. August. Pinkish red fruit. Crops heavily; susceptible to silver-leaf disease. Can also be regarded as an eating variety, though less well flavoured than the true dessert kinds.

Eating plums

Early Transparent Gage. D. Late August. Pale yellow skin with some red spots. Greengage flavour.

Farleigh Damson. Late April, early May. Self-fertile. Mid-September. Small blue-black fruit. Rich flavour. Makes good orchard boundary hedges.

Jefferson. B. Early September. Golden yellow, spotted red. Delicious, greengage-like flavour. Cross-pollinator with River's Early Prolific.

Kirke's. C. Mid-September. Dark purple fruit. Excellent sweet flavour. Cross-pollinates with River's Early Prolific (B)—there is sufficient overlap in flowering time.

Ouillin's Golden Gage. D. Mid-August. Dull golden skin, pale yellow flesh, not true greengage. Note late flowering and less likelihood of being caught by frost.

Quetsche. Late April, early May. October. Long oval, black. When stewed has the flavour of Carlsbad plums.

Reine Claude de Bavay. B. Late September–early October. Large, green-yellow, of true greengage flavour. Hardy, a prolific wall plant even in northern districts.

Severn Cross. C. Mid to late September. Large, oval, greenish yellow skin. Flesh pale yellow, juicy.

PESTS AND DISEASES

Plum gall mites   These spend the winter in the scales of the buds and come out to feed on the foliage in spring, which then turns a silvery colour, or reacts by producing blisters. Unfortunately well-intentioned birds will strip off the buds in winter in search of the mites. Therefore protection with nets will have to be given. To spray with lime sulphur is usually recommended, but is more trouble than it is worth, and will kill predators. It is best to fall back on picking off affected leaves.

Red plum maggot   This is similar to the codling moth found on apples. It lays its eggs in late June and July on the fruit stalks. The red caterpillars which then hatch bore into the developing fruit and, when gorged, pupate in the bark or in cracks in tree stakes. Attacked fruit will rot or fall prematurely. Spray derris in July or August to kill hatching caterpillars before they go to ground in the fruits; the timing is crucial. By July and August there will be no plum flowers to interest the bees, but none the less make it routine always to use derris in the evenings.

Aphides   Several species of these can cause a great deal of damage, in particular the leaf curling plum aphis, whose feeding results in the leaves curling over very tightly, making it difficult to penetrate them with sprays. Other aphides stunt the new growth severely by their feeding; badly affected shoot tips and leaves are best cut off completely and removed, and derris sprayed in the evenings when the bees have gone.

Plum slugworm   See pear slugworm, p. 229.

Silver leaf A fungus disease. This is responsible for the silvery appearance of the leaves which sometimes appears and can be confirmed if a dark stain shows in the wood when a branch is cut transversely. This infection gets a hold through wounds, and badly affected trees will die. Sometimes, however, they can recover of their own accord. Cut off the affected branches either at a main fork or flush with the trunk and paint the wounds with Arbrex or white lead paint. Burn the diseased prunings. Increase the supply of food by giving compost or decayed manure, and add lime if necessary to bring up the *p*H to 6·5–7·0.

Bacterial canker See cherries for detailed description of the disease. More serious on plums, and whole trees can be killed in a matter of days. Cut away affected wood in the spring when the trees are growing strongly. Plums should not be pruned in winter.

SPECIAL REFERENCE Bulletin No. 119, *Plums and Cherries*, 1961, Ministry of Agriculture, Fisheries and Food.

Quince   *Cydonia oblonga (Rosaceae)*
                                                                     Tree

Quinces with their curious, indescribable flavour, are yet another old-fashioned fruit that was once commonly known, now you must grow them yourself if you wish to enjoy them. They ripen in the open in October, and should be left hanging on the tree until then.

CULTIVATION Quinces grow in moist soil conditions. They flourish on the sides of streams. They are cultivated and sold by nurserymen as bushes or half-standards, on their own roots. For once they are not budded or grafted. In fact, quince is used as a stock for pears.

Probably a single tree, or two or three trees, will be enough for a small- or medium-sized garden, but if a number are needed plant bushes 3 m (10 ft) apart, standards and half-standards from 3·6 to 6 m (12 to 20 ft) apart. Plant in the same way as for apples and pears, if possible in moist soil or close by a pool or stream, in November. Standards and half-standards and large bushes will need to be staked.

Prune by thinning in autumn as soon as the leaves have fallen, take out crossing branches and remove enough growth to keep an open centre. Cut out straggling and dead wood. Quinces tend to make confused and twiggy growth which needs to be thinned out. Hard pruning in autumn and winter will stimulate vegetative shoot growth and it can be carried out in the first years, but as soon as the tree starts bearing, reduce the severity of the pruning to permit flower and fruit production. Quinces are self-fertile.

PICKING Leave the fruit on the tree until the end of October. Then store it in a frostproof shed. After they have turned yellow they will keep from two to three months. Try to store them apart from other fruits because their smell is extremely strong, and can influence the taste of apples and pears. If no separate shed is available for storing it is better to turn them at once into quince jelly, with its delicious and unique flavour.

VARIETIES

Bereczki, large pear-shaped, golden yellow, strongly flavoured. Bunyard conjectured that this may be the same as Vranja, which is included in some nurserymen's lists.

Champion, large, apple-shaped.

Meech's Prolific, fairly large, pear-shaped, vigorous, golden yellow.

Portugal, large, oval, light orange coloured.

PESTS AND DISEASES Aphis and caterpillar, see apple, p. 186.

Raspberry   *Rubus idaeus (Rosaceae)*
                                                                    Shrub

When they are ripe, raspberries are so fragile that the sheer weight of the upper layers in a fruiterer's punnet will damage those at the bottom. It is not surprising that they are unsatisfactory as well as expensive to buy. But picked in the garden just before lunch, scarcely handled, for they need no washing, they come to the table whole and full of their own deep-toned flavour (the more appreciated by a mature palate). They are one of the most delicious fruits of high summer, yet very cheap and easy to grow with some protection from the birds, and not particularly dependent on a good summer (the wild raspberries of the north, in Scotland and Finland, are flourishing examples of this fact). The fruit will be ready from early July to mid August, with some varieties fruiting in autumn. They need a little time to become established, but will then bear a good crop for many years.

Cultivated raspberries have been bedevilled by virus diseases, and it is essential to buy certified plants from a nursery that has been inspected for virus infection. Before the advent of certification, new canes would almost always become infected from other raspberries in the neighbourhood already infected, and have to be replaced every few years, but now there is no reason why your original ones should not bear good fruit for a long time.

CULTIVATION   Raspberries succeed best at a pH of 5·5–6·0 and they will put up with a certain amount of shade, though they do best in sun. Light soils which tend to dry out, are not very suitable unless irrigation is available.

In August or September prepare the cropping positions in your fruit cage by forking in rotted farmyard manure previously spread to a depth of at least 15 cm (6 in). Make certain that the ground is completely clean of perennial weeds. Put in wire supports, preferably two rows of wire, the lower one 60 cm (2 ft) above the ground and the second one 1·2 m (4 ft) above it, secured to posts 60 cm (2 ft) into the ground and strutted. After planting 37 cm (1¼ ft) apart in rows 1·5 m (5 ft) apart in late September or October, cut them down to about three buds above soil level. The canes which grow after this will spend the first summer reaching 1·8 m (6 ft) and bear fruit in the following summer. Ensure a generous water supply, especially in dry summer weather, otherwise the crop of new season's canes will be very sparse. Keep weeds hoed out but use the hoe gingerly because some of the roots remain near the surface, or mulch with straw through the growing season.

Mulch regularly with compost to retain the moisture in the soil and cut out the old canes in the autumn, leaving the new growth to bear fruit the following year. Remove weak new canes and thin out the remainder if crowded; this helps to prevent the spread of fungal diseases. Suckers can be dug up and replanted to fill in any gaps in the rows. Destroy plants affected by virus.

VARIETIES

Malling Exploit, early, abundant, vigorous, but susceptible to botrytis (grey mould) in wet weather.

Malling Promise, early. Tall-growing, abundant new growth. Susceptible also to botrytis, but fairly resistant to virus.

Lloyd George, mid-season and autumn. Tall-growing. The best flavour. Susceptible to virus.

Malling Jewel, mid-season and later. Fairly resistant to virus and botrytis. Plant slightly closer than other varieties, as it throws fewer canes and is less tall.

Glen Clova, early to mid-season. A fairly new variety. Bred at the Scottish Horticultural Research Institute. Good for preserving.

September, the latest from America. Bears fruit after the end of August, but cut down all canes in late winter, or early spring, to ensure later fruiting.

PESTS AND DISEASES

Raspberry beetle Small brownish beetles lay eggs in flowers in June and white maggots which hatch from these feed on the outside of the fruitlets, and later feed on the 'plug'. They pupate and mature in the soil and the adults emerge in spring to feed on the flower buds. Much damage is done. Derris can be used in the evening when the bees have gone, spraying ten days after the flowering begins and again ten to fifteen days later if an attack was severe the previous year.

Aphides and capsid bugs. Aphides spread virus diseases by their feeding; capsids feed on the leaves also, and may kill the growing points—they cause much trouble in Scotland.

Raspberry moth The small red-brown grub feeds inside the young fruiting sideshoots near the tip for four to six weeks in late spring, and buds and shoots gradually wither and die, so that the crop can be considerably depleted. It then pupates and hatches into the adult moth (small and brownish) which lays eggs on the open flowers. The grubs overwinter in a cocoon. Hand pick withered shoots and destroy them, and spray with derris in early April to trap the grubs as they move up the stems.

Spur blight A fungus disease, first showing in July–August; dark purple patches appear round the buds on the new canes and the buds are killed by the following spring, thus depleting the crop. Thin out canes to ensure plenty of air circulation, and cut out badly-infected canes completely and destroy.

Cane spot A fungus disease also, in the form of small round or oval spots on the canes from early June. Not usually very serious, though the spots can become cankered. Lloyd George is a susceptible variety. In severe outbreaks the cane size is reduced and tips killed, thus reducing fruiting. Cut out badly-affected canes completely. If the disease becomes very bad, spray with Bordeaux Mixture just before bud burst in March, and again just before flowering, but it is often the case that both this and spur blight will die out the following season, with thinning of the canes and less favourable climatic conditions. Both tend to spread in cool, damp weather.

Virus diseases Raspberries can suffer badly with these, particularly mosaic, which produces light green or yellow mottling of the leaves, dwarfs in which a number of short, weak canes are produced, and leaf curl when the leaves are very dark green and markedly curled downwards. Spread by the feeding of aphides and leaf suckers, it is best to obtain certified stock, as virus-infected plants cannot be treated and need to be grubbed and destroyed. Soil-living eelworms also carry some viruses, so replanting of new clean canes should be in a different site.

Red and White currants   *Ribes sativum (Saxifragaceae)*
                                                             Shrub

Bunyard, in his *Anatomy of Dessert,* wrote of red and white currants: 'their decorative value is great and a dish of either in the limelight is a temptation to an elegant trifling by a delicate hand'. Sadly, white currants are becoming as extinct as salsify and seakale at the greengrocer's. Even the more ordinary red currants seem to appear in smaller quantities and shorter seasons each year. Luckily you can grow your currants and not depend on the lowest common factor of public taste for supplies.

Red and white currants are picked from the open ground in July. Like blackcurrants they need to be grown in a fruit cage to protect them from birds. The bushes will last up to fifteen years.

CULTIVATION   In August and September prepare the cropping ground in an open position, if possible with shelter from strong winds, on strong loam, deep for preference, lighter than that needed for blackcurrants. Enrich this with garden compost or rotted farmyard manure previously spread to a depth of 10 cm (4 in) or, failing this, prick in hoof-and-horn meal, bonemeal and potassium sulphate at 56 g per sq m—about 2 oz per sq yd.

In the middle of October or, if really unavoidable, up to the middle of March, plant the bushes, usually supplied as three-year-olds on a short 15-cm (6-in) leg, and preserve this leg at the time of planting. Plant more shallowly than blackcurrants. Put them in 1·5 m (5 ft) apart in rows 1·8 m (6 ft) apart. After planting prune the bushes hard to outward pointing buds and cut out the leading shoot completely. Keep the leg clear of suckers. Spur prune the laterals back to 2·5 cm (1 in). Prune the subsequent laterals in the second and third winters to make a main framework of eight to ten leaders, and aim to create an open centre. Red and white currants produce their fruits from spurs on wood older than the previous year's shoots, and spur pruning is necessary each winter.

Red currants can also be grown as cordons and can be bought trained in this way from some nurserymen. Train these on wires or against walls 37–45 cm (1¼–1½ ft) apart, and spur prune them.

Red and white currants can also be cultivated as half-standards with clear stems of 60–90 cm, about 2–3 ft. These, with their delicate pendulous heads, are decorative in a kitchen garden designed with an eye to visual as well as alimentary pleasure.

VARIETIES
Red
Earliest of Fourlands, early, moderate, good size, good quality.

Laxton's No. 1, a little later than the above, but still early. A heavy cropper.

Red Lake, mid-season to late. Very large and juicy, with long bunches. Regarded as an outstanding new variety. Introduced by the University of Minnesota Fruit Breeding Farm.
White
White Dutch, mid-season. Pale yellow fruit.

PESTS AND DISEASES
Currant clearwing moth, aphids and capsids　See blackcurrants, p. 193.

Coral spot　A fungus disease. The leaves wilt on one or more shoots and later red raised dots appear on dead wood. Cut the latter out and burn it.

Rhubarb　　　　　　　　*Rheum rhaponticum (Polygonaceae)*
　　　　　　　　　　　　　　　　　Herbaceous perennial

Rhubarb is the perfect seasonal fruit. It is delightful to eat in the spring—rhubarb for Easter is an old country saying—yet one hardly regrets its passing, for by then there are so many more exciting fruits in the garden.

It is the stalks which are eaten, not the green leaves, which have been known to cause poisoning. The stalks contain oxalic acid and are not recommended for those whose kidneys are likely to form oxalate stones.

Rhubarb is available from January to August, if the early crop is forced. A rhubarb bed with its characteristic umbrella-like leaves will be a permanent part of your vegetable garden, and takes no part in the rotation of crops.

CULTIVATION In March make up a bed in an unshaded open position. Provide deep rich soil, well laced with decayed manure or garden compost to a depth of 15 cm (6 in) and lightly fork this in.

In April obtain roots from a nearby nursery or from friends who have an older garden. Plant these 75–90 cm (2½–3 ft) apart in both directions, 5 cm (2 in) below ground level.

In course of growth, hoe out weeds and make sure that there is no shortage of water.

Allow these roots to establish themselves, and pull no stalks the first year. The second, like asparagus, pull with some restraint.

Thin, pink stalks are obtained through blanching and gentle forcing. The old method was to cover the plants in January and February with special rhubarb pots. You may be able to improvise something similar. Another way is to lift whole plants in November, packing them into boxes of light soil or peat and putting these in a shed or under the staging of a greenhouse, covering them with an inverted box of the same size to exclude the light in order that blanched pink stalks are produced.

The sturdier greeny pink stalks come from unforced outdoor rhubarb, pulling of which can start in early April. A little litter will protect their first shoots and speed them along for the table. Remove flowering stems as they appear.

If roots are not readily available, build up your own stock by sowing seeds in a nursery bed in March in 2·5-cm (1-in) deep drills in light soil, in a frame or under cloches. Thin the developing plants progressively to 15 cm (6 in) apart, and in the following year transplant 90 cm (3 ft) apart to cropping positions in soil prepared with farmyard manure or garden compost as referred to previously. Do not pull stalks in the first year after planting.

VARIETIES
Seeds
   Holstein Bloodred, vigorous with dark, blood-red stalks.
   Prince Albert, early, tender.
   Champagne Early, bright scarlet, early.
   Victoria, a well-tried variety.
Roots
   Timperley Early.

DISEASES   Rhubarb plants can be affected with a mosaic virus
exhibited by yellow marbling of the leaves; by crown rot in which
the crown of the plant begins to rot and become soft and brown;
certain leaf-spotting fungi causing brown spots on the leaves (not
serious) and also by botrytis, on forced plants. The best policy is to
dig up and burn badly-affected plants.

Strawberry   *Fragaria xananassa (Rosaceae)*
                                       Perennial herbaceous plant

'Doubtless God could have made a better berry,' said Dr Boteler
according to Izaak Walton in *The Compleat Angler*, 'but doubtless
God never did.' He sums up everybody's opinion of strawberries.
To pick your own, in abundance, from your own garden, adds a
new dimension to the pleasure of eating them.
   Strawberries are picked from the open ground from about June
through the summer until early August, and you can hurry some
along under cloches to ripen two or three weeks earlier. You can
also lift some runners and force them in the greenhouse for some
very early strawberries, but although these bring pleasure by being
the first-comers, it must be admitted they are not so sweet as the
out-of-door crops. Perpetual fruiting varieties can be had from
about mid-August until the first frosts.

CULTIVATION   In July prepare the fruiting positions, not in
frost pockets (see p. 36), digging in garden compost or rotted
manure spread 15 cm (6 in) deep. Strawberries need rich soil,
slightly acid, with a pH between 5·5 and 6·5. Therefore fertile peat
or decayed leaf soil may be useful to lower the pH if necessary.
Thoroughly clean the ground of weeds, particularly perennial
kinds.

At the end of July consolidate the ground lightly by treading and then rake it to an even surface.

In August, in moist soil, put in the plants, obtained from a trustworthy source and certified as free from disease. These can either be runners with bare roots lifted from the open ground or pot plants. In either case put them in 40 cm ($1\frac{1}{4}$–$1\frac{1}{2}$ ft) apart in rows 75 cm ($2\frac{1}{2}$ ft) apart. Using a trowel, make a hole large enough to accommodate the full spread of the roots without folding them, and in the middle of the hole leave a slightly raised area on which to place the underside of the crown, thereby allowing the roots to droop downwards. Make sure of keeping the growing point above soil level. Firm in the plants by hand and water them. Continue to give adequate water. Keep the weeds hoed out. Cut off runners that may develop. If it proves impossible to put in plants before the middle of October, defer planting until the following spring.

In October, while the ground is still warm, hoe off weeds and put on a 5-cm (2-in) mulch of organic material.

In April lightly prick the soil between the plants, and remove any annual weeds, and when danger of frost is over, lay down straw for the developing fruit to rest on. Barley straw is most pliable and useful. The reason for delaying the strawing is to allow the soil to warm up naturally around the developing new fruits. If in spite of all there appears to be a danger of frost, cover all the plants with a layer of straw or litter and remove it the next morning. Alternatively, instead of strawing, black polythene sheeting can be used to keep the fruits clean.

Protect against slugs with soot, crushed egg shells, or grapefruit or orange hulls sunk in the ground and filled with beer. If not already done, rig protective netting against birds. Remove runners shortly before picking, except those required for increase.

Plants put in in early August will give some fruits the following summer. Plants put in in the following spring should have their blossoms removed just before they unfold to build up the plant for the following year's production.

Strawberries are useful for three years, one small crop in the first year if planted in the previous August, and two good crops in the second and third years, after which you should burn the plants and start a new bed as far away as possible.

After fruiting, tidy the beds by removing the straw. Most of this will go for litter, a small proportion can go into the compost

1

1

1

1

bins. Hoe between the plants gently and cut off the old large leaves to give light and air to the young leaves. Remove any runners present, except in the third year if you wish to renew your stocks. To produce your own potted runners, first earmark healthy plants and remove their blossoms, then fill small 7·5-cm (3-in) pots (peat pots are excellent) with a growing compost made up of sphagnum peat, sand and your best garden soil, sieved in equal quantities by volume. Sink these full pots into the ground under the runners and peg the runners down on to them with hairpins or wire hooks (Fig. 22). When they are rooted into the pots, cut off the umbilical connection and plant the new potted runners in

FIG. 22. Layering strawberry runners into pots; note the wire hook to hold down the runner stem

a new strawberry bed as far away as possible from the old one. You can make your own open ground runners simply by pegging down the stolons and allowing the plantlets to root into the ground, detaching them as before and planting the young bare-rooted plants in the new bed.

Earlier crops can be produced under cloches. Put these over maiden plants in February and enclose the ends. Allow some cracks for rain to penetrate. Tent-shaped glass cloches are best, see p. 46, but commercially, large use is made of polythene tunnels (see also p. 47). Watering may be necessary under cloches or tunnels.

To force strawberries, transfer established runners into 15-cm (6-in) pots filled with a rich growing compost mixed with a third of its bulk of rotted manure, leave them out until the end of November and then put them into greenhouses as near to the glass as possible. Here they will be very susceptible to variations in moisture. Therefore, keep a close eye on water requirements. In Sutton's old *The Culture of Vegetable and Flowers*, it is stated that a few inches (9-10 cm) of rotted manure laid down as a carpet for the pots to rest on will create more suitable moisture conditions and allow the plants to root there. A moderate temperature of about 16°C (60°F) is needed in which a fair crop of berries will be formed. Hand pollination may be necessary. At this stage take off any remaining flowers and increase the temperature to 18°C (about 65°F), and as the berries begin to take colour allow the temperature to rise to as much as 27°C (rather over 80°F). In this way I always achieve the first pick by May 18th.

VARIETIES (all are self-fertile)

Cambridge Vigour, early. Liable to be infected by red core disease in some districts. Well flavoured, rather soft.

Cambridge Favourite, heavy cropping and reliable. Probably the most widely grown by commercial growers. Large fruit, firm flesh, pine flavoured. It is not susceptible to mildew, but it is not resistant to strains of red core disease.

Cambridge Prizewinner, early. Good quality fruit. Suitable for cultivation under cloches.

Grandee, early. Crops heavily and produces very large berries 5 cm (2 in) and more in diameter. A large, strong growing variety needing wider spacing than usual.

Redgauntlet, mid to late season. Heavy cropping, but a little lighter than Talisman. Makes a compact plant.

Talisman, mid to late season. Small- to medium-sized fruit, good flavour and texture. Heavy cropper. Will produce a light autumn crop in some seasons, with protection. Resistant to red core disease and mildew.

Templar, a fairly new variety, mid to late season. Good flavour, resistant to red core disease, but susceptible to mildew.

Crusader, a smaller version of Templar and resistant to red core disease.

Royal Sovereign, first introduced towards the end of the last century. An early mid-season strawberry, considered to be the best flavoured. It has large scarlet fruit. Produces a great deal of leaf and forms a large plant, needing wider spacing than usual.

Hampshire Maid, St Claude, both are remontant or perpetual.

If blossoms are removed until June, the plants will bear fruits from August until the frosts. Runners are produced less freely on these varieties.

Baron Solemacher (Alpine), this does not make runners, but trim, small bushes, 25 cm (10 in) high with evergreen foliage. The little finger-nail-sized fruits are dark crimson and are borne until November. Delicious with cream. Tedius perhaps for adults to pick, but beloved by properly-brought-up children. They make a good edge in a potager and will put up with a fair amount of shade. Easily grown from seed sown in spring or autumn.

PESTS AND DISEASES Like many of the most prized and succulent, and consequently most highly-developed, fruits and vegetables, strawberries suffer from many afflictions, some of which are intractable within the limits applied by ordinary responsible civilized gardeners.

Aphides These are chiefly dangerous from the fact that they are vectors of virus diseases. There is a plethora of organophosphorus cures, some of them systemic, but it is better to leave these alone and try your best with derris and even pyrethrum; in both cases use in the evening.

Red spider mite Seen chiefly under glass and to some extent also under cloches. Tetradifon is an organochlorine acaricide which is not acceptable. It is better to maintain moist conditions and syringe the plants as often as possible.

There is some hope on the horizon through biological control. The predatory mite, *Phyloseiulus persimilis*, is now being used for the control of red spider mites in commercial and private greenhouses, and has been found also capable of controlling the pest on strawberries growing out of doors both under cloches and unprotected. Supplies of the predator are available to Fellows from the Royal Horticultural Society, and can be had from the Director, R.H.S. Garden, Wisley, Ripley, Surrey. They are also supplied from the Horticultural Training Centre, Dartington Hall, Totnes, Devon.

Strawberry or Tarsonemid mite Mites feed on the young folded leaves causing rust-coloured curling, wilting and withering. Plants look as though affected by drought. It is most likely to attack plants under cloches but can also occur in the open. Persistent organochlorine materials have been found satisfactory, but are not recommended for private gardeners. Dusting with flowers of sulphur is a help.

Eelworms Leaf and stem eelworms can cause damage; leaves become wrinkled and puckered, stems shorten and thicken, and the main crown may become blind. The best protection is to make sure of obtaining healthy plants, and never take runners from your own infected plants. Soil fumigation practised by large-scale growers is not suitable for private gardeners because it is strongly irritating to skin, eyes, nose and mouth. Hot-water treatment means maintaining an exact temperature—higher than which will kill the plants, lower is ineffective—and is impractical for the gardener.

Strawberry seed beetles These can eat the seeds on the surface of the fruits, making a clumsy job of it and eating the flesh also, whereas linnets which also take the seeds, tweek them out neatly without damaging the flesh. This is the way of distinguishing which pest is causing the damage. Slug pellets have been recommended but their disadvantages outweigh their value (see p. 42). Damage is more likely where the strawberry bed has become weedy, or where there is much rough grass and weeds surrounding the beds.

Wingless weevils The white grub-like larvae feed on the roots and the base of the crown of the plant, and cause it to collapse. There is no satisfactory control beyond organochlorine drenches.

Botrytis cinerea (Grey mould) A fungus disease infecting the fruits, exhibiting a soft squashy grey appearance. Prevent it by avoiding overcrowding, deleafing heavily foliaged plants, and under glass make sure of proper ventilation. Remove infected berries as soon as seen, and any which are damaged or with brown patches.

Mildew A fungus disease resulting in a greyish deposit on the plant. Can be checked by dusting with flowers of sulphur.

Red core A soil-borne fungus disease. Affected plants appear first to be suffering from lack of water, in early summer, but if the roots are examined it will be seen that the fibrous feeding roots have rotted away, leaving the fleshy main roots which, if cut lengthwise, show red or brownish red discoloration. The outer skin of the main roots can easily be rubbed off. There is at present no cure for this disease, and even the rotation of crops will not always ensure that the disease has been eliminated. Infection is worse after a wet autumn and winter, and on land where the drainage is restricted. Some varieties are resistant to the disease.

Virus diseases Yellow edge, and leaf crinkle virus are the main ones and are spread by aphides and soil-living eelworms. The best safeguard is to cultivate immune or nearly immune varieties, and to buy certified stock. Affected plants should be lifted and burnt.

SPECIAL REFERENCES

Bulletin 95, *Strawberries*, 1970, Ministry of Agriculture, Fisheries and Food.

Short Term Leaflet No 78, *Continuous Polythene Tunnels for Early Strawberry Production*, 1968, Ministry of Agriculture, Fisheries and Food.

Advisory Leaflet 580, *Virus Diseases of Strawberries*, 1970, Ministry of Agriculture, Fisheries and Food.

Advisory Leaflet 414, *Eelworms of Strawberry*, 1972, Ministry of Agriculture, Fisheries and Food.

Advisory Leaflet 410, *Red Core of Strawberry*, 1969, Ministry of Agriculture, Fisheries and Food.

Walnut *Juglans regia (Juglandaceae)*
Tree

The name derives from *Jovis glans*—Jupiter's nut. The walnut tree will grow to 18 m (60 ft), and apart from the value of its nuts when these can be harvested is a handsome landscape tree. The leaves have a splendid aromatic iodine scent when crushed between the fingers. Walnuts do not take kindly to being transplanted, and once put into position should not be moved again. If rooks and squirrels in the end have their way with the nuts, the timber is of great value. Trees can be planted 12 m (40 ft) apart to 'grow into money' for succeeding generations.

Walnuts are ripe for gathering when they fall from the tree in October.

CULTIVATION Walnuts succeed in good deep garden soils. They may do better over chalk and with a fairly high *p*H, over 6·0. They flourish best in warm congenial situations not likely to be visited by spring frosts, which can damage young foliage.

Plant them in November in well-prepared tree positions, as for apples, 1 × 1 × 1 m (3¼ × 3¼ × 3¼ ft) deep, and fix to stout chestnut stakes, not less than 12 m (40 ft) apart and at least in pairs, for the reason that walnut flowers do not readily self-pollinate because female flowers are sometimes produced before the pollen from the male catkin on the same tree is released on the wind. One or more extra trees will give a better chance of some male pollen getting on to the female flowers.

If you put them in open fields, protect them from cattle by tree guards. Metal tree guards will give reasonable protection but the trunk should also be surrounded with a plastic 'rabbit protector' which fits like a stocking round the base of the tree. The best ultimate protection against cattle eating the lower branches is a proper post and rail compound.

Prevent squirrels from taking the nuts by fixing a collar of wire netting round the trunk, 1·5 m (5 ft) up and bending it outwards to prevent them running up the tree. This, however, will be no good if there are other trees close enough to the walnut to allow squirrels to jump through the air from one to the other.

If, in spite of protection against squirrels, the nuts are taken by rooks, which are particularly fond of them and have good memories from year to year, pick them off the tree in July before the shells harden, and pickle them.

Pruning after planting is as for plum trees in the first few years, thereafter little or none except to thin crowded shoots.

VARIETIES Nurserymen generally offer only 'walnuts', but there was a time when connoisseurs paid attention to different varieties. A present-day enthusiast might be able to obtain wood from one of the special varieties and graft it on to ordinary walnut stock. Bunyard[1] gives:

Charberte, a large oval nut, smooth shell, firmly sealed, of good flavour. A French variety much grown in the walnut districts of the Midi.

Fertilis, small nut, fair flavour, dwarf. Suitable for cultivation as a bush. From France.

Franquette, large, rounded, thick shelled, very good flavour. Late flowering, a fact which may save it from spring frosts. Also from France.

[1] *A Handbook of Hardy Fruits, Stone and Bush Fruits, Nuts, etc.* John Murray, 1925.

Mayette, fairly large, moderately thick skinned, good flavour. Familiar in the Department of Isére, France.

DISEASE   Bacterial Blight.   Evidenced by small black spots on the foliage and the young nuts.   Cut out the affected shoots which you can reach in winter.

CHAPTER SEVEN

The Gardener's Calendar

JANUARY

Aubergines sow under glass for the earliest crops

Brassicas prepare beds for planting in 3 months' time

Broccoli sow early-maturing varieties under glass

Cabbage, summer sow under glass

Cauliflower, summer sow in heat under glass

Lettuces thin and transplant those sown under cloches in October; sow seed under frames and cold glass

Onions sow seeds in a cool greenhouse or frame for planting out in April

Peas buy pea-sticks

Tomatoes sow seeds in a warm greenhouse for May picking

Grapes finish pruning of greenhouse kinds as soon as possible

Melon sow seeds on hot-beds under glass for a May crop

Rhubarb begin to blanch out of doors

FEBRUARY

Artichokes, Jerusalem plant tubers

Aubergines sow under glass

Beans, broad sow Windsor types

Broccoli sow early-maturing varieties in cool greenhouse or cold frame

Cabbage, summer sow under glass

Carrots, early sow under glass

Cucumbers sow in heated greenhouse

Lettuce sow early in the month under cold glass

Onions sow seeds out of doors, towards the end of the month

Peas   sow early, round-seeded varieties out of doors

Potatoes   begin to chit tubers in trays, and plant early varieties at the end of the month

Peppers   sow seeds in a warm greenhouse

Shallots   plant in the garden

Spinach   sow seed out of doors

Tomatoes   sow seeds in heat under glass for picking in June

Grapes   increase greenhouse heat

Melons   sow seeds early in the month in a heated greenhouse for fruits in May

Rhubarb   begin to blanch out of doors

MARCH

Artichokes, Jerusalem   plant tubers

Aubergines   sow under glass

Beans, broad   sow Windsor types out of doors

Beans, French   sow under glass

Brussels sprouts   sow out of doors in the south

Cabbage, winter   sow out of doors

Carrots   sow in a cold frame

Celeriac   sow under glass

Celery   sow under glass

Garlic   plant cloves

Leeks   sow out of doors

Lettuce   sow out of doors

Marrows   sow in a warm greenhouse

Onions   sow out of doors

Parsnips   sow out of doors

Peas   sow out of doors; plant out November-sown kinds

Peppers   sow in a warm greenhouse for an early crop

Potatoes   plant out early varieties

Radishes   begin to sow out of doors, for first crop

Salsify   sow out of doors

Scorzonera   sow out of doors

Seakale   plant, or sow seeds if plants are unobtainable

Spinach   sow out of doors
Spinach, New Zealand   sow seeds in a cold frame
Swedes   sow out of doors
Tomatoes   sow in a warm greenhouse for July cropping
Turnips   sow out of doors for a summer crop

Angelica   sow under glass
Basil, sweet   sow under glass in heat
Bergamot   plant out of doors
Borage   sow seeds out of doors, or put in bought plants
Caraway   sow seeds out of doors
Chervil   sow seeds out of doors
Dill   sow seeds out of doors
Horseradish   plant pieces of root out of doors
Lemon balm   sow out of doors
Lovage   transplant
Mint   plant out of doors
Parsley   make first sowing out of doors
Thyme   sow or plant out of doors

Figs   plant trees out of doors
Melons   make up a hot-bed under glass for July-September crops

APRIL

Artichoke, globe   plant out of doors
Asparagus   plant out of doors
Beans, French   sow under cloches in early April, and out of doors towards the end of the month
Beans, haricot   sow out of doors
Beans, runner   fix bean poles
Beetroot   sow seeds late in the month
Broccoli   sow seeds of later-maturing varieties towards the end of the month
Brussels sprouts   sow early varieties in the North
Cabbage, red   transplant
Cabbage, Savoy   sow seeds out of doors
Cabbage, winter   sow seeds out of doors

Cardoons   sow seeds late in the month

Carrots   sow out of doors

Cauliflower, autumn   sow out of doors

Cucumbers   sow frame varieties under glass

Fennel, Florence   sow out of doors

Kohlrabi   sow out of doors

Lettuce   sow out of doors

Onions   plant sets

Peas   sow out of doors

Peppers   pot on seedlings, sow seed in heat

Potatoes   plant maincrop varieties

Radish   sow seed out of doors

Sorrel   sow seed out of doors

Spinach   sow out of doors

Spinach beet   begin successional sowings out of doors

Sweet corn   sow seeds in peat pots under glass in a warm greenhouse

Tomatoes   sow seeds under glass in a warm greenhouse; plant young plants in a cool greenhouse

Basil, sweet   sow under glass in heat

Bay, sweet   plant out of doors or in a pot

Chives   sow seeds out of doors

Coriander   sow seeds late in the month out of doors

Fennel   sow seeds late in the month out of doors

Lemon verbena   plant out of doors

Marjoram   sow seeds out of doors

Rosemary   plant out of doors

Sage   plant or sow seeds out of doors

Savory, summer   sow seeds out of doors

Savory, winter   sow seeds out of doors

Tarragon   sow out of doors late in the month

Thyme   sow or plant out of doors

Melon   sow seeds under glass for July–September crops

Rhubarb   plant out of doors

MAY

Beans, French   sow out of doors

Beans, runner   sow out of doors towards the end of the month

Broccoli   plant out early-maturing varieties; sow later-maturing varieties out of doors

Brussels sprouts   plant out of doors in the south

Cabbage, Chinese   sow out of doors

Cabbage, Savoy   sow out of doors

Cabbage, spring   transplant out of doors

Cauliflower, summer   sow out of doors

Celery   transplant or put in bought plants out of doors towards the end of the month

Chicory   sow out of doors

Cucumbers   sow out-of-door varieties

Endive   make first sowing out of doors

Kale   sow out of doors

Lettuce   sow out of doors

Marrows and courgettes   prepare a hot-bed out of doors for seed sowing later in the month; plant out at the end of the month

Peas   sow out of doors

Radish   sow out of doors

Sorrel   sow out of doors

Spinach   sow out of doors

Spinach, New Zealand   transplant out of doors

Sweet corn   sow out of doors at the end of the month; transplant peat-sown plants from under glass to the garden

Tomatoes   put out bought or home-raised plants at the end of the month

Basil, sweet   plant out of doors in cropping positions

Balm, lemon   sow in boxes under glass

Marjoram   make repeat sowing out of doors

Parsley   make repeat sowing out of doors

Pelargonium   plant out of doors at the end of the month

Thyme   take cuttings

JUNE

Beans, runner   sow out of doors

Broccoli   transplant later-maturing varieties

Brussels sprouts   buy or transplant out of doors in the north

Cabbage, winter   transplant or put in bought plants out of doors

Celeriac   transplant or put in bought plants out of doors early in the month

Chicory   sow seed out of doors

Cucumbers   put out home-grown or bought out-of-door varieties

Endive   sow out of doors

Lettuce   sow out of doors

Marrow   plant out of doors

Peas   sow out of doors

Tomatoes   plant out home-grown or bought plants

Turnips   sow for winter keeping

Lemon verbena   take cuttings

Marjoram   make repeat sowing out of doors

Pelargonium   plant out

Rosemary   take tip cuttings

Melons   plant out of doors

JULY

Beans, French   make a second sowing

Broccoli   transplant later-maturing varieties

Cabbage, Chinese   sow out of doors

Cabbage, spring   sow out of doors

Cabbage, winter   transplant or put in bought plants

Carrots   sow out of doors for late crop

Kale   transplant out of doors

Leeks   transplant out of doors

Lettuce   sow out of doors

Radish, winter   sow out of doors

Shallots   lift and store later in the month

Swedes   sow out of doors

Parsley   make repeat sowing out of doors

Pelargonium   take cuttings

Rosemary   take tip cuttings

Apples   summer prune restricted forms

Pears   summer prune restricted forms

Plums   summer prune established trees

Strawberries   peg down runners into the open ground or pots

AUGUST

Cabbage, spring   sow out of doors

Cardoons   begin to blanch

Corn salad   sow out of doors

Garlic   lift and put into dry store

Lettuce   make first sowings in a cool greenhouse also sow about the 20th of the month for spring cropping

Onions   bend down tops of mature foliage, lift crop 3 weeks later, dry and store; sow seeds out of doors to stand through the winter

Spinach, winter   sow out of doors

Turnips   sow for spring turnip greens

Angelica   sow out of doors

Bay   take half-ripe cuttings

Strawberries   plant out runners pegged down in July; pot plants for greenhouse forcing

SEPTEMBER

Cabbage, spring   transplant

Cabbage, red   sow out of doors or in a frame

Lettuce   sow out of doors and in a heated greenhouse

Potatoes   clear and store maincrop varieties

Spinach, winter   sow out of doors

Lovage   sow out of doors

Strawberries   plant out of doors

GICI—I

OCTOBER

Beans, broad   sow earliest Aquadulce varieties

Beetroot   lift and store

Cauliflower   sow in a cold frame

Chicory   lift and start to blanch

Garlic   plant cloves

Kohlrabi   lift and store

Lettuce   sow under cloches or in a frame early in the month or under cold glass

Onions   prepare cropping positions between now and January

Seakale   lift for blanching by second method

Swedes   lift and store at the end of the month

Bergamot   divide established plants and replant

Pelargonium   lift and pot under glass

Blackcurrants   plant between now and the end of March

Gooseberries   as above

Grape vines   plant out of doors

Peaches and Nectarines   plant between now and the end of March

Plums   as above

Raspberries   as above

Red and white currants   as above

NOVEMBER

Beans, broad   sow earliest varieties, Aquadulce and Longpods

Lettuce   sow under cold glass

Peas   sow earliest varieties in a cold frame or under glass

Seakale   plant between now and the end of March

Apples   begin winter pruning established trees

Apples   plant between now and the end of March

Apricots   as above

Cherries   as above

Loganberries and blackberries   as above

Medlars   as above

Mulberries   as above

Nuts   as above

Pears   as above

Quince   as above

Rhubarb   lift and begin to force

Walnuts   plant between now and the end of March

DECEMBER

Aubergines   sow in heat under glass

Lettuce   transplant those sown in frames in October; sow under cold glass

Potatoes   order seed and prepare chitting trays

Strawberries   bring in potted plants for greenhouse forcing

Seed catalogues   order supplies for following season

The Gardener's Jargon

Gardeners share a common language that is a kind of shorthand to anyone else. Here is a brief glossary of their more obscure terms. You will soon find yourself using them.

Blanch to whiten stalks and take out some of the bitterness. You cover the plant with soil, litter or a pot to exclude the light. Celery stalks are usually blanched.

Bolt go quickly to seed, usually without producing a crop on the way. Lettuce can bolt to seed without making a firm head.

Casing of soil, a covering of soil, usually over a hot-bed of fermenting manure for melons and mushrooms.

Cropping position the place in the garden where the plant is to mature to harvest.

Drills the shallow little valleys in freshly-raked soil 'drawn' out with a hoe for sowing seeds.

Earth up heap the soil round the stem, often for blanching. (To increase the crop for potatoes.)

Harden off gradually to accustom a greenhouse or frame-grown plant to the rigours of the garden by exposing it for longer and longer periods to out-of-door temperatures.

Nursery bed a place in the garden where seeds are sown and thinned, and from which they are subsequently planted on into their final cropping positions.

Prick out to lift tiny seedlings from their crowded germinating positions and transplant them further apart, either into their final cropping positions or into boxes, as a preliminary to final planting out.

Thin out to remove intermediate and weak seedlings, leaving the remainder correctly spaced for final cropping.

Trench much deeper than a drill, made with a spade for planting out vegetables that later need to be earthed up like celery and potatoes.

PART TWO

Cook It

_____

The pleasures of the table belong to all times
and all ages, to every country and every day;
they go hand in hand with all our other pleasures,
outlast them, and remain to console us for their loss.
                    JEAN-ANTHELME BRILLAT-SAVARIN

CHAPTER EIGHT

An Outline of Nutrition:
Vegetables and Fruit in Perspective

Nutrition—what it means

We are what we eat: our nutrition is the deciding factor in our weight and our height, in our physical and mental health, in our resistance to disease, in the way we behave and in how long we live. Our total growth and health is decided by the nutrients, and there are more than fifty of them, that are the chemical ingredients of the food we eat.

The physical effects of nutrition are obvious to us. One of the earliest discoveries was that scurvy is caused by a lack of vitamin C in fresh fruit and vegetables; one of the latest is that an infinitesimal amount of the mineral Fluorine will substantially help to prevent tooth decay. Now the logical progression is towards the effect of nutrition on our minds. Nerve and brain cells are as directly affected by foods as any other body cells, so it is not surprising that doctors are now having some success with massive doses of B vitamins for mental patients. Ethel Austin Martin[1] says it is 'increasingly likely that severe and prolonged nutritional deficiencies in early life may have a permanently crippling effect on the intellectual potential and learning ability of children'. These are both extreme examples, but isn't it possible that just as there is sub-clinical scurvy caused by lack of vitamin C so there may be sub-clinical depression, irritability and anger caused by lack of the B vitamins in a faulty diet? That same faulty diet will undoubtedly lead us to senility or an early death. If we eat properly we can prolong our lives into an old age that is physically and mentally active. More than all this, if you eat right, you feel good.

---

[1] *Nutrition in Action*, Holt, Rinehart and Winston, 1963.

Yet many of us simply do not know that we have such a powerful weapon to wield both to our own advantage and for the benefit of our children. To understand how to use it, we must know how all nutrients, not only fruit and vegetables, contribute to our growth and health.

Nutrients—what they are

There are six classes of nutrients—carbohydrates, fats, proteins, vitamins, minerals and water. The following chart describes their main functions:

Nutrient	Chief functions	Main sources
Carbohydrates* (sugars and starches)	Burnt by the body to release energy. When not needed, stored mainly as fat—alas.	Sugar, syrup, bread, flour and other cereals, jams, root vegetables and potatoes, fruits.
Fats*	Provide twice as much energy as the same amount of carbohydrates. Include fat-soluble vitamins A, D and E, and essential fatty acids.	Butter, margarine and other fats, whole milk and cheeses, meat, salad and cooking oils.
Proteins	The stuff of life: make new tissue, combine to form essentials like hormones and enzymes.†	Meat, eggs, cheese, milk, fish, poultry, soybeans, wheatgerm, brewer's yeast, some vegetables.

* The energy produced by carbohydrates and fats is measured in Calories which are units of heat. They are properly called kilocalories, defined as the amount of energy needed to raise the temperature of one kilogram of water one degree centigrade. When we change over to the metric system we will use kilojoules, more refined units of measurement. One kilocalorie is equivalent to 4·19 kilojoules.

† Chemically, enzymes are complex protein molecules synthesized by the body. They are substances which must be present for metabolism to proceed correctly. They are catalysts which take part in, but are unchanged by, the reactions involved in digesting food.

Nutrient	Chief functions	Main sources
Vitamin C (ascorbic acid) water soluble	Forms collagen that literally holds us together. Speeds healing from cuts and surgery, helps fight infection. Lack causes scurvy.	Nearly all our supply comes from fruits and vegetables—red peppers, broccoli, blackcurrants, rosehips in particular.
B vitamins Thiamine (B1) Riboflavin (B2) Niacin (nicotinic acid) Pyridoxine (B6) Folic acid Cyano-cobalamin (B12) Pantothenic acid Biotin Choline Inositol all water soluble	All needed for nerves, good digestion, healthy skin and blood cells, and for the release of energy from carbohydrates—thus aids slimming. Extreme deficiencies of these vitamins causes diseases like beriberi, pellagra and anaemia.	Whole-grain foods, liver, wheatgerm, brewer's yeast, leafy green vegetables, lean meat and milk, molasses, pulse vegetables (peas and beans).
Vitamin A fat soluble	Needed for eyesight, for skin and linings of body cavities and passages.	Liver, butter, margarine, carrots, cheese, eggs, leafy green vegetables.
Vitamin D fat soluble	Needed to absorb calcium and phosphorus and so make strong bones and teeth.	Sunlight makes it on bare skin, also present in margarine, butter, eggs.
Vitamin E fat soluble	Needed for skeletal muscles, lack can cause leg paralysis and failure to reproduce.	Vegetable oils, cooking fats, margarine and eggs.
Vitamin K fat soluble	Needed for blood clotting.	Leafy green vegetables.
Calcium	Makes strong bones, sound teeth, healthy blood. Deficiency causes rickets.	Milk, cheese, green vegetables, fortified flour.

Nutrient	Chief functions	Main sources
Copper	Needed to absorb iron.	Liver, shellfish, nuts, raisins and dried peas and beans.
Fluorine	Prevents tooth decay.	Fluorine-rich water or toothpaste.
Iodine	Essential: a deficiency causes goitre.	Vegetables grown on iodine-rich soil, salt-water fish or iodized table salt.
Iron	Makes red blood cells: too little causes anaemia.	Beef liver, dark green leafy vegetables, dried prunes and apricots, egg yolks and whole-grains.
Magnesium	Works with protein, calcium, vitamin D and phosphorus.	Grains and cereals, vegetables, milk, meat, eggs and fish.
Phosphorus	Works with calcium, helps to release body energy.	Lean meat, milk, cheese, fish, peas and beans, whole-cereals and eggs.
Potassium, Sodium and Chlorine	Form fluids inside and outside cells, concerned with nerves, and messages from nerves to muscles.	Sodium chloride is ordinary salt; potassium is found in many foods, dried prunes are the richest source.
Sulphur	Works with protein.	Proteins and dried apricots.
Trace elements Cobalt Manganese Zinc Selenium Molybdenum Chromium Strontium	are all trace elements; dieticians suppose that normal healthy eating will provide enough of them.	
Water	Needed in every tissue and for every body-building activity. Two-thirds of an adult's weight is water.	

Vegetables and fruits in nutritional perspective

Vegetables and fruits provide nearly all (94 per cent) of our vital vitamin C, vitamins from the B group, minerals, some proteins, as well as much energy-producing starch and sugar.

Vitamin C is the major reason for growing our own produce. It is present in all green-growing things and is the easiest vitamin to destroy: vulnerable to attack from oxygen, hurried along by the enzymes active in raw fruits and vegetables especially in warm temperatures. It is also destroyed by strong light, by alkalies like soda, and by copper. So you should harvest garden produce as late as you can, keep it cool and dark and cook it quickly without contact with copper or soda. Even using the most careful methods, it is difficult to avoid losing at least half the original amount—one good reason for eating a salad every day.

The B group vitamins are all soluble in water.

Thiamine (mainly in vegetables such as peas and potatoes) is also extremely easy to destroy during cooking—up to 30 per cent by toasting a thin slice of bread, up to 20 per cent in baked foods, a third or more in meats. You lose thiamine by careless handling, by soaking and draining, in cooking water and fat. The best way to preserve it in cereals is to cook them at a moderate temperature until they absorb all their liquid. Thiamine is one reason why it is important to save and use all your vegetable cooking water and to make gravy and sauces from the meat juices left in the pan after cooking. It is destroyed by bicarbonate of soda (by itself and in baking powder) and by sulphite. (Bulk-peeled potato chips are dipped in sulphite to stop them discolouring; sausages contain a lot of sulphite.)

Riboflavine (some in broccoli, spinach, peas, beans, and other vegetables) is not harmed by ordinary cooking temperatures, but it does dissolve in water—so can be lost in cooking water and meat drippings—and it is destroyed by any kind of light. (You have no control over the time your milk travels about with the milk-man in broad daylight, but you can put it straight into a dark fridge as soon as he delivers it, or ask him to leave it in a dark box outside.)

Other B vitamins found plentifully in vegetables and fruits are pantothenic acid (some in peas and beans, less in most other vegetables), pyridoxine (B6) (some in most vegetables) and biotin[1] (most vegetables and some fruits).

The fat-soluble vitamins, A, E and K, are all found in vegetables and are not so easy to destroy by careless handling and cooking.

We eat *vitamin A* in two forms—vitamin A named as such is present in animal foods only, and carotene is in both animal and vegetable foods. Vitamin A is undamaged by cooking, but is destroyed if the food is dried in air, and by rancidity in fats. (Antibiotics and mineral oil laxatives decrease our absorption of vitamin A.) You can recognize vitamin A in some foods by its yellow colour, in apricots and leafy green and yellow vegetables, for example. Carotene is so called for its carroty colour, which is a little ironic, for the carotene in carrots is surrounded by indigestible cellulose, so the carrots must be cooked before all the vitamin A is available to us (shredding for salads, or thorough chewing, will also help to break down the cellulose). We store vitamin A in the liver, and too much, in the form of supplements, is toxic.

Vitamin D is needed to make strong bones and teeth. It is formed by the action of sun on the skin, and also in milk and dairy produce generally, including eggs. Some is present in animal fats and oils and in other salad oils.

Vitamin E is a tocopherol. Deep-fat frying destroys it, as does any commercial processing involving oxidation. There is also some loss in storage, even in a deep freeze, also due to oxidation. It is an anti-oxidant, so we need vitamin E in proportion to the amount of fats we eat. Some of our supplies come from fruit and vegetables (and some from grain products, in particular wheatgerm; also salad oils, cooking fats and margarine).

Vitamin K is essential to make our blood clot, although the amount we need is not yet certain. We eat it in a wide variety of

---

[1] Raw egg white contains a substance called avidin which combines with biotin to make a substance we are unable to digest; so, as a general rule, you should cook without using raw egg whites.

green leafy vegetables (and egg yolk, cow's milk and liver). We also manufacture it with the bacteria in our stomachs.

Minerals are all present in varying quantities in fruits and vegetables—long-rooted vegetables in particular (e.g. parsnips) reach down and draw up valuable minerals for us.[1] These minerals will all leach into water (iron and calcium less than the others) and so may be lost at the last if you do not save and use your cooking water.

Proteins

Only plants can make protein; the rest of us, animal and human, must obtain our supplies directly or indirectly from plants. Meat is the best-known source of protein but there are cheaper, less obvious sources of protein to experiment with. They include soya beans and soya flour (more than 40 per cent protein, compared to the 25 per cent of best steak), brewer's yeast, skim milk powder, and wheatgerm which is the millings from whole-grains.

The quality of protein is important, too. For under the umbrella-word 'protein' shelter twenty-two amino acids, eight of them essential to our diet. That is, all eight of them are needed in the right proportion by our bodies *at the same time*. Incomplete proteins do not hang about waiting for their complement to be made up later, they are immediately discarded—wasted in effect. Animal proteins are complete for human purposes, whereas plant proteins (soya beans being an exception) may not be.

Individual plant proteins are different in quantity and ratio; a vegetarian can eat them in the correct proportions if he chooses a careful variety of vegetable foods. (Macrobiotic eaters have died on a diet of brown rice alone, because the proteins were incomplete.) Best of all is to mix animal and vegetable proteins, for they have a way of complementing each other—cereals and milk, rice with meat and so forth.

Children have a special need for protein in order to grow

---

[1] The absorption of calcium is hindered by oxalic acid, which is present in spinach and rhubarb. Oddly, spinach, always 'so good for you', actually locks out its own calcium. It does not lock out any other calcium, so if you cook spinach in milk you can restore this loss.

properly—particularly when they are learning to sit or stand up. Their bodies will use what protein is available to maintain the *status quo* before making any growth, so they must have enough to do both. Pregnant women and women breast-feeding their babies need plenty of protein too.

A note on fats and cholesterol

As well as providing calories, some fats give us important fat-soluble vitamins (vitamin A in butter for example) and others provide linoleic acid, a polyunsaturated fatty acid that is essential to our diet. Safflower oil and sunflower oil both have upwards of 70 per cent of linoleic acid, while animal fats like beef and lamb provide less than 5 per cent. Poor growth and skin troubles in babies have been traced to lack of linoleic acid. So too has a high cholesterol blood count in adults. We hear a lot about cholesterol these days: it comes from animal fats and the body needs some, but not too much of it, in the nervous tissues, fluids, blood and bile. In fact it is such a needed substance that we can make it internally, and would still have some in our systems if we ate none at all. But too much cholesterol in the artery linings is thought to cause coronary thrombosis. Linoleic acid appears to be able to keep cholesterol within the right limits, hence our need to eat salads dressed with safflower or sunflower oil, and to use a poly-unsaturated margarine as well as butter (see also p. 281).

One thing is plain from this brief summary of the work of nutrients in our bodies, and it is that if we are concerned with a proper diet it must be a complete diet. The work of proteins, minerals and vitamins are so interlocked and their proper functions so dependent on the right supplies of everything all the time, that to concentrate on eating proteins and to ignore the minerals, say, or to eat some vitamins but forget others, is a complete waste of time.

Yet nutrition is not simply a question of putting the required number of grams and micrograms into one's mouth. Eating has always been a highly complex activity in every civilization, in-volved with tribal taboos and social overtones that usually have nothing to do with nutrition. Traditional ways of cooking foods are handed down through the generations, preserving, or more likely destroying, nutrients quite accidentally. We, as a western-civilized people, think we know better than the African tribe that suffered from a permanent and severe protein deficiency because of its taboos connected with cows and cows' milk. But what about the traditional British method of preparing vegetables hours in advance, keeping them 'fresh' in a pan of water and then boiling them for up to half an hour without a lid before draining away all the cooking water? Our own ignorance of water-soluble, heat- and light-unstable nutrients means that we could hardly have eliminated them more efficiently if they had been poisonous. Nutritionally it would be better to throw away the vegetables and drink the water.

Children learn their eating habits and preferences from their parents and they learn them very early in life, if not before. I think there is a possibility of prenatal influence here. So parents have a duty to learn and to practise good eating habits—although it is much harder to alter eating habits as an adult—for the sake of their children as well as themselves. The will to do so makes it easier, and soon the beginnings of good health, weight loss where it is needed, and a feeling of well-being will make it a positive change for the better.

There is a powerful psychological aspect to eating. Good diges- tion is encouraged by pleasant mealtimes, good conversation and appetizing food. Don't force yourself or your children to eat something that is disliked, just because 'it's good for you'. If you don't like it, it isn't.

CHAPTER NINE

Good Cooking and Good Eating

We cannot afford to waste vegetables and fruits through ignorance and carelessness. They play a major part in good nutrition. There are three ways to damage your freshly grown vegetables: in the kitchen equipment itself, in the way you prepare your produce and in the way you cook it.

Kitchen equipment

Before you can begin to cook for maximum nutrition you must examine your kitchen equipment, perhaps add to it, perhaps reject some items. Copper destroys all vitamin C on contact, so hang your pretty copper pans on the wall where they will decorate your kitchen but not harm your food. (Even if they are tinned, the tin will eventually wear through from cooking acid foods—tomatoes for example.) Choose pans according to the kind of stove you cook on, but make sure that they all, including the frying pan, have a tight-fitting lid. There is some evidence that aluminium pans may be harmful and also, possibly, non-stick surfaces. Cast-iron pans can be beneficial, in that small traces of iron find their way into food. Good quality, hard-enamel pans are safe too, but you should avoid the cheap, soft-enamel ones which can deteriorate at the seams or chip to release harmful substances, such as antimony salts, into the food. Lead is often present in cheap enamel pans and in glazes for earthenware casseroles and bowls; acid food, such as lemonade, can dissolve out a considerable amount of lead. Cadmium can be released from the orange enamel-coated lids of otherwise harmless hard-enamel pans. However, new regulations now ban the sale of dangerous pots and pans likely to release lead and cadmium into our diet. It is only in old equipment that there could still be a danger.

Pressure cookers preserve vitamin C because they shorten the cooking time.

If you haven't already got one, invest in a steamer. Mine cost less than 50p; it looks like a saucepan with holes in the bottom, fits neatly into an existing pan and produces the most delicious steamed vegetables that come to the table with all their delicate flavours intact. (If you steam vegetables, you are cooking them with minimal contact with water—just the steam that condenses on them—so you avoid dissolving out too many nutrients. However, some experts argue that because the vegetables heat up more slowly in steam than in boiling water, an oxidase in plant cells has more time to destroy vitamin C. But when you boil the vegetables you can lose anywhere from 40 to 80 per cent of the vitamin C, so it is hard to save it either way.) The steamer is also useful for skinning fruits and vegetables: a few seconds' steam, along with the other vegetables (provided they are not powerfully flavoured, like onions) if you are cooking, and the skins slip off magically.

Buy a deep-fryer. Mine also cost less than 50p and doubles as a blanching basket when I am freezing vegetables. Quick-frying in hot oil will seal in most nutrients effectively (vitamin B1 will be lost) although too much oil eaten along with fried food is fattening.

You need your own favourite vegetable knife, which you should keep sharp and keep to yourself. 'If you are so imprudent as to use another man's knife it will cut you,' says Nicolas Freeling, 'each knife has its character, its especial feel and balance. Once used it bends to the owner, to the way he holds it and sharpens it. If you pick it up, all unity and movement is at once gone, the hand is stiff and awkward, and a cut is as good as inevitable.' A well-sharpened knife will destroy fewer vitamins than a blunt one: in a growing plant the oxidase is kept apart from vitamin C until the cells are damaged by bruising, cutting or grating. A sharp knife will mash the cells less.

You should also have a liquidizer powerful enough to deal with raw vegetables and a *mouli-légumes*, which performs the same sort of function with the extra advantage of separating out the stringy, fibrous parts when you are making soups. Patience and a large sieve are the only alternatives. Cook, or freeze, or eat liquidized raw vegetables as quickly as you can, because liquidizing is the ultimate mashing which lets the oxidase loose on vitamin C.

A salad-spinning basket with a rubber suction foot is the hardest-working piece of equipment in my kitchen. It throws the water from a washed lettuce by centrifugal force.

If you are growing produce on any scale you must consider adding a deep-freeze to your equipment. Freezing, much more than pickling or bottling, preserves the goodness in food, especially if the vegetables are frozen within a few hours of picking, and if you are freezing your own produce you can ensure that this is so. (Unfrozen food starts to deteriorate faster than fresh food, so it is important to cook it straight from the freezer where possible.) A deep-freeze will take care of a glut of vegetables (there are some ideas for a dearth on pages 328–332). My freezer was new last year to catch the spare broad beans and peas, and the pounds and pounds of runner beans that went on growing right up to the first frost. The first nip in the air sent me out at dusk to strip the runners by torchlight—luckily, for the next morning the grass was white and all the tender plants limp and transparent. A bag of home-frozen beans tastes quite exotic in midwinter if they have been blanched carefully before freezing and later cooked while still frozen. (Blanching means plunging vegetables first into boiling water and then into iced water to stop the enzyme action. There are different timings for different vegetables. *The Home Book of Food Freezing* by Pat M. Cox will tell you more about this.)

The quality of your frozen vegetables will depend on how quickly your machine can freeze them. As the temperature falls from $32°F$ ($0°C$) to $25°F$ ($-4°C$) the actual cells become damaged: the longer vegetables stay within this temperature range the more liable they are to unfreeze with a poor, soggy texture. The quicker the vegetables pass through this danger-area the better the results, so turn your control to the coldest setting before freezing, and follow the manufacturer's instructions about quantities to freeze at any one time—usually 10 per cent of the total freezing capacity.

With a freezer you can also make delicious ice-creams and water ices from your own fresh fruit juices in the summer, and frequently an extra cooked dish to save yourself kitchen time—prepare double quantity of any recipe, and freeze half. If, as sometimes happens, you have food all ready cooked and nobody to eat it, it is far better to freeze it for future use than to keep it warm and losing nutritional value until it is time to dish up.

Preparing vegetables and fruit

Light and warmth and water are the major enemies of garden vegetables once they are picked, ironically since these are the three things they need most on the stalk. But when picked, the enzymes that once worked for the plant will attack its structure, especially at room temperature. Boiling kills these enzymes (chilling only inhibits their activities) so you must cook vegetables and fruits as soon as possible after harvesting. If you do this you will be surprised to find that vegetables you would ordinarily avoid because they are dull, have a crispness of texture and delicacy of flavour that is not even a memory in shop-bought vegetables. (One Scottish gourmet even insists that his tiny new potatoes come into the kitchen in a box of soil, so that there is no drop in either temperature or moisture content before they are cooked.) By contrast, 'fresh' vegetables that have travelled to and from a wholesale market and then been displayed at the local greengrocer, actually contain less vitamin C than those frozen within twenty-four hours of picking.

If you cannot cook your vegetables right away, clean them, wrap them and store them in the refrigerator or a cool, dark place as fast as you can. Root vegetables need to be scrubbed and dried, vegetable leaves rinsed quickly and wiped, or spin-dried. Any moisture that remains on the vegetables will dissolve out nutrients. Knowing that my vegetables have been grown without poison sprays, I don't bother to wash any of the high-growing ones like tomatoes, cucumbers, raspberries (fatal to wash these), currants or beans, unless they have been mud-splashed by heavy rains. I reckon I am washing away more than imaginary dirt.

Vegetables and fruits are protected in nature by their skins and peels and pods, so save yours from the damaging effects of warmth and oxygen by podding and peeling them as late as possible and shredding and chopping them at the very last minute.

In any method of cooking, the smaller the vegetable pieces the quicker they will cook and the less vitamins and minerals they will lose. But the fewer vegetables you peel the better. Many nutrients lie directly under the skin and get thrown away with the peelings. Here you have a great advantage with home-grown vegetables, for most of them either have no skin at all, or else a very thin one. Carrots fresh from the garden simply do not have a skin,

neither do new potatoes; they acquire them through exposure
to air.

Vegetables shouldn't be prepared hours in advance and kept
drowning in a pan of cold water until it is time to cook them. If
you are accustomed to doing this, you should plan your schedule
to leave the vegetables till the last minute. Even if you are enter-
taining, this can be arranged; most guests will cheerfully lend a
hand to pod some last-minute peas, or slice a cucumber. It is no
longer a social disgrace to be caught cooking, in fact it is quite the
reverse. In Jane Austen's time the unfortunate Mr Collins, at
dinner in *Pride and Prejudice*, 'begged to know to which of his
fair cousins the excellency of its cooking was owing. But here he
was set right by Mrs Bennett, who assured him with some asperity
that they were all very well able to keep a good cook, and that her
daughters had nothing to do in the kitchen.' Mrs Bennett would
disapprove of my informal kitchen and dining room which makes it
easy to mix the jobs of cook and hostess.

Cooking vegetables and fruit

There are some basic cookery rules that apply to all vegetables.
The first is that you must cook them in the absolute minimum time
and the absolute minimum liquid. If you want 'boiled' vegetables
you must either steam them or put them into a very small amount
of lightly salted, fast-boiling milk or water, just enough to stop
them sticking. A pan full of steam or water-vapour from one of
these methods will exclude much damaging oxygen and the
vegetables will reach boiling point in the quickest possible time.
Cover them tightly and cook them only until they are *al dente*,
slightly bitey in texture. Green vegetables take on an olive-ish,
school cabbage tinge when they have been overcooked. Test them
by spearing a fragment from the pan—put the lid back on of
course—but remember that the leaf part will taste cooked while
the spiny centre will need a minute longer. When they are done,
tip the vegetables into a colander placed over a bowl to catch the
cooking liquid (keep the liquid from the steamer too). If you are
accustomed to serving your vegetables in butter or margarine, try
them without any for once: you will find they have a fresh, clear
taste, and will be less fattening as well. Otherwise, melt some
butter or margarine in the hot pan, tip the drained vegetables

back in, hold the lid on and shake with a firm circular movement to coat the vegetables evenly and serve them as soon as you can.

Sauté-ing or stewing vegetables means that there will be some loss of vitamins and minerals into the pan juices—in a risotto or a *bœuf à la bourguignonne* for example—but as these juices usually get eaten as well, this doesn't matter so much. Stir the vegetables you are sauté-ing as soon as you put them in the pan, to give them a protective coating of oil.

Baking and roasting will destroy some nutrients, too. You can minimize this by baking onions, beetroot and potatoes in cooking foil—pull it back for the last 15 minutes if you like a crisp jacket to your potatoes. If you are roasting vegetables alongside the joint, turn them carefully until they are coated with fat, which will protect them from damage.

However carefully we prepare and cook them, vegetables in general (fruits less so because they contain more acid) will be damaged a little in the process—carrots are an exception to this rule. So I include many salad recipes; they are every cook's pleasure to prepare, decorative, appetizing and supremely nutritious.

Even so there is an important place in our diet for cooked vegetables. We can concentrate their bulk to eat more of them at a time (you can manage far more spinach cooked than raw). Cooking also sterilizes food and makes it more digestible. It improves its appearance and brings out new, appetizing flavours to stimulate our gastric juices—the psychological aspect of eating again.

I think everyone seriously concerned with cooking, whether it is regular family food or an occasional party piece, feels that she must make a contribution of time and skill to the presentation of food. This should not take the form of laborious cooking, over-elaborate recipes, too many rich butter and cream sauces. You know that the more simply you present your ingredients, the more delicious they will be. Your contribution of time and skill both to the health of your family and the enjoyment of your guests will be in the growing of your own fruit and vegetables, and in their presentation as whole food. There is no conflict between good eating and healthy eating. And this is in no way cranky. Elizabeth David demonstrates that French food at its best (the accepted ideal for all cooks) is usually at its simplest as well.

A classic French example is an hors-d'œuvre, a selection of raw or barely blanched vegetables, each presented separately and served in a different dressing. It might consist of shredded carrots in a slightly sweet dressing, sliced cucumbers in a lemony one, finely sliced green peppers, tomatoes halved and filled with dressed crab in a tomato mayonnaise, tiny peas, some slices of garlic sausage, or a *pâté de campagne*, all arranged on a bed of crisp lettuce leaves on a big plate. I was surprised by just such a one at Le Touquet airport once. In my ignorance I had no idea the restaurant was famous until I unfolded a clean yellow napkin and turned to confront the hors-d'œuvre. The whole was simple-seeming but carefully planned, and had taken someone a lot of loving time to prepare so thoughtfully.

So if you enjoy cooking and like to spend time on it, turn your attention to salads like these sometimes. Re-examine all your favourite recipes in the light of your knowledge of nutrition. Substitute yoghurt for cream in some recipes, a polyunsaturated oil (p. 281) for olive oil in another. If vegetables have to be blanched before another cooking process, save the water and use it in soups and gravies.

The stock from cooking vegetables is rich in taste and in minerals, sugars and B and C vitamins. You can use it to thin a flour-based gravy for a roast joint, or as the liquid for stews, meat pies and home-made soups. Potato water is good for making wholemeal bread (p. 358).

Whole food in general

Once beyond the idea that white is right you can use wholemeal flour in many dishes. What is more absurd than thickening a gravy with white flour and then colouring it with gravy browning? When you need white sauces and pastries use the 81 per cent stoneground flour, which is next best to the wholewheat.

In fact you should re-think all foods in terms of wholeness. As food is refined for whiteness or peeled for smoothness, important nutrients are invariably left behind. You can put back some of these by buying the refinings—blackstrap molasses from sugar, wheatgerm from wholewheat, for example. You can serve food as whole as possible—baked potatoes, brown rice. (If you prefer white rice, choose a brand that has been treated to drive the nutrients into the grain before milling.) You can make many high-starch, high-sugar foods more than 'empty calories' by the addition of extras like soya flour (it has the highest percentage of protein in any food), dried skim milk powder (rich in calcium, vitamins and protein, low in fat), blackstrap molasses (full of B vitamins), brewer's yeast (B vitamins and protein) and yoghurt (protein, calcium and valuable stomach bacteria). Make your own yoghurt (p. 356).

But it is important to be subtle with these additions. If you continually heap in the same extras you will find that all your dishes taste alike, and that they have lost their variety—the most important gastronomic pleasure. Blackstrap molasses and brewer's yeast in particular have very distinctive and pervasive tastes. Try them out sparingly at first.

It is vital to make your dishes appetizing, and the first requisite for this is careful seasoning. Herbs play a major part here; they are described in detail in Chapter Ten.

Seasonings

Owing to the widespread interest in cooking encouraged by writers such as Elizabeth David and Robert Carrier, a peppermill for black peppercorns, a saltmill for grinding up large sea-salt crystals and a string of garlic bulbs are in many kitchens these days. There is little difference between natural rock salt and sea salt—they are both sodium chloride. Table salt contains a little magnesium carbonate to keep it running freely; too much magnesium is not very good for us and there is little need for it in a warm dry house. Too much and too little salt are both equally bad for the human body. Black pepper, freshly ground, is a true aromatic spice, essential to good cooking, and bears little resemblance to the sneezy white powder you buy in perforated tins. You can experiment with other kinds of pepper: freshly ground white peppercorns (they are the black ones picked ripe and husked) are useful in any white dish where specks of black pepper would show; the red pepper, Hungarian paprika, will add a gentler flavour to food, and if you sprinkle it generously over a chicken before roasting, it will brown the skin beautifully.

Mustard is the third basic condiment (weight for weight, mustard actually contains more protein than grilled steak, although the quantities you consume are, of course, much smaller) together with salt and pepper. Along with these you will need a judicious sprinkle of Worcestershire sauce (it has blameless ingredients, mostly vinegar) or soy sauce (contains protein extracts), an occasional squeeze of tomato purée or fresh lemon juice. Whatever seasonings and flavourings you choose, try to use them as whole, as authentic and as fresh as it is possible to obtain them. Vanilla, for example: once you have used real vanilla pods, long, black and flexible, to flavour a recipe, you will never again return to the bottled essence. Although the pods are expensive, they can be used again and again. You simply wash them and dry them and put them away; if you keep them in a jar of sugar they will flavour it deliciously for later use in cakes and custards. Nutmeg, too, is much more distinctive when it is freshly grated each time. And fresh ginger root has a sweet, almost lily-like smell, far removed from the peppery powder we are more accustomed to.

When you prepare your own dishes from the beginning, and wherever possible use your own fresh vegetables and herbs, you know that they are free from all the sinister additives we see listed on processed food labels—the ubiquitous monosodium glutamate (a general savoury taste intensifier), and sodium nitrite and sodium nitrate (*known* to be poisonous in concentration), anti-oxidants which stop food going stale. Your dishes don't need any chemical dressing up. Freshly cooked food has its own bright and natural colours, it tastes as good as it looks and it won't be around long enough to go stale.

Sugars and starch

We are the biggest sweet eaters in the world, way ahead of the Swiss who are next on the list. We cram ourselves with starch and sugars; even the British sausage can legally contain as much as 50 per cent bread filling. (Don't imagine you are feeding your family much protein when you cook them sausages.) Yet our bodies cannot make starch and sugar into body tissue as they can protein; starch and sugar can be transformed only into energy or, more often, stored as fat. In the beginning starch and sugar cause serious tooth decay, later they create all the diseases associated with obesity. People, especially active, growing children, need starch and sugar in their food (children actually need starch to provide the energy for proteins to build cells), but only as part of a balanced diet that also includes the necessary vitamins, proteins and minerals. Too often, and wrongly, starch and sugar take first place. Give your children sweets, biscuits and cakes only sparingly; make your own ice lollies and ice-creams so that some vitamin C, calcium and protein are included in the recipes. Hand out apples, carrots, sticks of cheese and celery for school break.

If there is any food value in most breakfast cereals, apart from a lot of starch and some of the added B vitamins, it is as a vehicle to get milk into children. Instead of corn flakes, give them home-made muesli, cheaper and fresher than the bought kind, to eat with hot or cold milk (p. 360).

Instead of steamed and sugary puddings you will find it quicker and less starchy to serve yoghurt with a fruit purée, with black-currant syrup or with a dollop of honey (yoghurt and honey is supposed to be the original ambrosia). Honey is a better sweetener than either brown or white sugar. Apart from the magical powers associated with it, it contains a monosaccharide, more easily digested than sugar, and traces of protein, iron, calcium and B vitamins. You will find that there are many recipes where you can use honey instead of sugar. You can also buy a sugar extracted from fruit (monosaccharide fructose as opposed to sucrose) which is white and fine-grained, and makes an undetectable alternative to castor sugar in cooking.

Other valuable alternatives are the polyunsaturated fats and oils for butter and olive oil. I found a taste for them easy to acquire, as their chief crime is their blandness. Polyunsaturated fats are considered valuable to control blood cholesterol levels. A recent American study showed that men on a diet high in polyunsaturates had nearly one-third fewer coronaries than those on a normal diet; but they also showed an increased *risk* of developing cancer. No causal link has yet been found between cancer and an excess of polyunsaturates, but perhaps it is wise to steer a middle way. I use butter, or a margarine made of sunflower oil or any vegetable oil, such as safflower oil, high in polyunsaturates, indiscriminately. I prefer safflower oil (over 70 per cent linoleic acid) for cooking and salads, and the delicious, nutty-flavoured, but expensive walnut oil (60 per cent) to the more usual olive oil (only 10 per cent) in salad dressings (see also p. 354).

CHAPTER TEN

Cooking with Herbs

THE distinctive and subtle flavours of herbs (technically known as their essential oils) make all the difference between plain, dull food and delicious dishes. I cannot overemphasize their importance if you want to feed a healthy family. Paradoxically there is little nutritive value in herbs—with the outstanding exception of parsley—yet they form a most important part of every cook's vegetable garden. The addition of a bundle of herbs, a clove of garlic and the end of a bottle of red wine will make a boring beef stew into *bœuf à la bourguignonne*; with a chosen handful of fresh herbs you can produce an *omelette fines herbes* in an instant (p. 328). French names apart, you will find that plates are thoroughly emptied and often passed up for more when you have taken the care to season your dishes imaginatively. And this is surely the point for someone seeking a positive satisfaction from the work of cooking.

A *bouquet garni* is the little bundle of herbs—classically a bay leaf, and a sprig or two of parsley and thyme—tied by the stalks so that they can be fished out at the end of the cooking time. There are endless variations on a *bouquet garni*, and rightly so. With a flourishing herb garden you will want to experiment with the addition of herbs such as marjoram, savory, lovage, tarragon, sage, or whatever is available and has an affinity with the dish you are preparing. Make different *bouquets garnis*—and make them up just as you need them—or everything you cook will take on the same universal herb flavour.

A careful choice of herbs will add a fillip to all your cooking. A green salad made only of lettuce leaves, tossed in a French dressing, to which a teaspoon of chopped herbs has been added, is the correct and elegant accompaniment to a rich meat dish.

Here are just a few of the myriad uses for your herbs. A mayon-

naise *fines herbes* is made by chopping a selection of herbs into
home-made mayonnaise (p. 354) to accompany a cold chicken;
or serve piping hot herb buns (p. 359) instead of potatoes with a
winter Sunday joint. Mince up some herbs into your nutritious
home-made liver pâté: you can greatly vary the basic recipe
by the amount and kinds of herbs you incorporate. You can
make delectable herb butters very quickly, by mixing a tablespoon or so of finely chopped herbs with some softened butter
or margarine. Chill it well and put little pats on grilled meats,
just before they come to the table. Chive butter (or sour cream
with chives) is a standard accompaniment to baked potatoes. A
stuffing, too, can be a simple mixture of herbs, brown breadcrumbs
or brown rice with an egg to bind it. Sage and onion is the best
known, but you can also make a tarragon stuffing, a parsley and
thyme one, or experiment with any combination of herbs in your
garden. These stuffings absorb meat juices during cooking and
flavour the dish with their aromatic oils. They are quick to prepare
and they will make an economical cut like shoulder of lamb more
acceptable; they are especially good in a cold chicken on a picnic.

You can make your own tarragon vinegar, and many other herb
vinegars, very quickly and effectively in the summer when supplies
are plentiful. Loosely fill a wide-necked jar with tarragon, basil,
marjoram, or any herb you like—leaves, stalks and all—fill the jar
with (preferably cider) vinegar, put the lid on and leave it to infuse
for a couple of weeks. Strain off the vinegar into a clean bottle, and
push a long decorative stalk of tarragon or whatever into the bottle.

Many recipes call for herbs to be chopped. There are gadgets
you can buy to help you do this, but I have come to the conclusion
that the most successful way to chop most herbs is by hand on a
board, holding the knife blade in two hands and scraping the
chopped herbs into a little heap when they become scattered.
This way they are not mashed beyond flavour and recognition. I
scissor chives straight into the dish.

Drying and freezing herbs

We need herbs all the year round, but like most other growing
plants they are much more available in the summer months. I
greatly prefer them fresh, particularly for salads, and I can find
quite a few fresh ones all the time. In January I had some sage,

rosemary, thyme and lemon thyme, perennial marjoram, winter savory and even some lemon balm and early spears of mint under a sheltered wall. You can pot some herb roots, parsley for example, and keep them on a sunny windowsill or in the greenhouse. Mint and chives are hard to keep flourishing because they die down naturally, but you can freeze these two. Chop or scissor them, blend with a very little water and pack them into ice-trays. When they are frozen solid turn them out and store them as cubes in a plastic bag. Parsley also freezes well.

Other herbs must be dried. For the best results (for potpourri ingredients, too), cut the herbs on a dry sunny summer morning, picking each one just before it is due to flower when the maximum amount of essential oils will be concentrated in the leaves. Tie them in bunches and put them head downwards into ordinary paper bags, tie up the necks and hang the bags in a warm airy place to dry (under 100°F) until you need them. Crumble the brittle leaves between your fingers and use only as much as you need each time. The essential oils are best preserved in the whole leaves. Herb and spice glass jars in a wooden rack are decorative on the kitchen wall, but if they contain herbs ready chopped and exposed to the deteriorating influence of daylight, they will not contribute to your cooking.

If a recipe calls for a particular herb which you don't have, try a different one. One herb will often be an alternative—not a substitute—for another. Above all, experiment. The flavour of a herb is the hardest thing to describe, the easiest to enjoy.

Angelica is chiefly known for its green candied stalk—invaluable along with glacé cherries, as a trifle decoration. You can also put a piece of the fresh stalk with fruit to be stewed; it is said to reduce the tartness a little.

Basil is an important culinary herb. It has a curious almost-nutmeg flavour, and a special affinity for tomatoes, and therefore all dishes that feature tomatoes—like tomato aspic, pizza, tomato salad. Cut some stems and dry them for winter use. You can also make basil vinegar.

Bay leaves are essential to every *bouquet garni* for every soup, stew, or stock in the kitchen. Traditionally a bay leaf decorates the top of a pâté. I always add a leaf to my risotto, others recommend a small one in a rice pudding. Bay leaves dry well.

Bergamot, as 'Oswego Tea', was once a common drink in America, reputed to have been drunk after the Boston Tea Party. Try it with pork dishes.

Borage with its delightful star-shaped blue flowers is perhaps best known as a garnish for Pimms. Try the leaves chopped in salad to add a cucumber flavour, but pick them before they become uncomfortably large and hairy. I like to pick long-flowered stems and use them to decorate salads and cold meats.

Caraway's little spicy seeds are an invaluable flavouring for baking—seed cakes, breads and buns. Some pickles contain caraway seeds, and they are a small but important finishing touch to coleslaw.

Chervil is an alternative to parsley, best used fresh, for it has a delicate flavour. Good in *fines herbes* combinations, chopped in salad dressings and sprinkled over potatoes.

Chives are a hurried cook's delight. With no peeling, no crying and little chopping, they will produce the taste of onions in a fraction of the preparation time. Scissor them on to green salads, tomato salads, potato salads; add them to *fines herbes* mixtures for omelettes and mayonnaise. Make cottage or cream cheese mixtures with your own fresh chives: these will have a lively green colour instead of the limp grey specks you find in the commercial kinds. Scissored chives are a vital garnish for the delicious cold summer soup, vichysoisse (p. 311). They are better eaten fresh, they wilt when they are kept or cooked, and they dry poorly. Freeze them in an ice-tray for winter use.

Coriander seeds are hot and spicy, much used in Roman cookery and an ingredient of curry powder. Crush them in marinades and dressings for mushrooms and meat dishes.

Dill for me is a northern herb, as well as one of my favourites. In Finland old ladies sell great feathery armfuls of it at local markets, and the Finns serve it with all kinds of fish. They have a special dish of raw salmon marinated with dill which is quite incredible. As well as using the foliage in summer, you can save the seed heads and make dill vinegar (about $\frac{1}{4}$ oz or 6 grams of seed to a pint) or your own dill pickles:

Sterilize your jars and put 1 peeled clove of garlic, 6 peppercorns, 1 clove and 3 or 4 sprigs of dill with seeds into the bottom of each. Pick your outdoor cucumbers when they are not more than 3 to 4 inches long, wash them and pack them into the jars. Make a pickle by boiling together one pint of water to two pints of cider vinegar and a generous handful of salt. Let it cool a little and pour into the jars of pickle. This makes strong, sour pickles. If you like them sweeter, add a generous handful of sugar to the vinegar mixture.

Fennel has a strong aniseed flavour. As a herb it is traditionally associated with fish. You can use it in a court bouillon when you are poaching a fish; slip a feathery stalk alongside a fish baking in the oven, or chop the fennel and put it in a white sauce in the manner of a parsley sauce. If you have the chance to grill freshly caught fish out of doors, put some dried fennel stalks into the fire. Fennel dies right down in the winter, so store some of these stalks in a jar.

Horseradish You can make your own horseradish sauce, at once more pungent and less peppery than the bottled kind. Simply grate the root into a little whipped cream. Some people also like the shredded root on its own with both roast beef and smoked trout.

Lemon balm has a delicate lemon fragrance, pleasant to crush between the fingers, but a little pallid for cooking. Chop it into salads and dressings. Disappointing to dry.

Lemon verbena is mainly important for potpourri. Dry a generous amount of these leaves to bring a lemony tang to your own mixture. Traditionally, a leaf is also placed in the bottom of a cake tin.

Lovage is a herb much used by the Romans, but one that I have only just discovered. Its leaves and stalks have a lovely curried-celery taste that make them endlessly useful as a celery-substitute in the summer. I use it frequently in *bouquets garnis* for meat stocks and stews, and in preference to celery in a chicken salad. This is an American dish, to my mind not well-enough known over here, because it is both versatile and delicious: it can either be a fast way of using up a leftover cold chicken, or the planned party-piece at a fork supper. Simply dice cooked chicken and green peppers and a few small lovage stalks into a bowl, add a grated shallot and enough mayonnaise to coat the ingredients. Use the proportions you prefer. Season it well with fresh lemon juice, salt and ground black pepper.

Lovage dries fairly satisfactorily.

Marjoram is the British version of oregano, which lends its distinctive taste to the garnish on pizzas, marinaded kebabs, and on the vodka-and-bouillon cocktail called a Bullshot. Marjoram is also excellent chopped on salads, in omelettes, *bouquets garnis* and as marjoram vinegar. I grow the perennial variety because it is available all the year round.

Mint has associations at once with English Sunday lunch and the wilder shores of Middle Eastern cooking. Mint sauce for roast lamb is made by chopping a good handful of leaves, mixing them with a teaspoon or so of sugar or honey and then adding just enough vinegar to make a liquid. A sprig of mint may also be dropped into the cooking water for peas and new potatoes, and you can sprinkle the cooked potatoes with chopped mint (or better still a mixture of mint, parsley and chives) just before you serve them. Mint is an essential for a Mint Julep and other summery drinks—add a chopped handful along with the tea-leaves to your teapot on a hot afternoon. Mint freezes well in ice-trays, but it loses its lovely brilliant green colour.

Eau de Cologne Mint and Pennyroyal, which is also a kind of mint, are both useful in potpourri, but too scented to be much use in cooking.

Parsley is the only herb that is immensely nutritious, being rich in calcium and in vitamins A and C. Yet traditionally parsley is a decorative herb, used to surround plates of cold meats and sandwiches, or chopped and scattered on top of dishes just before they come to the table. The more of the decorations you can eat the better. Parsley sauce (a white sauce with lots of chopped parsley stirred in at the last moment (p. 356)) goes well with quickly cooked broad beans, especially if they have been left by mistake in the garden until they are rather large and leathery. Try deep-frying sprigs of curly parsley and serving them as a vegetable. You can also add it to almost every salad and *bouquet garni*. More unusual is a delicious prawn and mushroom salad in which parsley is an essential ingredient (p. 313).

The cool green taste of fresh parsley combines well with lemon juice, to make an interesting sorbet. In *La Belle Epoque* a sorbet was often served between courses, to rest the stomach before a renewed attack on its digestive capacity. These days we eat less, but a sorbet or water ice is still welcome, particularly to people who prefer not to finish with an oversweet dessert (p. 338).

Pelargonium (scented geranium leaves). I use Pheasant's Foot (*Pelargonium denticulatum*), but any will add a curious old-fashioned sweet savour to milk puddings like egg custard and rice puddings. Elizabeth David finds they have an affinity with blackberries in jellies and water ices. Keep a pot in the greenhouse or on a windowsill for winter use.

Rosemary is a Mediterranean herb. I remember in Sainte Maxime once being privately horrified to see a large sprig of rosemary go into the court bouillon to poach some *langoustines*. Of course they were delicious. Even so, in Britain the only use I have for rosemary is in conjunction with garlic to cook the classic *gigot d'agneau*. The leaves of rosemary are spiky and indestructible, so I strain them out before serving the meat juices as gravy. You can pick rosemary fresh all the year round.

Sage, to my mind, is a maligned herb. I like to use it fresh from the garden, when it has little of the bitterness associated with the dried leaves. It has a special affinity with liver and liver pâté, pork, and stuffing for poultry, where it counteracts the greasiness of duck or goose. I use it when I need a fairly strong *bouqet garni*—in meat stocks or stews, for example.

Savory is a powerfully flavoured herb; a sprig or two goes well in a *bouquet garni*, a *fines herbes* mixture or a herb-flavoured salad dressing, but it should be used discreetly. Traditionally it is associated with broad beans. I grow the perennial kind because it is available most of the year.

Tarragon is an important pot herb. All cooks specify the true French tarragon, with its distinctive flavour that reminds me of new cotton fabric. Tarragon goes with chicken—*poulet à l'estragon* can be a variety of chicken dishes, incorporating tarragon in the cooking, the sauce or the stuffing. You can make delicious tarragon vinegar and tarragon butter. It is an ingredient of *fines herbes* for an omelette and it dries well for the winter.

Thyme is an essential of a classic *bouquet garni*. There are many kinds of thyme, but I find myself always returning to the delicate-scented Lemon Thyme, for stuffings, in stews and stocks, minced-meat dishes like Shepherd's Pie, and liver pâtés. The lemon overtones help to counteract any greasiness in these dishes. Thyme dries well.

The Recipes

'Food for pleasure and not just nourishment, is best cooked in one's own kitchen and eaten with the feet under one's own table. Still, in good restaurants there are things unthought of at home as being too much time and trouble, or simply needing more skill and imagination than one possesses.' Like Nicolas Freeling, crime-writer, gourmet and restaurateur, I feel that restaurants do some things better, and two of them are Chinese and Indian food. So the recipes that follow are generally in the main line of European cookery, offshoots, however distant, from the classic French stem. The emphasis in the recipes is always on cooking to retain the maximum nutritional value; healthy eating and delicious eating are the same thing. They are an arbitrary and personal selection, each one pegged to a particular fruit or vegetable. There is an additional chapter at the end for flexible dishes that you can make with a handful of almost any vegetables, together with recipes for dressings, sauces, breads, pastries, muesli and yoghurt.

All the dishes are intended for the enjoyment of produce freshly picked, and most of them are simple enough for the cook to have a life of her own outside the kitchen. The detailed recipes are calculated for four greedy people. Since we shall soon be changing over to metric measurements, these equivalents are given in the brackets. The exact metric conversions of 28·35 grams to an ounce, 567 ml to a pint, are extremely difficult to work out, so I have rounded the conversion down to 25 grams to an ounce, 500 ml to a pint, and so forth. Therefore, measure your ingredients in pints and pounds, or in litres and grams, don't skip from one to the other, or the amounts will not be in the correct proportion.

The oven temperatures I give are as accurate as possible, but must be considered as only approximate to your oven. Everyone's oven has it idiosyncrasies, and you are the best person to know yours. Your own good sense, and sense of taste and smell, will tell you more about how well cooked your dishes are than any amount of charts.

These recipes are intended for a beginner cook to follow with confidence, always allowing that however hard one tries to include every detail, even the most precise recipes can have 'a hidden side, like the moon'.

Vegetables

Artichokes

Globe Artichokes A whole large artichoke per person makes
a dinner-party first course. You just trim the stem (Cordon Bleu
cooks also trim the tops of the pointed outer leaves, presumably
to make the artichokes look neater) and cook them covered, in
boiling salted water with a squeeze of lemon juice or a teaspoonful
of vinegar, for 20 to 25 minutes. Lift an artichoke up by a leaf,
and if the leaf pulls out and the artichoke falls back into the water,
it is cooked. Leave them upside down for 5 to 10 minutes for all
the water to drain out of the leaves. Serve them hot with melted
butter or Hollandaise sauce (p. 356) or cold with vinaigrette.
You can also eat the tiny, sideshoot artichokes, either raw as do
the Italians, boiled as above, or preserved raw in oil. In the unlikely event of there being any left over, the hearts, in a French
dressing, are delicious as a salad.

Jerusalem artichokes Jerusalem artichokes do not taste the
same as their more aristocratic namesakes; they are a strongly
flavoured, I think delicious, and useful root vegetable in their own
right, both cooked and grated raw in salads. You can peel them
with a potato peeler (they are fiddly) and serve them like new or
mashed potatoes, or drop them into a stew, or make them into a
subtle, velvet-smooth, very *haute cuisine*, soup:

Artichoke Soup
1 oz (25 g) butter or margarine   1 medium onion
½ lb (200 g) artichokes (peeled weight)
½ pint (250 ml) chicken stock   ½ pint (250 ml) milk
salt and pepper

Peel and chop the onion and cook it gently in the butter until it is
soft, add the chopped artichokes, and continue to cook for a

minute or two. Add the stock, the milk and the seasonings, and simmer, covered, for 10 to 15 minutes, or until the artichokes are tender. Liquidize or sieve, reheat if necessary, and serve with croûtons.

Asparagus

In my view there are only two ways to eat asparagus: plain boiled hot or plain boiled cold. Wash the stems carefully (it spoils everything if the asparagus is at all gritty) and tie them in bundles with all the tips facing in the same direction. Stand these in a tall pan in a little boiling salted water and put the lid on, so that the tips are cooked by steam, not damaged by bubbling water (or steam them if they will fit into your steamer), for 15 to 20 minutes, until a fork will pierce the stems. Drain the asparagus, untie the bundles and serve with a lot of melted butter and a lot of table napkins. (Some people like asparagus with Hollandaise sauce, p. 356, but I think it's a waste of time.) If there are any left over, which there won't be, serve them cold with a vinaigrette sauce—Elizabeth David suggests an oil and lemon, not vinegar, one. If there aren't enough to go round, eat them yourself when no one is looking.

If you feel, altruistically, that you want your supply to stretch a little, you can roll the cooked spears in thin slices of buttered brown bread, or use them in a delicious asparagus quiche (p. 329).

The only asparagus that needs any other kind of cooking is the tiny, bitter, wild kind that grows in the spring in the south of Spain: it is quite unforgettable, but unfortunately not to be found in an English garden. It is served as a first course baked in the bottom of a cocotte dish with an egg broken over it.

Aubergines

Aubergines contain bitter juices, so before you start on a recipe, slice or dice them and sprinkle them with salt. Leave them to drain for half an hour or so in the refrigerator, then rinse them quickly under a cold tap and dry them in a teatowel. Unlike most other vegetables, they are perfectly horrible to eat raw.

You need aubergines for Ratatouille (p. 306) and for the Greek version of Shepherd's Pie, Moussaka, which makes an interesting variant for Sunday's leftovers:

Moussaka

1 large onion, chopped	1 clove garlic, sliced
Cooking oil	
1 lb (400 g) cooked, minced lamb	
½ lb (200 g) mushrooms, sliced	
4 large tomatoes—preferably Marmande—peeled and chopped	
salt and pepper	Tomato purée
¼ pint (125 ml) meat or vegetable stock	
4 aubergines, sliced lengthways, salted and rinsed	
flour	grated Parmesan cheese
2 eggs	¼ pint (125 ml) yoghurt (see p. 356)

Sauté the onion and garlic in cooking oil until soft, add the lamb and the mushrooms, cook for a minute or two, then add the tomatoes, seasonings, a squeeze of tomato purée and the stock, and cook gently. Flour and fry the aubergine slices in hot oil until they are crisp, and dry them on a bed of kitchen paper. Line a baking dish with the slices, add a layer of mince mixture, a layer of aubergines, and so on, ending with aubergines. Sprinkle the top with grated cheese. Beat the eggs with two tablespoons of flour and then beat in the yoghurt. Pour this sauce over the dish and bake in a fairly hot oven (410°F, Mark 6) until the top has browned.

Beans

Broad beans   Most gardeners pick out the delicate bunched leaf tops of their broad beans to discourage the ubiquitous black fly, and these pickings make delicious bean-flavoured greens cooked very quickly in a little boiling salted water. You can also cook the pods, beans and all, when they are a couple of inches long.

When the beans themselves are ripe, harvest them small, and cook them the same way. (I sometimes find that at the beginning of the season there are not enough of any one vegetable to go round, so I make a dish of mixed spring vegetables—broad beans, peas and tiny pale carrots—cooked separately but served together. They are particularly appropriate heaped into the centre of a crown roast of lamb.)

If your beans have become a little leathery with age, cook them and serve in a hot parsley sauce (p. 356), or cool and turn them in a sauce made of yoghurt (p. 356), a generous handful of chopped parsley and plenty of salt and pepper, for an unusual salad.

Runner beans, French beans (haricot verts) and Haricot beans (haricot blancs) Whatever the summer, your runner bean plants will reliably produce enough to eat fresh from early August until the first frost, to fill the freezer for winter Sunday lunches, and still more besides to give away. The dwarf and climbing pencil-podded French beans are more aristocratic, but less prolific. Pick both kinds when they are young and tender—there is no pleasure in a bean that has become tough, stringy and full of parchment—and I have always found that continuous and almost brutal picking increases the crop. To prepare your beans, you top and tail them, pulling off any attached strings at the same time. Older beans need to have their side strings pared off with a knife.

I prefer the English scarlet runners very simply boiled to accompany traditional English dishes, like roast meat. The French serve tiny French beans that have been par-cooked (dropped into boiling water for a very few minutes) and then finished off in the pan juices of the joint, so that they absorb some of the meat flavours.

Both kinds of bean also make excellent salads and may be parcooked first. They can be served along with other *crudités* (raw, young vegetables, see p. 331) such as peas, radishes or tiny carrots, each in a separate little bowl, with no dressing at all. They are an ingredient of *Salade Niçoise*. They are particularly good tossed in a French dressing along with a very little grated onion and a generous handful of chopped walnuts.

Haricot beans, from the variety *Comtesse de Chambord*, are the small white kidney-shaped flageolet beans. When they are really fresh, you can simmer them until tender and then turn them in a French dressing with chopped parsley and grated onion, for a delicious salad. But their prime purpose is to provide the identifying ingredient in a *cassoulet*, a rich stew of pork, mutton, sausage and sometimes goose or duck, that originates from around Toulouse. It is a marvellously filling dish, one that can be conjured out of the oven on your return from some bleak expedition, because it must be made well ahead, and may be done in stages. It will restore tempers and inspire compliments on your cooking. I hesitate to give a recipe for this, because there are so many variants, depending on the ingredients available beside the necessary beans. If you want to do a cassoulet in style, starting with your own home-made sausages, undertake the one in *Mastering the Art of French Cooking* by Simone Beck and Julia Child. Here is a simpler one, to use as a basis for your own improvements:

Cassoulet

1 lb (400 g) white haricot beans
3 pints (1½ litres) water   salt
1 clove garlic
2 large onions, stuck with 6 cloves
2 or 3 carrots   *bouquet garni*
4 oz (100 g) salt pork, diced   cooking oil
chopped shallots
A combination of raw lean pork, lamb cut into cubes, garlic sausage—cooked duck or, correctly, preserved goose (*confit d'oie*) if you can get it—about 1 lb (400 g) altogether, but kept separate (see method)
chopped stalk of two celery
a generous squeeze tomato purée
seasonings
dry white wine (¼ bottle), or the leftover heel of a bottle will do

Bring the beans to the boil in the salted water, take them off the heat and let them soak for an hour. Add the garlic, carrots, onions and cloves, bouquet of herbs and salt pork, and simmer for an hour. Skim any scum from the surface.

Heat the cooking oil in a separate pan and sauté the chopped shallots until softened, add the cubed lamb and pork and the celery, and fry gently until cooked on all sides. Tip into the bean pot, with seasonings, tomato purée, chopped garlic sausage and any wine. Continue cooking until the beans are almost tender, add cooked duck or *confit d'oie*, put everything in a large casserole (earthenware if possible) and bake in a moderate oven for a further half-hour.

Beetroot

The leaves of beetroot are tremendously rich in vitamin A, with useful amounts of vitamins B and C as well. They make an acceptable green vegetable that tastes like a milder version of spinach if they are cooked in the same ways (including the salad recipe with bacon crumbs on page 323) using only the tender inside leaves.

Beetroot itself is a good accompaniment to a mixed salad, both grated and raw, or cooked and sliced in a vinegary dressing. For the winter when lettuces are scarce, there is a recipe for Celery, Beetroot and Apple Salad on page 305. Whenever you cook your beetroot, wash and trim them (not too close or they will 'bleed') and then bake them in a low oven for a couple of hours (according to size) wrapped in foil. They are cooked when they 'give' slightly when pressed. The skins will rub off, and the beets will have a sweet, faintly earthy flavour which would be dissolved out into the water if they were boiled.

Beetroot are the basis of every variation of the famous and delicious Borscht—*The Joy of Cooking* (by I. S. Rombauer and M. R. Becker) says that there are as many versions of this soup as there are Russians. I spent a recent summer looking for a bowl of Borscht through Leningrad and Finland with absolutely no success, so I came home and tested some of the many recipes I found. I make no apology for giving two of them here: they are so totally different—one a sophisticated summer dinner-party soup, the other a filling winter lunch by itself. Another cookery writer says: 'The choicest varieties of the vast borscht family require forty-eight hours of preparation by an army of scullery wenches.' Happily, neither of these is so demanding.

Borscht I (Summer)   ½ lb (200 g) cooked beetroot
   juice of 2 lemons   1 pint (500 ml) good beef stock
   4 dessertspoons yoghurt   salt and pepper
    or sour cream

Liquidize or sieve the beetroot with the beef stock, add the lemon juice until the liquid has a good sharp taste, season it and chill. (If you have liquidized your soup and used home-made beef stock that jells in the refrigerator, chill the soup in the blender goblet and whizz it once more just before serving.) Place a dessertspoon of yoghurt or sour cream in each soup bowl and ladle on the Borscht. Sprinkle on a little chopped dill if you like.

Borscht II (Winter)   3 large carrots
  1 large onion   2 large beetroots
  1 pint (500 ml) good beef stock
  2 or 3 cabbage leaves   4 tomatoes, skinned
  margarine, butter, salt and pepper
  4 dessertspoons sour cream for serving

Peel the onions and beetroots, scrub the carrots. Chop them all
very finely and simmer them in the beef stock until almost tender
(about 15 minutes). Add a knob of butter, the cabbage leaves
very finely shredded, the tomatoes quartered, salt and pepper.
Continue to simmer the soup until the cabbage and tomatoes are
cooked. Serve with a dessertspoon of sour cream for each bowl.

Broccoli and Calabrese

Cut your broccoli while the heads are still firm and tight, not
breaking into flower. Trim off any woody-looking ends, tie the
stems into helping-sized bundles, and steam the broccoli until the
stem can be pierced with a fork. Untie the bundles, arrange them
neatly on warmed plates, and serve them as a first course with a
Hollandaise sauce (p. 356). You may also serve them as an accompanying vegetable, with or without the Hollandaise. Broccoli is
also good to eat raw as a salad: pick small tender sprigs and par-
cook them (3 minutes is enough), or let them marinade in a
French dressing before you serve them. Broccoli freezes well; I
freeze mine tied in bundles, so that I can cook it with the minimum of trouble.
  If you have any left-over broccoli, try the following soup, either
hot or chilled:

Cream of Broccoli Soup   1 large onion, chopped
  1 carrot, chopped
  $\frac{3}{4}$ pint (375 ml) chicken stock   sprig of lovage
  1 clove garlic
  $\frac{1}{4}-\frac{1}{2}$ lb (100–200 g) cooked broccoli
  salt and pepper
  $\frac{1}{4}$ pint (125 ml) thin cream, or top of the milk with tablespoon
    dried skim milk beaten in
  4 teaspoons yoghurt

Simmer the raw vegetables in the chicken stock until they are tender. Turn them into the blender, add broccoli, garlic, lovage, seasonings and cream. Blend thoroughly, and either return them to the pan to warm through or chill them and serve with a dollop of yoghurt in the centre of each soup bowl. If it sets too thick on chilling, add a little more top of the milk or cold chicken stock.

Calabrese   This is almost indistinguishable from broccoli—its colour is perhaps a paler green and its flower-heads a little more tightly bunched. Its main advantage is that it starts the season early, from September to November, by which time your early broccoli should be ready. Treat it exactly like broccoli.

Brussels sprouts

Brussels sprouts, like peas, are vegetables we enjoy for their shape as much as their taste. So to my mind it is meaningless to make them into soups or purées or anything else that destroys their delicious, miniature-cabbage appearance.

The season for Brussels sprouts begins with the first frost, and I find them addictive. ('I must go home and eat some sprouts,' I once announced towards the end of a long summer holiday, suddenly needing what the whole of Spain could not provide.) I like them fast-cooked and turned in a little melted butter, or served with little peeled and boiled chestnuts, with the Christmas turkey. Sprouts freeze well, but we never have enough left over.

Cabbage

Spring cabbage, savoy, etc   If you actively dislike cabbage, or are just bored by it, try it once more, cooked very briefly indeed. If it is a large one, slice it fairly thinly; if it is a small light spring cabbage, you can simply quarter it and cook each section on the stem. Plunge the cabbage into a few inches of boiling slightly salted water and cook it until it is barely wilted (the stem or leaf rib will take on a transparent look when it is cooked). Drain it (save the liquid), melt a little butter or margarine in the pan, turn the cabbage back in and season it with a twist of the peppermill. Serve it at once. The cabbage will have a springy texture and a bright green colour; it will taste delicious and it will be a home-

cooked speciality. No restaurant I know takes the trouble to serve
cabbage so freshly cooked.

You can fry cabbage, like the Chinese. By itself this recipe will
accompany many dishes, or you can make it into a self-sufficient
supper by serving it with long thin strips of fried beef or pork,
on a bed of fried rice.

Chinese Fried Cabbage
    1 medium-sized firm white cabbage
    oil for frying   2 teaspoons soy sauce
    salt, pepper and sugar

Slice the cabbage into thin strips, wash and drain it if necessary.
Heat some oil in a frying pan, toss in a handful of cabbage, keep
turning it to stop it burning, and add more oil circumspectly, as
the cabbage soaks it up. Keep adding more cabbage as the previous
lot cooks down, until it is all done. Season with sugar, salt and
pepper and soy sauce and serve as fast as you can.

You can stuff cabbage leaves with the mixture for marrows
(p. 312). Roll them up, secure with toothpicks and bake in a
casserole with some beef stock poured over them.

Coleslaw is a basic, cheap daily salad when you have not the
ingredients for a green salad in your winter garden and you find
lettuces expensive as well as tasteless to buy. I make fresh coleslaw
almost every lunchtime in winter, and find we never become tired
of it.

Coleslaw
    1 medium-sized firm white savoy cabbage
    1 tablespoon cider vinegar   2 tablespoons mayonnaise
    1 tablespoon yoghurt   seasonings
    caraway seeds
    green peppers, celery, carrots, if you please

Shred or slice the cabbage as thinly as possible into a bowl. Add
vinegar, mayonnaise, yoghurt, a sprinkling of caraway seeds and a
generous seasoning of salt, pepper, Worcester sauce, and sugar or
honey. Turn it all together and serve at once. You can vary your

basic coleslaw by adding extra raw chopped vegetables like celery, green peppers or grated carrot.

Treat Pe-Tsai, Chinese cabbage, like ordinary cabbage. You can also boil the thick ribs and serve them with melted butter as a first course.

Red Cabbage This is so different from green cabbage that it deserves a section to itself. You can shred it into salads (try a calico coleslaw, with a mixture of red and white), but its leaves are thicker than ordinary cabbage, and its stem tougher, so it lends itself more to casserole cooking. A sweet and sour cabbage goes well with goose, with spare ribs or pork chops, to make a cheering winter dish.

Sweet and Sour Red Cabbage 1 medium onion
  2 cooking apples   2 tablespoons of brown sugar
  half a medium-sized red cabbage
  vinegar   oil, salt and pepper

Use a casserole that will also go on top of the stove, if you have one. Chop the onion and sauté it until transparent in the oil, add the peeled and chopped apples. When it is softened, add the brown sugar and stir till the apple and the onion are coated in it. Add the shredded red cabbage and stir to coat it in oil. Cook it for a moment or two, then add the vinegar, seasoning, and a little water. Put the lid on the casserole and cook it in a slow oven (310°F, Mark 2) for an hour or until the cabbage is cooked. This dish is even better if it is cooled and reheated before serving.

Calabrese see Broccoli

Cardoons see Celery

Carrots

Carrots, in their various stages, are a vegetable for all seasons. The tiny pale new ones mix with the first broad beans and peas to make a dish of mixed spring vegetables. The old dark woody ones will add their interesting sweet flavour to every winter stew, stock, soup and plate of mixed diced vegetables.

The cellulose in raw carrots makes their rich supply of carotene (provitamin A) largely unavailable to us. Cooking, or grating if you want to serve them raw, will break this down, and of course thorough chewing helps. A little heap of freshly grated raw carrot in a lemony French dressing is a delicious component of any hors-d'œuvre. The nutrients lie just below the skin of carrots, so you should scrub them, whenever possible, rather than peel them. The small new carrots are best cooked whole, in a very little boiling salted water. For grand occasions you can finish them in a sugar and butter mixture—an ounce (25 grams) of each to the pound—with the lid off for a few minutes, to make a delicious glaze. The old ones take a long time to cook, so are best diced first. Like most root vegetables, carrots also make a good winter soup, this one rather more delicately flavoured than some of the others. The French call it Potage Crécy, because their best carrots are grown around there. Perhaps the Black Prince drank it.

Carrot Soup   1 medium onion
  1 oz (25 g) butter or margarine 1 large potato
  ½ lb (200 g) carrots
  1 pint (500 ml) vegetable cooking water or chicken stock
  seasonings

Peel and chop the onion and cook it until it is transparent. Peel and chop the potato and add it to the onion. Scrub and grate the carrots and add them to the pan: cook them for 5 minutes or so, until they too start to soften. Add the stock and seasonings, and simmer, covered, for 15 to 20 minutes or until the potato pieces and carrot shreds are soft. Liquidize or sieve, reheat if necessary, and serve sprinkled with chopped parsley.

Cauliflower

Raw cauliflower makes an unusual, and relatively unfattening, cocktail-party snack: gently break the white head up into tiny florets, pile these on to a big dish with a bowl of spicy mayonnaise in the centre (p. 355). If you like to expand on this idea, add tiny cherry tomatoes, leaving their calyxes to pick them up by, thin strips of green pepper, red pepper, scrubbed radishes with neatly trimmed stems, celery, and carrots cut into matchsticks (see p. 331

for more about these crudités). Serve this hors-d'œuvre either with pre-dinner drinks, or as a first course.

Another unusual hors-d'œuvre, *Caulifleur*, is made by breaking the white head into small florets and then cooking them until they are just *al dente*, in a little salted water. In a bowl you assemble a layer of florets (well seasoned with salt and pepper or the dish becomes too bland), a coating of home-made mayonnaise (p. 354), another layer of cauliflower, another of mayonnaise, finally sprinkling a generous handful of cooked shrimps over and round the top mayonnaise layer.

More traditionally cauliflower is cooked and served as a vegetable or made into cauliflower cheese, an excellent, informal supper dish. To preserve as many nutrients as possible, break the head into florets and cook the cauliflower in the milk you later use to make the cheese sauce (p. 356) and add a couple of tablespoons of skim milk powder to the mixture for some extra calcium and protein.

Celeriac

For a crunchy winter salad, scrub the celeriac roots and peel off the fibrous skin, and then cut them into matchsticks. They can be a salad on their own with a dressing, or make part of a combination salad.

Whole celeriac takes as long as beetroot to cook, so dice yours fairly finely and it should be cooked in about half an hour. It is good with melted butter, and in a cheese sauce, and in a celeriac soup, also called

Potage Savoyarde
½ lb (200 g) celeriac, peeled and diced
1 medium onion   1 large potato
2–3 leeks
1 oz (25 g) butter or margarine
salt and pepper   ½ pint (250 ml) chicken stock
½ pint (250 ml) milk

Peel and dice all the vegetables very finely. Put them in a pan with the butter and stir until they turn transparent. Add the stock, milk and seasonings, and simmer, covered, until all the vegetables are soft. Liquidize or sieve, reheat if necessary and serve.

Celery and Cardoons

Celery To me, celery is important for its crunch, so braised celery, limp and unhappy, seems as pointless as cooked lettuce. The only exception to this is the addition of a handful of coarsely diced celery to any stuffing of poultry and game.

There are lots of delicious and unusual ways of serving raw celery (as well as the simplest of all, carefully scrubbed, in a tall jug, with cheese) and it is an important and necessary salad vegetable during the winter.

Waldorf Salad (p. 353) is one way and another is:

Celery and Beetroot Salad   a head of celery—inside stalks
  3 medium-sized cooked beetroots
  3 eating apples   oil, vinegar, seasonings

Dice all the vegetables and fruit and mix them together with the dressing ingredients (see p. 354) for proportions. Serve the salad before the apple has a chance to become soggy.

You can also fill the curved stalks with any cheese mixture—the cream cheese one on page 308 is good, or mashed-up blue cheese —and slice them up carefully, to serve at cocktail parties.

The flavour of celery is a classic addition to meat dishes, so save the stringy outside stalks and the leaves for flavouring soups, stocks and stews. Save the seeds from your home-grown plants to use in breads, pickles and chutneys, or grind them up with sea salt to make your own celery salt.

Cardoons have a crisp, unusual flavour that makes them an alternative rather than a substitute for celery. You can use them in the same ways.

Chard

Chard, the blanched stalks of globe artichoke plants, are cooked and served like asparagus—although their flavour is not so special. Tie the stalks in bundles and cook them gently until they can be pierced with a fork. Serve them with melted butter.

Chicory

For me, chicory is primarily a salad vegetable. You can wash and slice the heads and serve them in a French dressing or mayonnaise. If you like it cooked, it is refreshing with game, and easy to bake at the same time. Put the clean, whole chicory heads in an oven-proof dish with a little water, a chopped onion if you like, and some seasonings. Cover with a lid or with foil and cook in a medium oven (380°F, Mk 5) for about 30 minutes or until the heads are soft, not soggy. You can serve the liquid with the chicory.

Corn Salad

Corn Salad or Lamb's Lettuce, is a green, leafy vegetable that will provide a winter salad crop if it is sown towards the end of August. Treat it like lettuce.

Courgettes

If you pick courgettes when they are little bigger than a fat cigar, the skins are tender and should not be peeled. Slice the courgettes into rings and steam them if you like their delicate flavour by itself. You can also sauté them in plenty of oil, salt and garlic to make a delicious vegetable accompaniment to any summer meat dish—fried chicken, grilled cutlets, what you will.

You can expand your sautéed courgettes into the delicious and unusual Provençal dish of ratatouille, a summer vegetable stew that is equally good hot or cold. Its taste benefits from being made with fresh garden produce.

Ratatouille

a clove of garlic   1 large onion
1 large green pepper, or 2 small ones
an aubergine, diced   about 6 courgettes
about 6 tomatoes, skinned and chopped
a squeeze of tomato purée, salt and pepper
Cooking oil or olive oil (do not use any fat or this will congeal and thoroughly spoil the dish when it is cold)

This dish is good made in an earthenware pan if you have one. Peel and chop the onion and garlic and melt them in the oil until they are transparent. (Do not let them, or anything else in this dish, brown.) Add the chopped peppers, then the aubergine, then the diced courgettes and finally the tomatoes. If the dish shows signs of sticking, add more oil, but by the time the tomatoes are put in the cooking should have changed from sautéing to stewing. Season the dish, stir in the tomato purée, cover it and allow it to stew very gently until all the vegetables have coalesced into a delicious and colourful mass.

Cucumbers

It is a great pity that cucumbers cannot be frozen in any form. Instead we must use them as they grow in as many various ways as possible. The Glasshouse Crops Research Institute has recently concluded that the taste of a cucumber lies largely in its skin. Therefore serve them unpeeled as much as possible—except, of course, those outdoor varieties with bitter or prickly skins. (I can find no nutritional substantiation for the paradoxical theories that cucumber is indigestible if you peel it, and indigestible if you don't peel it. Both folklores abound.)

Perhaps because of their legendary coolness, cucumbers play an important part in Eastern cookery. This salad is intended to cool off a hot curry, but it is good with anything on a hot day.

Cucumber and Yoghurt Salad Grate a whole greenhouse cucumber or two (smaller) peeled garden ones fairly coarsely, straight into a dish. Add a good handful of chopped mint and a crushed clove of garlic, salt and plenty of freshly ground pepper, and mix in about $\frac{1}{4}$ pint (125 ml) of plain yoghurt. Serve at once.

This same recipe can be expanded into an equally delicious and cooling soup for a summer's lunch.

Cucumber Soup Cut the cucumber (or two garden ones) lengthwise and remove the seeds with a spoon. Grate it fairly coarsely into a deep bowl. Stir in chopped (a teaspoon per person) mint, a dessertspoon each of cider vinegar and salad oil, salt, pepper and about $\frac{3}{4}$ pint (375 ml) of plain yoghurt (see p. 357), with a little milk, according to the yoghurt's thickness, to make a soup consistency. This soup has a slightly chewy texture, owing to the grated scraps of cucumber, and this adds to its interest. If you liquidize or sieve the cucumber, I think it becomes too bland.

You can also stuff your cucumbers, either for a first course, for part of an hors-d'œuvre, or for canapés at a cocktail party. Cut the cucumbers in half lengthwise and scoop out the seeds. Slice them into sections—very small ones if you are making canapés—and fill them with a mixture of cream cheese or sieved cottage cheese, and chopped anchovies, chopped chives and dill, mixed with a dash of Worcester sauce and plenty of salt and pepper.

Endive (see Lettuce)

Fennel

Florence fennel is a root vegetable that looks like plaited celery, and shares with its herbal relative a clean, aniseed flavour. Fennel is a valuable crisp salad vegetable in the early spring when lettuces are limp and expensive, it is good sliced and served either by itself or as part of a mixed salad with a French dressing. You can also try it chopped, quickly cooked in water and served in a cheese sauce.

It also makes a delicately flavoured and unusual soup—follow the method for artichoke soup (p. 293).

Garlic

'Now there is no cooking except with garlic—but in the hands of a bad cook it is poisonous. It must be used with extreme care. The most reckless are the English: once they take to cooking with garlic they use it so freely it's impossible even for an Italian to eat it,' growls Ludwig Bemelmans. Perhaps because it has been too much used in the past, garlic has become the focus of objection for people who usually have never tasted it. The effect of a little garlic in dishes like stews, soups and risottos will be to intensify the flavours of the other ingredients: when you have cooked dishes such as these with garlic you will find them wishy-washy without it. You may vary the intensity of your garlic according to your taste or mood, by the way you use it. It will be strongest squeezed through a garlic press, less strong crushed with the flat of a knife and mixed with a little salt, barely present if you slice it very thinly. If you think you do not like it, use it this way first.

Rub a clove of garlic round the inside of your salad bowl (preferably a wooden one) if you like no more than a hint in your salads. If you like a lot more than a hint, try a Caesar salad (p. 312). Slice a clove or two and slip them into slits in the skin of your leg of lamb, and roast it with a sprig of rosemary for *gigot d'agneau*. If you enjoy garlic, explore some of the Provençal recipes which lean heavily on garlic—bouillabaisse, the rich fish stew, *aigo bouido*, garlic soup, or best of all *aioli*, crushed-garlic mayonnaise (p. 355) which you can serve with a selection of your raw or cooked summer vegetables—French beans, artichokes, potatoes, beetroot, or what you have freshest in the garden.

For a party, serve garlic bread made with a French loaf, hot and succulent with garlic and butter. You can prepare it the day before, which is a great advantage when organizing food in quantity.

Garlic Bread   Calculate that a long French loaf will feed about four people. Each loaf will need 2 to 3 cloves of garlic and about 3 oz (75 g) of butter or margarine. Cut the loaves in slices that stop just before the crust, so that they remain in one piece. Crush or pound the garlic and mix it into the softened butter. Insert a generous blob into each slit, sprinkle some salt on the top, wrap each loaf securely in foil and refrigerate them until they are needed. Bake them in a hot oven (410°F, Mark 6) for 20 minutes or until they are crisp-crusted, with the garlic butter melted and absorbed inside.

Kohlrabi

You can eat the green tops of kohlrabi, quickly cooked in boiling salted water, like cabbage. The root looks like a green turnip but it has a subtler, nutty flavour of its own and a useful amount of calcium. Wash, peel and chop them and cook them in boiling salted water until tender. You can also grate the peeled root or cut it into matchsticks to make a winter salad, and serve it with mayonnaise or French dressing. The matchsticks are good mixed with matchsticks of dill-pickled cucumbers with rice salad.

A good kohlrabi winter soup is made in the same way as Jerusalem artichoke soup on p. 293.

Leeks

Unless you are entering one of those largest-leek contests, leeks are better eaten when they are fairly small. Dig them out carefully and leave the muddy outer skin and roots on your compost heap. The leeks will still need to be washed cary carefully, as they seem to grow round the soil, trapping it between their skin layers. If you do not need them whole, slice them longitudinally to check that there is no grit left inside. Dry and refrigerate them until needed or else the outer skin will go dry and the inner ones limp, with lying about.

You can serve leeks plain, particularly hot with a roast joint of meat, or cold as a first course with a vinaigrette sauce. Boil or steam them gently until they can be pierced with a fork and then leave them to drain in a colander placed over a bowl for a few minutes; then turn or shake them to release more liquid, for the layers of skin will also trap a lot of water. This will also spoil the consistency of a cheese sauce when you are serving them *au gratin*. Leeks *au gratin* can be expanded into a main course as sausage and leek pie if you pour cheese sauce over cooked leeks and cooked sausages arranged in an open pastry case, and bake it till it is lightly browned. It is good, but involves four different cooking processes, so I consider it only if I have one or more of the items already prepared.

But to me leeks have a far more important role as one of the really important flavourings for meat dishes: any stew is improved by the addition of a few leeks; they improve its consistency as they disintegrate, as well as its flavour. The classic *bœuf à la bourguignonne* is not, in my view, complete without a hint of leeks in its rich savour. Yet it is paradoxically in the summer time, when leeks are all but out of season, that they are needed most of all. The smooth, delicious iced potato and leek soup, Vichyssoise, is a wonderful early summer dish, easy to make and extremely effective to serve, but totally dependent on a supply of leeks. Either cook and freeze your almost-completed vichyssoise at a time when leeks are available, or leave a cramped-up row of them in the garden to harvest in late May. If they are going to seed and have a hard woody stem in the centre, use only the outside layers of skin, and strain everything carefully because although the flavour is good these are very thready.

Vichyssoise
3 potatoes, medium size
4 or 5 leeks
1 pint (500 ml) good chicken stock
2 oz (50 g) butter
¾ pint (375 ml) single cream, a little milk
a handful of chives   salt and pepper

Melt the butter in a saucepan but do not let it brown. Add the peeled, diced potatoes and shortly afterwards the washed and sliced leeks. Stir them attentively until they are transparent, but on no account let them brown. Pour in the hot chicken stock, taste the mixture, season it, and simmer until the vegetables are cooked. Liquidize the soup and sieve it to be on the safe side. Chill it thoroughly. Freeze it at this point. Just before serving mix in the single cream and a little milk if the consistency is too thick. Ladle the vichyssoise into individual chilled soup bowls, and scissor chives on to the surface of each one.

Like all good dishes, this one is versatile: if it is bleak and rainy for your summer lunch party, leave out the cream and chives and serve the soup as piping hot leek and potato soup to warm everyone up.

Kale
Strip off the leaves, unless your kale stalks are very young and tender, and cook them for a little longer than cabbage, just until they are done, and serve with plenty of melted butter or margarine. In Scotland, where they are a useful, hardy winter vegetable, they make Kilmany Kail, a dish of rabbit pieces, kale, a piece of salt pork and seasonings, stewed slowly in some water until tender, and served with oatcakes.

Lettuce and Endive
Lettuce is almost inseparable from salad, and to my mind it is pointless to cook it. As a change from the usual tomato and cucumber and French dressing kind, try a Caesar Salad, imported from California. If you have never tasted it, the recipe sounds almost too revolting to contemplate. Many visitors have had to be coaxed into tasting it, only to ask for the recipe afterwards. Try it: it makes a filling lunch dish without too much starch.

Caesar Salad

    2 lettuces, one cabbage lettuce and one cos, if possible, or one
      endive
    oil, lemon juice, seasonings   3–4 oz (75–100 g) blue cheese
    2 cloves garlic   4 pieces toast
    1 egg yolk

Wash and dry the lettuces and put them in your salad bowl. Make
a dressing in a large cup of two parts oil to one part lemon juice,
a shake of Worcester sauce, salt and pepper. (This should be a
tart, strong dressing.) Cut up the blue cheese and stir it into the
dressing with a fork until it is all broken up and makes a thick,
grey mess. Peel and slice the garlic and rub it hard over both sides
of the toast; cut the toast into small squares and add to the lettuce.
Pour the dressing over the salad, put in the egg yolk and toss until
each leaf glistens. Serve it at once.

Marrows

The delicate green flavour of a marrow is preserved by steaming.
Simply peel and cut it into rings, scooping out the seeds and pith
and cook the rings until they are just tender.

Stuffed marrow is a classic English dish, and you can invent
many variations to make it more interesting. My family enjoy a
recipe, originally Jewish, for sweet and sour stuffing in their
marrows.

Sweet and Sour Stuffed Marrow Prepare the marrow by
peeling it, and cutting off a longitudinal lid. Scoop out the seeds
and pith from the centre of both pieces.

Stuffing for a medium-sized marrow:

    1 large onion   clove of garlic
    cooking oil   1 lb (400 g) minced beef
    2 or 3 skinned, sliced tomatoes
    a squeeze of tomato purée
    tablespoon of vinegar
    tablespoon of blackstrap molasses
    salt and pepper

Peel the marrow, cut the end off and scoop out seeds and pith. Chop the onion and garlic and melt them gently in the oil; when they are transparent add the beef and stir until it has lost its bright red colour, add the tomatoes, the tomato purée, molasses and vinegar and seasonings. Taste the mixture, it should have a distinct sweet and sour flavour. Adjust it if necessary. Spoon the mixture into the hollow marrow, put the lid on and wrap it tightly in foil. Bake it in a moderate oven (370°F, Mark 4) for an hour or so, until the marrow has turned translucent and pierces easily with a fork.

Mushrooms

Cooked mushrooms—in stews, in stuffings, stuffed, with kebabs, in risotto—are almost as familiar an accompaniment to meat dishes as are onions, though in a very different way.

Half the pleasure of mushrooms is in their texture, so they also lend themselves well to being eaten marinaded but not cooked: they have a capacity for absorbing the flavours of the marinade while remaining firm-textured. Three tablespoons of oil, one of vinegar, some crushed coriander seeds and a pinch of salt makes a good spicy marinade. Leave some button mushrooms in this for a day or two in the refrigerator and then serve them as part of an hors-d'œuvre. You can also make the following excellent first course for a dinner party:

Prawn and Mushroom Salad   The difference in taste, texture and colour between the prawns and the mushrooms is emphasized by the sharp, parsley-flavoured dressing.

$\frac{3}{4}$ lb (300 g) prawns, thawed out very slowly if they are frozen
$\frac{3}{4}$ lb (300 g) mushrooms—small, firm, fresh ones that need not be peeled
1 big bunch parsley and a sprig of fennel
1 crushed clove garlic   4 tablespoons oil
2 tablespoons lemon juice   seasonings

Make a dressing of the garlic, oil, lemon juice (no vinegar) and seasonings. Wipe and slice the mushrooms thinly and leave them to marinade for an hour or so in the refrigerator. At the very last minute add the prawns and the chopped herbs, toss gently and serve.

Mushrooms, more than any other garden crop, are subject to gluts and dearths. Luckily they freeze easily, so you can simply pack your spare ones into polythene bags—they do not need to be blanched—for a continuous supply of this mysterious 'vegetable'. If you are interested in other edible fungi, toadstools and the like, read Richard Mabey's *Food for Free* to identify them growing in the wild.

(See also my recipe for a stir-fried Chinese dish on p. 323.)

Mustard and Cress

Mustard and cress is at its best in home-made brown bread sandwiches for tea, seasoned only with a sprinkle of salt. Remember to scissor it or chop it into short lengths, otherwise the sandwiches pull apart as you eat them. You can also scatter a good scissored handful on to leek and potato soup (Vichyssoise, p. 311), as a change from chives.

Onions

Onions are easy to grow, easy to store; they contain useful calcium, vitamin A and some vitamin C. Yet even the necessary onion is more crisp and juicy sliced straight from the garden, when this is possible in the late summer months. Boiled, fried, stewed, or baked (a neglected but delicious and simple way of serving them) they are the ubiquitous accompaniment to meat cookery and provide huge scope for an adventurous cook.

Used raw, they bring an American accent to food. Try crisp, raw onion rings with a home-made hamburger consisting of nothing but patties of twice-minced beef, lightly fried. A Jewish-American delicacy consists of raw onion and tomato rings with smoked salmon on a bagel (a kind of salty bun); this turns a helping of smoked salmon from a first course into a meal. You can also make an irresistible cocktail-party dip by mixing some grated raw onion, a carton of cream cheese, some chopped olives and a dollop of tomato purée. Serve it in a bowl surrounded by little biscuits or celery sticks.

Gazpacho, the iced soup originally from Andalucia, is another summertime delicacy which needs crisp, raw onions to complete its flavour (p. 318).

French onion soup survived the demise of Les Halles in Paris, whence it originally became famous. This soup is impossible to eat with any delicacy, the rings of onion slide up the spoon, strings of melted cheese stick to one's chin, but it is wonderfully warming to eat after a cold winter outing or round a frosty bonfire.

Onion Soup   4 large onions
1 oz (25 g) butter or margarine
1 dessertspoon brown sugar   1 tablespoon flour
1½ pints (750 ml) good beef stock
salt and pepper
4 slices oven-toasted French bread
Gruyère cheese

Peel and slice the onions into thin rings. Melt the butter in a big heavy pan, add the onion rings and the brown sugar, and stir carefully till the onions are a golden brown colour. Sprinkle on the flour, stir till it has absorbed the remaining butter, add the stock, slowly at first so that the flour does not form lumps, season, and simmer the soup gently for half an hour or so. Place a slice of oven toast covered in grated Gruyère cheese in the bottom of each bowl and ladle hot soup over it. If you like your soup really thick and gooey, put the toast and cheese into an oven-proof casserole, pour the soup over it and bake it in a hot oven (440°F, Mark 7) until the cheese bubbles.

If you are troubled by onion tears, try the old Cordon Bleu trick of holding a slice of stale bread between your teeth while you slice the onions: it will soak up the fumes as they rise. When you have finished slicing, wash your hands with soap and cold water, and they will not smell at all.

Shallots and Pickling Onions   Shallots are another branch of the onion family, a little less overpowering when you need an onion flavour for a fish dish. I also use the small ones interchangeably with button onions to sauté in butter and brown sugar and add in the last half-hour to a *bœuf à la bourguignonne*, and I

use them interchangeably with overgrown spring onions to make
a winter supply of pickled onions.

Pickled Onions   Peel 1 lb (400 g) onions or shallots and soak
them in a brine solution, of 2 oz (50 g) salt to 1 pint (500 ml) cold
water, for two days. Meanwhile prepare your vinegar pickle, because it must be cold before you use it. To each pint of malt
vinegar add 1 tablespoon of pickling spices and 4 oz sugar. Cover
and boil for 15 minutes.

   Drain, rinse and shake the moisture from the onions, pack them
into jars, pour over the vinegar and seal carefully.

Spring Onions   Plant plenty of spring onions and pull them
thin and green to serve in a glass as an accompaniment to cheese,
in the radish recipe on page 320, or in a mixed summer salad. Any
that are overlooked and grow too bulbous can be lifted and pickled,
along with shallots, at the end of the summer.

Parsnips

Parsnips are winter root vegetables that go well with meat dishes,
particularly beef. You need a few parsnips if you are making a
classic *pot au feu*. When you are roasting beef, simply peel a
parsnip per person, cut them in half lengthwise and place them
flat side down around the perimeter of the roasting pan so they
absorb some meat juices as they cook. If you are cooking pork,
try glazed parsnips as a change from apple sauce:

For 4 parsnips:
   2 oz (50 g) brown sugar
   1 oz (25 g) butter or margarine, melted
   squeeze of lemon juice   3–4 tablespoons cider
   salt

Peel and par-cook the parsnips in salted water until they are soft
(about 10 minutes). Drain them and slice in half, then lay them
in a buttered baking dish. Mix the remaining ingredients together and pour over the parsnips. Dot with a little extra butter
and bake in a medium oven (370°F, Mark 4) until they are golden
glazed.

Peas

You must pick your peapods when they are fat but still green and juicy, or the peas inside will be large and metallic-flavoured. A pound of them will yield about half a pound of peas, which will serve two people.

Every child will tell you that peas are best eaten secretly, straight from the vine. I like them raw, tossed by the handful into a green salad or an omelette. If you want to cook them, steam them or cook them briefly in a little milk—they should not wrinkle. I find that mint is too powerful with them, but you can try instead the delicious French method of adding a few pearl-sized onions (boiled separately) at the last moment (about a dozen to a pound of peas). Serve your peas with any and every dish while they are still in season—both ham and duck are traditional, and they go well with lamb as well. If you find your first pickings are scanty, make a mixed dish of spring vegetables—peas, tiny carrots and small broad beans all together—perhaps heaped into the centre of a crown roast of lamb for a dinner party.

Instead of composting your peapods (provided that they have not turned into tough, overripe parchment) you can turn them into a delicious and thrifty summer soup. Make it quickly after shelling, while the pods are still juicy.

Peapod Soup
½ pint (250 ml) milk
salt and pepper

1 lb (400 g) peapods
½ pint (250 ml) good beef stock
top of the milk

Put the pods, the milk and the stock into a saucepan, cover and simmer until the pods are tender. Put them through the medium disc of the mouli, or rub them through a sieve, taking care to leave the stringy bits behind (a blender won't do), and reheat the delicate green soup that results. Season it and stir in a little top of the milk. You can serve it chilled, but I prefer it hot.

Mangetout Peas These are the ones you eat pod and all and are almost a different vegetable, and very well worth growing. I have only ever seen them on sale for a very brief season, yet they are delicious, and above all easy. Pick them while the pods are still flat and the shape of the peas barely beginning to bulge, and they need no washing, no preparing. Just cook them briefly in lightly salted water and wait for the exclamations of pleasure that this unusual vegetable always invokes. Guests of mine have to be persuaded to try them and have then come hurrying back for more.

See also my recipe for a stir-fried Chinese dish, on page 323.

Peppers

Together with tomatoes, cucumbers and lettuce, peppers have become a standard ingredient of mixed salad. You just cut them in half, take out the seeds, and then slice them into strips. You can also cut the tops off, remove the seeds and stuff them—raw. They are good filled with the cream cheese mixture for cucumbers, chilled and sliced (p. 308); cooked, you can use the sweet and sour recipe for marrows (p. 312). They are also essential to the classical French dish, ratatouille, a stew of vegetables that can be eaten hot or cold, as a first course or as an accompanying vegetable, but one that must be made with fresh, full-flavoured vegetables (p. 306).

Gazpacho, the Spanish iced soup, must also be made with good fresh vegetables if it is not to be a pallid imitation of its Andalucian original. This soup takes a little time to prepare and it must be done in time to chill it before serving. You can speed this by suspending a polythene bag full of ice in the bowl, or putting it very briefly into the freezer.

Gazpacho Andaluz   1 large onion
  1 large green pepper   1 cucumber
  4 large ripe tomatoes—preferably Marmande
  tomato juice—19 fluid oz (540 ml) tin
  oil—about a tablespoon
  juice of a lemon, salt and pepper
  butter or margarine
  2 slices stale bread   1 clove garlic

Reserve about a quarter each of the onion, cucumber and green pepper, and one tomato. Liquidize or sieve the rest, together with the garlic, lubricating with some tomato juice as you go. If you have used a liquidizer, pour the results through a sieve into a bowl, so the soup is completely smooth, with a thickish consistency.

Dilute it with a little more tomato juice if you need to. Stir in seasonings, lemon juice and oil. Chill the soup until you serve it. Melt the butter or margarine in a frying pan and cut the bread into small squares. Fry them briskly on both sides until they are golden (these are croûtons). Put them in a small bowl. Dice the remaining vegetables (peel the tomato) and put each one in its own bowl. When you serve the soup each guest scatters a few croûtons and some of each of the diced vegetables over his plate.

Potatoes

Potatoes are richest in vitamin C when they are harvested. As they are stored through the winter the vitamin C is gradually destroyed, so if you like potatoes, but feel you should not eat too many, enjoy them small and freshly dug in the early summer, and eschew them later in the year.

The nutrients of potatoes lie directly under the skin, so as often as possible they should be cooked scrubbed, but not peeled. Baby new potatoes have no skins to speak of when they are eaten straight from the garden. For older potatoes Constance Spry suggests cooking and then peeling them quickly by hand to serve piping hot—a painful counsel of perfection. But you can do this when you are making potato salad, if you let them cool a little first. Dice them and dress them with mayonnaise or vinaigrette while they are still warm. Old potatoes are most nutritious when they are scrubbed (so you can later eat the skin), foil-wrapped and baked: if you are in a hurry, stick a long, clean nail into each one, the metal will quickly conduct the heat to the centre. You can make any number of delicious garnishes for them with chopped herbs mixed into butter, margarine, or sour cream. If you like really crunchy roast potatoes with a joint, peel them, parboil them for five minutes, drain them (saving the water for gravy) and let them dry for a moment or two before putting them into the oven in their own heatproof dish, with a little oil or dripping in it. Turn them over at half time. If you like pale, fluffy mashed potatoes, there is one certain method you must follow. After the potatoes are boiled, drain them, and put the empty pan back on the heat. Add a couple of inches of milk and a knob of butter or margarine and let the milk come to the boil. Tip the potatoes back into the pan and beat them with your electric mixer or a wooden spoon, until they are light and standing in peaks. The boiled milk makes all the difference to the final result.

Potatoes are also very good sliced and baked in a casserole, either as a necessary part of Irish stew, or as a separate vegetable dish with alternating layers of onion rings, a little milk or stock to moisten them and seasoning. A 1-pint casserole dish will take about 1 hour to cook in a moderate oven. The top should be a crisp brown crust.

Besides the multitude of cooking methods—European cookery must have been very odd without them—potatoes are essential to the smooth delicious texture of classic soups like vichyssoise, and they provide a natural thickening agent for more pedestrian winter soups.

Radishes

Radishes are a sideline in most salads, adding colour and crunch almost incidentally. Here is one where they contribute to a good and satisfying slimmers' lunch dish:

Radish, Cucumber and Cottage Cheese Salad
2 8-oz (200 g) cartons of cottage cheese
a bunch red radishes   half a cucumber
a handful of chives or spring onions

Turn the cottage cheese into a bowl. Dice as finely as possible the radishes, cucumber and spring onions (or scissor in the chives). Mix it all together with some black pepper. This is quite different from the commercial chive cottage cheese with little grey specks in it.

The big, black winter radishes can be scraped and peeled, thinly sliced and served as a salad in a French dressing, or with horse-radish sauce.

Salsify and Scorzonera

Salsify and Black Salsify, or Scorzonera, are spindly root vegetables (the former with white roots, the latter with black). They are less popular now than in Mrs Beeton's day, but are interesting, delicious and unusual vegetables. Salsify is sometimes called the vegetable oyster, on account of its subtle flavour.

Wash, scrape (like a carrot) and chop your salsify into about

2″ lengths, and drop these into cold water to which you have
added a little lemon juice or vinegar—the pieces will otherwise discolour very rapidly when exposed to oxygen. Cook the salsify in a
little boiling water, with salt and vinegar, until it is soft (about
30 minutes). It can be served with melted butter or a white sauce.

Scorzonera, like beetroot, bleeds a lot if it is peeled before
cooking, so scrub it and cook it whole, peeling and chopping it
afterwards.

You can make a salsify or scorzonera soup with the same basic
recipe, although their colours will be quite different.

Salsify or Scorzonera Soup   1 onion
1 oz (25 g) butter or margarine
½ lb (200 g) cooked salsify or scorzonera
1 pint (500 ml) chicken stock
1 egg yolk   3 tablespoons cream
salt and pepper

Peel and chop the onion and sauté it in the butter until it is transparent. Add the chopped salsify, chicken stock and seasonings
and simmer until the onion is cooked. Purée the mixture in a
blender, or rub it through a sieve; return to the pan and stir in
the cream. Beat the egg yolk in a bowl, beat in a little of the hot
soup, and then stir the contents of the bowl into the pan. Do not
let it boil, but serve it hot.

Seakale

Seakale looks like skimpy celery, but you treat it like asparagus.
Wash the stalks, trim the ends and tie them into helping-sized
bundles (about 4 oz (100 g) per person). Cook them, covered in
boiling salted water with a squeeze of lemon juice in it, until they
are easily pierced with a fork (20 minutes or so). Serve with melted
butter, or margarine, or a hollandaise sauce (p. 356) as a first
course, or coated in a cheese sauce (p. 356) for a supper dish.

Sorrel

Sorrel is an interesting, highly nutritious vegetable, with a cool
acid taste that makes it an alternative, not a substitute, for spinach.
I find it something like a vegetable lemon in flavour. It cooks like

GICI—L

spinach, and you can serve a sorrel purée with any liver dish or, traditionally, coarse fish. This is too acid for me, and I prefer a few leaves added to an omelette *fines herbes*, or better still shredded into a plain lettuce salad.

Sorrel is the vital ingredient of *Germiny à l'Oseille*, a cream of sorrel soup that greatly delighted Ludwig Bemelmans, who called it 'the Queen of all soups in the world'. It is a classic French cream soup—rich, a little time-consuming to make, but essential if one is to understand what Bemelmans was talking about. This is a dinner-party soup that will be specially appreciated because you do not find it in a restaurant:

Germiny à l'Oseille

3 tablespoons chopped onions
1 tablespoon butter or margarine
½ lb (200 g) washed, shredded sorrel
1 tablespoon flour
1¼ pint (625 ml) hot chicken stock
1 egg yolk   ¼ pint (125 ml) cream
seasonings

Soften the onions in the butter or margarine until they are transparent, stir in the sorrel and cook it gently until the leaves wilt and lose their bright green colour. Stir in the flour and continue cooking until it is all absorbed. Remove the pan from the stove and beat in the hot stock.

In a mixing bowl, blend thoroughly the egg yolk and the cream, beat in the hot soup, very cautiously at first to avoid it curdling. Return it to the pan and stir, without allowing the soup to boil, for a few minutes to cook the eggs. Serve hot, or chilled. If it sets a little in cooling, stir in some top of the milk to thin it.

Spinach and Spinach Beet

Pick your garden spinach before the leaves get thick and tough and, to save yourself time, twist or snip them off at the top of the stalk. Wash them quickly and thoroughly and spin or shake them dry. Then shred them—or else the leaves turn into a solid 'plate' at the bottom of the pan—and cook them gently in a little milk or milk and water. The milk will soften the very acid flavour. Spinach cooks down quite alarmingly, so you need two pounds to feed four people. If you like it puréed, put the cooked vegetable through your mouli, or liquidize or sieve it.

You can serve spinach or spinach purée with almost any dish—particularly eggs, where their blandness will counteract the sharp taste of the spinach. You can place a couple of tablespoonsful in the centre of an almost-cooked omelette, or you can make a spinach soup by substituting spinach for sorrel in the preceding recipe. For a supper dish, place poached eggs on a bed of spinach, cover them with either a cheese sauce (p. 356), or some thick cream and grated cheese and bake until just heated through and the cheese begins to melt.

If, like many people, you hate spinach, try it in a salad that is made from small fresh spinach leaves, a scattering of crisply fried crumbled bacon and a French or Roquefort dressing. It tastes delicious and bears no resemblance to cooked spinach—and of course you don't eat anything like the same volume.

Sprouting Seeds

Seeds you have sprouted yourself are a delight to add to every salad, and many cooked dishes. They need little washing—only a little picking over—and, nutritionally, should be eaten seed and all. You can make a low-calorie 'spaghetti' with an interesting texture by using soya bean sprouts instead of pasta and serving them with a meat or meat and tomato sauce. You can bake bean sprouts with your bread dough to make California Sprouted Wheat Bread, or you can mix bean sprouts with some other barely cooked vegetables—onions, mushrooms and chopped green and red peppers, for example—and layer them into a strudel pastry with some thin cheese slices to make a savoury spring roll. A most delicious recipe is for:

A Stir-fried Chinese Vegetable Dish Heat some oil in a frying pan and add in order, chopped onions, chopped mushrooms, mangetout peas and bean sprouts. Fry the vegetables over a fairly high heat, stirring continuously to prevent them sticking and burning. When they are almost cooked add a very little water, cover the pan and cook for 3 more minutes. Toss in some raw prawns, about 2 ounces per person, and cook them through very briefly. Serve the dish with fried or pilaff rice (p. 332).

Swedes

I like swedes cooked; I find them unsuitable for a winter salad,
although I have seen recipes for swede salads. Like many other
winter root vegetables, they are hard and take a long time to cook.
If they are scrubbed and peeled and then diced fairly finely, they
will be soft in under half an hour. You can serve them like this,
turned in a little melted butter or margarine, or as part of a mixed
diced vegetable dish, along with carrots and turnips. (This combination, puréed, also makes a good winter soup, p. 331). I think
swedes are best drained, returned to the pan with a little milk and
butter or margarine, and mashed like potatoes. Their orange,
slightly fibrous texture will not fluff up like potatoes, but they
taste good anyway.

When your swedes sprout orange shoots in the spring, allow
the shoots to grow fairly fat and then cook them and serve them
with melted butter—this is a nearly forgotten nineteenth-century
delicacy.

Sweetcorn

Sweetcorn must be home grown to be appreciated at its very best.
Addicts of fresh corn recommend the cook to run from kitchen-
garden to boiling pot, stripping off the covering leaves on the way.
This is an exaggeration of course, but you must harvest your corn
at the latest moment before you cook it, and above all refrain from
refrigerating it, because the little kernels will become wrinkled and
sad, and will not recover by cooking.

Harvest your corn as soon as the silk hanging from the green-
sheathed cobs is dark brown and dry, then the kernels will be a
delicate pale yellow, sweet and tender. You can boil your cobs,
or steam them, covered, for some 4 to 8 minutes, according to the
size. Add a pinch of sugar to the water, not salt, because it toughens
the kernels. They are cooked when a kernel feels tender to the
prong of a fork. If you are eating out of doors, corn tastes delicious
baked in its leaves and a protective coating of foil, in the embers
of the fire.

Corn is usually served in Britain as a first course, on the cob,
with plenty of butter or margarine and salt. Americans eat it as
an ordinary vegetable with the main course.

If you have a bumper crop and are looking for a more adventurous recipe, try this adaptation of a Vietnamese soup, a little like the sweetcorn soups in Chinese restaurants:

Cream of Corn Soup
3 ears of corn
1 pint (500 ml) chicken stock
sugar, salt and pepper
4 tablespoons cream

Boil the corn cobs for about 10 minutes or until very tender. Let them cook a little, and then standing the cobs on end cut the kernels off, downwards, with a sharp knife. Liquidize or sieve these with a little of the chicken stock and the seasonings. Return the soup to the pan, reheat it and stir in the rest of the chicken stock. Pour the soup into a big bowl or individual dishes and swirl the cream into the top.

Tomatoes

Tomatoes were made for salads—every kind of salad. The quickest salad I know is made from tomatoes sliced into a dish with crisp onion rings and dressed with a tart vinaigrette. Or you can leave out the onions and garnish the tomatoes with scissored chives or chopped basil—a herb that has a special affinity with tomatoes. Add a hunk of crusty French bread, a wedge of Brie and a glass of wine and you have an unequalled five-minute lunch. Raw, sliced in their skins, their taste, texture and above all their colour make them the perfect complement to lettuce, the other basic salad ingredient.

Cooked tomatoes impart their own distinctive flavour (too loosely termed 'Provençal' by menu-writers) to every dish they appear in, and their acids help to make the meat fibres tender. They are so very obtrusive that it is best to make them a feature of the dish (see the section on green peppers for a ratatouille recipe) or leave them out altogether.

Another Mediterranean dish which is successful over here is a tomato sauce (no relation to ketchup) to accompany a chicken, a white fish or a dish of pasta.

Tomato Sauce

    2 lb ripe tomatoes, the big Marmande are best—if you use
        tasteless ones you will make a tasteless sauce
    2 tablespoons safflower oil   1 small finely chopped onion
    1 crushed clove garlic
    1 tablespoon or so of cider vinegar and, if you have it, the heel
        of a bottle of red wine
    seasonings (see method)

Scald (pour boiling water over) or steam, skin and quarter the tomatoes; cut out any hard, tasteless white cores. In a pan (a French or Spanish earthenware one is good for this) heat the oil and add the garlic and onion. Cook them gently until they are soft and transparent but not browned. Add the tomatoes, vinegar, wine and seasonings. These might be a bay leaf, a spray of parsley, sage, lemon or ordinary thyme, a twist of lemon peel, salt, freshly ground black pepper, a teaspoon of honey, a dash of Worcester sauce. Cover and simmer slowly, stirring occasionally to stop it sticking or burning, until the whole has cooked down into a tasty, slightly lumpy sauce.

If you have a glut of tomatoes, you can turn some of them into your own tomato juice. Simply put a pound or two of tomatoes in a heavy pan, cover and cook them on a cool stove or in a cool oven and let them simmer gently with no extra water. Stir occasionally if they look like sticking. When they are well cooked down, put them through the mouli or liquidize them and then sieve them, add a little salt and sugar, and chill before serving. The result is not quite the same as the canned kind, but good in its way.

    Totally different is a delicious messy sandwich lunch which precisely illustrates the American flair for combining unusual flavours, known to Americans as BLT.

Bacon, Lettuce and Tomato Sandwiches The secret is to combine all the ingredients while they are at their peak of hot, cold, crisp and so forth. Serve one sandwich at a time as the toaster pops, rather than keeping everything waiting and cooling.

    8 slices wholemeal bread, toasted
    butter or margarine and mayonnaise

4 large tomatoes sliced and seasoned with a sprinkle of salt,
freshly ground black pepper and sugar
8 slices crisply grilled bacon
large washed green lettuce leaves

Butter a slice of toast, cover it generously with mayonnaise, cover
that with some lettuce and sliced tomatoes. Lay two slices of bacon
on that, then more lettuce, more mayonnaise and the second piece
of buttered toast. Press the sandwich together and cut firmly in
half. Serve with plenty of napkins and put some more bacon under
the grill for second helpings.

Turnips

You can eat the green tops of turnips cooked like cabbage; they
are rich in vitamins A and C and calcium. Small summer turnips
can be cooked whole, but the large roots must be scrubbed, peeled
and diced, and cooked like swedes. Turnips are a necessity for a
well-flavoured *pot au feu*, and good in any winter vegetable soup.

Mixed Vegetables in Search of a Recipe

Even with a flourishing kitchen garden there will be times when you find yourself with a small quantity of several vegetables to transform into one good dish. You may need a prop for these, in the way of flour or eggs. For example:

An Omelette with a filling of chopped herbs, or slightly cooked tomatoes or mushrooms, or a handful of tiny peas or beans, or sorrel (superb), or what you will. An omelette, to my mind, is a far more instant dish than anything more elaborate you need time to unfreeze, and one you need never feel ashamed of. Omelettes are also very easy to make, contrary to the mist of awe that has grown up around them. Buy yourself a proper omelette pan with curved sides and a good treated surface. Mine is 9 inches in diameter, it makes a 4-egg, 2-person omelette, and if I am feeding more, I simply make another one. Keep your special pan for omelettes only; use it and clean it without scratching the finish (Fig. 23).

Put the omelette pan on a good heat and melt a tablespoonful of butter or margarine in it. Break 2 eggs per person into a mixing bowl, beat them with a fork while you count to thirty, they should be broken up, well mixed but not particularly foamy. Season them lightly with salt and pepper.

Pour the mixture into the hot pan and leave it for a moment. When the bottom has set solid, lift up a corner and let some of the runny egg mixture pour underneath it, to set likewise. When the whole is nearly cooked, scatter on your filling (pre-cooked if necessary) then lift the pan and slide the omelette on to a hot serving plate. Tip the pan at the last moment to fold the top half over the bottom. Serve it at once, with a green salad and a hunk of home-made bread. The inside should be slightly runny, the outside firm but not leathery.

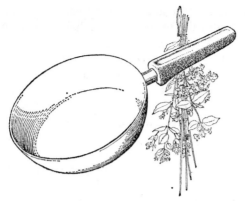

FIG. 23. An omelette pan

A Quiche This is a pastry flan case that may be filled with any variety of raw herbs or just-cooked vegetables, chopped chives, mushrooms and bacon, onions, spinach, asparagus—you name it— with a creamy egg or egg and cheese custard baked on the top. You can use a yeast pastry (p. 359) for this, or a shortcrust one (p. 359), both calculated for an 8-inch flan tin. When you have lined the tin with pastry, turn in your chosen filling and pour over the following custard, liquidized or rotary-whisked until smooth.

4 oz (100 g) cottage cheese
2 tablespoons dried skim milk powder
2 eggs   ¼ pint (125 ml) milk
salt and pepper

Bake in a fairly hot oven for half an hour or until the custard rises and the edges of the pastry are seen to be cooked. Serve at once or the custard will fall.

Pancakes You can fill little pancakes with the same mixtures you use for quiches and omelettes. For the batter you need:

4 oz (100 g) flour (81 per cent)
salt and pepper   1 egg
½ pint (250 ml) milk
a little cooking oil for frying them

Sift the flour, salt and pepper into a bowl. Make a dip in the middle, drop in the egg, mix it in with a wooden spoon and then add the milk, to make a smooth runny batter. If you have time, leave it to stand in the refrigerator for half an hour or so. On a good flame heat a little cooking oil in your frying pan, swirl it round to coat the whole surface, and pour off any extra. Put a tablespoonful of batter in the pan and let it cook until solid. Turn it gently with a palette knife and cook the other side.

Spoon the vegetable mixture on to your pancakes and fold them up. They are good covered with a cheese sauce (p. 356).

If you add a teaspoon of sugar with a good pinch of salt but no pepper to your pancake mixture, and fill them with cooked fruit, you will have sweet instead of savour pancakes.

Make a Pizza This Italian bread dough has delectable slices of vegetables, and fish or meat, half submerged in it and is frequently covered in melted cheese and marjoram. It has cousins all round the Mediterranean: the Provencal Pissaladière omits the cheese, the Mallorquin Coca di Verdura substitutes local-caught sardines for anchovies. There are so many variations that you can make yours as you please—with tomatoes, mushrooms, green peppers, artichoke hearts, French beans, capers, part-cooked onions, garlic, and anchovies, olives, ham, cheese, tunafish, shrimps, whitebait, sardines . . . anything, but not everything, goes. Select your ingredients to complement one another.

Take one quarter of the bread dough (p. 359) and let it rise for an hour or so in a cloth-covered bowl and a warm place. Flatten the dough and work it by hand to a round flat shape, some ½ inch thick, 8 inches in diameter. Transfer it to a greased baking sheet, and spread your ingredients over it. They might be sliced tomato rings, scissored snippets of anchovies and thinly sliced cheese and/or a sprinkling of grated Parmesan cheese, or tomatoes and green peppers with sliced mushrooms, or what you will. Always finish your pizza with a generous handful of chopped fresh marjoram, which will create the authentic pizza smell as it comes out of the oven. Sprinkle it with cooking oil and bake in a moderately hot oven (400°F, Mark 5) for 20 minutes or until the edges of the pizza are crisp, any cheese is bubbling and the toppings look cooked. Serve at once. This pizza will feed 4 medium-hungry people: if they are all pizza fanatics, they will demolish two of them.

A mixed vegetable soup makes a warming bowlful, especially in midwinter when the vegetable garden is pretty uninspiring. Experiment will tell you which vegetables you like together. (I find that parsnips are a bit too obtrusive.) Begin with the following:

2 lb (1 kilo) mixed onions, leeks, carrots, turnips, celery
2 oz (50 g) butter or margarine
4 pints water   mixed herbs
salt, pepper, sugar, Worcester sauce

Where necessary peel and chop the vegetables quite small. Melt the butter in a large pan and cook the onions and leeks until soft and beginning to brown. Add the rest of the vegetables and cook for a few minutes more. Add the water, herbs and seasonings and simmer with the lid on until the vegetables are tender (about 20 minutes). This makes a good quantity of soup—but you can save half of it as it is, and purée the rest in a liquidizer or sieve for the next day. It also makes an excellent vegetable stock if you strain off the juice and use it independently.

An Hors-d'œuvre or plate of *crudités* (pp. 277, 296, 303) is yet another way of presenting a variety of vegetables in an appetizing manner. These are generally a quantity of salad vegetables—perhaps tomatoes, cucumbers, beetroot, cauliflower florets, shredded carrots, with possibly some hard-boiled eggs or garlic sausage—chopped into individual dishes or arranged decoratively on one big plate. To look and taste inviting, the vegetables must be very freshly sliced, and either dressed individually if they are in separate dishes, or placed round a bowl of spicy mayonnaise (p. 354). The result should make a thoughtful combination, not a shovelled together heap of leftovers.

A Salade Niçoise is just such a typical flexible feast, that will alter its requirements to suit what is available in the garden. The secret of this salad is to bring it to the table arranged carefully in the bowl, before jumbling up all the ingredients by mixing in the dressing. Line the bottom of the bowl with several layers of lettuce leaves, pile in a selection of the following: sliced tomatoes and green peppers, radishes, barely blanched French beans, herbs, cooked potato chunks, and hard-boiled eggs, anchovies, black olives, or tunafish. Dress it generously. With a glass of chilled white wine and some French bread this is a perfect summer lunch.

Tomato aspic The Americans love their salads as aspics—particularly tomato aspic which is another interesting way to present a collection of vegetables.

> 2 level tablespoons gelatine
> $1\frac{1}{2}$ pints (750 ml) tomato juice
> minced or finely chopped vegetables, like celery, green peppers, grated onion, grated carrot or beetroot, and so forth

Sprinkle the gelatine on the surface of the tomato juice, let it soak for a few minutes, then warm it gently, stirring too, until it dissolves. Mix in the chopped vegetables and pour the aspic into a mould. Let it set in the refrigerator, or faster still, in the freezer. If you use a ring mould you can turn it out and fill the centre with tunafish, shrimps in mayonnaise, chicken salad or what you will.

Rice Salad is a more substantial way of stretching your collection of vegetables. Rice cooked as a pilaff is good for eating cold, as the grains remain separate, and no nutrients are lost by rinsing it. Always use twice the volume of stock to rice.

Rice Pilaff $1\frac{1}{2}$ pints (750 ml) chicken stock
  1 medium onion   salt and pepper
  1 lb (400 g) long grain rice   oil

Heat the oil in a deep pan. Chop the onion finely and sauté it until it is transparent. Add the rice and turn it in the oil until each grain is translucent. Pour in stock and the seasonings, put the lid on and cook it in a medium hot oven (400°F, Mark 5) for 20 minutes. The rice will have absorbed all the liquid. Transfer the rice to a cold bowl to stop it cooking, dress it with a French dressing while it is still warm and then mix in your chopped vegetables.

Other Garden Foods

LONG before primitive man learnt how to grow food crops, he was living off random-growing wild plants. There are still many of these around today; both the wild versions of our cultivated vegetables and others that we may not know we shall enjoy eating. I list here a few of the ones that are likely to be in everyone's garden.[1]

Nettles, for example. For all their vicious sting, nettles have valuable properties to the herbalist, and are useful on your compost heap. You can turn them into nettle beer, and nettle soup—a curious, green-specked, faintly-fishy tasting soup—when you pick the very young and tender green tops. Make it like *Germiny à l'Oseille* on p. 322.

Sunflower seeds are rich in protein and polyunsaturated oil. I like to eat them by the handful; you can also put them into your home-made muesli, scatter them over salads, and serve them with cocktails.

Poppyseeds add a nice touch sprinkled on the crust of home-made bread and rolls.

Nasturtium petals bring a peppery taste and a gay colour when they are torn up in a green salad. The leaves are also good in salads and sandwiches. You can pickle the seeds and use them like capers.

Marigold petals also look good scattered into salads and have an unusual flavour.

---

[1] Many more edible wild plants are detailed in Richard Mabey's *Food for Free*.

Dandelion greens are highly prized in France as a salad vegetable in the early spring. Cut off the whole plant with a sharp knife at soil level and wash it in several changes of water, spin the leaves dry and serve them in a French dressing.

Watercress makes a delicious soup. Follow the rule for Vichyssoise (p. 331), using a big bunch of watercress instead of leeks. Serve the soup hot. (Don't pick your watercress anywhere near sheep: an infinitesimal water snail may transmit their liver fluke to you.) In any event, wash it very thoroughly under a running cold tap, and pick it over extra carefully.

Fruits and Nuts

'THIS makes me wonder more than all the rest, that at this time of year, when every tree is barren of his fruit, from whence you had these ripe grapes,' said the Duke of Anholt to Dr Faustus. (Mephistopheles had just produced them from the other side of the world.) We would take the Doctor's miracle for granted, but in mediaeval times lack of fruit and vegetables, with scurvy as a result, was commonplace towards the end of winter. Freezing and air freight have made an important difference to our daily diets, but I still feel there is a special and appropriate pleasure in enjoying fruits in their own season. When they are freshly picked from your own garden, many need no added cooking to enhance them. If you have fruit which is ripe, whole and enough to go round, don't search for an elaborate recipe, simply pile it into a bowl and put it on the table. If it is clean and you know the fruit has not been sprayed with chemicals, it will not even need to be washed.

If you have a variety of fruit available, and perhaps not quite enough of any one, you can invent your own fruit salads. A little sugar, or honey, and water heated until the sugar melts, and then cooled, will supplement the fruits' natural juices. I like these fruit salads chosen by colours: the most elegant one I ever had was all of red fruits—cherries, strawberries and raspberries, and a sprinkling of red currants to add an acid bite. It sounds simple: it tasted memorable.

If you have to cook fruit—rhubarb, for example, or hard cooking pears—it is encouraging to know that because it has a higher acid content than vegetables, the nutrients of fruit are less damaged by cooking. We are also accustomed to eating cooked fruit along with the juices, so any vitamins and minerals that have leached into the syrup are automatically included. I like to 'melt' fruit very gently in a covered pot with no more than a couple of table-spoons of water and a little sugar, preferably in a low oven. In this way the fruit keeps its shape and the juices are thick and delicious. (Plums, particularly, give out a resinous juice, as do their trees.) You can serve this compôte as it is with cream or yoghurt, or in-corporate it in pies and tarts, or purée it before mixing up your own fruit yoghurts, jellies, mousses and ice-creams.

Fruit with pastry—pies and tarts and crumbles—is the British standby for a cooked fruit pudding. I give the basic recipes for pastry and crumble on pages 359–360. Instead of our usual 'deep dish' (as the Americans describe them) fruit pies with pastry on top, try for a change reversing the order and making an open fruit tart *à la Française*. An ordinary tart can become a delight to make with the fruit sliced and carefully arranged in the flan case, and finished with a professional glaze of warmed and sieved jam (p. 341), or a rich egg custard—you can make this with plums and cherries and apricots as well as apples.

Ices, Ice-Creams and Ice Lollies   Making ices and ice-creams out of your own fruit is a kind of anti-cooking with its own rules. The difficulty is to achieve at home the smoothness of commercial ices, as these are made by a continuous stirring process that pre-vents the formation of large ice crystals. An older generation, mainly American, swears by grandmother's hand-cranked ma-chines, where the ice-cream container was packed in coarse salt and chipped ice, and everyone took a turn at the handle till it would move no more and the ice-cream was ready.

The equivalent today is an electric ice-cream maker. There are several kinds of these which fit into the freezing compartment of the fridge or into the coldest part of the freezer, with a thin flex that shuts in the door, to provide the power to drive the paddles. These turn continuously in the freezing mixture until it is so stiff that they cut out automatically. They cost some £9 and upwards, and you can buy an extra container to make double quantities if you like. They are a great pleasure for a family that enjoys ices. With one you can easily make your own nutritious ice-creams and water ices, and so avoid feeding your children the commercial kind full of artificial flavourings, emulsifiers and vegetable 'cream'. If you do without one of these you must take out the freezing mixture two or three times before it is hard, and beat it with a fork, scraping away all the ice crystals that have formed on the sides, and breaking them up. A teaspoon of gelatine (dissolved in a little water) added to each pint of liquid will help keep the ice-cream smooth. Too much sugar in the mixture will slow up the process, and also cause it to taste much too sweet when it is frozen, so remember to adjust your sugar and water quantities if you are using fruit that has been frozen in sugar or sugar syrup.

Correctly, a water ice is a fruit purée mixed with a little sugar syrup and frozen. A sorbet, or sherbet, is the same recipe with a beaten egg white folded in half way through the freezing process. It gives the sorbet a faintly fluffy consistency and a whitish, more opaque colour than the water ice. But raw egg white is a 'lock-out' food; it contains a substance called avidin which combines with the B vitamin biotin in the stomach to prevent it from reaching the blood. So I give no sorbet recipe; the simple water ices are just as delicious. An ice-cream is, properly, a flavoured egg custard or a fruit purée folded into loosely whipped cream and frozen. This is high in cholesterol, laborious and expensive too, so I give an alternative but equally good recipe for ice-cream. The very distinctive taste of evaporated milk is masked by the fruit flavours, and the consistency is excellent.

As I suggest plenty of ices and ice-creams, I give here the usual quantities for making any of them. The amount of fruit depends on how ripe and strongly flavoured it is when you pick it, so it is always wise to taste your mixture and add a little more fruit purée if you find it pallid. The sugar you need may also be varied, according to your taste and the sweetness of the fruit.

Basic Fruit Ice-Cream Recipe
1 lb (400 g) fruit
6 fl oz (150 ml) evaporated milk, thoroughly chilled
about 3 oz (75 g) sugar
1 teaspoon gelatine sprinkled on to 2 tablespoons warm water and left to dissolve
4 tablespoons dried skim milk powder

If necessary cook the fruit in the sugar and liquidize it. Or liquidize it raw with the sugar. Rub it through a nylon sieve with a wooden spoon (contact with metal will cause some fruits to discolour and taste odd). Whisk the chilled evaporated milk and the dried skim milk powder until it thickens, add the fruit purée and finally the gelatine, and freeze.

Basic Water Ice Recipe   1 lb (400 g) fruit
½ pint (250 ml) water
approximately 4 oz (100 g) sugar

Boil the sugar and the water together for 5 minutes to make a good syrup, otherwise the texture of your water ice will be terrible. When the syrup is cooked, stir in the fruit, puréed as above, and freeze.

A parsley and lemon ice is another version of this recipe, very cooling and refreshing at the end of a summer dinner party.

Parsley and Lemon Ice   2 lemons
2 oz (50 g) sugar   ¾ pint (375 ml) water
a big bunch parsley (about 2 oz or 50 g)

Pare the lemon rinds very thinly, add them to the sugar and water and boil briskly for 5 minutes. Allow the syrup to cool, then strain off the rinds, add the juice of the lemons and the parsley, de-stalked and very finely chopped. Follow the rule above for freezing.

For children you can buy an ice lolly kit: some little plastic pots and a bundle of sticks that fit into them. You can fill the pots with ice-cream, with water ice or, if you are in a hurry, with some strong blackcurrant drink (diluted with a little water), rosehip syrup or real orange juice. They are endlessly popular, and rich in vitamin C.

I cannot emphasize enough that ice-cream making is rewarding but quite complicated and time-consuming, and it needs practice. One of the problems I found with my electrically made ices is their timing: they are at their best up to half an hour after the paddles have stopped. After that it is a matter of dodging the box in and out of the freezer to keep its contents at the right consistency. Ideally, an ice-cream is not a dessert that can be prepared hours, if not days, beforehand and then forgotten until the very last minute. (Fruit ice-creams do keep well, but they definitely have a better texture when they are freshly made.) Different machines, different mixtures and quantities all take different times to freeze, so it is important to time and then note each one down at the end of the recipe.

Although fruits are customarily turned into jams and jellies, I have deliberately omitted any detailed recipes for these. There is a place for them, in small quantities, in our diet, but the large amounts of sugar, and the long boiling time with no lid on, which destroys vitamins and minerals, makes them 'empty' calories, not nutritious food. I prefer to freeze spare fruit wherever possible.

Apples

The apple crop, like the runner beans, is one that seldom fails in an English garden. If you grow good sweet eating apples you need only enjoy them raw. Autumn finds every country housewife turning her windfalls into chutneys, stuffings, purées and jellies, freezing them,[1] baking them, stewing them, and thinking about Apple Charlotte, Apple Betty and all the host of traditional English apple dishes. Because they are plentiful, apples are used as the base for many more exotically flavoured preserves, like mint jelly, rose-petal jam, geranium jelly and mulberry jam. Everyone has her favourite apple recipes, so I must be forgiven for choosing mine.

Apple sauce is essential for me with both pork and pork sausages; I like it made moments before serving, by liquidizing peeled raw apples with a tablespoon of lemon juice and a very little sugar. This sauce has a wonderful green taste. Big, whole cooking apples are good for baking, cored but not peeled, with a 'waist' cut round their middles to stop them exploding in the oven. Fill the core-holes with anything you please—dates, nuts, sultanas, honey, brown sugar, syrup—and bake the apples just until they puff up

---

[1] You can freeze apples as a purée, or whole. Damaged cooking apples can be salvaged if you peel and slice the sound parts, dropping them straight into cold water and a little salt (1 dessertspoon to a quart) to prevent oxidation. Then pack them into bags or boxes and freeze them fast. They will need the barest cooking time when you take them out.

and turn fluffy inside (in a fairly hot oven, 380–400°F, Mark 5). Marvellous with very cold vanilla ice-cream.

Apple pies and tarts need a book to themselves. They are considered to be traditional both by the Americans and the British. The Americans call ours, with the pastry on top, 'deep dish apple pie'. You can flavour them with cloves or cinnamon, orange or lemon peel, or a quince. 'I think no apple tart is perfect without a quince to flavour it,' says Constance Spry.

Deep Dish Apple Pie   For a 2-pint, 3-inch-deep pie dish:

   shortcrust pastry (p. 359)
   2–3 lb (1 kg–1,400 g) cooking apples (according to how much
      they shrink in cooking)
   brown sugar
   Flavourings—quince, cloves, cinnamon, orange peel, what you
      will

Make the shortcrust pastry recipe on page 359. Cover the dough and leave it in the refrigerator until you need it.

Peel, core and slice the apples and layer them into the pie dish with brown sugar according to their tartness and add the flavouring you prefer. Cover the pie dish, with foil if necessary, and put it in a cool oven for 30 minutes or so, to cook the fruit gently. The apple slices should keep their shape, not disintegrate into apple mush. If the fruit has shrunk a lot in cooking, add some more and mix it well in. Wet the edges of the pie dish. Roll out the pastry roughly to the size and shape of the pie-dish top, spread it over—with a 'blackbird' in the centre if it seems likely to sag—trim it and press it firmly on to the wet dish edge with a fork or the back of a knife. Traditionally, apple pie crusts are decorated with all sorts of elaborate pastry leaves and flowers. If you have time you can experiment with your trimmings and stick the decorations on with a drop of water. Bake the pie in a moderate oven until the crust is cooked—about 45 minutes. Serve it hot or cold.

If you enjoy decorative cookery, make a French apple tart (Fig. 24). This is a shallow pastry flan filled with very thinly sliced dessert apples arranged in an overlapping spiral. It is finished

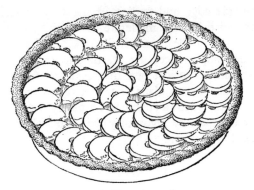

FIG. 24. A French apple tart

with a glaze of melted and strained apricot jam. If you do this carefully, and serve it with cream, it will make a highly praised dinner-party dish from very simple, cheap ingredients.

French Apple Tart For a 7-inch tin, ¾-inch deep (using the quantity of pastry given on p. 359); if you have a deeper tin, you can begin by spreading a layer of cooked, sweetened apple sauce in the bottom:

Shortcrust pastry (p. 359)	1 lb (400 g) dessert apples
1 tablespoon cider vinegar	castor sugar
2 tablespoons apricot jam	

First make the shortcrust pastry, with a good teaspoon of sugar in the mixture. When you have made the dough, cover it in the bowl and set it in the refrigerator—or freezer if it is for a short while—until you need it.

Quarter, core and peel the apples, then slice them very thinly—they should be translucent enough for you to see the shadow of the knife through them—and drop them into a bowl of cold water laced with the cider vinegar.

Roll out the cold pastry very thinly, as quickly as you can, twirl it round the rolling pin and lift it on to the tin. Spread it over, press it gently into the edge of the base and trim the top neatly. Decorate the edge with a fork or the back of a knife. Drain the apple slices and wrap them in a clean tea-towel while you select the most perfect crescents to make an overlapping spiral starting from the outside edge and ending in the centre. Sprinkle with castor sugar and bake in a moderate oven for 15 to 20 minutes, or until the edges of the pastry look cooked and the tops of the sugar-sprinkled apple slices are starting to caramelize. Melt 2 good tablespoons of apricot jam in a pan and when it bubbles sieve it into a bowl, then glaze your tart round the pastry edges and over the apples with a spoon and a pastry brush, taking care not to apply the glaze so vigorously that you disturb the pattern of the slices. Serve warm.

Apricots

Like all exotic fruit, apricots are best eaten raw, but they have an affinity with poultry, and you can make an apricot and rice stuffing for chicken and duck. Apricots also make good water ices and ice-cream (recipes, pp. 337–338)—use a generous amount of fruit for a good strong flavour—and delicious flat French-style tarts. (Use the pastry recipe on p. 359 and fill the shell with stoned, halved apricots, and the custard on p. 348). But if you want to show off, an apricot soufflé is very impressive. It is extremely light and delicate to eat and, like all soufflés, must come to the table the moment it leaves the oven.

Apricot Soufflé

$\frac{1}{2}$ lb (200 g) apricots, flavoured with a little sugar and stewed until just soft

lemon juice   1 tablespoon apricot brandy
3 egg whites

Stone and purée the apricots. Rub the mixture through a fine sieve with a wooden spoon to remove any scraps of skin and stir in the liqueur and lemon juice. Crack the stones, remove the kernels, and peel and chop them finely. Beat the egg whites until stiff; gently, with a metal spoon, fold in the apricot purée and the chopped kernels. Turn the mixture into a greased soufflé dish and bake in a moderate oven (370°F, Mark 4) for 20 minutes or until the soufflé is risen high and the top is golden brown. Serve it immediately.

Blackberries and Loganberries

Blackberries have a traditional affinity with apples: the apples have a complementary flavour, and they will usefully increase a small quantity of painfully picked blackberries, particularly in a blackberry and apple pie. Urban Americans have never tasted blackberries, so visitors from there often find this very traditional dish wildly exotic. In any other recipe—blackberry and apple jelly, for example—I find the presence of the apple simply dilutes the flavour of the blackberries. If you have plentiful home-grown blackberries use them neat.

Blackberries make an incredibly delicious water ice and ice-cream (recipes pp. 337–338)—two dishes that have to be made at home; certainly I have never seen them for sale commercially. Blackberry water ice, particularly, has an unrivalled delicacy of flavour, if you follow the usual rule for water ices and Elizabeth David's suggestion to cook and cool the fruit with two or three scented geranium leaves. (I use Pheasant's Foot, *Pelargonium Denticulatum.*)

Loganberries are very similar in flavour—not so strong—as blackberries, and can be used in place of them. Any extra pounds will make delicious jam.

Currants

Blackcurrants *Glace à la Russe* is a pale blackcurrant-flavoured water ice, made from the young leaves of blackcurrant bushes—an unusual and useful dessert, because it will fill a gap in garden supplies between the last of the rhubarb and the first of the strawberries. The quantities are slightly different than for the usual fruit purée water ice.

Glace à la Russe   1 pint (500 ml) water
8 oz (200 g) sugar
2 or 3 good handfuls young blackcurrant leaves
juice of 3 lemons

Melt the sugar in the water, bring to the boil, add the blackcurrant leaves and boil briskly for 5 minutes. Cool the syrup with the leaves in it, then add the lemon juice, strain it, and freeze as usual.

Blackcurrants themselves are rich in vitamin C, as well as being a versatile summer fruit: they need to be cooked gently with a little sugar, and then they taste good as water ices (p. 337) and ice-creams (p. 338), and in tarts (p. 359), pies and mousses. They also freeze well for winter use.

Red Currants Red currants, dangling like tempting little red beads, have such a brief season in the helter-skelter of a summer kitchen garden that their unusual acid flavour seems gone before we have had enough time to enjoy it. A handful of them, raw, will add distinction to a fruit salad. They are also a necessary ingredient of summer pudding, a very traditional dish that seems in danger of being neglected among the many convenience foods we can choose from.

Summer Pudding For a 2-pint bowl you will need:

> 1½ lb mixed raspberries, red or white currants and black-currants, or raspberries with any one of the other currants
> a little sugar   a little milk
> about 7 slices bread (white or brown but not too fresh), according to the loaf size, not wafer thin, with the crusts removed

'Melt' the fruit and sugar in a covered dish in a low oven until it is softened. Allow to cool. Sprinkle the bread slices with milk and then use them to line completely the bottom and sides of the bowl. Overlap the bread at the joins so there are no cracks. Pour off excess fruit juice and then spoon the fruit into the bowl. Cover it with a lid of bread slices, protect this with greaseproof paper or foil, and put a plate or saucer that fits into the bowl on top of that. Finally put a heavy weight—some 2 pounds—on the plate and refrigerate the pudding overnight. Turn it out—a delicious dome of fruit in juice-soaked bread—and serve. You can pour over the extra juice, or use it for yoghurt or what you will.

If you have any red currants to spare, turn them into your own red-currant jelly to serve with roast lamb, venison or jugged hare throughout the winter.

White currants, which are hard to find in the shops, can be used in the same way.

Cherries

In the South of France, they close their eyes and wish on the first cherries of the year.

Your own home-grown sweet cherries are not likely to get as far as the cooking pot. Quite rightly they will all be eaten, ripe, juicy and delicious, straight from the stalk. If, however, you have any of the acid Morellos they can be improved by being turned into a cherry tart—little individual tartlets are nicest (pastry recipe, p. 359).

Kirsch is the cherry liqueur, and goes well with hot, cooked cherries, very gently simmered in sugar syrup (stoned first if you have the patience). You can warm the kirsch separately. Pour it over the cherries and set fire to it, if you want to impress some-one.

Figs

I must confess I detest figs, so I am quite the wrong person to write about eating them. However, I gather from people who do like them, that they should be eaten raw, and in as large a quantity as possible. I have to admit that they are decorative fruit when ripe, with their purplish skin and wound-coloured interior, and for connoisseurs make a dessert that needs no improvement.

If you have a quantity of the small, unripe green figs, you can stew them gently with a little sugar and water and serve them as a compôte, or turn them into a rich 'preserve' of sliced figs in a thick syrup, to enjoy during the winter.

Gooseberries

The big, pinkish, squashy, dessert gooseberries need no cooking and are usually eaten as they are.

The small green gooseberries, the kind that need to be cooked, are a wonderfully versatile fruit.

If it is a blazing summer day you can make a delicious gooseberry ice-cream (p. 337) that has a delicate pinkish colour, or an unusual sharp gooseberry water ice (p. 338). If it is a bleak grey June there is nothing nicer than a hearty hot gooseberry crumble: fill your oven-proof dish with gooseberries and a little sugar and bake it in

GICI—M

a moderate oven (370°F, Mark 4) topped with crumble mixture (p. 360).

You can also make a Gooseberry Tansy (p. 350).

Gooseberries have an affinity with elderflowers. These big creamy-white flower heads produce the flavour of Muscat grapes when steeped in sugar syrup. You can try adding a couple of heads to the syrup for your water ice, removing them when it has cooled. Gooseberries are also associated with mackerel, either as a stuffing inside the cleaned fish, or as a puréed sauce to accompany them.

Grapes

A freshly cut bunch of grapes, with the bloom still upon them, is a rare pleasure that needs only grape-scissors and perhaps finger-bowls to set them off, not any lily-gilding from the kitchen. I prefer the sweet 'white' grapes, especially when they are just about to turn brown with ripeness, indeed I never get enough of them. 'There *were* going to be grapes for dessert,' our Spanish Maria used to say accusingly, 'but the Senorita Margherita has eaten them again.' I learnt to get to the icebox before my companion. I find that black grapes, although their bloom is more beautiful, sometimes have tough skins. (This bloom is not dust, as the little girl who didn't know any better exclaimed, but in fact the wild yeasts which will ferment to make wine.)

In cooking, green grapes will complement both meat and fish dishes. *Sole Veronique* is a classic fish dish that needs some grapes in the white-wine sauce, and game, particularly pheasant, is delicious stuffed with peeled stoned grapes. (This is a tedious business: skin the grapes after scalding them with boiling water and then halve them and remove the pips with a fork-tine or the tip of a small sharp knife.)

Medlars

You have to wait until your medlars are almost rotten or 'bletted' before you can eat them. If you like them, you can split open the brown fruits and spoon out the flesh, or bake them, or turn them into jam and jelly.

Melons

If you have grown sweet delicious melons in your own greenhouse
or frame, you will not want to do more than chill them and enjoy
them as they are. Melon and transparent slices of raw Parma ham
(or Spanish *Jamon Serrano*) make an incomparable, because not
over-filling, first course at a dinner party.

In this climate, however, such perfection can be difficult—the
melons are often small and less ripe and juicy than those grown
by the Mediterranean. If so, you can improve on nature. Serve a
whole melon to a person. Cut it in half and lift out the seedy centre
with a spoon, then sprinkle the melon with sugar to sweeten it a
little, and fill the middle with an elegant fruit salad, its components
chosen for their colours: green and black grapes for example, or
raspberries and strawberries with kirsch. Cream is a mistake with
melons.

Mulberries

Mulberries are odd, watery, mediaeval berries. If you like them
you can eat them raw, or make them into tarts, jelly, and jam. (Use
equal quantities of mulberries and apples.)

Theodora Fitzgibbon suggests a refreshing dinner-party
dessert made from mulberries and oranges. You need an orange
per person. Cut the tops off the oranges, and take out the fruit
with a very sharp knife. Separate the flesh from the pips and pith,
and chop it in a bowl. Carefully turn in the mulberries, some
kirsch and sugar to taste, and pile the mixture back into the orange
shells. Chill thoroughly before serving.

Peaches and Nectarines

Peaches Just eat them. The pale, greenish-fleshed English
peaches in particular have too delicate a flavour to bear any cooking process. It is the more robust tasting, yellow-fleshed variety
that makes such delectable peach ice-cream in America, but I have
not found it successful here. So serve your peaches whole and
raw as a dessert that needs no improvement, whenever possible.
If you have only a few, or some damaged ones, make them into a
fruit salad; they can be peeled easily after a few minutes in the

steamer. Unripe peaches can be improved by being baked, very slowly (310°F, Mark 2), in a covered pot, with a sprinkling of sugar and a couple of tablespoons of water. You can serve these hot with some brandy stirred into the juices, or ice cold.

Nectarines Nectarines are smooth versions of peaches, but to me they are like a rose without a thorn—a bit too good to be true. Other people prefer them to peaches. Eat them whole and fresh whenever you can. Otherwise use them as you would peaches.

Pears

If you are lucky enough to grow your own dessert pears, eat them as they are. Their juicy, grainy flesh is spoiled by any cooking. But if, like me, you inherited a tree that bears, erratically, a crop of hard wooden cooking pears, they will need some attention to make them edible. Peel them (core them if you can, otherwise leave them whole) and pile them into a casserole with a few tablespoons of water and sugar. Put the lid on and bake them until they turn pink, for a couple of hours in a slow (310°F, Mark 2) oven. You can improvise variations to improve the juices—Elizabeth David suggests red wine; we also enjoy brown sugar and a vanilla pod which is removed and washed for re-use. These pears are delicious served hot with a bowl of cold yoghurt to counteract their sweetness.

Plums

Fat, ripe dessert plums need only a bowl and an appreciative family. Ripe greengages also need little improvement. Less sweet ripe plums, especially sharp little damsons, will take happily to tarts and pies. For a special occasion make a French open flan (p. 340), and fill it with plums halved and stoned, and placed cut side down. Pour over them a custard of egg yolk, sugar and cream whisked together (1 egg, 1 tablespoon of sugar and 1 tablespoon of cream for an 8-inch tin) and bake it gently (370°F, Mark 4) until the pastry is golden and the custard set—about half an hour. The sharp plums will be perfectly set off by the bland pastry and sweet custard.

Damsons and other cooking plums will all make delicious home-made plum jam to store away until winter tea-times. The natural colour of fruit and sugar exposes the unlikely synthetic pink of commercial plum jam.

Quinces

Quinces are not fruit that can be eaten raw. And even cooked, I cannot like them. The Romans thought them worth preserving. Constance Spry insisted on a quince in her apple tarts, other people adore quince jam, quince cheese and quince jelly—the latter is very thick and glutinous. You might try a dish of quinces and raisins, cooked in butter until soft, and finished with a glass of sweet sherry.

Raspberries

There is no substitute for raspberries and sugar and cream. For a dinner party you can chill them and sprinkle them with kirsch; for a birthday tea you can serve them warm from the garden. Cooking fresh raspberries turns them effectively into jam. I would advise anyone with too many to fill up the freezer first. Raspberries freeze well, either turned in a little sugar, or packed in sugar syrup, or, best of all, frozen plain and spread out on flat plates, and packed into boxes when they are hard and easy to handle. (This method shortens their freezer life a little.)

If it is the beginning or the end of the season and there are not enough raspberries to go round, a raspberry shortcake will stretch the supply a little. (This is officially a strawberry shortcake, so the recipe is on p. 351.)

A raspberry water ice (p. 338) or a raspberry ice-cream (p. 337) is a delicious summer dessert. You can buy them, made on the premises, at roadside cafés in France, where they make a wonderfully refreshing break to a long journey. You can make your own at home, whether from fresh fruit in season, or from frozen raspberries at any time. Raspberries always unfreeze a little less firm and separate, so they are well suited to a purée. They improve with a squeeze of lemon juice in the mixture.

Another recipe combines raspberries with oranges to make a very distinctive fruit salad with a wonderful cool, sharp flavour. We have it traditionally after our hot ham on Christmas Eve, when its acid coldness provides the perfect contrast to the rich, greasy main course.

Pamela's Fruit Salad

  6 oranges, or more if they have very thick, obstinate skins
  $\frac{1}{2}$ lb (200 g) raspberries. Let them thaw very slowly overnight in the fridge if you are using frozen ones.
  red food colouring   sugar
  brandy and Grand Marnier, miniatures will do, but more is better

Prepare the oranges in completely skinless segments, any pithy pieces spoil everything. (Immerse them in boiling water for a few minutes to remove all pith very easily.) Add them and their juice to the raspberries in a bowl. Mix equal quantities of sugar and water, enough to cover the fruit, in a saucepan, with some red food colouring and the brandy and Grand Marnier. Scrape the pith from some orange peel and cut the peel into *julienne* strips (tiny matchsticks). Add these to the pan, and slowly stew them, covered, until they are soft. Pour the contents of the pan over the fruit, and serve the dish very chilled. The fruit salad should have a wonderful bright raspberry red colour with contrasting orange segments in it.

Rhubarb

Rhubarb is something you either love or loathe, so I always take care to provide an alternative pudding for guests with unknown tastes. I always serve it either as a pie or a crumble (p. 360), for the tart taste of rhubarb demands a bland, sweet accompaniment. Because the stalks are watery, I cook them gently in a slow oven and then pour off some of the water before sweetening the fruit and putting on the topping. Rhubarb, like spinach, contains oxalic acid—which makes its calcium content unavailable—so add a generous tablespoon of dried skim milk powder to your pastry to compensate for this.

    Rhubarb freezes well, and you can also use it for making wine.

    You can also make a rhubarb tansy—and a gooseberry one—from a very old recipe for a rich fruit custard, where the eggs and cream effectively neutralize the sharpness of the fruit.

Rhubarb Tansy   1 lb (400 g) rhubarb
¼ lb (100 g) butter or margarine
sugar   2 egg yolks
¼ pint (25 ml) cream—whipped

Cut up the rhubarb and stew it in a covered pan with the butter, a little sugar and a tablespoon or two of water until cooked. Take the pan off the heat. Beat the two egg yolks and mix them into the fruit mixture, then turn in the whipped cream, allow the dish to thicken for a moment or two without boiling.

Strawberries

Strawberries, like raspberries, need little improving beyond sugar and cream, so serve them like this while you have plenty. Towards the end of the season the berries will be smaller, and this is the moment to turn them into purées for your home-made strawberry ice-cream (p. 337) and water ice (p. 338) (the water ice, particularly, has a delicate clear flavour, not at all sickly). They are both better made with a good squeeze of lemon juice.

Another way of stretching the strawberry supply a little is to make a strawberry shortcake. This was originally a British recipe that emigrated to America, and has lately and enthusiastically been re-imported:

Strawberry Shortcake   12 oz (300 g) strawberries
7 oz (175 g) self-raising flour   1 oz (25 g) soy flour
2 teaspoons baking powder
4 tablespoons soft butter or margarine
1 tablespoon sugar   salt
milk to mix   butter and cream

Sift together flour, soy flour, baking powder, salt and sugar. Fork in the softened butter and enough milk to make a soft, rather un-manageable dough. Divide it in two, pat each half into a fairly deep 8 or 9 inch round, and bake them in a fairly hot oven (380°F, Mark 5) for 10 to 12 minutes. When they are cooked, let them cool a little and then spread one with butter. Cut the strawberries in half, pile most of them on to the shortcake, put the other shortcake on top, and decorate it with the remainder of the strawberries, sprinkled with sugar and embedded in whipped cream. A good strawberry shortcake should be served warm.

Wild strawberries are a rare delicacy that again ask for no more than sugar and cream.

Nuts

Walnuts and Hazelnuts Nuts are high in protein (in fat too), good to eat by themselves and useful in cookery. Their quality of crunchiness adds as much to the texture of a recipe as their delicious flavour does to the taste. They are used in both sweet and salt dishes, including your own muesli mixture.

To keep them through the winter, first gather them as they ripen and fall to the ground—September for cobnuts, October for walnuts. Take off the outer walnut husk and scrape the nuts to remove any lingering pabulum for fungus to grow on, dip the shells in a bleach solution to preserve them, and allow them to dry. Spread out both kinds of nut on shelves covered in paper and when they are dry pack them into the old type of earthenware crock if possible, or otherwise into large jars, sandwiched between layers of salt. Keep them in a cellar or a cool place until they are needed.

Hazelnuts will improve your poultry stuffings, and they are also good in cakes, particularly in conjunction with chocolate, in a rich shortcake dish with egg custard and apricots, and in meringues.

Hazelnut Meringues
a pinch of cream of tartar
4 egg whites
4 oz (100 g) icing sugar
4 oz finely chopped or ground hazelnuts
4 oz (100 g) castor sugar
a pinch of salt

Beat the egg whites, salt and cream of tartar until they are stiff and dry, standing up in rigid peaks when you lift the beaters out. Using a metal tablespoon, fold in the sugar and the nuts. Spoon the mixture on to greased baking trays as separate meringues, or pipe it to fill in a bigger pre-drawn circle on greaseproof paper if you want to make a meringue cake. Bake *very* slowly in the coolest imaginable oven (250°F, Mark ½) until they dry out but do not colour brown. Sandwich the individual meringues with whipped cream or serve them with a fruit compôte. The bigger meringue can be spread with fresh fruit—raspberries are delicious—and topped with whipped cream.

Walnuts are used in, as well as on, cakes. You can chop them and scatter them over salads like the one for runner beans on page 296. You also need them for Waldorf Salad, an import from America, as simple to make as it is effective to serve:

Waldorf Salad   3 eating apples
  1 head celery, inside stalks
  1 generous handful chopped walnuts
  mayonnaise

Dice the apples and the celery, add the chopped nuts and dress with mayonnaise.

In France they grow walnuts in such abundance that they press them to make the delicious nutty-tasting salad oil that is sadly expensive to buy in Britain. You would need a veritable forest to produce your own oil in any quantity.

Some General Basic Recipes

DRESSINGS, sauces and mayonnaise put the finishing touches to your home-grown, home-cooked vegetable dishes. They will make them special-tasting and tempting to even the most uninterested palate. If they are made from good, nutritious ingredients they will complement the fresh flavours of your produce.

French dressing is the best known and hardest worked of all the salad dressings. At its simplest it consists of oil and vinegar in the proportion of three to one, with salt, pepper and mustard. You can vary this by using lemon juice instead of vinegar; you can elaborate on it with Worcester sauce, garlic, tomato ketchup, chopped herbs of almost any kind, a little sugar or honey. Choose the ingredients of your French dressing to complement the salad it is to cover, and the dish the salad is to accompany. But always remember to spoon the oil over the salad first, and toss it till each leaf glistens. This will protect the nutrients from the damaging effects of air and vinegar. Salads should be dressed only moments before they are eaten, at the table if you like. After this, turn in the vinegar and seasonings. A simple French dressing for a lettuce salad for four is:

3 tablespoons oil
½ teaspoon dry mustard
1 tablespoon vinegar

1 small clove garlic
salt and pepper

Toss the leaves in the oil. Put the crushed garlic, dry mustard, salt and pepper in a cup, mix thoroughly, then mix in the vinegar and add that to the salad.

Mayonnaise is the other basic salad dressing, creamy and opaque, unlike the unobtrusive French dressing. In my view, there is only one way to make mayonnaise. All short cuts with a blender have been useless in my experience and it has taken longer in the end to repair the damage than to make the mayonnaise my way. It is not difficult to make mayonnaise, but it needs time and patience and above all a calm frame of mind. If you have never made it before, ask someone to show you the first time. You need oil, vinegar, lemon juice and seasonings, and an egg yolk—two are easier if you are a beginner (use the spare whites to make meringues, p. 352). Separate the egg, put the yolk in a small bowl and beat it with a fork or one leg of your mixer. Beating all the time, dribble some oil into the yolk, pause till it's all mixed in, dribble some more, very cautiously, until you have doubled the volume of the egg yolk and it is holding together in a firm mass, showing the trail of the whisk. You can now be a little bolder with the oil. When it gets too stiff, add a little vinegar or lemon juice to thin it. Continue until you have enough mayonnaise for your purpose, or have added about one-third of a pint of oil. (You can beat in more, but it may start to separate out again if you leave it to stand for longer than an hour or two.) Season it, and thin it if necessary. 'A mayonnaise is as good as its consistency' is the rule of thumb. If your mixture curdles, start again with a clean bowl and a fresh egg yolk. Beat in the curdled mixture as if it were oil.

You can use this basic mayonnaise as it is, or add any variety of chopped herbs for a mayonnaise *fines herbes*, or turn it into either of the two ubiquitous American salad dressings, Roquefort and Thousand Island Dressing. Roquefort Dressing combines mayonnaise with plenty of crumbled blue cheese and Worcester sauce. Thousand Island adds chili sauce, tomato purée, chopped green peppers and minced onions. Both these dressings should taste quite powerful by themselves. They are calmed by a bland green salad. You can make a spicy mayonnaise to go with a plate of *crudités* (see pp. 277–296 and 303) by stirring in lemon juice, salt, paprika, chopped herbs including plenty of parsley, grated onion or chopped chives, a good pinch of curry powder and some Worcester sauce.

If you like a lighter mayonnaise you can mix it half and half with plain yoghurt for any of these recipes.

For **aioli,** the delicious Provençal garlic mayonnaise, begin your mayonnaise by pounding or thoroughly crushing two good-sized garlic cloves in the bottom of the bowl. Add the egg yolks and proceed as before.

Hollandaise sauce is another that is surrounded by imaginary terrors. Again it needs only time and self-confidence. You need an egg yolk, about 4 ounces (100 grams) of butter or margarine, cut into small pieces, a teaspoon of cold water, lemon juice, and a double saucepan (improvise one with a mixing bowl over a pan of hot water, if necessary). Fill the pan with steaming hot water, not boiling, and keep it like that. Off this heat, put the egg yolk and the cold water in the top of the pan, beat it with a fork or a wire whisk, then place the pan over the water and begin adding the butter pieces very slowly. Beat each piece in before adding the next. If you think it is getting too hot, lift the pan off the heat for a moment or two. If you let the egg scramble, you are sunk. When you have beaten in all the butter the sauce will be thick and creamy. Add some lemon juice and salt and pepper to taste. Keep it warm in the double pan until it is time to serve it, but turn the heat off, or you will have scrambled eggs after all.

White sauces (plain, cheese, parsley, etc.) or English gravy, are all made on the same principle of a roux—flour and butter—base. For a white sauce melt an ounce (25 grams) of butter or margarine in a saucepan, stir in an ounce (25 grams) of flour, vigorously, until it is all taken up by the butter and has a dry, bready look. Immediately begin to add half a pint of cold milk very slowly, stirring each addition until the lumps have gone. When it is all in, let the sauce come to a good boil for a moment or two, to cook out the flavour of raw flour. For a cheese sauce, stir in 4 ounces (100 grams) or so of grated cheese, and a little Parmesan to intensify the flavour, and seasonings. For a parsley sauce, chop a generous bunch and add it at the last moment. English gravy is made the same way, only you use vegetable water instead of milk, in the roasting tin. Put the cooked joint on a warm plate, pour off most of the fat and as little of the meat juices underneath it as possible. Mix in enough flour to absorb the fat, stir it and let it brown for a moment or two before adding vegetable water or stock, and seasoning. Remember to let this boil, too.

Yoghurt Making Yoghurt is an important food for healthy eating—low in fat, high in protein, calcium and valuable digestive bacteria. Most people like the commercial kind, but it is cheaper and uses less sugar if you make your own yoghurt at home, and mix your own flavours too. Rhubarb and yoghurt is a marvellous combination for example.

Yoghurt is a cultured milk, the bacteria thickening the milk as they multiply. As with bread, I had a few failures before I got the knack. You can buy the famed *Lactobacillus Bulgaricus*, that has reputedly kept individual Bulgarians alive for a hundred years and more, or any plain unsweetened pot of natural yoghurt; it is all 'live' and may be used as a starter. It takes so long to make yoghurt—in time, not in continuous effort—that it needs a little planning before you start. Many times I have found myself ringing home from a call box or waking up with a jump in the night, when I have remembered a bowl 'yogging' quietly away in some corner. For if you 'over-yog' you will get a thick deposit with a thin whey floating over it instead of a homogeneous consistency. If the culture is too old it will cause the reverse to happen—a thick crusty top floating over a thin liquid. Some starter pots do this straight away: it means they have been sitting too long in the shop. It is a good idea to change your culture every six weeks or so, as the conditions for growing yoghurt are also good for typhoid.

Two pints of plain yoghurt
    2 pints (1 l) milk, preferably skimmed (ask your milkman)
    4 oz (100 g) skim milk powder
    1 tablespoon yoghurt from a pot or last week's bowl

Whisk all the ingredients in a mixing bowl with a fork until they are smooth. Cover with a clean cloth and set to 'yog' in a warm place—a linen cupboard, boiler room, storage radiator. (Yoghurt bacteria multiply best at a temperature between 90°F and 105°F. Below this they lie dormant, above 120°F they die.) This will take about five hours. When the mixture thickens into a homogeneous cream put it into the refrigerator. If you use whole milk, lift off the skin. You can speed up the process by warming the milk a little.

You can use yoghurt instead of sour cream or fresh cream with cold food. If you heat it, it will separate. As a cream substitute it is useful for anyone concerned about cholesterol.

Once you have mastered yoghurt, you will want to tackle yeast, another way of cooking with 'live' food.

A basic bread recipe It is immensely satisfying to make your own bread: the smell fills the kitchen, the loaves cool proudly on their rack. For years I tried to bake with yeast and every attempt was a dismal failure. My husband tactfully blamed the Esse cooker and called a halt to all bread making. Then one day a guest effortlessly knocked up a pair of delicious brown loaves and, by copying her every move, I did the same. Now we bake twice a week and try to keep a spare loaf in the freezer against extra guests. (Bread freezes well but gets stale very quickly once it is thawed.) For anyone who is a beginner with yeast, my only advice is to keep trying. If I can make bread, anyone can.

Wholemeal Bread   For two 9-inch bread tins

> 2 lb (1 kilo) plain wholemeal flour
> 2 oz (50 g) wheatgerm
> 4 level tablespoons dried skim milk
> 2½ teaspoons salt
> 1 ounce (25 g) fresh yeast (ask any baker) or half the amount of dried yeast
> 2 teaspoons brown sugar
> 1⅛ pints (550 ml) warm water or warm potato water

Mix the flour, wheatgerm, skim milk powder and salt in a big bowl. Cream the yeast with the sugar in a cup then pour into the flour mixture and add the liquid. Mix and knead until you have a firm elastic dough that has taken up all the flour and does not stick to the sides of the bowl. Divide the dough into two and press into well-greased bread tins. Cover them with a clean, dampened tea-towel and set to rise in a warm place—a linen cupboard or a boiler room. When the dough has risen to the tops of the tins, place them in a hot oven (440°F, Mark 7) for 15 minutes. (If the dough sags a little on the way to the stove, let it prove for 15 minutes on the side.) Lower the heat slightly (410°F, Mark 6) and cook for another 45 minutes. Tip the loaves out—they are cooked if they knock hollow on the bottom. Dry them upside down in the oven with the heat turned off and the door ajar, for 10 minutes. Cool them on a rack.

If you use freshly ground wholemeal flour, you will make delicious and nutritious loaves that bear no resemblance to the pliable white slices from commercial bakers. Flour should not only be stone-ground (the heat generated in electric milling destroys nutrients) but freshly stone-ground—like everything else flour goes stale.

You will soon want to extend this basic bread beyond loaves to buns, pizzas and rolls. Make the same recipe and let the dough rise in the mixing bowl covered with a cloth. Then divide it in half. One half will make two pizzas (p. 330), the other a dozen small rolls, or herb buns.

Chop a tablespoon of the herb you have chosen for each bun, 'knock down' (reknead briefly) the dough and mix the herbs in thoroughly. Divide the dough into twelve equal parts, shape each one into a bun and place on a greased baking tray. Cover them and leave them to prove for 20 to 30 minutes. Bake in a hot oven (410°F, Mark 6) for 10 to 15 minutes or until the top is browned.

If you like a substantial fruit pie, or savoury quiche, raised without baking powder, which destroys B vitamins, mix a richer dough from 9 ounces (225 grams) of 81 per cent flour, 1 ounce (25 grams) soy flour, $\frac{1}{2}$ ounce (12$\frac{1}{2}$ grams) yeast, 3 ounces (75 grams) of butter or margarine, 2 eggs, 2 teaspoons of sugar and a pinch of salt. Stir the softened butter and then the eggs into the flour and salt. Cream the yeast in the sugar and proceed as for bread. When it has risen, roll out the dough very thinly and shape it by hand into your flan tins (these quantities will make two 8-inch pies), press it down firmly round the edge, fill with partly cooked fruit and juices, and bake them in a fairly hot oven (380°F, Mark 5) for half an hour or until cooked.

Shortcrust pastry makes a neater shell for your savoury quiches and fruit pies. I use the same basic recipe all the time, with the addition of a teaspoon of sugar for sweet pies and, on occasions, an egg for a richer one.

Basic Shortcrust Recipe For an 8-inch flan tin

4$\frac{1}{2}$ oz (112 g) plain flour, 81 per cent if you can get it, or whole-wheat, which makes brown, slightly crumbly pastry
$\frac{1}{2}$ oz (12$\frac{1}{2}$ g) soy flour   salt
2 oz (50 g) butter or margarine
1 tablespoon dried skim milk powder
cold water

Sieve the flour, soy flour, salt (and sugar) into a mixing bowl. Add the butter or margarine cut up into little pieces and rub it quickly in, using the tips of your fingers. Mix in the egg if you use it, and enough cold water to make a dough. If possible now rest the dough in the refrigerator or the freezer for half an hour or so. Roll it out quickly and fairly thinly.

If you are in a hurry, a crumble topping for fruit like rhubarb and apples is a great time-saver, as you can cut out the rolling and sprinkle the crumbs straight on to the filling—pre-cooked a little, if necessary. The following recipe will top a 2-pint pie-dish:

Basic Crumble Recipe
3 oz (75 g) flour, plain or wholewheat
1 oz (25 g) soy flour
2 oz (50 g) sugar, brown or white
3 oz (75 g) butter or margarine

Put all the dry ingredients into a mixing bowl, add the cut-up butter or margarine and rub it in until the mixture has the texture of fine crumbs. Sprinkle these thickly over the surface of your filling and bake it for half an hour in a moderate oven, or until it is crisp on the top and cooked through.

Bread and pastry are two starchy staples that can be made into more than empty calories. Breakfast cereal is another: the commercial kinds are often standard rubbish foods with a few of the cheaper synthetic B vitamins added as a sop to the advertising copy. Instead you can give your family a nutritious, crunchy, home-made muesli. Mix it up in small quantities or the fruit shrivels.

Muesli
½ lb (200 g) uncooked porridge oats
2 tablespoons each: dried skim milk powder, wheatgerm, soy flour
2 tablespoons each of most of the following: ground almonds; chopped, mixed nuts, your own if possible; desiccated coconut; sunflower seeds; dried apple flakes; raisins, sultanas, currants—

read the packets and try to buy the kind that are not separate with liquid paraffin (known to be carcinogenic in quantity); demerara sugar.

Mix all the ingredients together and serve with milk or yoghurt. Serve also some fresh fruit or fruit juice, to bring some vitamin C to breakfast.

Equivalents

To convert Fahrenheit to Centigrade: subtract 32, multiply by 5 and divide by 9.
To convert Centigrade to Fahrenheit: multiply by 9, divide by 5 and add 32.

F°	C°	F°	C°	F°	C°
0	−18	36	2	72	22
4	−16	40	4	76	24
8	−13	44	7	80	27
12	−11	48	9	84	29
16	−9	52	11	88	31
20	−7	56	13	92	33
24	−4	60	16	96	36
28	−2	64	18	100	38
32	0	68	20	212	100

(Centigrade equivalents have been rounded off to the nearest whole degree)

Oven equivalents

F°	C°	Gas mark	F°	C°	Gas mark
250	120	$\frac{1}{2}$	375	190	5
275	135	1	400	205	6
300	150	2	425	220	7
325	165	3	450	230	8
350	180	4	475	245	9

(Centigrade equivalents have been rounded off to the nearest 5°)

Other equivalents

	exact	working
1 pint	567 ml	500 ml
1 gallon	4·546 l	4·5 l
1 ounce	28·35 g	25 g
1 pound	0·454 kg	0·5 kg
1 cwt	50·80 kg	50 kg
1 inch	25·40 mm	25 mm
1 foot	30·48 cm	30 cm
1 yard	0·914 m	1 m
1 acre	0·4047 hectares	

Suppliers

General

Many garden centres supply seeds, plants, tools, thermometers (including soil thermometers), ready-mixed composts, peat, fertilizers, insecticides, fungicides and, in some cases, also cloches, frames, greenhouses and fruit cages, beside the usual run of hose, watercans, labels, canes and sticks. The name of your nearest approved garden centre can be had from the Horticultural Trades Association, 18 Westcote Road, Reading, Berks.

Seeds and plants

Seeds:
Samuel Dobie & Son Ltd, Upper Dee Mills, Llangollen, Denbighs
Suttons Seeds Ltd, Reading, Berks
Thompson & Morgan Ltd, Ipswich, Suffolk
W. J. Unwin Ltd, Histon, Cambridge

Asparagus crowns:
Asmer Seeds Ltd, Evesham, Worcs
Elsom's Ltd, Spalding, Lincs
Suttons Seeds Ltd, Reading, Berks

Globe artichokes:
C. Smith & Son, Caledonian Nurseries, Guernsey, C.I.

Herb plants:
E. & A. Evetts, Ashfields Herb Nursery, Hinstock, Market Drayton, Shropshire

Mushroom spawn:
W. Darlington & Sons Ltd, Station Road, Rustington, Littlehampton, Sussex
Samuel Dobie & Son Ltd, Upper Dee Mills, Llangollen, Denbighs

Composts, peat, organic materials, seaweed fertilizers, etc.

Alexpeat, Burnham-on-Sea, Somerset

Chase Organics (G.B.) Ltd, Shepperton, Middlesex (seaweed fert.)
Compost Supply Company, Agriculture House, Knightsbridge, London SW1 (seaweed fert.)
Fisons Ltd, Harston, Cambridge
Fritted Trace Elements, Lindsey & Kesteven Fertilisers Ltd, Saxilby, Lincoln
Frit No 253A: Ferro Enamels Ltd (through horticultural sundries-
                 men)
                 Medlock Chemicals, The Grove, Stubbington, Hants.
ICI Garden Products, Woolmead House, Bear Lane, Farnham, Surrey
Pan Britannica Industries Ltd, Britannica House, Waltham Cross, Herts
Organic Concentrates Ltd, Chalfont St Giles, Bucks, HP8 4AP
Wilfrid Smith (Horticultural) Ltd, Gemini House, High Street, Edgware, Middlesex, HA8 7ET (Marinure—seaweed)

Equipment
Cloches:
Expandite Ltd, Western Road, Bracknell, Berks, RG12 1RH
Manna Engineering Products Ltd, 67 Jeddo Road, London W12 9EH
Q-Cloche Ltd, Willowbank Wharf, Ranelagh Gardens, Putney, London SW6
Continuous polythene tunnels:
British Visqueen Ltd, Stevenage, Herts
Plant Protection Ltd, Woolmead House, Bear Lane, Farnham, Surrey
Frames:
Access Frames, Yelverton Road, Crick, Rugby
Alton Glasshouses Ltd, Alton Works, Bewdley, Worcs, DY12 2UJ
Pluie Frames, Surrey Rose Farm, Guildford Road, Chobham, Surrey
F. Pratten & Co. Ltd, Midsomer Norton, Bath BA3 4AG
Q-Cloche Ltd, Willowbank Wharf, Ranelagh Gardens, Putney, London SW6
Greenhouses:
Alitex, St John's Works, Station Road, Alton, Hants
Alton Glasshouses Ltd, Alton Works, Bewdley, Worcs, DY12 2UJ
Baco Leisure Products Ltd, Windover Road, Huntingdon, PE18 7EH
Crittall-Hope Ltd, Braintree, Essex
Robert H. Hall & Co. (Ltd), Paddock Wood, Kent
Hartley Clear Span Ltd, Greenfield, Oldham, Lancs
Marley Buildings Ltd, Guildford, Surrey

F. Pratten & Co. Ltd, Midsomer Norton, Bath BA3 4AG

G. F. Strawson & Son, St Andrews Works, Charlesfield Road, Horley, Surrey

C. H. Whitehouse Ltd, Buckhurst Works, Frant, Sussex

Greenhouse heating equipment and thermostats, propagators, blinds, extractor fans, automatic ventilators, etc. (electrical):

Roberts Electrical Co. Ltd (Humex Products), 5 High Road, Byfleet, Surrey

Simplex of Cambridge Ltd, Sawston, Cambridge CB2 4J

Greenhouse heaters, oil:

Aladdin Industries Ltd, Greenford, Middlesex

Charles Parkway & Son Ltd, Halstead, Essex

Nets and fruit cages:

W. Oliver Allen & Sons, Porthleven, Cornwall (netting)

Netlon Ltd, N.E. Wing, Bush House, Aldwych, London WC2B 4PX

C. Sutton (Sidcup) Ltd, Bridport, Dorset

William Wood & Son Ltd, Bath Road, Taplow, Maidenhead, Berks

Pots, peat and whalehide:

Jiffy Pot (U.K.) Ltd, Trulls Hatch, Rotherfield, Crowborough, Sussex

Root-o-Pots, Ambassador House, Brigstock Road, Thornton Heath, Surrey CR4 7JG

Tomato ring culture pots: Fyba Pot Co., Malvern Road, Knottingley, Yorks

Bibliography

WE are indebted first of all to the Royal Horticultural Society's *Dictionary of Gardening*, the essential starting point for all further investigation, and the soundest source of really practical information.

The Royal Horticultural Society, *Dictionary of Gardening*, Oxford University Press, 1951

The Royal Horticultural Society, *The Vegetable Garden Displayed*

The Royal Horticultural Society, *The Fruit Garden Displayed*, 1968

The Royal Horticultural Society, *Fruit Present and Future*, Vol. II, 1973

The Royal Horticultural Society, *Gardening Chemicals*, 1967

The Royal Horticultural Society, *Practical Aspects of the Manuring of Fruit in Gardens*, 1963

The Royal Horticultural Society, *Model Fruit Gardens at Wisley*

The Royal Horticultural Society, *A Select List of Vegetables for Gardens*

Atkins, F. C., *Mushroom Growing Today*, Faber, 1972

Bagenal, N. B., *Fruit Growing*, Ward Lock, 1939

Beck, Bertholle & Child, *Mastering the Art of French Cooking*, Penguin, 1966

Brillat-Savarin, Jean-Anthelme, *The Philosopher in the Kitchen*, Penguin, 1970

Bruce, M. E., *Common-sense Compost Making*, Faber, 1973

Bunyard, Edward A., *A Handbook of Hardy Fruits, Apples and Pears*, John Murray, 1920

Bunyard, Edward A., *A Handbook of Hardy Fruits, Stone and Bush Fruits, Nuts, etc.*, John Murray, 1925

Bunyard, Edward A., *The Anatomy of Dessert*, Chatto & Windus, 1933

Carrier, Robert, *Great Dishes of the World*, Nelson, 1963

Carson, Rachel, *Silent Spring*, Hamish Hamilton, 1963

Cox, Pat M., *The Home Book of Food Freezing*, Faber, 1972

David, Elizabeth, *Salt, Spice and Aromatics in the English Kitchen*, Penguin, 1970

David, Elizabeth, *French Provincial Cooking*, Penguin, 1964

David, Elizabeth, *Summer Cooking*, Penguin, 1965
Davis, Adelle, *Let's Eat Right to Keep Fit*, Allen & Unwin, 1960
Davis, Adelle, *Let's Cook It Right*, Allen & Unwin, 1970
Fitzgibbon, Theodora, *Weekend Cooking*, André Deutsch, 1956
Flower & Rosenbaum (eds), *Apicius Roman Cookbook*, Harrap, 1958
Fraser, H., *The Gardener's Guide to Pruning*, Collingridge, 1966
Friede, Donald & Eleanor (eds), *Bemelman's La Bonne Table*, Simon & Schuster, 1964
Furner, Brian, *Fresh Food from Small Gardens*, Stuart & Watkins in conjunction with The Soil Association, 1969
Furner, Brian and Rodale, Robert, *The Basic Book of Organic Gardening*, Pan/Ballantine, 1971
Furner, Brian, *The Kitchen Garden*, Pan, 1971
Genders, Roy, *The Complete Book of Vegetables and Herbs*, Ward Lock, 1972
Goldberg & Waldo, *The Molly Goldberg Cookbook*, Doubleday, 1955
Goold-Adams, Deenagh, *The Cool Greenhouse Today*, Faber, 1969
Hartley, G. S. and West, T. F., *Chemicals for Pest Control*, Pergamon Press, 1969
Hemphill, Rosemary, *The Penguin Book of Herbs and Spices*, 1966
Heptinstall, William, *Hors d'Œuvre and Cold Table*, Faber, 1959
Hills, Lawrence D., *Fertility Finder*, Henry Doubleday Research Association, Bocking, Braintree, Essex
Hills, Lawrence D., *Fertility without Fertilizers*, Henry Doubleday Research Association
Hills, Lawrence D., *Grow Your Own Fruit and Vegetables*, Faber, 1971
Hills, Lawrence D., *Pest Control Without Poisons*, Henry Doubleday Research Association
Howard, Albert, *An Agricultural Testament*, Oxford University Press, 1940
Howe, Robin, *Soups*, Wine and Food Society, 1967
Lawrence, W. J. C. and Newell, J., *Seed and Potting Composts*, Allen & Unwin, 1952
Mabey, Richard, *Food for Free*, Collins, 1972
Manual of Nutrition, H.M.S.O., 1970
Mendelstein (ed.), *Vitamins*, Churchill Livingstone, 1971
McCance, R. A. and Widdowson, E. M., *The Composition of Foods*, Medical Research Council, H.M.S.O., 1969
McKay, C. D., *The French Garden*, 'Daily Mail'
Martin, Ethel Austin, *Nutrition in Action*, Holt, Rinehart & Winston, 1963
Masefield, G. B., Wallis, M., Harrison, S. G. and Nicholson, B. E., *The Oxford Book of Food Plants*, Oxford University Press, 1969
Mellanby, Kenneth, *Pesticides and Pollution*, Collins, 1967

Ministry of Agriculture, Fisheries and Food, *Agricultural Chemicals Approval Scheme, 1973 List of Approved Products and Their Uses for Farmers and Growers, Insecticides, Fungicides*

Ministry of Agriculture, Fisheries and Food, *Modern Farming and the Soil*, Agricultural Advisory Council, H.M.S.O., 1970

Ministry of Agriculture, Fisheries and Food, *Toxic Chemicals in Agriculture and Food Storage*, H.M.S.O., 1961

Organic Gardening and Farming, Rodale Press, Emmaus, Pa., U.S.A.

Pauli, F. W., *Soil Fertility*, Adam Hilger, 1967

Poincelot, Raymond P., *The Biochemistry and Methodology of Composting*, The Connecticut Agricultural Experiment Station, U.S.A.

Pullar, Philippa, *Consuming Passions*, Hamish Hamilton, 1970

Remington, J. S. and Francis, W., *The Manure and Fertilizer Handbook*, Leonard Hill, 1955

Rombauer & Becker, *The Joy of Cooking*, Bobbs-Merrill Co. Inc., U.S.A., 1931

Rudd, Robert L., *Pesticides and the Living Landscape*, Faber, 1964

Sinclair, Hugh M. and Hollingsworth, Dorothy F., *Hutchison's Food and the Principles of Nutrition*, Arnold, 1969

Spry, Constance, *Come into the Garden, Cook*, Dent, 1946

Sutton and Sons, *The Culture of Vegetables and Flowers*, Simpkin, Marshall, Hamilton, Kent & Co. Ltd, 1902

White, Florence, *Good Things in England*, Cape, 1962

Whitehead, George E., *Grow Fruit in Your Greenhouse*, Faber, 1970

Whitehead, Stanley B., *Fruit from Trained Trees*, Dent, 1954

Index

Cabbage, Chinese, cultivation, 83
preparation, 301
Cabbage, red, cultivation, 83
preparation, 302
Cabbage, savoy, cultivation, 84
preparation, 300–1
Calabrese, see Broccoli
Calcium, 265
Calendar, gardener's, 251–9
Caraway, cultivation, 158
preparation, 285
Carbohydrates, 264
Cardoon, cultivation, 88–9
preparation, 305
Carrier, Robert, 279
Carrot, cultivation, 89–90
preparation, 302–3
Cauliflower, cultivation, 85
preparation, 303–4
Celeriac, cultivation, 90–1
preparation, 304
Celery, cultivation, 91–3
preparation, 305
Chards, see Artichokes
Chase cloches, 46
Cherry, cultivation, 194–200
pests and diseases, 200
preparation, 345
pruning, 195–8
varieties, 198–200
Chervil, cultivation, 158
preparation, 285
Chicory, cultivation, 93–4
preparation, 306
Chives, cultivation, 158–9
preparation, 285
Chlorine, 266
Cholesterol, 270
Chromium, see Trace Elements
Cloches, 45–9
bell, 45
Chase, 46
polythene, 46–7
PVC, 48

Cobalt, see Trace Elements
Cobnut, see Nuts
Compost, garden, 21–6
Berkeley 'Two-Week' Process, 25
hot bed, 28
Indore Process, 22
organic materials, 26–31
Composts, sowing and potting, 33–4
Connecticut Agricultural Experiment Station, 27, 28
Copper, 266
Coriander, cultivation, 159
preparation, 285
Corn Salad, cultivation, see Lettuces
preparation, 306
Courgette, see Marrow
Cow manure, 27
Crop rotation, 37–8
Cucumber, cultivation, 95–9
preparation, 307

Damsons, see Plums
Dandelion greens, 334
David, Elizabeth, 277, 279, 288, 294, 343, 348, 366
Derris, 41–2
Dig-for-Victory Campaign, 37
Dill, cultivation, 159
preparation, 285–6
Diseases and Pests, see under specific vegetable or fruit entry
Dutch light frame, 49

Egg Plant, see Aubergine
Encarsia formosa, 99, 152
Endive, cultivation, 99–100

Fats, 264, 270
Fennel, cultivation, 160
preparation, 286

Index of Recipes

For general preparation of fruit and vegetables see main index.